1495

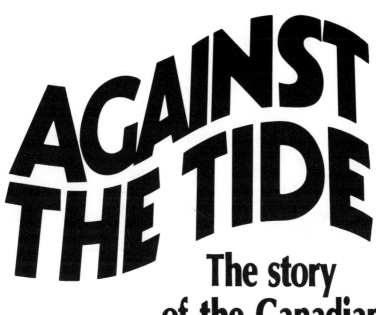

AGAINST THE TIDE

The story of the Canadian Seamen's Union

Jim Green

Progress Books Toronto 1986

Cover design: Dan Hammond

Published by Progress Books
71 Bathurst Street
Toronto, Canada M5V 2P6

Published in conjunction with the Tim Buck - Norman Bethune Educational Centre

Printed and bound in Canada ⬤ 28

Canadian Cataloguing in Publication Data

Green, Jim, 1943–
   Against the tide : the story of the Canadian Seamen's Union
Includes index.
ISBN 0-919396-49-6

1. Canadian Seamen's Union - History. 2. Seafarers' International Union of Canada. 3. Banks, Hal, 1909–   . Title.

HD6528.S4G74 1986   331.88'113875'0971   C86-094382-8

Contents

Drawings by Bill Stapleton
    After pages 184 and 240

Foreword

AT LONG LAST the history that many of us have awaited for so long has become a reality. Many people have talked about writing a history of the Canadian Seamen's Union, but Jim Green has done it. He took on an enormously taxing and time-consuming job and has provided us with an important record of labor history that is long overdue.

In terms of the overall Canadian labor scene, the history of Canada's seamen and their struggles to lift themselves from virtual peonage to movers and achievers in the labor movement is of comparatively short duration, but few groups of workers have had the political and historical impact that they have had.

My first trip to sea was on an oil tanker in November 1939. I was fortunate to join the union soon after, in early 1940. By that time the CSU was already well-established on the Great Lakes thanks to the work of men like Dewar Ferguson of Toronto and Pat Sullivan in Montreal. But there were other factors which made the winter of 1940 a propitious moment to join the union. The war had begun, making a deepsea shipping fleet vital not just to Canada but to the Allies as a whole. The war years were a period of expansion for the union, when branches were opened in such ports as Saint John, New Brunswick, and Halifax, Nova Scotia. Above all, the war years gave me and others a sense of commitment to a Canadian merchant marine and to an independent Canadian union.

There was another factor which shaped my commitment to the CSU. Because I got my start as a sailor on a deepsea ship, I immediately gained experience of the unique factors which made the CSU an especially militant and close-knit group of workers. We on the ships lived and worked together for weeks and months at a time, sharing grievances which went beyond those of low wages and long hours to include poor food and sleeping accommodations. We felt these grievances as a whole crew and not just as individuals. This created a solidarity, a feeling of brotherhood and comradeship, which was far greater than that of shoreside workers.

Although the CSU made big gains for the seamen during the war, we in the union knew that with the winning of peace we faced our biggest problem: the threat of scuttling the Canadian fleet. For it was then that the shipowners began hiring foreign seamen and switching the Canadian flag to foreign flag registration. This was followed by the signing of an illegal back-door agreement with an American gangster-controlled union. Thus not only the CSU but the very existence of the seamen's livelihood was at stake.

This threat produced the world-wide deepsea strike of 1949. It was an historic battle in more ways than one. The militancy and courage displayed by CSU crews was accompanied by unparalleled unity and support from foreign dockworkers and others in such far away places as Great Britain, South Africa, New Zealand, Cuba and Australia.

Outstanding among these supportive actions by fraternal workers on foreign shores were the actions of the British dockworkers. When CSU striking seamen advised the dockers that a Canadian ship was in port with scab labor, the dockers immediately declared the ship "black." This meant that all dockers would refuse to work these ships.

These actions made the British and Canadian shipowners furious. Determined to break the strike and the solidarity of the dockers, they told the dockers they would not be allowed to work any ship until the Canadian ships were unloaded. The result was that hundreds of ships were idle and thousands of dockers were out of work.

The government introduced the Emergency Powers Act and brought in thousands of soldiers to unload the ships. At the same time the press unleashed a campaign against the CSU, claiming the strike was a communist plot to sabotage the Marshall Plan!

The British dockers continued to support the seamen despite the government's campaign against them and despite economic hardship. The dockers returned to work only after the CSU decided to end the strike in British ports. This was a saga of solidarity the Canadian seamen will never forget.

Such international solidarity, as well as the militancy and national pride displayed by Canadian seamen, set an example for the rest of the labor movement in Canada. This made the CSU a potential sparkplug for the Canadian labor movement as a whole and thus a thorn in the side of the Canadian government. This explains, though nothing excuses, the literally treacherous and criminal actions of a government bent on our destruction.

This is a fascinating story and Jim Green tells it well. In closing I must pay tribute to a few of the CSU officials who literally devoted their lives to the cause of the union. There was Eric Atkins, port agent in Halifax; Eddie Reid, business agent in St. John; Bert Meade, national organizer in Halifax; Dan Daniels, editor of the *Searchlight*; Conrad Sauras, port agent in Montreal. With the publication of this book, the thousands of rank and file members who displayed outstanding leadership and heroism on the strike-bound ships all over the world receive their tribute.

HARRY DAVIS
President
Canadian Seamen's Union
1947-51

Preface

I NEVER thought of myself as a writer and when I took on the task of writing the history of the Canadian Seamen's Union I had no idea what I was getting into.

In 1972 I was living in Vancouver's waterfront community in the Downtown Eastside, studying at the University of British Columbia and working as a casual longshoreman.

The Seamen's Union and the Fishermen's Union halls were down the street. The pubs that were frequented by longshoremen, shipyard workers, seamen and fishermen all were within walking distance. The Patricia Hotel's rear entrance was just a few steps across the lane from my back door.

Many seamen had lived in the local hotels for years. The Pat was a favorite and many seamen had been living there for more than 25 years. But it was in the pub of the Columbia Hotel at the corner of Cordova and Columbia that I got involved with the Canadian Seamen's Union.

I was sitting with a couple of waterfront workers. The crowd kept changing. A couple of guys had to turn to at midnight and left to get their gear. Others appeared. A young switchman took off and came back with half a dozen orders of fish and chips from the Only Seafood Restaurant. We talked about the Socreds, the NDP, football and hockey.

Finally I was asked why I was going to UBC if I had no plans to be an academician. I admitted that although it gave me an opportunity to do some studying, the main reason was that I had a Canada Council fellowship and it wouldn't hurt to finish my master's degree.

Joe Hendsbee, a seaman who had spent time in the Teamsters, was at the table. He had also spent six months in the slammer as a result of an altercation on the Marine Workers' picket line at Allied Engineering in 1962. Also with us was Al Chadwick. Like Hendsbee, he was a seaman who had joined many picket lines over the years. He had done a lot of boxing during the war and had been with Hendsbee on the Allied line. He had been involved in the altercation but did not do time. Both guys had a rough and ready reputation and they started in on me. "Quit school or do something about it." "Straighten out your act." "What about the CSU?" "Yeah!" "Quit the bullshit and write the CSU history." Unfortunately I knew almost nothing about the CSU. I had heard it mentioned in semi-reverent tones. I did know that it had been a militant union and that it no longer existed, but that was about all. Chadwick was relentless about the CSU and I finally agreed to give it a look.

I began to meet others who had been active in the CSU. Tommy McGrath was then president of Local 400 (Seamen's Section) of the Canadian Brotherhood of Railroad, Transportation and General Workers' Union. He urged me on and introduced me to several more ex-CSUers. Among them were three men who truly are working class heroes — Tommy Burnett, Jimmy O'Donnell and Andy "Jock" Brogan. Among them they accounted for more than 100 years of trade union experience. What really moved me, however, was their dedication to principle, their sense of humor and, above all, their love for the Canadian Seamen's Union. I knew that if these three were involved, the CSU was definitely a story worth telling.

What I didn't know at the time was the enormous task I had undertaken. The CSU was a tiny union begun in the mid-30s by a handful of seamen on the Great Lakes. It grew to one of the most important and powerful unions in Canada during the Second World War and represented seamen from coast to coast. It saw its leadership jailed, then elected to top positions in the Canadian labor movement. It faced betrayal, both from within its ranks and from the labor movement. It took up the historic task of defending the Canadian merchant marine from elimination. It fought to save thousands of jobs on Canadian vessels and in Canadian shipyards. In an unparalleled epic struggle, it sought to keep Canada a leading maritime nation.

To save the Canadian merchant fleet — the third largest in the world — the CSU mounted a world-wide strike that directly involved more than one million workers in a global picket line the magnitude of which has not been seen before or since. It was a battle the seamen could not win but one they fought to the final bell.

By its very nature the Canadian Seamen's Union was a serious threat to the shipowners, to "business trade unionism" and to the Canadian and American governments it confronted. Its challenge to the shipowners threw down the gauntlet to men who were entrenched in Canada's economic and political élite. Its reliance on rank and file democracy, solidarity and political action was the antithesis of the business union philosophy pursued by the labor aristocrats, especially in the American labor movement, who dominated North American trade unions. Its demand for a Canadian merchant marine defied federal government policies that were dictated by a determination to put our country at the service of American imperatives in the emerging Cold War.

The CSU, which brought democracy to a racketeer-ridden industry, was defeated by a powerful alliance that restored the rule of the club to the Canadian waterfront, but the repercussions reached far beyond the docks. Every tactic from shotguns to the courts was used to put down the Canadian seamen. The defeat of the CSU required an all-out assault on the democracy and autonomy of the Canadian trade union movement. Canada acted not as a sovereign nation but as an agent of U.S. interests and policies. The battle lost by the seamen was a defeat for all Canadians.

A history of a rank and file union requires close contact with those involved and very thorough research. The Canadian Seamen's Union History Project Committee was established in 1975 with local committees in Montreal, Toronto and Vancouver. Stan Wingfield from Montreal was elected national coordinator and an office was set up in a building overlooking Pigeon Park in the Downtown Eastside of Vancouver. The committee raised funds for expenses, collected research materials and put on socials to bring the seamen together. In Fishermen's Hall in Vancouver more than 150 supporters, including seamen from all over the country, attended a 1975 gathering. Telegrams of support came from CSUers in New Zealand and Australia. The roast beef dinner was cooked and served entirely by former CSU cooks. It was a fine reunion that was followed through the years by get-togethers across the country.

The committee collected photos, leaflets and other materials from the seamen and all the remaining files from the CSU's National Office were turned over to the committee. The committee also reviewed all material that I wrote and sent their criticisms along to me. Quite a few people warned that a book of this nature could not be written "by a committee." Too many personalities and egos would clash and I would spend most of my time caught between various factions. Although there definitely were different viewpoints represented on the committee, no one ever attempted to dictate or interpret to me. We worked together to make this history as factual and accurate as possible. The committee members had been there and I had not. They kept me on course.

Obviously a main source of information was the seamen themselves. There were two major ways the seamen's knowledge contributed to this history. There were hundreds of interviews that were taped or recorded by pen and pad. There were also thousands of hours working on jobs, attending union meetings — I have been a member of the Marine Workers and Boilermakers Industrial Union for several years — and serving on committees and community organizations with former members of the CSU.

What has contributed the most to my feelings for the CSU was the way that I was accepted by its members. I travelled from coast to coast to learn the seamen's history. Of all the days on the road, I spent only one night in a rented room and that was in the only town I visited where I didn't have a name of a seaman I could look up in the book. I never really asked for anything. I would just mention the letters CSU and every door would swing open to me. It was not merely hospitality that I received. I was treated like a brother, or in some cases like a son. It was this warmth that touched me most. I will never be able to erase the picture of Scotty Munro telling his story of how Canadian seamen were gunned down on the Halifax waterfront in 1949. As he described this bloody struggle he had his arm around Kay, his 15-year-old grand-daughter, while his 19-year-old granddaughter Karen snuggled in between her mother and grandmother. Three generations were present in that room as the CSU story was told. There is an aura about the CSU that attracted me from the beginning. Gerry Tellier, Moose Mozdir, Stan and Jeannette Wingfield, Nick Buszowski, Stringer McDonald and Tommy Burnett have been among my closest friends.

One problem in writing a history about people you care for and respect is how to maintain objectivity. A second problem is how to make the history stand up to the scrutiny of the CSU's detractors.

I have declared my bias and will state categorically that I believe the CSU represents the best model of democratic and rank and file organizational structure. I have attempted to understand that structure by analyzing material that has been written about the CSU and by studying the people who produced, developed and defended it. Many hours were spent in the archives at Dalhousie University, the Public Archives of Canada and the British Columbia and Ontario Archives. In addition, thousands of newspaper clippings from newspapers around the world were collected and studied. Many first-hand accounts of events by pro- and anti-CSU participants were taken from sworn affidavits.

The Canadian Seamen's Union has always been a controversial subject. In this book there has been very little presented that is not backed up by documented references. (The text is peppered with footnotes that contain these sources. The notes, however, contain no additional information other than source references. A reader may read this book without referring to the notes.)

The people who lived the events speak in these pages, but this book is not "oral history." The participants' recollections are woven into material from all other available sources to try to create an objective picture of the CSU and its time.

The story of the Canadian Seamen's Union needs to be told not only because it provides a major lesson to be learned from Canadian history, nor solely because knowing it will enable us to understand the developments that left Canada without a merchant marine. Equally important is the need to know how the spirit of the CSU has stayed alive and fresh some 35 years after the source of the light has been legalistically extinguished. The CSU did not simply transfer that spirit to the seamen, it had the ability to reflect their own light back upon them.

Because it really was Canadian and because it really was the seamen's union, the CSU was outlawed in its own land. Even though it was crushed under the iron heel of authority, it survived in the hearts and minds of the membership. Thirty years after the CSU was smashed, Fred Skelhorn, who remains an active trade unionist, spoke for a lot of seamen when he told me "the CSU is in my heart. We've made mistakes and anyone who says he hasn't made mistakes is a goddamn liar. We've made a few but we are still the greatest thing that ever hit this goddamn continent. It's impossible to ever bring anything like that back again. It was just so great you can't hit it again. Impossible! If you do, it ain't going to be in my lifetime. If it is in my time, I won't be able to recognize it anyhow, 'cause I'm going to forget how great it was. I'll be too goddamn old."[1]

Acknowledgements

THIS BOOK could never have been written if it had not been for the unselfish contribution and support of many individuals and organizations. William (Moose) Mozdir, who collected every scrap of information on the CSU for more than 30 years, Bud Doucette, Tommy McGrath and Stan Wingfield made this book possible by getting the seamen involved and keeping me on course. Lis Partington was there from the beginning and helped with research, production and advice.

CBRT Local 400, ILWU Local 500, the United Fishermen and Allied Workers Union, the Vancouver local of the Canadian Union of Postal Workers and Vancouver Co-operative Radio (CFRO) all gave support and invaluable assistance to this project.

Geoff Meggs proved to be not only a fine editor but the person with the right personality to keep me in line and to see to it that this book would become a reality.

There were many others who helped in this work. I am deeply grateful for their assistance, but there is no space to acknowledge all contributions and a partial list must suffice: Bert Johnson, Mike James, John Hamm, Ken Doyle, Evert Hoogers, Carolyn Lee, Chris Brown, Linda Field, Mike Marino, Danny Daniels, Jeannette Wingfield, Tommy Burnett, Nick Buszowski, Grace Doucette, Charlie Murray, Kay Murray, Harry Davis, Muriel Davis, Paddy Jones, Jaquelin Rutherford, Mike Linke, Danielle Dionne, Glenn Bullard, Paula Butler, Gerry Yetman and family, Madeleine Parent, Stuart Rush, Zanzy Rutherford, Jimmy O'Donnell, Al Chadwick, Dave Fairey, Geneva Biggers, Gerry Tellier, Kathy Schultz, Gerry McCullough, Sheila Linke, Dave Crain, Two Points Murray, Roberta Hawken, Gerard Fortin, John Shayler, Helen Mellieur, Brenda Ferguson, Dave Forsyth, George Brandak from Special Collections at UBC and Danny Moore of the Public Archives of Canada.

I alone am responsible for factual errors or questionable interpretations that may appear in the text.

CHAPTER ONE

Shipping Out

THERE IS AN UNDENIABLE romance about the sea but anyone who ships out in search of a cushy job is in for the shock of a lifetime. The entire history of the industry has been one of brutality and violence. Most people have read *Les Miserables* or other novels which describe the days when many ships were powered by prisoners chained to the oars. In ancient times it was not uncommon to use slaves. Slaves and prisoners were very cheap labor, requiring the absolute minimum to stay alive. They were easily replaced if they starved to death or died of injuries and the ships were a perfect place to get rid of religious heretics or political dissidents. Instead of stirring up trouble ashore, they could be pulling profits at sea.

Forced labor at sea continued into the mid-17th century in Europe and until the mid-19th century in North America. One of the most important benefits to the shipping interests from the use of slaves and prisoners was the downward pressure it exerted on wages in related industries ashore. It was difficult for a longshoreman to expect fair compensation for his labor when his brother on board ship was in irons.[1]

Oar power was not suited to long voyages or heavy cargoes and eventually sailing vessels predominated on the sea lanes. Slaves and prisoners gave way to men who went to sea to earn a living, but the traditions established in earlier periods persisted. Conditions at sea were so terrible that only dire necessity would drive men to ship out. Seamen generally were not free to choose which vessel they would take and if they were known to be seamen the choice of ship often was decided by a club wielded by the press gangs who roamed the waterfront in search of crews. The press gangs were so common in the United Kingdom that as late as the Second World War the Royal Navy was still known to the seamen as "Andrew." The name referred to the notorious press ganger Andrew Miller, who did his job so well that it was said he had impressed enough seamen to make up his own navy. History tells of the great admirals who gave their lives in wars at sea but for every naval officer who died there probably were a thousand seamen on the bottom whose names were not recorded.

1

On merchant ships, as in the Navy, discipline on board was authoritarian and brutal. No complaint from a crew member was tolerated. The seamen, often kidnapped by thugs and carried on board unconscious, worked for wages determined by the shipowners and the Crown, spending months or years at sea under intolerable conditions working endless hours on deck and aloft. The authority of the captain was absolute. To disobey the most trivial or absurd command meant punishment that could more properly be called torture. Seamen were flogged, staked out in the sun or abandoned in strange ports with no means of ever returning home. A favorite trick was keel-hauling and most pirate movies spend a few frames depicting this officers' sport.

These were the occupational hazards which seamen generally endured as part of their calling. Most accepted these conditions as permanent, but for those who did not the law stated that organization of any kind by seamen was illegal. By the same statutes, the captain was granted the power of life and death over any seaman who stepped out of line or violated an officer's orders. Mutineers faced the death penalty and such rebellions usually were limited to a single ship. They were sporadic, spontaneous outbursts, not the calculated resistance of men organizing to improve their situation.

It was men and women toiling under conditions like these who helped build Canada. Our country always has depended on water transport for its foreign trade. Our economy relies on the export of raw materials and the import of manufactured goods. Before the railways opened Canada's interior to development, the government spent millions on canals to allow maritime trade to penetrate to the heart of the continent.

Today Canada has only a handful of ocean-going ships. There are no Canadian seamen to move our goods to foreign markets and our shipyards are idle or closed. But it has not always been so.

Three times Canada has built merchant fleets that ranked among the world's largest and three times the fleets have been scuttled. In 1878, Canada possessed the fourth-largest merchant fleet in the world consisting of 7,196 vessels. But as steel ships replaced iron steamships and wooden clippers, our position as a maritime nation declined. By 1900 the Canadian merchant marine had ceased to exist for all practical purposes.[2] Canada failed to build a viable steel industry, shipyards were closed or restricted to repair work and Canada's transoceanic cargoes were shipped in foreign bottoms.

The First World War made the rebirth of the Canadian merchant fleet a necessity. In response to orders placed by the British Imperial Munitions Board, 23 ships were built in Great Lakes yards, 12 in British Columbia, four on the St. Lawrence and two in the maritime provinces. They were delivered to managers appointed by the British government.[3]

Canada's canal system received a major overhaul in the same period. Beginning in 1913 the government undertook a 20-year reconstruction of the Welland Canal, the vital link between Lake Ontario and Lake Erie that skirted the cataracts of Niagara Falls. Only 43 kilometres long, the canal lifts ships from Port Weller on Lake Ontario up the 93-metre rise to Port Colborne on Lake Erie with a system of eight locks. The new Welland Canal was linked to existing systems at Cornwall and along the St. Lawrence to Montreal.

These sparks rejuvenated Canada's shipyards. As space became available the Canadian government utilized the yards to build its own steel ship merchant marine to come to the aid of British shipping during the war. The war ended before the Canadian ships were called into service but the government believed the project was profitable and continued launching vessels for a peacetime merchant marine. By 1921, 63 vessels had been built in Canadian yards. They flew the Red Ensign and were manned primarily by Canadians. The fleet was completely government-owned and operated under the Canadian Government Merchant Marine Ltd.[4] To the seamen, the line was known simply as the CGMM.

THE CREATION OF THE CGMM may have moved the country's merchant marine into the 20th century, but conditions for the men who worked the ships remained abysmal. The seamen's lives were dominated by the Canada Shipping Act and the ship's articles, which ensured that seamen who no longer were shackled to oars were chained to their ships by legislation. The act, which remains in force to this day, reflected the contempt that shipowners had for their workers.

"We were 'the scum of the waterfront'," recalls Joe West, who spent his life at sea on ships as varied as Nova Scotia fishing schooners and deepsea freighters. "I think that comes from the ancient times. The way they used to crew ships was you'd be shanghaied from the shore, merely knocked out and brought aboard. That's why even today you have the hardest time trying to make a steamship company come to terms because they never got out of the habit: 'We used to get them for nothing.' "[5]

Although press-ganging had disappeared, ship's articles made up the loss. Throughout the English-speaking world, seamen were bound to the ship by the articles — otherwise known as the Agreement and Account of Crew, the Articles of Agreement or the Crew List — which they signed before the voyage began and when "paying off" at trip's end. The articles were a legal contract of employment between master and crew.

Articles on a typical foreign-going vessel set down the maximum length of time the seaman could be required to serve on the vessel before being legally signed off. One or two-year articles were the norm. The document might include a minimum scale of provisions and allowable substitutes. It gave the size of the crew and the minimum number of qualified able seamen to be carried. It also contained clauses reinforcing the legal authority of the ship's master, required the seamen to be diligent and tractable and provided fines or other penalties for alleged disciplinary infractions. Names of each crew member, from master to galleyboy, were accompanied by his age, nationality, last ship, rating, rate of wages and dates of engagement and discharge.

Failure to be on board at sailing time, "desertion" in foreign ports, death and injury, discharge during the voyage because of illness (or by mutual agreement between master and seaman) were other items generally recorded in the articles as well as in the official ship's log.

In Canada as in other nations, the ship's articles were only one of the two documents that ruled the seamen's lives. Almost every shoreside worker, for example, has been late to work or missed two or three days without prior permission from an employer. Such absence without leave from a ship — in peace or in war, at home or abroad — was a violation of the Canada Shipping Act. If the ship's master so wished, the absence without leave could be designated desertion. Either offence carried penalties of up to three months of imprisonment at hard labor.[6]

If the master determined that a seaman had deserted or was absent without leave, the Shipping Act stated that the "master, any mate, the owner, ship's husband or consignee may, in any place in Canada, with or without the assistance of the local police officers or constables (and those officers and constables are hereby directed to give assistance, if required) and also at any place outside Canada, insofar as the laws in force at that place will permit, arrest him without procuring a warrant."[7] If the seaman, once apprehended was taken before a judge instead of directly back to the ship, he was required to pay out of his wages all costs incurred by his captors.[8] If he was sentenced to do time at hard labor, the master or owner could have him removed from prison and returned to the ship.[9] There was no escape. The act also spelled out that tavern owners must turn over names of seamen being sought by the authority.

To leave no doubt about the master's power, the act ruled that if a seaman was "guilty of wilful disobedience to any lawful command, he shall be liable to imprisonment for a period not exceeding one month." What was a "lawful command"? What was "wilful disobedience"? The decision was left to the captain. As former seaman Danny Daniels puts it, "the regulations are so written that if you don't kiss his boots, you can be charged with failing to obey an order."[10] This was the catch-all clause which allowed the master to impose his will, no matter how dangerous or absurd. Every moment on board ship a seaman was at the whim of the skipper.

The Shipping Act did provide a procedure for the seamen to follow in raising complaints, particularly on questions of water and food. The procedure for each was essentially the same. If there was a water complaint, it had to be supported by at least three crew members. It had to be addressed to another ship's captain, a consular officer, a shipping master or a chief officer of customs. If none of these authorities was available no complaint could be filed. If the officer decided to check the water and found it substandard, he notified the ship's master. "If the master and the said officer or person certify in that statement that there was no reasonable ground for the complaint," the act continued, "each of the complainants shall be liable to forfeit to the owners out of his wages a sum not exceeding one week's wages."[11]

"The whole act worked against us," recalls Stan Wingfield, whose career at sea began during the Second World War. "What possible chance would seamen have against two officers, one of whom was your own master, in a case like that? They would taste the water, tut-tut a bit and say, 'I find nothing wrong with this water. I'd drink it myself.' Of course, it was the seamen who would have to drink it, while working like dogs. Not only would they be sentenced to drink shitty water for the voyage, they'd lose a week's pay into the bargain."[12]

AND THE SEAMEN did work like dogs. Nick Buszowski shipped deep sea for 20 years and did almost every job there was. The officers or licensed personnel, he recalls, were served their meals by messmen. The rest of the crew — the unlicensed personnel — were served by mess-boys. "You were a 'man' if you served the licensed," Buszowski says, "and a 'boy' if you served the crew. You got a lower rate if you served the crew. Then there were the stewards, who catered to the passengers on passenger vessels. Their rates were probably about the same, but the passenger stewards got tips. They made the passengers' bunks and cleaned their cabins. On top of that, they served the passengers' meals. The stewards would make sure they were not doing the same passengers' rooms as they were serving. The passengers would have to double tip and the steward could pick up a couple of extra bucks."[13]

Most seamen worked as deckhands. The Deck Department was responsible for all the painting, chipping, cleaning and polishing required on a vessel as well as its operation while under way. The deck gang moved and docked the vessel and prepared it for loading and unloading. There were three major divisions in this department. The wheelsman or quartermaster steered the ship and did other routine deck work such as splicing, cleaning and repairs. In canals, he operated the snub winch which stopped the forward progress of the ship as it was being winched through the locks. The watchman's main function was to take orders from the mate and pass them on to the deck crew. He also was required to sound the ballast tanks a couple of times each watch. Most of the deck gang, however, were simple deckhands, on call 24 hours a day. They handled the ship's lines, ran winches, cleaned, chipped, painted and just about anything else that needed to be done.

On Canadian freighters negotiating the system of inland canals, a deckhand's work was long, hard and dangerous. Dave Crain spent his early years as a Lake deckhand and remembers every lock.

"From Montreal to Cardinal (at the west end of the St. Lawrence system near Cornwall) there are 26 locks. That's the lower canal. There would be three deckhands on each laker. Two of them would go ashore on a landing boom and one guy would stay and run the aft winch. A landing boom was a swinging boom that was used to put you ashore. There was a bosun's chair or a man rope — a rope with knots — on the end of the boom. The reason the guys are ashore is to get the lines, haul the wires on and put them in the bits.

"You are kind of pulling yourself along the canal and into the locks. You were walking from Montreal to Prescott. That's really what it was on the lower canal. Depending on how much traffic there was it would take you maybe three days to get through the 26 locks. It was okay in the summer because you could always jump in the river or the lake, wherever you were and kind of refresh, but you never got that much sleep. You'd get intermittent sleep, but there would never be anytime when you got eight hours sleep.

"There had been some instances when people going out on a landing boom ended between the ship's side and the canal and were squashed to death. There was a fair number of deckhands running around with two or three fingers off ... There were also a couple of instances that I knew about where people were down below (in the hold) sweeping off ledges and things like that when they were unloading grain and they would fall in. They never got them out alive. They would suffocate."[14]

Yet it was the engine room — called the stokehold and crewed by firemen and trimmers known as the black gang — that powered the entire system. Between 1920 and 1946, the Canadian fleet consisted almost exclusively of coal-burning steamships. At six feet two inches and 160 pounds, Stan Wingfield was well-built for the job he took in the engine room of a Canadian freighter in 1945 at the age of 16 and is well-qualified to describe the underworld hell of the stokehold. Soon after the Second World War, he shipped out on a 10,000-ton freighter called the *Withrow Park*.

"In the stokehold of a 10,000-tonner there were three boilers and three furnaces in each boiler. On watch there was one fireman for each boiler, a trimmer, and in the engine room was the engineer who was on watch. There was an oiler and, on days, a donkeyman. A donkeyman is what you would call a foreman ashore. The three main tools in the stokehold are a shovel, a slice bar and a rake.

"We were steaming down the St. Lawrence, going with the current. It's not too hard firing a boiler when you have the current with you. In Quebec City they brought a fireman aboard. He must have been hanging around the hall and he came aboard as a fireman.

"Anyway, this guy came down and he was green as shit. He didn't know a shovel from a slice bar or a rake or what have you. A shovel, amongst ourselves, we never called it a shovel. We called it a banjo. The reason for that is, of course, that it is shaped like a banjo, but also it sings. What I mean by that is when you are steaming and you open up your fires you would sort of slide your banjo along the steel plate to spread your coals properly. It would make sort of a 'zing.'

"It was very, very hot. We didn't find it that hot, of course. This guy was pretty green. He'd never sailed before. This kid was saying it was hot even before we got started.

"We dropped off the pilot at Pointe au Père and from there we started heading south. In about three days we were in the Caribbean. It started to get pretty hot. In front of those fires it was 130 degrees or more, especially when the doors were open. If you had a good fire going, your fire was white hot. After your fires were cleaned and pitched, you would take a slice bar. You'd open your doors. The slice bar has one end like a wedge. You'd wedge this underneath your clinkers and raise them ever so slightly. This is to let the air get at your fires.

"It's very hot. While you are doing this you have smoke and flames billowing out. If you'd been able to take a bird's eye view of the stokehold, what you'd see is a bunch of guys black with dust, except for maybe the streaks of sweat running down their backs. The gasses are gagging your mouth. You usually chew a sweat rag. We'd hold one end of this rag between our teeth while we were slicing the fires or cleaning them. Usually we just had jeans on. Some guys wore shirts. I never. Heavy boots. We had a canvas rag in our hands to hold the slice bar and to handle the hot furnace doors.

"When we went down to the stokehold there were two landings of grates. You couldn't go down like on ordinary steps, you don't go one step at a time. We would slide down on the handrails, from one landing to the next, very rapidly. If you went down trying to hold the railing, you'd burn your fuckin' hands. You wouldn't burn the skin off, but the rails were too hot to hold. Your hands became like hard leather, anyway, from handling slice bars.

"After slicing, you'd close the door and let that burn, then you'd start over. We had to keep the steam 'on the blood.' There was a steam gauge on each boiler and the gauge was, I believe, 210 pounds. 'On the blood' was when it hit there. If you went over the blood, you'd blow the fuckin' safety valve and your steam would go way, way down. You couldn't go too low, because if you did, you'd slow the engines down. It was a routine balance thing you had to work at — pitch, slice, rake, and repeat this throughout the watch.

"The trimmer, his job was to see that the firemen were supplied with coal from the bunkers. There were coal chutes on each side, except for the center boiler. He had to take a wheelbarrow, fill it up and take it to the center fireman. Then his job was to take buckets of salt water and throw the water on the ashes that were being pulled. This would cause gasses and smoke and dust to fly up all over the place. As you were coming down, it would hit you in the face.

"This new guy — he thought he was in Dante's fuckin' Inferno or something. It wasn't that bad, but this guy he broke down and cried. He literally got down on his knees and started crying. Of course, we were kidding with him. We said, 'If you refuse to work, it's mutiny.' They put him in the galley. As big and as muscular as he was, he couldn't handle it at all.

"You had to keep up the steam. Usually you would just follow one another. You didn't have to be told. Nobody would say, 'Let's get up and give it a pitch.' You didn't do it individually, you did it as a team. It would be bang, like that. It was beautiful unionism of the guys, the way we used to work it.

"You weren't down there but for four hours, but in those four hours there wasn't much time for resting. You had to keep working like a workhorse. Your body was so drained from the heat and all. I'd flop in my bunk and I'd just close my eyes when the oiler would be there shaking me to get up for our watch. I'd look at him and swear that I had only slept for five minutes. You'd drag your ass up to the messroom. They'd call you 25 minutes before your watch. You'd have a coffee and you'd go down to face that bloody smoke and dust and dirt again. The sweat would pour into your eyes. Your heart would be pounding. It sometimes felt like it was in your throat. Sometimes when we were eating, I'd see guys fall off to sleep they were so fagged out."[15]

THE CGMM'S STATED PURPOSE was to carry Canadian cargoes, to provide employment in the post-war period and to develop new trade routes.[16] It successfully laid the foundation for regular service to the

United Kingdom, South America, the West Indies, France and the coast of Newfoundland. Within two years it was achieving its goals, producing jobs and opening important trade routes, but the CGMM vessels, built in an inflated wartime economy from a near-obsolete design were unable to compete with more efficient and faster vessels.[17] Bad management compounded CGMM's problems. On one occasion, shipments of Canadian apples were carried to Britain in Norwegian bottoms while Canadian ships were making the trip carrying only ballast. In another case, 15 CGMM ships were tied up in Halifax for repairs when none were needed — an administrative error.[18] Not surprisingly the CGMM was not profitable, particularly in the first years of costly investment to secure new routes.

Determined not to subsidize CGMM, the government sold off its fleet. The CGMM was scuttled.[19] Fifty-six of the vessels were sold to foreign shipping interests for $2.4 million and six were acquired by the Canadian National Steamships (West Indies) Ltd. for $900,000.[20] The sale of the fleet virtually ended Canada's participation in deepsea shipping. Canadian National operated only 11 ships and Imperial Oil maintained a few deep water tankers. As late as 1939 there were only 38 ocean-going vessels of more than 1,000 tons operating under Canadian registry.[21]

For the Canadian seamen who worked the CGMM fleet, the end came without warning, often in foreign ports thousands of miles from home. When shipowners needed seamen's labor they were tied to the job by the laws of the country and by personal contracts, but when they had outlived their usefulness, they were discarded without a second thought. Smiler — he never used his second name — was a crewman on the *Canadian Settler* when the ship was transferred to foreign registry in 1925. The vessel was sold while she was tied up in the port of Avonmouth in the U.K. Smiler and a number of the crew were sent to Cardiff for passage back to Canada on another CGMM ship.

"When we went there," he recalls, "the shore captain or agent who was representing the company put us in a truck loaded with straw. 'Get in there, boys,' he says. We could see then, not that we weren't used to a lot of this stuff, the way they were going to treat us. According to what we knew about shipping acts ourselves, we said, 'We're entitled to passage back, they sold the ships from underneath us.' Well, the captain said, 'What's this? You're getting passage back.' He took us aboard then and you know where he took us? To the cattlemen's quarters just white-washed with a few old bunks thrown in for a few cattlemen when they're taking cattle over. He pushed us in there. We said, 'No, no, no, we don't take this, we're entitled to something better than this.' Of course, we've got no union. We said we would go to the Board of Trade. He said he didn't care what we did. 'This is what you are supposed to have and that's what you are going to have.'

"All in one group we walked up to the Board of Trade. He had a car and he got there before us and made arrangements as to what we were to receive. When we got there the Board of Trade said, 'We're sorry, but you'll have to go there. We've already had the argument from your agent. You'll have to take it.' " Undaunted, the Canadians appealed to the port warden. "He took us down to the ship and he looked at it and said, 'Not fit for a pig, much less a man.' " But when confronted by the mate with the decision of the Board of Trade, the port warden backed off. Triumphantly, the captain ordered the seamen to appear at the shipping office the next day. "He says, 'I want to sign you on under my command,' " Smiler remembers. "He was starting to put on airs.

"We went to the shipping office. There was a Newfoundlander by the name of O'Toole. He was a very old guy. He was the first guy they called to sign on. Just as he was to sign on I said, 'Hold it.' It was just something that came to my mind. 'What's this?' says the shipping master. 'I've had enough trouble with you fellows.' I said, 'I'd like to ask you a question. Can a man be on the articles of two ships at the same time?' He said, 'Certainly not.' 'Well,' I said, 'We're still on the articles of the other ship. We never signed off.'

"The commissioner came down and asked what happened. He looked at the captain and said, 'Captain, it seems to lay with the boys now.' He then started to explain: 'Of course, you're not coming under his command to do any work. It's just that he must have control over his own ship. He has to be the master of his own ship. He can't carry anything he can't control.'

"I said, 'We're entitled to a better passage than what we're getting. We should be going across as passengers, not thrown into an old tub and pushed around that way. I know there are better ways of getting home than this and we're entitled to it.' Finally the old man offered (the men) a sum of money and they accepted it. They broke down. There wasn't unity among the bunch. That was an instance before there was unions."[22]

When the deepsea crews returned they found a country that could no longer offer them jobs on deepsea ships. It would be another 15 years before Canadian workers could again ship deepsea. As the merchant marine died the seamen turned to the coastal and inland waterways for the few jobs that remained.

When Smiler returned to Canada he was able to land a job on the Lakes. "I made the last trip of the season on this Lake boat in Port Colborne. I think I walked up and back. It was $60 a month. There was no such thing as 'hours'. The only sleep you got was on Lake Ontario for a couple of hours or so. Then the captain would have you out and if he could get you to do some deck work he would. Then you walked, you may as well say, all the way to Port Colborne. You had 15 locks in a row. That took a lot of come-uppance at that time of the year. You were slung out on a boom, put on the dock and you took the lines. You were there rain or shine. It was very slow moving up 15 locks especially at that time of the year. It was crowded with ships trying to make the last trip of the year. You just kept walking through the old Welland Canal.

"You got fed pretty well in those days. They did carry pretty good cooks. The wages weren't too bad at $60 a month for a deckhand or $72 for a wheelsman, but you got very little sleep."[23]

With the beginning of the Depression, conditions deteriorated. By 1935 wages had sunk to two-thirds of the 1929 level. Work became more demanding and unemployment among seamen increased as the ship-owners cut crews in order to minimize costs and to maximize profits.[24] In 1936, a wheelsman was making only $55 as month, a deckhand only $40.[25] With the deepsea fleet gone and wages and working conditions reduced to the minimum, the seamen were forced against the wall. Finally they fought back.

CHAPTER TWO

Beginnings

THE CANADIAN SEAMEN'S UNION was born on the Great Lakes, created out of the seamen's determination to build an organization that would represent them and protect their interests. It arose during the 1930s from the very nature of the industry, which compelled the seamen to work 24 hours a day under constant supervision, confronted them with every conceivable hazard from shipwreck to the slow death of black lung, and then threw them on the beach for the winter to fend for themselves as best they could.

Death hung over the Lakes like a fog. Safety had improved little from the time of the five-day storm of 1913 which wrecked 24 ships and claimed the lives of 300 Canadian seamen.[1] U.S. government statistics showed that seamen in the 1930s had the highest death rate of any group of workers. This was attributed to overwork, the effects of breathing coal and cargo dust, inhaling paint chippings, overheating in the stokehold, the presence of excess carbon dioxide and long working hours without sufficient rest.[2]

The seamen, unlike most shore workers, lived at their job site under the constant rule of the employer. For 24 hours a day they were denied the personal and private activities most other workers take for granted. Food, leisure and sleep were all under company control. A rigid class structure dominated shipboard life, with the officers eating and sleeping separately from the unlicensed personnel. Racism and divisions between Anglophones and Francophones were encouraged. The seamen needed unity to confront the shipowners, and unity could come only from a rank and file organization.

Instead, the seamen were stuck with the National Seamen's Association, headed by one Capt. H.N. McMaster. An operating manager of the Canada Steamship Lines before he moved into the more lucrative field of "representing" seamen, McMaster was backed up in the NSA executive by his daughter, who was secretary-treasurer.[3] McMaster had long forgotten the rigors of life at sea and tried to hide his 250-pound bulk under a soft-brim cap and dark glasses. Seamen laid off at season's end or simply put ashore at the whim of the skipper were easy pickings for the Captain, who offered the only way back to a paying job.

Gus Genetis was 16 when he joined McMaster's association to land his first shipboard job in Montreal. "You went into his office, you paid five bucks and you got a job on the ship," he recalls. "He was recruiting for the companies. In fact, he drove you to the ship wherever it was, in Cornwall or anywhere. It was just a place to get a job. It was an office, you went up to the second floor, you paid him $5 and you went aboard the ship he put you on."[4]

George Dagesse was 19 when he shipped out on the *Lucius W. Robinson* during the 1930s. "I didn't even know there was such a thing as a union then. I was a trimmer. First thing I knew, I had to sign a card for McMaster's 'union.' I had not been in a union before and that was one of my first jobs. The captain of the ship was working for McMaster and gave me the card to sign. I said I didn't want any part of it, because I had heard about it, but I was forced to."

In his six months on the *Robinson*, there was never a union meeting on the vessel. Did he ever meet a union representative other than the captain? "No, none at all." Was there a ship's committee? "No, none at all." Were there ship's delegates elected from the different departments? "No, none at all." Did he have to pay dues? "I had to pay dues."[5]

McMaster was more than a crimp, the name seamen gave to the shore-based racketeers who rounded up labor for the shipowners. He had another more sinister function. With the National Seamen's Association in place and McMaster at the helm, the shipping interests could claim their seamen had a union. They could set wages, working hours and conditions which suited them and eliminate any grievance procedure. With McMaster's assistance, the shipowners had a free hand to push their vessels and their workers to the breaking point. Safety was left up to the ship's master and regulations were ignored to keep the ship moving at all costs. The seamen had to battle the shipowners on one hand and McMaster on the other. As Stan Wingfield puts it, "The seamen were being bit in both balls by the bourgeoisie."[6] Was McMaster on the shipowners' payroll? If he wasn't, he was a fool, for he served them well.

During Dagesse's time on the *Robinson*, the vessel encountered a storm between Sydney and Halifax with 30-foot waves. He was certain they would not survive. The ship would roll to 39 degrees and water would pour into the boiler room from the air intakes. As the ship crested the waves, the propeller would break out of the water and freewheel, threatening to break the driveshaft and put the vessel at the mercy of the storm. As the waves swept the ship, bow and stern would leave the water simultaneously, leaving the ship supported only at midships and in danger of breaking up. It was a flat-bottomed Lake boat and in

Dagesse's opinion the "company did everything in its power to sink that ship." Under the circumstances, Dagesse considered McMaster and his helpers no better than murderers.[7]

The seamen's constant layoffs brought them into contact with the unemployed organizations and gave them their first taste of real trade unionism. The seamen were stuck with McMaster's company union while at sea, but they could belong to a legitimate organization while they were "on the beach" between jobs. Through the unemployed organizations, the young seamen learned the value of organization and the fundamentals of unionism. For many it was a turning point. When the season was about to open on the Lakes, the seamen would congregate at the major ports — Montreal, Toronto, Port Arthur, Thorold or Cornwall — as well as smaller ports where they might be able to pick up a Laker. Season's end would find them laid off in the same ports. Often they wound up at one of the Single Men's Unemployed Association offices.

In Montreal during the Depression just finding a meal could be a major task. "What a lot of us used to do," remembers Smiler, "because it got so bad for seamen, was go aboard some of the passenger ships and eat. It wasn't hard to walk into the dock area. The trick was knowing how to get aboard the ships and where to go and look. When you got aboard a passenger ship, you've got to go down a couple of decks. Of course, if the master-at-arms catches you, he runs you off. So we used to have our little fun evading him. With what was left, the crew always fed us. When the crews were all finished eating, they would say okay. There might be six or seven of us. We'd go in and clean up after in the messroom."[8]

As members of the unemployed organizations, they learned more than survival tricks. They learned to organize and they came into contact with experienced trade unionists. They learned the value of collective action in achieving a common goal. They worked together and assisted other unions in their struggle as members of organizations rather than as individuals. Jimmy Bell, who rose to be secretary-treasurer of the Nova Scotia Federation of Labor, was secretary of the Single Men's Unemployed Association in Toronto in the 1930s. He worked closely with the unemployed seamen and recalls how they supported themselves:

"We were able to feed ourselves by tin canning. We used to do odd jobs. Different organizations like the Steel Workers Organizing Committee were started up. If they needed a couple of fellows to hand out leaflets, we'd help out. Or we'd follow workers home, find out their names and turn them over to the organizer for him to follow up. We'd go up to the General Steel Works in Toronto and pick a couple of fellows and follow them home. You could sort out the fellows who were a bit interested against those who wouldn't be. Some would take the leaflet and read it. We'd go after them and not the ones who took the leaflet and threw it away. We'd compile a list of employees and give it to the union organizer. That's the type of auxiliary services we would perform. Instead of paying the fellows they'd make a donation to the unemployed organization."[9]

The seamen took their new-found skills back to the ships. They began raising their grievances and demanding action. McMaster decided he had to make a move if he was to continue to hold the seamen in his grip. In the summer of 1935 he put out a letter warning the shipowners to give the crews a raise or face a general strike on the Lakes by August 1. The shipowners understood the charade, but unfortunately for McMaster the seamen took him at his word and abandoned the ships.[10]

Although the seamen had many legitimate grievances, the walkout centered strictly on economic matters. Canadian seamen had watched their wages drop by as much as 50 percent between 1929 and 1935. Hours of work had increased and the crew size had been cut back in order to realize a greater profit for the coupon clippers ashore. The *Globe and Mail* reported that seamen were seeking a reduction in working hours to 12 hours a day from 24.[11]

As seamen began to tie up their ships and join the picket lines around the canals and Lake ports, T.B. Enderbee, general manager of Canada Steamship Lines, panicked. Apparently fearing that McMaster had changed sides, he called a news conference and exposed the Captain as a fraud. He informed the press and the CSL employees that McMaster's outfit was not a union but a fundraiser for the Captain. The National Seamen's Association, he said, and McMaster's National Association of Marine Engineers, were not legitimate unions. Neither were registered with the Registrar General of the Dominion of Canada in accordance with the Trade Union Act.[12] Enderbee was telling everyone what most seamen already knew — McMaster was a phony.

The Captain's reply was true to form. Instead of backing the seamen, he denied that he had anything to do with the walkout. He hurried to the Ministry of Labor and pleaded that it was all a mistake. He claimed he had cancelled the walkout, but his message was not received.[13] McMaster had opened a Pandora's Box for the shipowners. Once on strike for legitimate demands, the seamen were not prepared to give in to the companies because of the Captain's mistake. His credibility had worn very thin. Despite his betrayal, they had developed their own leadership during the brief strike, inexperienced and untutored but born out of the ranks and ready to learn.

The seamen were abandoned on the docks by the NSA. They faced being blacklisted for life and were worried that because they were under articles and did not have the support of a union they could be charged with mutiny.[14] The strike crumbled. The defeat was particularly bitter for the seamen of the *S.S. Chippewa*, who saw their vessel sail out of Toronto, undermanned and with a scab crew as they stood on the dock cursing McMaster and holding useless picket signs. Among the striking seamen was Dewar Ferguson.

Although McMaster had deserted the strikers, they discovered support in other quarters. The first person to come to their aid was J.B. Salsberg, organizer for the Workers Unity League, who came to the picket lines and suggested the seamen use the WUL hall as their strike headquarters. They moved in immediately.

Created under the leadership of the Communist Party of Canada, the Workers Unity League had been formed in 1929 to respond to the need for militant, rank and file industrial union organization to meet the gathering economic crisis of the Depression. The main goal of the WUL was organizing the unorganized in mass production industries. It had an explicitly revolutionary program aimed at mobilizing workers to defend their working and living conditions and ultimately of overthrowing the capitalist system. Unlike its mainstream rivals, the WUL admitted trade unionists regardless of political affiliation or links to international unions. The Trades and Labor Congress of Canada, by contrast, accepted only affiliates of the American Federation of Labor. The All-Canadian Congress of Labor accepted only Canadian unions. Both were hostile to left-wing unions and both believed it was impossible to organize or to win strikes during the Depression.[15]

These policies were of little immediate importance to the striking seamen. What mattered most to them was the tangible help they received from the WUL when they needed it badly. It was at the WUL hall that Ferguson and others active in the strike found support from rank and file trade unionists — from their own class. Ferguson later described those early days:

"We set up a soup kitchen right in the Workers Unity League hall. There were two women there — one was Lil Greene and the other was Lily Himmelfarb — who were working with the Workers Unity League, and they were of great assistance to us. We didn't know anything about collecting money, or asking people for money for strike funds, or anything like that. We had no experience. I was elected to speak on behalf of the seamen down at some of the meetings and the first meeting I spoke at was down in the garment center, at Camden and Spadina Avenue, at noon when the workers all came out of the clothing shops. We discussed the conditions of the seamen and the strike, and J.B. Salsberg got up and introduced us and gave us the outline and then had me speak.

"Well, I had never spoken at a meeting before, and when I got finished

I didn't know what I said, but they said it was all right. I told them about the conditions aboard ship and this is what they wanted to know. The women, along with some of the seamen who were with me on the committee, passed cans around and to our surprise, people were putting quarters and dollars into the strike fund, you know, in the cans. I had never seen this before and it really gave us encouragement. Joe Turnbull went with the committee to go around to the stores to ask for food to feed the striking seamen and he told me later, he said, 'Fergie, I never seen anything like it.'

"He said, 'We went into these little Jewish stores all along Spadina Avenue and up around College and Dundas and when we told them what it was all about, you'd be surprised the amount of groceries we got,' and he showed us the tins of groceries, beans, all sorts of food, coffee, tea and that, and he was really inspired and so were the rest of the committee who went with him. There were three or four seamen and when we reported in, we had collected $65 at two meetings in the garment center, which was a lot of money in those days. And the amount of food we had from the stores was quite considerable and it impressed the seamen very much."[16]

Nevertheless, the strike was lost and the seamen attempted to get back on the ships. They agreed to organize on board and to convene a meeting in the fall to establish a new union. The returning seamen would set up committees on the ships and keep in touch with the organizing office, which would be staffed by Ferguson and Turnbull and located in space provided by the Union of the Unemployed. Ferguson and Turnbull were elected to stay behind because of their leadership qualities and because both had undoubtedly been blacklisted by the companies.

The two organizers faced a tough task. Charged with organizing the fall convention, they also had to sign up any crews that stopped in the Port of Toronto. The ship committees were the seeds of a new union, but the Toronto office was the stable home base. Turnbull soon left for the Mackenzie-Papineau Battalion to fight Franco and fascism in Spain. He was replaced by Bert Whyte, a blacklisted miner and part-time writer for the Communist Party's newspaper the *Clarion*, who helped Ferguson patrol the waterfront. The two shared a tiny room on Augusta Street where Ferguson often cooked up a stew for visiting seamen on a two-burner gas stove in the hallway.[17]

"During that period," Ferguson later recalled, "the Union of the Unemployed was very active and they were in the office just upstairs from us. They would give us a great deal of help. I must say that without their help, the organizing in the early stages would have been very difficult." Ferguson reciprocated that aid when he could, speaking at outdoor meetings, addressing the unemployed and seamen in particular. He already knew Salsberg and Whyte and soon he met Harvey Murphy, later a leader of the Mine, Mill and Smelterworkers Union. All three were communists. Their dedication to the working class impressed him and it was not a difficult decision in 1935 when Bert Whyte asked him to join the party. Ferguson's application for membership marked the first direct involvement of the Communist Party with the seamen's organization.

For Danny Daniels, the seaman who eventually became one of the editors of the Canadian Seamen's Union paper the *Searchlight*, there is no mystery to the quick links that grew between the communists and the seamen. From the earliest days of human society, ships had been treated as a dumping ground, he says, a place to send "the jailbirds or the people who had violated the codes of that particular society. It was one of the most oppressive areas of work other than the mines. There was a radicalization, of necessity, of the people involved. This radicalization has shown itself in country after country, and it involved not only merchant seamen but navy seamen.

"If you look at the history of England, you find major mutinies which occurred on the British fleet, but not in the Army. Indeed, the Shipping Act came into being after one such mutiny when Captain Bligh lost his second ship. So there is radicalization. In the Soviet revolution, the seamen were a vanguard, so to speak, of the working class. It is not because they were more brilliant men, it's because of the conditions and because you had a lot of time to think on long voyages. There was no way someone was going to tell you 'if you work hard, you are going to become a boss and have your own ship.' You never saw your shipowner and yet he had his own ship and perhaps many others. You were working hard and never managing to get a ship, not even the skiff you were always dreaming of. It wasn't because you fucked off and spent money all the time, it was because your wages were so small.

"There's that radicalization. Why am I putting so much emphasis on this? It is because of this: had the Communist Party not been involved, then there would have been another radical grouping. The seamen of necessity would have sought out some effective organization ashore with which they could ally.

"In the United States, for example, and certainly on the West Coast, there was the influence of the Wobblies, the Industrial Workers of the World. Even during the time when the Communist Party was regarded as a revolutionary organization by the seamen, there was the great romantic influence of the IWW on all of us. Had it not been the CP, it would have been a radical Socialist Party or a radical anarchist party, but it would have been a radical group. In this case it was the CP. Why? Because the CP had the initiative to be present when the struggle started on the Great Lakes against the shipowners and McMaster.

"The seamen looked around and said, 'These guys are going out of their way to help us. They are on our side. They talk our language. They put out for us, put us up in their homes, they lay out bread for us. Hell, we'll look into their ideas.' And that's exactly what happened. The Communist Party became the most influential organization of shore-side people on the ships."[18]

The Ontario seamen held their first large meeting just before the 1936 shipping season opened on the Great Lakes in mid-April. There were more than 200 employed seamen present and they formed the Marine Workers Union of the Great Lakes,[19] an industrial union to cover all unlicensed personnel. Ferguson was elected president and general organizer, while Hugh Lawson, who had been a Wobbly, assumed the only other officer's position. The union set out to win improved working conditions, safer ships and higher wages. Organizing was concentrated along the Welland Canal and Georgian Bay.

Almost simultaneously, Ferguson heard rumors of another union being established in Montreal by two cooks who were reported to be working for McMaster. "We were wrong in this case," Ferguson said later. "We didn't pay much attention to it. We concentrated on our own organization and on learning the lessons of McMaster's sellout the previous year."

The Montreal organization actually had resulted from dissatisfaction with McMaster. Called the National Seamen's Union (NSU), it was headed by a cook named J.A. "Pat" Sullivan and had been chartered in 1936 by the All-Canadian Congress of Labor (ACCL). Like the Marine Workers Union, the NSU was an industrial union designed to bring all seamen into a single organization.[20] Sullivan had previously worked as an agent in McMaster's NSA, but quit when McMaster informed him the seamen could have no voice in the handling of funds and could not examine the association's books.[21] Like the Toronto organization, the Montreal union had close ties with the Union of Unemployed. Its president, J.D. "Jack" Munro, was not a seaman but had worked hand in glove with Sullivan to help the early organizing in Montreal.

Rank and file seamen were bringing the news of the two unions back to the ports of Montreal and Toronto. At Munro's urging, Sullivan wrote to Ferguson and proposed a meeting. They set a date in Toronto.

The meeting was held in the Charles Restaurant in Toronto on July 23, 1936. Exactly who was present, besides Ferguson and Sullivan, is not recorded, but it was decided that the interests of the seamen would best be served by amalgamating the two unions. For the time being, the new organization would be called the National Seamen's Union. Ferguson was president and Sullivan took on the job of secretary-treasurer. The

ACCL affiliation was maintained and headquarters of the new organization were established at 685, rue de la Commune in Montreal. A seamen's conference convened to endorse the merger called for the creation of a branch office at 8 Bay Street in Toronto and the establishment of other locals wherever they were needed.[22] The National Seamen's Union officially became the Canadian Seamen's Union in September 1936. The CSU had been born from struggle, but the pains of birth were nothing compared to the conflicts which lay ahead.

CHAPTER THREE

Victory on the Lakes

THE NEW UNION almost immediately clashed with the leadership of the ACCL. With no certifications and a small membership paying only 50 cents a month each in dues, the CSU fell behind in its per capita payments. An appeal to ACCL secretary-treasurer W.T. Burford for a reprieve was turned down. ACCL representative Joe Wall, a well-known right-winger, charged that he had reports from a CSU dissident that the union's funds were being improperly used.

Theoretically, relations between the CSU and the ACCL should have been harmonious. Composed of Canadian unions which had either been expelled or had withdrawn from the Trades and Labor Congress of Canada, the ACCL was dedicated to industrial unions.[1] More than 85 percent of the unions in the TLC, by contrast, were international unions affiliated to the American Federation of Labor with headquarters in the United States. The TLC unions were craft-based, organizing each particular trade into different unions. Under the TLC constitution, no organization could join if it sought jurisdiction already granted by the AFL to its affiliates. This meant that national Canadian unions could not belong to the TLC if an international union claimed the right to represent workers in that sector.

Yet Workers Unity League unions sought merger with TLC affiliates when the WUL dissolved in 1935. (The WUL and Communist Party had concluded that the WUL's goals of a militant, democratic trade union movement could best be achieved by uniting Canadian workers in a single organization around a militant platform.[2]) With Sullivan now a Communist Party member as well as Ferguson, the value of ACCL affiliation was actively debated within the CSU. Events soon settled the question for them.

Within months of its creation, the CSU found itself under all-out attack from the ACCL leadership. To defuse Wall's charges, Sullivan asked William Dodge, then chairman of the Montreal District Council of the ACCL, to examine the union's books. Dodge, who later became secretary-treasurer of the Canadian Labor Congress, concluded that "none of the charges concerning mis-use of funds could be supported.

All of the financial operations of the union were perfectly in order."

Burford would not give in. He moved to put the union under the administration of an ACCL official, possibly Wall or one of his informants. Sullivan agreed to an administrator, provided the person selected was acceptable to the CSU. He proposed a board composed of Dodge and D.A. Vannesse, head of the Firefighters Union, another ACCL affiliate. Burford ignored Sullivan and appointed a board unacceptable to the CSU.

According to Dodge, the financial dispute was the cover for an attempt to purge the fledgling union's leadership. "It may have been due to the fact that Sullivan was a recognized left-winger and it was suspected that colleagues of his were also of that persuasion. I was not a left-winger myself and never have been in that particular ideological group, but it didn't matter to me what Sullivan was. I thought he was running the union reasonably well and trying to do a good job for a group of people who needed organization very much. I thought myself that the financial aspect of it was largely an excuse for moving in on them because of their political views. Burford was a fanatical anti-socialist and anti-communist, an extreme right-winger. Wall was very much of that persuasion as well."[3]

Wall was not prepared to stop at checking balance sheets. He informed Sullivan that under an ACCL trusteeship all CSU leaflets and union publicity would be cleared through him. The CSU leadership decided Wall should state his case directly to the seamen. When they heard his pitch, he was asked to leave the building. The irate seamen passed motions dissociating their union from the ACCL and instructing Sullivan to make the necessary arrangements to affiliate the CSU to an international body.[4]

There were several possible routes into the Trades and Labor Congress. One was a merger with an existing affiliate, an inconceivable choice for workers who had just built their own rank and file organization. A second alternative was application for a direct charter, which could only be granted by a two-thirds vote of a TLC convention. Even if the vote were won, the CSU would live with the constant threat of an American-based affiliate seizing its jurisdiction. The only avenue open to the CSU was affiliation to an existing U.S.-based union. Under such an arrangement, no vote was required to affiliate to the TLC. Equally important was the fact that the AFL connection would give the CSU preferential jurisdiction over Canadian seamen. Rather than face the threat of attack by an international, the CSU would itself be protected from other internationals moving into its jurisdiction.

On September 12, 1936, Sullivan pulled out a piece of CSU stationery and started typing a letter to the TLC. The letterhead read "National

Seamen's Union, Chartered by the All-Canadian Congress of Labor" and bore the ACCL seal. But Sullivan was applying for a "charter through the Trades and Labor Congress of Canada to cover the seamen employed in this trade. We have already sent a communication to the ISU (International Seamen's Union)," he wrote, "but to date have had no reply.

"As you will notice by our letterhead ... we were formerly affiliated with the All-Canadian Congress of Labor. Since the first of September we have been independent of any affiliation whatsoever. Owing to the policy adopted by the ACCL, which we considered was detrimental to the movement in the forming of an organization of seamen, we the executive board believe that autonomy of the union should remain with the seamen, whereas the ACCL wishes to take control of this movement. It was decided for the betterment of our members that we should disaffiliate ... Notice of this change has already been publicly made through the press."[5]

The Canadian organization did not have long to wait. By return mail, the ISU granted a charter to the young union under the name of the Canadian Seamen's Union with jurisdiction over all unlicensed seamen and fishermen in Canada. Now, thanks to the decision of an American organization with absolutely no involvement in Canada, the CSU could organize without interference in Canada and gain admission to the Trades and Labor Congress without a vote.[6]

Bankrupt, moribund and racketeer-ridden, the ISU issued the charter almost by reflex. In the United States, it was engaged in a desperate effort to stamp out the newly-formed National Maritime Union, an American counterpart of the CSU. Canadian seamen were well aware of the ISU's condition, which was akin to a cadaver collapsing from within, and they were familiar as well with the struggle of American seamen to build an American rank and file organization. One Canadian seaman who had seen the new American union close up was Tommy Burnett.

Burnett was 15 when he first shipped out from British Columbia in 1930. During the following 50 years he sailed the coasts of Canada and the United States, crossed the oceans and visited most of the world's great ports. Some guys look like seamen. Tommy doesn't. He was a fireman, but he is not big like most stokehold veterans, nor is he small and wiry. He's somewhere in between.

During his career he belonged to virtually every west coast seamen's union from the Seafarers' Industrial Union to the National Maritime Union, through the CSU, the West Coast Seamen's Union and finally Local 400 of the Canadian Brotherhood of Railway, Transport and General Workers. In 1936, only 21 and blacklisted in the wake of the

1935 Vancouver waterfront strike, he set out on a voyage which would not return him to his native province for 19 years.

With his picket cards from Vancouver and a letter from the seamen's union president as his letters of reference, Burnett presented himself at the office of the Maritime Firemen's Union in San Francisco, where Harry Ferguson was the secretary.[7]

"I was flat on my ass and I had to do something. Ferguson said, 'This is a rank and file union, I'll call in a committee off the floor.' He called a committee in and as soon as they saw my picket cards, they said, 'Fuck, you're all right. What job do you want on the board?' There were two open jobs and I took the *Kentuckian*.

"I made one trip on her and when I came back the '36 to '37 strike was on. I spent the strike in 'Pedro and joined the same ship after, made another coastal trip, came back and paid off. I beat my way to New York and arrived there in the summer of 1937. The National Maritime Union had been formed and I went down to the NMU hall."

Using the alias Tommy Wilson to avoid deportation, Burnett attended the founding convention of the National Maritime Union. "It impressed me," he recalls. "It was all very high-spirited and rarin' to go. The rank and file ran the meetings, had actual control over the meetings. The chairman was elected at each meeting.

"The NMU, right from the very start, said no discrimination on account of race, creed, color, national origin or political belief. In all the southern ports in the ISU halls, they had a big white line up the center of the hall. The NMU never had that. They were the first halls to dispatch mixed crews."

This was the union the ISU was using all its energy to smash. Aware that any dues they sent the ISU would be used in the battle against their American brothers, the CSU members insisted on a unique arrangement. As Sullivan put it, "under no circumstances was the Canadian union to hand over any monies to the International Seamen's Union, but to make the excuse that the Canadian union needed the money for organizing in Canada."[8] The CSU arranged to pay its TLC per capita directly to the congress, rather than through the ISU. The seamen would have their cake and eat it too, using the American affiliation to join a Canadian labor center without paying a cent to the gangster-ridden U.S. organization.

The ISU leadership did not object. In 1921, the TLC had asked the ISU its position regarding Canadian seamen. On March 27, 1921, Frank Morrison, then secretary of the American Federation of Labor, advised TLC president Tom Moore that he "took this matter up with President Furuseth of the International Seamen's Union of America and he returned it with the following notation: 'We have spent money and time on the Canadian seamen and they will neither work together independently nor under our jurisdiction. We have given them up and told them to act for themselves.' "[9] This did not mean, the ISU hastened to add in a second letter two weeks later, that it surrendered jurisdiction.[10] That second letter, however, was the total organizational effort expended by the ISU in Canada between 1921 and 1936.

The ISU connection served another purpose for the CSU: it satisfied the desire of the seamen for an international link that would integrate them with the struggles of the broader labor movement. Madeleine Parent, who was associated with the CSU in its infancy in Montreal and dedicated her life to organizing independent Canadian trade unions, says the urge to join an international was understandable in the context of the time.

"Ever since the early 1920s, workers in Quebec found themselves threatened by the Catholic syndicates which at that time were dominated by the clergy, and through the clergy related to the employers and governments of the time. Those workers who didn't wish to be under such domination found that relating to the AFL gave them a certain independence which, of course, led to another dependence.

"There was what was for then a very strong Montreal Trades and Labor Council which we rallied around. There was a certain acceptance of the fact that you belonged to that group as against the Catholic syndicates... The Canadian Seamen's Union was part of the Trades and Labor Council as an affiliate of the TLC. Pat Sullivan and the representatives of the CSU were very much a part of the life of that movement and they were on the left wing. This grouping got support from a lot of rank and filers at the time. It wasn't what you would call just an AFL thing. There were Quebec workers fighting the battles on the waterfront and the factories and elsewhere within this organization."[11]

Now entrenched in the labor movement, the CSU was ready to approach the shipowners, but this time their hats would be on the back of their heads, not in their hands.

BY EARLY 1937, the new union could claim between 1,200 and 1,900 members.[12] Seamen were flocking to join because they saw the CSU as an organization made up of people like themselves who knew the score and dreamed of a better day. There was no time for the union to grow peacefully — issues were pressing and the CSU advised shipowners "they are not bucking any infant union when they buck us, but a full-grown outfit that knows all the points and is willing to show them when called on."[13] With that warning, the CSU convened its first annual convention March 27, 1937 in Toronto.

Delegates to that two-day gathering established the CSU's basic structure and elected its first full slate of officers. Munro took over the president's gavel while Ferguson and Jack Chapman filled the vice-presidencies. Sullivan was elected secretary-treasurer, the union's only full-time paid position. The convention also directed the officers to establish a newspaper to keep the membership informed of union activity. This paper was called the *Searchlight* and Pat Sullivan was the first editor. "An organ of rank and file expression and opinion," the *Searchlight* was to form an important link between the ships and the union ashore.[14]

The union's highest body was the membership, organized into locals with their own elected executives free to work autonomously on local issues. Conventions were to be held annually with delegates elected from the floor of local meetings and the national executive was to be elected by convention for a one-year term. The national office was in Montreal and locals were established in Toronto and Fort William. Others would be established as needed.[15]

The heart of the union was not ashore but on the ships, where the seamen worked. The 1937 convention established an institution which it hoped would guarantee democracy in every aspect of the seamen's lives and keep the union on a true course. Delegates issued a call to the crews on all ships to elect three-person ship's committees with one member designated ship's delegate. The ship's committee was "to settle all grievances on board ship, to draw every member of the crew into the union, to establish and maintain direct contact with officers of the union in the important ports and to act as consultants to the (union) officers."[16]

Ship's committees ensured that the union remained in the hands of the members. Grievances could be handled on the spot without long delays. Only if a settlement could not be reached would shoreside officials come into play. The committees, the seeds of a workers' government afloat, gave the seamen the dignity that only self-rule can bestow.

Shipowners and the government deeply resented the committees and constantly attempted to misrepresent their role. "There never was any thought in the CSU of competing with the 'navigational' power of the officers, or of the captain or of the companies," says Danny Daniels. "This is often what the shipowners misleadingly maintained. The ship's committees were an attempt to create a powerbase for the seamen concerning their working and living conditions. It was meant to give them a collective, democratic voice and leverage concerning their sea-homes. In this sense it was a challenge to the companies, who automatically assumed they had the right to treat the seamen as prison inmates. We were out to undo the prison approach."[17]

The convention also drew up the union's collective bargaining program: better working conditions, reduction of the working day to eight hours, wage parity with American seamen, lifeboat and firedrill on every vessel, union hiring, a closed shop, ship's committees on every vessel and the establishment of councils of maritime unions. It was an ambitious program, one the seamen were aware could not be won overnight.

Safety was a burning issue for the seamen, who vowed to force the installation of wireless radios on all ships in Canadian waters. Under the Canada Shipping Act, vessels under 5,000 tons did not require wireless. Was a person's life less valuable because he or she worked on a smaller vessel? Apparently it was, because the companies opposed any change in the regulations that would add a radio operator's wages to their overhead.

The result of the "profit before safety" equation was evident in the loss of the 1,664-ton lake vessel S.S. Calgadoc, which went down that year without a wireless and unable to call for help. Nineteen seamen drowned "like rats in a trap," said the Searchlight. "We will do everything in our power to see that no more of our brothers are needlessly sacrificed on the altar of profit and will do everything to see that the marine laws of the country are altered to give the seafarer in our Great Lakes at least the opportunity for his life."[18]

The shipowners showed no more concern for safety when paying passengers were involved. The CSU made a particular target in 1937 of the Canadian National Steamship Co., a subsidiary of the Canadian National Railway, which operated the passenger vessels Dalhousie City and Northumberland between Toronto and Port Dalhousie. Each carried liferafts and lifeboats capable of seating 224 people. Each vessel, when it was not undermanned, carried a crew of 26. On a normal run, the passengers numbered about 1,000. Simple mathematics indicated that most on board would be left to their own resources in the event of a disaster. To make matters worse, crews commonly worked 15 to 20-hour days. In one lifeboat drill, it had taken the crew 15 minutes to get one boat over the side.

Munro cabled Transport Minister C.D. Howe and Labor Minister Norman Rogers demanding an investigation of the two boats, but nothing was done until the refusal of the Northumberland crew to sail forced resolution of the safety issues.

The CSU's international ties helped win victories on another front. Wage parity with American seamen was a CSU goal, but with U.S. wages double the Canadian level on average, the increase could not be won in one jump. The first step, however, came in June 1937 when members of the International Longshoremen's Association (ILA) in the Port of New York refused to handle non-union Canadian vessels. The first vessel caught in the boycott was the Donnaconna Paper Co. vessel *ADC*, whose crew was unable to produce union cards.[19] The company contacted the CSU and offered to recognize the union as well as to grant a small wage increase. The CSU notified the longshoremen to proceed unloading the vessel. It was a small victory, but it gave the union a toehold it needed.

Fearing similar treatment, the Canada Steamship Lines, the largest Lake carrier, reached an agreement with the CSU June 28. It recognized the union and agreed to wage increases ranging from $5 to $10 a month. The CSU had truly come of age. In four short months, it had become the union of all the unlicensed seamen employed by Canada's largest shipping company.[20] The CSU was well aware that the American longshoremen had given them the boost they needed and within a month the Canadians had the opportunity to return the favor.

Members of the newly-formed Local 1477 of the ILA went on strike for union recognition in Thorold, Ontario, in July 1937. Seamen employed by the Scott Misener Steamship Co. were ordered to work the cargo or be dismissed. The CSU members immediately joined the picket lines and seamen who were not union members signed CSU cards and picked up placards as well. The longshoremen quickly won their agreement and unity between the seamen and the longshore workers grew.[21] But the unity at the rank and file level was in stark contrast to the attitude in the ILA's leadership.

Soon after the Thorold victory, Montreal longshoremen in the ILA went on strike. The employers responded by setting up a scab union to work the waterfront. Joe "King Joe" Ryan, president of the ILA, came up to Montreal from his New York office, revoked the charter of the striking ILA members and chartered the scab union in its place. The Montreal Trades and Labor Council, outraged by Ryan's tactics, directed council president Raoul Trepanier, along with delegates Kent Rowley and Pat Sullivan, to meet Ryan, demand that he revoke the scab union charter and insist that he support the strikers.

When the Canadians arrived at Ryan's hotel suite they were greeted by one of Ryan's gunmen, who stuck his pistol in Trepanier's stomach and backed him out the door. Seeing that it was not a climate conducive to the active exchange of ideas, the delegation left. Ryan's scab local not only shattered the longshore strike but seriously weakened all the waterfront unions, the CSU included.[22]

As the CSU's official spokesman, Sullivan became well-known and respected in labor circles. In 1937 he was elected to the executive of the Montreal Trades and Labor Council. In October, the CSU was instrumental in the creation of a council of waterfront unions known as the Transportation Federation. The development of such a council, to strengthen the waterfront unions and to build the CSU's links with other organizations, had been a goal of the first convention. Sullivan was elected secretary-treasurer, the council's highest position.[23]

As Sullivan's responsibilities grew, the daily administration of the union fell to other officials while Sullivan acted as the union's public face. He was a good speaker and an effective liaison with other trade unions. It was a division of labor which suited the union and served the seamen well.

Despite its growth and new challenges, the union remembered its roots. The halls in Montreal and Toronto were open 24 hours a day and the Fort William office stayed open until 11 p.m. to serve the membership's needs. It was not, however, just seamen who utilized the facilities. Jimmy Bell, of the Union of the Unemployed, remembers how the CSU aided the "Duke Street Boys," as Toronto's unemployed were known in those days. "Quite a few of our fellows, the Duke Street Boys, if they got stranded in the wintertime, would have to hang out (in one of the ports) until spring. They just didn't like the atmosphere of the pogies, you know, the city-operated pogies, where you had to be fumigated every night and you lived a rather vegetable-type existence. The CSU used to keep their halls open all winter and our fellows would go up there and flop."[24] The CSU halls served as social and political centers for the unemployed, the seamen just off a ship and for those waiting to ship out. Knowledgeable union organizers knew they could always count on the CSU hall for help on a picket line. This tradition began with the birth of the CSU and never was abandoned.

McMaster, always alive to the possibilities of profiting from seamen's misfortunes, tried to turn the plight of the unemployed to his own advantage. His National Seamen's Association established a "soup kitchen" in Montreal and asked grocery stores to contribute food to the needy. Telephone salesmen solicited donations to the kitchen in return for a 60 percent cut of the proceeds. McMaster raked off the remainder, but added a special twist to the scam for his shipowner friends.

Seamen on the beach were not always aware that the soup kitchen was connected to the Captain until it was too late. "I was unfortunate enough this past winter to be stranded in the city of Montreal," reported one seaman, "and had to apply to the Montreal soup kitchen for a meal. All I had was roughly nine meals and now I find that they are trying to claim that I must join their bogus organization in return for the few paltry meals I had."[25] The Montreal Trades and Labor Council brought pressure to bear on the Better Business Bureau and McMaster's racket was exposed,[26] but this did not stop the Norris Steamship Co. from demanding that seamen join McMaster's outfit as a condition of employment. Nor did it stop seamen from signing with McMaster, obtaining a job and exposing the shake-down to the CSU.[27]

Details of McMaster's rackets and a host of other developments important to the seamen were carried in the *Searchlight*, which rolled off the presses for the first time as a four-page tabloid on July 1, 1937. From the beginning the *Searchlight* carried articles in French. A couple of issues later it contained "La page française," and by October 15 it boasted "La section française." Although the leadership of the union was primarily English-speaking, the *Searchlight* noted that "the French Canadian seamen have shown themselves to be thoroughly conscious of the need for organization and have disproved the opinion held by some that the French Canadian sailors would be hard to win for the organization. This idea is fostered by all employers, since it plays into their hands and weakens the forces of the movement, but it has no foundation in fact."[28]

The *Searchlight's* modest beginning did not go unnoticed. The paper carried articles calling for German seamen to join with Spaniards fighting against the spread of fascism and the anti-fascist stance of the union was obvious. There were articles on the history of trade unionism and room for rank and file opinion, but not everyone cared for the opinions expressed. On November 10, 1937, the government of Premier Maurice Duplessis shut down the *Searchlight's* print shop under the Padlock Law, which allowed the Quebec authorities to close any operation suspected of advocating communism.[29]

"The intent of this law was unmasked in its operation," says Daniels. "It was used against any social or labor organization regardless of whether it was communist or not. Homes of journalists, like those of the *New York Times* correspondent in Montreal, were raided. Church groups leaning to liberalism and concerned about the steady growth of fascism were impeded in their operations. Halls and restaurants were threatened that if they allowed their premises to be used by any of these groups they would be padlocked. Unions like the CSU frequently had trouble finding adequate places in which to meet. The law was the first measure of a government leaning to fascism."[30]

The padlocking of the print shop was a setback for the *Searchlight*, but not a fatal one. The paper changed its form but did not miss an issue. A mimeographed emergency edition appeared November 15. It had been another stumbling block thrown in the path of the union, but the CSU was getting good at jumping hurdles.

CHAPTER FOUR

The Right to Choose

CAPT. McMASTER had been grasping at straws to keep his National Seamen's Association afloat. He treaded water for as long as he could and just when it seemed he had gone down for the last time, the shipowners would save him and put his experience as operations manager for Canada Steamship Lines to work.

Early in 1938, New York's *Journal of Commerce* reported that the CSU had blossomed to 5,000 members.[1] This growth was reflected in the mushrooming of locals along the inland waterway. By the time the CSU's second annual convention opened in Montreal on St. Valentine's Day, the union boasted 12 functioning locals.

The shipowners had to have an organization to combat the CSU's rapid growth, so McMaster surfaced once more. He proclaimed himself Governor of the Canadian Brotherhood of Ship's Employees (CBSE), and the tiny, right-wing Canadian Federation of Labor accepted this construction of recycled debris as an affiliate in January 1938.[2] This time, however, McMaster would not be satisfied with the unlicensed personnel. He wanted more. The CBSE was to include all people employed on Canadian vessels. It had three sections — the Mercantile Marine Officers Guild of Canada, the Canadian Brotherhood of Marine Engineers and his old standby, the National Seamen's Association.[3] His organizational approach was simple. The company and its captains would force the organization on their employees.

As McMaster labored to breathe life into the CBSE, 72 delegates to the CSU convention in Montreal were completing the adoption of a union constitution, a task begun by the founding convention a year before. A draft constitution had been circulated to the locals for criticism and amendment by the rank and file. The text adopted by the convention had some important features that made the CSU as different from McMaster's organization as night from day.

The CSU constitution dedicated the union to unity and to opposition to discrimination in any form. On its first page, the CSU stated that its purpose was "to unite in one union, regardless of creed, color or political affiliation, all seamen engaged in the Canadian shipping industry."[4]

What seems like a conventional statement of basic human rights today was a challenge to the status quo in the 1930s, when Native Indians and Canadians of Japanese or Chinese descent had no franchise at all and the women of Quebec were denied the right to vote in provincial elections. The convention was an example of the CSU's non-discrimination policy in action. Among the delegates were 10 Francophones, five from Montreal and five from Champlain. The CSU had already demonstrated its determination to recognize the language and cultural rights of its members by establishing the *Searchlight* as a bilingual paper from its first edition. This policy was extended to have the business of the convention conducted in English and French. The reason for this emphasis was spelled out in the constitution's preamble: "We have learned from bitter experience that the main aim and purpose of the employing interests is at all times to divide and keep apart organizations endeavoring to unite for their common interest."[5] The CSU was determined to avoid an internal split which the shipowners could exploit. McMaster saw things very differently from the CSU. In his union, Blacks were organized into separate locals. The Captain did not believe in placing Black seamen in jobs outside the catering department.[6]

Although the CSU was committed to struggle to improve the economic welfare of its members, it did not restrict itself to collective bargaining. Social benefits were at a minimum and the CSU constitution drew special attention to the need for struggle on the legislative front. The union was to "secure by legislation the benefits of old age pensions, unemployment insurance, hospitalization and enforcement of effective safety and health measures and any other social reform that may be of benefit to the seamen."[7] Another objective was changes in the Canada Shipping Act to render it "more equitable, an aid instead of a hindrance to the well-being of Canadian seamen." A top priority was amendments requiring "wirelesses aboard all vessels regardless of tonnage."[8]

Spirit was high at the 1938 convention. Given the phenomenal growth in membership and locals, the potential seemed limitless. The CSU had agreements with many of the major shipping companies and was well-established in local labor councils. The seamen had also built ties with licensed personnel. Representatives of the St. Lawrence-Kingston-Ottawa Pilots Association attended the convention as fraternal delegates, as did representatives of the captains, and both organizations pledged their full support to the CSU's undertakings.[9] The solidarity was welcome, but the seamen were to find the captains to be unsteady allies at best.

The job of president became a full-time, paid position and Sullivan easily won election to the position. Jack Munro was known to be a dedicated trade unionist who mixed misery with rye. Rumor had it that his drinking was interfering with his work and the seamen felt Sullivan was better-suited to the job. T.J. "Tom" Houtman was unanimously elected to Sullivan's old post of secretary-treasurer and Dewar Ferguson and Jack Chapman were elected vice-presidents.[10] From the election of officers, the seamen turned to the question of a safety program, but their debate was rudely interrupted by the announcement that McMaster had signed contracts with companies which already had agreements recognizing the CSU as the seamen's legitimate organization.

Hughie Edmonson, a 65-year-old seaman who had been a member of McMaster's NSA, took the floor. He denounced McMaster as an agent of the shipowners who was out to destroy the unity of the seamen and he recalled the days before the CSU when the seamen had no collective strength and lay at the shipowners' mercy. Edmonson told the delegates of the carriage driver who was very good at killing flies by flicking them off his horse's neck with a swat of his whip. A passenger in the carriage expressed his admiration for the driver's accuracy, but the driver kept silent, killing flies one by one until his companion saw a hornets' nest in the distance. "See if you can get the hornets' nest," the passenger suggested, but the driver firmly refused. "Why not?" the passenger asked. "Because, my friend, the hornets are organized."[11] The delegates received the story with laughter and applause. Nobody missed the point.

McMaster and the shipowners were challenging the CSU to a life and death struggle. The companies were refusing to hire known CSU members and were making membership in McMaster's organization a condition of employment. If the shipowners succeeded in terminating their agreements with the union and forcing the seamen to join the CBSE, the CSU was dead. The seamen knew they would have to bring the companies down hard. The convention decided to strike all vessels of companies refusing to honor the CSU agreement. Local meetings held on the heels of the convention endorsed the strike call right down the line.[12] There would be only one issue at stake: the democratic right of seamen to the organization of their choice.

Navigation had ended on the Lakes in December 1937 and was scheduled to resume at midnight April 15, 1938, when summer insurance rates for Lake vessels took effect.[13] Five major steamship companies and a number of smaller operators were forcing seamen to join McMaster's organization. Leading the assault were Norris Steamship Ltd., Mohawk Navigation Co., Paterson Steamship Ltd., Hall Corp. of Canada and North American Transport Ltd. Firms like Algoma Central and St. Lawrence Steamship Co. were biding their time, avoiding an open conflict but hopeful the CSU could be beaten. Companies like

Canada Steamship Lines and Tree Lines, which honored their CSU agreements, would not be affected by the strike.[14]

As the deadline drew near, many seamen were employed "working by," readying the ships for the coming season. Those working under the McMaster agreement had signed with the Captain's organization to obtain a job. The CSU claimed 90 per cent of the seamen working for these companies actually were loyal to the union. The companies, on the other hand, were insistent that the CSU had no membership and that their employees were loyal to McMaster. The CSU countered with petitions signed by hundreds of seamen pledging support for the CSU.[15] McMaster left no doubt where he stood, writing to Colonial Steamship Lines' president Scott Misener to "again (urge) upon vessel owners the absolute control of employment."[16] Ernie Donne, president of the CSU's Port Arthur local, replied that the strike was necessary to "protect the members of our union from discrimination and rid ourselves of racketeers, phoneys and labor fakers."[17]

The shipowners did not believe the CSU had the strength, support or expertise to pull off the strike and they had two weapons in their arsenal to help drive the CSU off the Lakes. One was the threat of blacklisting held over any seaman who supported the strike. The second was a smear campaign, launched in an effort to undermine the seamen's unity and confidence in their union. With 24 hours remaining until the deadline, the companies that had signed with McMaster's CBSE issued a joint statement declaring that "Canadian seamen have the right to join whichever union they prefer. We have the right to sign contracts with whichever union is representative of the seamen. We are not to be dictated to by a body that, right from the beginning, is controlled by outside interests."[18]

Outside interests? The *Montreal Star* elaborated. When the CSU had attempted to convince the shipowners to avert a strike by honoring their agreements, the companies had refused, the *Star* reported, "on the grounds that it was a 'foreign union' and that the union contracted by the shipping companies was a Canadian one, operated by Canadians, and furthermore, the Brotherhood of Ships' Employees was the union favored by the seamen on this side of the Great Lakes."[19] Playing on the CSU's AFL connection, the shipowners were wrapping themselves in the Red Ensign and rushing to defend their employees against an "international" union, hoping to portray their attack on the CSU as a fight between two unions.[20] Ten years later, they would reverse course and invite an international into the country to break the CSU.

The CSU was already in action. Meetings of the seamen were being held in every port and on the ships as news of the strike swept the waterfronts of the St. Lawrence, the canal systems and the Great Lakes.

In Toronto, for example, rank and filers spread out on the docks April 12, talking to seamen who were working by. They handed out leaflets advising the working seamen that "these companies are violating all the established rights of labor today in compelling seamen, Canadian citizens, members of our union, to join the company union and pay monies to it as a condition of employment."[21] Meanwhile, the union sought ways to avoid a tie-up. A request to the Department of Labor to arbitrate the dispute went unheeded. Through union lawyer A.W. Roebuck the CSU appealed to the operators to come to the bargaining table.[22] The companies, confident they could break the CSU, told the union to shove off.

On April 14, the CSU national executive held a telephone conference to complete preparations for a tie-up. From their home ports, the executive members listened to Sullivan's report. "We asked the shipowners to cease this tactic of forcing men to join a fake union," he said. "We appealed to them to agree to a government-supervised referendum on the boats which would easily prove what we already know — that over 80 per cent of the seamen belong to our union ... In view of this attitude of the shipping companies, we are duty bound to give leadership to the seamen that will protect their rights and interests. To permit a few unscrupulous companies to establish fake company unions would amount to a betrayal of our membership." The executive voted unanimously to carry through with the strike.[23]

The union claimed as members 1,800 of the 2,100 seamen employed by the anti-union steamship companies, but a spokesman for Norris Steamship stated that the company was aware of no strike and was signing on union men who were satisfied with working conditions and wages.[24] At the same moment, seamen were patrolling the waterfront emphasizing the necessity of strike action to get rid of McMaster and spreading the news that the CSU was guaranteed the support of the 50,000 longshoremen on both sides of the Lakes. Seamen were seen tearing up their McMaster cards and some pasted pictures of CSU leaders on the sides of the vessels tied up in port.[25]

Just hours before the strike deadline, two of the affected companies broke ranks and signed with the CSU. As a result, the union ensured the ships of Algoma Central and St. Lawrence Steamships would sail on schedule.[26] But at 5:30 that afternoon events took a different turn aboard the *F.V. Massey* as the crew washed up for dinner. They had been fitting out the ship for the first voyage of the season. As they sat down to supper, the first mate crept up to the bow and the second mate slipped to the stern. They manned the lines, which had been let go and merely looped over the bollards on the dock, slipped the vessel free and the *Massey* began to drift into Toronto harbor. The crew felt the movement and realized what was up. An oiler and two deckhands shot up from the galley, scrambled over the side to the dock and made fast the lines. The black gang then returned to the engine room. They banked their fires, swept up a bit of ash and bid the first engineer farewell. Although the officers all remained on board, the ship was tied up and a picket line thrown up on the dock.[27]

The *Massey* was owned and operated by Capt. James B. Foote of Toronto, who also was operations manager of the Union Transit Co. and the Lake Steamship Co. The Union Transit Company had named the *James B. Foote* in his honor. Within minutes of the attempt by the officers of the *Massey* to clear the dock, the licensed personnel of the *Foote* tried a similar stunt. The crew was at dinner and this time the officers were able to get the vessel 100 yards away from the dock before the inexperienced crew realized what was happening. The skipper dropped anchor in the harbor and awaited the midnight start.

The seamen in Toronto had already scheduled an 8 p.m. meeting that evening at the Labor Temple. The crew of the *Massey* made a full report and told how the *James B. Foote* crew had been shanghaied. Pickets poured out of the hall to cover the waterfront. Seamen on the ships joined the lines. The tie-up in Toronto was complete when the crews of 10 Norris Steamship Lines vessels hit the bricks.

There was still the *Foote*. As the hour of midnight chimed, the *Foote* began to steam for the harbor's Western Gap, the short and narrow channel that joins the western end of the harbor with Lake Ontario. Dewar Ferguson was at dockside as the ship got under way. He and five or six pickets piled into a car and took off in pursuit, reaching the gap just moments before the *Foote*. The pickets yelled to the ship and several heads appeared at the portholes. "Pull her up in the canal," Ferguson shouted, and he knew his message had been received. "They'll never get through the canal," he predicted. A couple of the pickets with him were not so sure. The *Foote* had a green crew. They might not understand what was needed, but there was nothing that could be done. The seamen on the *Foote* had heard a voice call to them from the dark. The question was whether or not they would act.[28]

The strike as a whole was solid. Toronto was tied up, as were 11 other ports. In most, seamen simply picketed the ships and all movement ceased. If the shipowners were looking for a test of the CSU's support they had their answer. Canada's inland waterways were paralyzed by strike action for the first time in history. The three-year-old union had proved itself the shipowners' equal in a crucial confrontation.

On ship after ship, seamen seized the initiative and consolidated the strike. In Fort William the 18 crew members of the Paterson Steamship Ltd.'s *Mantadoc* decided picketing was a good first step but that even tougher measures were required. They locked themselves in the galley and refused to leave until the CSU's conditions were met. When the company got rid of McMaster and recognized the CSU they would release the ship, they said, but not before. The crew was fed by the union's Women's Auxiliary and more than 100 pickets patrolled the dock. Police checked the picket line and the occupied ship, and seeing nothing to be alarmed about, they left the area.[29]

Only one struck ship, the *Foote*, was still moving. The shipowners saw it as the only gleam of hope in a dark situation. Colonial Steamships president Scott Misener declared April 16 that the seamen wanted nothing to do with a "union controlled by Max Rosens, alias Pat Sullivan, who has come from New York trying to force the men into the American-controlled organization." Sullivan was unruffled by Misener's use of threadbare and fascistic claims of an "international Jewish conspiracy." "A couple of years ago they were calling me that damn Irishman," he replied. "Now I'm a New York Jew ... And if Misener thinks his men won't have anything to do with the CSU, why are his ships tied up today?"[30]

W.T. Burford, formerly of the All-Canadian Congress of Labor and by now secretary-treasurer of the Canadian Federation of Labor, hurried to back up Misener on behalf of McMaster, who had affiliated his company union to the CFL. "There is no reason to fear any interruption of work in the shipping industry," Burford declared as the strike entered its second day. "If Mr. Sullivan has any members of his organization, called the Canadian Seamen's Union and purporting to be a branch of the International Seamen's Union, they are not in evidence."[31] He was right. There weren't many members of the CSU hanging around Burford's office in Ottawa. They were too busy picketing the Lakes.

The *James B. Foote* was struck by the crew in Welland Canal as Ferguson had predicted. The seamen went ashore and set up a picket line, but the captain pleaded with the strikers to move the *Foote* just as far as a nearby coal dock. The pickets reluctantly agreed to allow three crew members to return to the ship with the understanding that the *Foote* would once again be tied up at the dock. But with the volunteers aboard, the captain ordered the ship to be taken into the lake. The captain had hoodwinked the seamen into believing he was a man of his word and the *Foote* sailed into Lake Erie with the shanghaied crew aboard. Unfortunately for the captain, the *Foote* was so short of coal that she had to return to the Port Colborne coal dock on April 17. The crew immediately struck and the *Foote* escapade ended with the captain being charged with kidnapping. That was the last vessel to move and the CSU's strike was a complete success.[32]

The next day the companies acknowledged defeat. A lawyer representing the shipowners signed a letter agreeing to allow the men to join the union of their choice and stating they would meet with the representatives of the CSU.[33] There was jubilation on the waterfront. In Toronto the striking seamen had been living and eating in the CSU Hall at 95½ Church Street, downstairs from the offices of the Taxi Drivers Union, who also were on strike. During the CSU strike, the drivers had used their cars to shuttle pickets between the hall and the waterfront. With news of the victory, the cabbies rounded up the seamen from the rainy picket lines and rushed them to the Labor Temple for a victory celebration. Ferguson and Sullivan arrived to the strains of For He's A Jolly Good Fellow. Mike Nichols, leader of the striking taxi drivers, and J.B. Salsberg, by then a Toronto alderman, clambered onto the stage to extend their congratulations.[34]

For the shipowners, there was not only the humiliation of signing agreements to give the CSU a free hand to organize. Far worse, from their point of view, was the fact that the "scum of the waterfront" had developed a new pride and self-respect. The seamen had won nothing new in a material sense. They had not won a wage increase or improved working conditions. But by forcing the companies to accept their democratic rights, the seamen laid the foundation for other improvements. As Ferguson said, "the next step is to build our union and (to win) better wages and working conditions for all members of the marine transport industry."[35] The CSU could only grow and thrive as long as it was strong enough to insist on recognition by the shipowners, its right to organize and to bargain for seamen. It was a right that could not be guaranteed by legislation. It was a right that had to be won first and foremost in the minds and hearts of the seamen and then defended on the picket lines.

THERE WAS LITTLE TIME to relax after the April victory. North American Transport Ltd. and its sister companies, Mohawk Navigation and Inland Lines, hoped to evade the hard-won agreement and reports came into the national office that these companies continued to force seamen to pay dues to McMaster as a condition of employment.[36] McMaster himself would come aboard on paydays and collect his $6 from each as the men were paid off. Those who refused to pay were signed off.[37] Matters reached a head in June 1938, when three seamen were dismissed on the spot for defending their contract and refusing to give McMaster a cut of their wages.[38] The fired seamen went before Local 1 in Montreal and told their story. The local instructed the leadership to put a stop to the intimidation, and Sullivan and a handful of rank and filers set out for Cornwall to do the necessary groundwork. An office was established in the Cornwall Labor Temple to serve as a strike headquarters if necessary.[39]

The union knew the shipping schedules and expected the Inland

Lines *Damia* in Cornwall any day. On the morning of June 5, Sullivan and Jack Chapman watched the vessel move into the locks. When she was in the lock, Sullivan spelled out the situation to the crew. The seamen immediately walked off the ship and the strike was on. Movement in the canal came to a standstill.

Before long, the people of Cornwall heard of the goings-on and began to line the banks of the canal to watch the action.[40] The CSU had home field advantage. Cornwall had a strong trade union history and the strike had been called on a Sunday, the one day off for the people of Cornwall. The mills and the factories were closed and a partisan crowd gathered to enjoy the entertainment. The CSU put on a good show — canal traffic backed up some eight miles.[41]

Negotiations between the union, the company, the Department of Labor and the General Superintendent of Canals began immediately. The *Damia* owners were in a corner. Their ship was tied up and the CSU was confident it could maintain the strike for as long as necessary. The CSU's position strengthened with each passing moment as ship after ship piled up in the canal behind the plugged lock. Inland Lines now had to face the growing wrath of other shipowners who saw their profits evaporating because of Inland's refusal to accept the CSU agreement. Although the Department of Labor insisted that the canal be cleared, Inland was unable to do more than move the vessel out of the lock without a crew. Shipping still was reduced to 50 percent of the normal level. After 48 hours of hand-wringing, Inland realized its only course was to honor its agreement with the union.[42]

This time the CSU would not be satisfied with a simple written pledge that the company would live up to its agreement. It insisted that Inland write to the Minister of Labor in Ottawa guaranteeing the conditions of the settlement. J. Arthur Mathewson, attorney for Inland, Mohawk and North American Transport, dutifully complied. In a letter to the federal government June 7, he pledged there would be no more discrimination on the part of the companies and that the case of the three fired seamen would be investigated. He further promised "wholehearted cooperation with you in your efforts to foster mutual trust and confidence with the men, and if investigation shows any injustices done, we will do our best to remedy them."[43]

But Mathewson was also busy on another front. In June 1938, seaman John Osborne was unemployed and hanging around the Montreal waterfront. Osborne held a CSU card. He was not active in the union, but he knew his way around. He had been approached by McMaster's men before and turned them down. But on June 21, Frank Valiquette, a well-known McMaster flunkey, asked Osborne to accompany him to an office on St. James Street. Osborne agreed.

According to his subsequent sworn statement, Osborne found the office "being occupied by one J.A. Mathewson, K.C., Capt. Herbert Newbolt McMaster and one Mr. Wilson, who I was informed was also a King's Counsellor. McMaster then approached me with the idea of forming a new organization to be named the Marine Workers' Protective League of Canada, the object of this organization being to wreck the present existing union, namely the CSU. Mr. McMaster informed me that I would be put on the 'Black List' and would never sail on a vessel again unless I consented to assist them in the formation of this group. Mr. Mathewson then stated that I, or any other organizer, would be well paid; and that if I accepted the position as General Organizer that he would personally see that I received $22.50 per week and the other delegates were to receive $10 per week, the said payroll to be received each week at Mr. Mathewson's office along with an incidental expense account.

"Sooner than be on the beach all summer and the threat of the black ball being held out, I consented to become the General Organizer and a meeting was held the same day."

The meeting decided to put out a leaflet attacking Sullivan and the CSU. By June 24, Osborne received a parcel from Mathewson containing 500 membership cards of the Marine Workers' Protective League and 1,000 leaflets "attacking Sullivan's character." Osborne also received a suit and the "necessary accessories in order to be able to approach the personnel aboard the ships" from McMaster.

"During the week of June 27 to July 1 we diligently performed our duties," Osborne continued, "as laid down by our financial backers, Mr. J.A. Mathewson and Capt. H.N. McMaster. But when I approached Mr. J.A. Mathewson on Saturday, July 2, for the payroll, he was absent. Mr. Wilson, his partner, informed me that we had not collected the money that they expected, therefore they could only allow me $12 and advised me to see Capt. H.N. McMaster, who could possibly pay me more." It was the beginning of a long morning for Osborne. When he arrived at McMaster's office, the captain was absent, but his daughter typed out a receipt for $36 and asked him to wait. At length, the Governor himself arrived and ushered Osborne into his private office. "He informed me that he had no money but that if I would continue working with him in his efforts to smash Sullivan, that he had an important position waiting for me as secretary of the Montreal Council of the Canadian Federation of Labor with a possible salary of $5,800 a year plus expenses. Upon me informing him that this did not feed my delegates, who had worked all week, he then informed me to call Mr. Wilson on the phone, as he thought the money might be there for me." Not so, replied Wilson's secretary. "Capt. McMaster then informed me that I should give the men

One ($1.00) Dollar each in order to keep them quiet."[44]

Osborne's confession allowed the CSU to put the Marine Workers' Protective League out of commission but did not clear him with the union. He was named "an enemy of the seamen" and left for a healthier climate.[45] McMaster and the shipowners had lost another fraudulent organization but not their burning desire to defeat the CSU and its president, Pat Sullivan.

The shipowners singled out Sullivan because of his many responsibilities. He was president of the union and on the executive of the Montreal Trades and Labor Council as well as the Transport Federation. It was Sullivan who headed the negotiating committees that faced the companies across the table and it was Sullivan who represented the CSU in many Trades and Labor Congress bodies. Conditioned by years of experience with business unions and power exercised from above, the shipowners believed that with Sullivan out of the way, the CSU would crumble. But through the ships' committees and the union's democratic structure, the CSU was evolving the ability to regenerate leadership. The executive, the local leadership and the members themselves were learning how to keep their union working on the picket line, at conferences and in the day-to-day struggle for better conditions on board ship. Behind Sullivan stood such seasoned veterans as Theodore Roy, Ernie Donne, Cyril Lenton and Aage Antonsen, as well as many others.

It was this innate strength of a rank and file organization that both baffled and angered the shipowners. Their contempt for seamen was so profound that McMaster felt sure Osborne's finks could be bought and paid for with a dollar bill. The outstanding unity of the seamen during the 1938 strike came as a sickening surprise to the shipowners, who seemed to believe that the seamen would work with a will once they had been spirited away from the nefarious influences of the Sullivans, the Fergusons and the Salsbergs. The strike on the *Damia* seemed even more threatening and incomprehensible: a single crew answering the strike call of a handful of organizers standing at the side of the canal had paralyzed Canada's Lakes. There could be only one explanation: outside agitators! From the tool of cynical American union organizers the CSU was turned in company propaganda in 1938 into a finely-tuned weapon of sabotage wielded by the Communist Party of Canada. Outsiders — perhaps Jews, definitely communists, certainly not from the ranks of the seamen — were creating chaos on the Lakes to suit their own interest. It was a theme the shipowners developed with greater sophistication and persistence as time went on.

More than 15 years later the *Damia* strike was transformed from a relatively insignificant incident in a larger struggle into a Communist Party experiment to test the possibility of plugging the canals by striking a vessel in the locks. The absurdity of such a theory should have been obvious. Even a schoolchild could have deduced that stopping a vessel in the locks would block the system. Proof, if any was needed, had been provided by the crew of the *Foote* just two months before. The *Foote* incident, however, did not suit the propaganda purposes of the shipowners, who quickly recovered from their shock at the seamen's unity to devise an explanation that diverted attention from the real causes of the strike.

With the Lake contract secured, the seamen could turn their attention to broader issues. Eleven CSU delegates travelled that September to the TLC convention in Niagara Falls armed with numerous resolutions about the maritime industry. But the growing international threat of fascism and the fight for Canadian trade union autonomy dominated the meeting, the TLC's last peacetime convention for seven years.

In Spain, where Canada's Mackenzie-Papineau Battalion had been fighting side-by-side with the Spanish Republicans to stop the fascist machine, and in China, where Imperial Japan's armies were sweeping all before them, the engines of war were being fed with iron, steel and other material from Canada. The Congress pledged its full support to the peoples of Spain and China in their wars against fascist aggression. Seamen well knew the fate of trade unionists under fascist regimes. The CSU urged the convention to make the support more than verbal, proposing that the congress stand firmly behind the seamen and longshoremen when they refused to handle goods destined for the aggressor nations. The CSU amendment failed.

Yet even this debate was overshadowed by an ultimatum from the American Federation of Labor, which had expelled unions of the Committee for Industrial Organization from the AFL during the previous year. The CIO had been formed in 1935 by eight AFL unions determined to meet the growing demand among American workers for strong, militant industrial unions organized across craft lines. By 1937, the CIO had been established in Canada and was organizing workers in the electrical and steel industries while the CSU took on the job of organizing seamen. After their expulsion from the AFL in that year, the CIO became the Congress of Industrial Organizations and stepped up the task of organizing millions of workers in basic industry.

Now, led by the AFL, American-based international unions in the TLC told the congress that it must either purge the CIO unions from its ranks or face the withdrawal of the internationals, which constituted 80 percent of the TLC's membership. Forty-five unions put forward resolutions urging unity. A composite resolution rejecting a split in the Canadian House of Labor passed by a comfortable margin.[46]

The AFL's response was not long in coming. Resolutions adopted at its October 1938 convention in Houston, Texas, were designed to reduce the TLC's status to that of a state council of the AFL. The TLC, one resolution declared, was "maintained as a Canadian legislative mouthpiece for the American Federation of Labor by the international unions affiliated with the American Federation of Labor..."[47] The AFL delegates unanimously adopted two resolutions giving the federation absolute power over the TLC. The AFL was to have the sole right to issue charters to provincial and local labor councils in Canada; TLC officers were to be ordered to turn over all members of national unions to international unions where there was overlapping jurisdiction; all labor councils would be required to hold AFL charters to be considered legitimate; and all charters issued up to that time could be suspended or revoked at any time by the AFL executive.[48]

For the moment the CSU was insulated from the AFL attack by its connection with the ISU, but the union's delegates must have felt uneasy as they returned to their ships. Despite the gains of the past three years, the CSU could ill-afford to rest on its laurels.

All unions needed solidarity to win decent agreements, but the seamen were particularly reliant on their fellow maritime workers. The 1938 Lake strike had shattered McMaster's company union, but the willingness of the tiny Canadian Federation of Labor to dignify the Captain with a trade union charter proved that the shipowners did not have to go far to find allies even in the ranks of the labor movement. Without strong internal organization and solid backing from a militant and democratic Canadian union movement, the seamen would be doomed. They decided to step up their efforts on both fronts.

CHAPTER FIVE

Knowledge is Power

IN 1939, the CSU entered a period of relative calm. The agreement signed with the Canadian Lake Carriers Association, which represented the majority of the Lake shipping interests, was not to expire until 1940. The Scott Misener interests ignored the agreement and began to hire off the docks, in violation of contract clauses guaranteeing preference to union members. The CSU took the issue to arbitration and won, but it took the threat of a strike to win Misener's compliance.[1]

The 1939 convention, held in Windsor, Ontario, set consolidation as the main objective of the union's work. "Every ship must become a union stronghold manned by conscious CSU men," the *Searchlight* said. "That is what consolidation means and this is the goal for which we must set our course."[2]

The convention adopted the slogan "Knowledge is Power," and resolved that the *Searchlight* should begin the consolidation program with a series of articles on trade unionism. Dewar Ferguson took on the job and the first sentence of the first article identified the basic unit of the trade union movement — the shop committee.

In the seamen's union, the shop committee became the ship's committee and the emphasis on the on-the-job committee was part of what differentiated the rank-and-file oriented CSU from a bureaucratic or business union. In the CSU's book, direction came from the committees and any union that failed to act in this manner could not be truly considered "rank and file."[3]

A second plank of the consolidation program was the establishment of ships' libraries, which made books on politics and trade unionism available on board ship. Reading would lead to discussion and discussion would lead to a more developed understanding of problems and their solution. The books could be purchased for about 50 cents each from the National Office and they became the core of the ship's library. By making libraries the expense of individual crews and members, the CSU allowed crews to develop collections most suited to their needs. Those not interested could remain outside the plan. Among the first books made available by the Publicity and Education Department were

One-Fifth of Mankind by Anna Louise Strong, *School for Barbarism*, an anti-nazi work by Ericka Mann, Leo Huberman's *Labor Spy Racket* and *Fontana*, by Ignazio Silone. It was a modest but solid beginning.

Heading the Publicity and Education Department, also established by the 1939 convention, was Dave Sinclair, who had been editing the *Searchlight* on a part-time basis. Now he also was charged with editing newsletters, Ship's Delegate Bulletins and strike publicity, as well as the job of researching for negotiations and briefs.

The Ship's Delegate Bulletins were designed to complement the union educational work aboard ship. Mimeographed and produced at least once a month, each carried the legend, "Use this bulletin as a basis for your current meetings." They commented on union news — dress buttons were available, meeting dates, when to expect the next *Searchlight* — but there were no political references. The purpose of the bulletins was to encourage on-board discussion and meetings. One bulletin suggested regular question periods on any topic during crew meetings. Questions that could not be resolved with the resources of the crew could be forwarded to headquarters for a written reply.[4]

Loyalty can be purchased in any pet shop. That was not the type of loyalty, however, the CSU wanted from the rank and file. It wanted an educated, critical membership knowledgeable of political and trade union events. Changes were made in the *Searchlight* to make it more of an organ of rank and file opinion. The discussions and debates which began in on-board meetings were circulated throughout the union and others were drawn into the arguments. Union officials, individual seamen and crews could air their views on an equal basis. Two debates which raged in the pages of the paper in 1939 give an idea of the general flavor.

There was still a great deal of unemployment in 1939. For tens of thousands of Canadians, the Depression remained a reality and the CSU allowed unemployed seamen and others out of work to use the union halls as a flop. Shipping had been especially slow in the beginning of the year because of late ice conditions, weak grain markets and loss of cargoes to foreign vessels which had begun to work the Lakes.[5] As a result, there were more unemployed men than usual around the halls, and the *Searchlight* received complaints from two or three crews about the untidy conditions of the halls and the large number of unemployed hanging around. The letters started a heated discussion.

The union agreed that the halls were not as clean as they might be and pledged that they would be better maintained in the future. There was a very small budget to work with and the officials would do the best they could given the financial situation. Then Ferguson jumped into the debate. It was a rank and file union, but elected officials were not only entitled to spout their opinions, they were expected to. "A number of our sailors are on relief," he wrote, "not because they want to be, but because of the slack season in the industry this spring. These men hang around the hall for the purpose of trying to find employment so that they can get off relief. A married man sailing on the Great Lakes, outside of the licensed officers and the first cook, does not earn enough money in a season to keep a family the year round, and unless he is fortunate enough to get work during the winter months, the man is forced to apply for relief if he is to keep a roof over his head and keep the kiddies' tummies full.

"Of course, some may argue that these men have no right to marry and have children if they can't provide for them. Well, to this I say it is only right and natural for every healthy and red-blooded Canadian to marry and have a family. And if he, through no fault of his own, cannot find work, then he is entitled to relief. And it is our duty as an organization to carry on a persistent fight for federal unemployment insurance, not only for married men but for every adult who is forced into the ranks of the unemployed, so that they will not be forced to beg for their meals and will have a decent bed to sleep in and will maintain their self-respect."[6]

There were more beefs about the conditions of the halls, but there were no more about the unemployed. Billy Boyd may very well have been one of those unemployed seamen who were seen around the halls that winter. Like many Lake seamen, he did his turn on the beach in the late 1930s when unemployment insurance was still a distant dream. It was often tough to survive.

"Some guys couldn't bum salt in Salt Lake City," he recalls. "We'd go and bum for grub. Guys who had never bummed in their lives, when they got hungry, well, they'd go and bum. I bummed plenty. You could always go aboard passenger ships in the summer time. You had to go up their cargo nets. Of course you got a run-around from the master-at-arms, the bastards. They'd chase you all over the place. But the crews were good. They'd say, 'Fuck him, come on in here, mate,' and they'd give you whatever they had left. It wasn't always that good, but when you are hungry, anything is good.

"I met a guy down there once who had some kind of little business right around by the Seamen's Club in Montreal. I was standing there one day and he came by. He was well dressed and had his own car. 'Who are you,' he said. 'A seaman?' I said, 'Yeah.' 'Pretty hard to get a job?' I said, 'Yeah.' We talked for maybe half an hour and he said, 'Here, here's a dollar. Go and have yourself a feed.' Well, I thanked him very much. 'Be here tomorrow at noon,' he said. The next day at noon he gave me another dollar, and the next, and the next. The only days I didn't get a dollar was on Sundays...

"Then there was this little hole-in-the-wall across from the freight yards where a guy had a restaurant. You could get sandwiches and soup, but you had to stand up to eat it. I got to know him pretty good. 'Come on over, I got a bunch of stuff for you. I've got a bunch of sandwiches all made up. I've made money out of it. Take 'em and give 'em to the boys down there where you are at.' He was a Frenchman and a damn good fellow. I'd take 'em down to the shack. There was about nine guys down there and they'd all dive in... there used to be another one on McGill, where you could really get a bowl of soup. I'd say to the guy, 'Well, I've only got a nickel.' 'That's all right, keep the nickel.' He'd give me a big bowl of soup anyway. He was a waiter. He didn't give a shit, and he didn't have to pay.

"Then on the Main for 10 cents you could get a big bowl of stew and a big stack of bread. But sometimes it was pretty hard to get that 10 cents, I'll tell you that."[7]

Another issue that provoked a storm of controversy in the columns of the *Searchlight* was raised by the crew of the *Sheldon Weed*. The crew of the *Sheldon Weed* had been critical of the messy union halls, the unemployed and "communist" views in the *Searchlight*, but the incident that really aggravated the *Weed* men was a decision of the 1939 CSU convention that approved a $3 a member annual strike fund assessment, along with $1 a member a year to cover the expenses of the *Searchlight*. The crew of the *Sheldon Weed* was bitterly opposed to the *Searchlight* levy and they let everyone know it. One of their points — the failure of crews to receive the paper regularly — hit home. The executive responded to the complaints by reducing the *Searchlight* levy to 50 cents, but the crew of the *Sheldon Weed* could not be bought off so easily. The ship's delegate reported to the paper that a meeting had been held on board the vessel and all the members had brought their dues up to date. They refused, however, to pay the *Searchlight* assessment. The meeting concluded with the entire crew standing and shouting, "More Power to the CSU."[8] The *Sheldon Weed's* campaign against the *Searchlight* took more space than any other single issue that year and quite a few seamen were angered by the continued opposition to the union paper. One member's reply to the *Weed* crew filled an entire page.[9]

Democracy was served by the debates in the *Searchlight*, but one group's opposition to a particular policy was not allowed to deflect the union from the course the membership directed. As members of a democratic organization, the crew of the *Sheldon Weed* was obliged to accept the decision of the majority. Ferguson pointed out that if they remained opposed to the assessment, they could change it through democratic procedures. In the meantime, they had to pay the assessment to remain members of the union in good standing. They had won a reduced assessment and improvements in the paper's distribution and they dropped their protest.[10]

The columns of the *Searchlight* were not all politics and debate. One issue in 1939 told the story of the "pompous judge who glared sternly over his spectacles at the tattered prisoner, who had been dragged before the bar of justice on a charge of vagrancy. 'Have you ever earned a dollar in your life?' the judge asked in scorn. 'Yes, your honor,' was the response. 'I voted for you in the last election.' "[11]

ON SEPTEMBER 10, 1939, Canada declared war on Germany. The CSU, like many trade unions, had long been warning of the danger posed by Nazi Germany and had done all in its power to stop shipments from Canada to the aggressor countries. Many CSU members had friends from the labor and unemployed movements who had volunteered for the Mackenzie-Papineau Battalion and fought fascism in Spain. But as Pat Sullivan observed in the *Searchlight*, even at the union's 1939 convention the seamen "did not foresee that our country would make a formal declaration of war."[12] The CSU was not alone. William Lyon Mackenzie King, the man who announced to the nation Canada's commitment to the war, had planned in July to be in Germany in November as a guest of Adolph Hitler.[13]

The CSU responded quickly to the changed situation, notifying the government immediately that it was willing to do all it could to aid the war effort. But the union made it clear from the outset that its support was not offered without qualification. In late October, Sullivan updated the seamen on the national executive's proposals to the King government.

"We have informed the Canadian government that we are quite prepared to collaborate with them in seeing that the transportation industry, insofar as water transportation is concerned, operates without interruption," he wrote, "but at the same time reserving the right to call upon the government to sit with us in a conference with the shipowners to protect the economic rights of our membership, having in mind the fact that the cost of living has already jumped by some 15 to 20 percent and that the wages now being paid are not sufficient for our seamen to maintain the standards of living that we were enjoying prior to the declaration of war. With this proviso, we again reaffirm our desire to cooperate with the Dominion government and the shipowners in seeing that there is no interruption in navigation during the crisis we are now going through."[14]

The union was suggesting a tripartite board to govern the industry during hostilities. It was a dangerous situation. The CSU knew from experience that governments usually side with those it represents, and King's government could not be mistaken for a friend of labor. But in this situation there was an added complication. The Canadian state was itself a shipowner, constantly at odds with the CSU. The union was like a boxer entering the ring with the third man — the referee — backing its opponent. In self-defense the union added the condition that the economic rights of the seamen had to be protected. The CSU was prepared to bend in the new situation, but would not allow the war to be used as an excuse to break the seamen's organization.

Two weeks after the declaration of war, the CSU's executive met to put the union on a wartime footing. It decided to intensify the consolidation effort already begun. The union was to develop strength through democracy and the rank and file was to remain the driving force of the organization. "Based on the premise that the union must be maintained and ready to protect the interest of its membership during the crucial days ahead," the *Searchlight* reported, "the plans of the executive envision the closest cooperation on the part of the individual crew members and their elected representatives aboard ship."[15]

Jack Chapman was dispatched to Ottawa to take up the idea of a tripartite board with the government and the shipowners. He was to discuss the inflation which was eroding the CSU's wage scales. He also was to argue for war risk bonuses for crews of the Canadian National (West Indies) Steamships which sailed from Halifax to the Caribbean, as well as for crews of Lake boats that were being transferred to Atlantic coastal runs as part of the war effort.

With the war declaration, the CSU shore delegates began to run into resistance when they attempted to board ships to handle crew grievances. Shore delegates often were barred from ships for "security reasons" under war-related legislation. The union realized this club could be used against maritime unions for the duration of the war. The union gave the ship's committees the task of maintaining links with the shore organization. "Stress was placed on the fact that the ship's delegate and individual crew members will be the decisive factor in any sure-fire contact between the CSU and the seamen at a time like this."[16]

According to the executive, the union faced a war on two fronts. "If this is to be a real war against fascism," Chapman told the members, "our first duty is to ensure that the home front will not be left exposed to the danger of attacks by the forces of reaction under the guise of emergency measures. This means that our trade union movement must be on hand to guarantee the preservation and extension of all our democratic rights. The Nazi regime has executed 46 seamen because they were engaged in building the illegal seamen's union among their shipmates. This is nothing unusual for fascism, which can maintain itself in power only by destroying the trade unions and all other democratic organizations. Would it not be contradictory, therefore, to fight

Hitler without at the same time fighting to preserve and strengthen our union?"[17]

The CSU had good reason to fear "attacks under the guise of emergency measures." Within hours of the Nazi invasion of Poland but nine days before Canada joined the conflict, the King government invoked the War Measures Act, taking unto itself sweeping powers of censorship, including full control and suppression of writing, publications, maps, photographs and communication; powers of arrest, detention, exclusion and deportation; and powers to control harbors, ports, territorial waters and the movement of vessels.[18] Given its experience with the *Searchlight* under Duplessis' Padlock Law, the CSU could be forgiven for fearing it could once again be the target of repressive legislation.

A look at King's personal career would confirm their fears. Before the First World War, King had served John D. Rockefeller as a labor relations expert. He was given the task of clearing up the great miners' strike in Ludlow, Colorado, where Rockefeller goons had gunned down miners' wives and children in April 1914. The miners remained on strike, demanding only that their union be recognized. King advised his boss to wait the miners out. By the end of the war, he reasoned, they would be so weak that Rockefeller could settle on his own terms.[19] Throughout his labor career, King had championed the "Colorado" plan of industrial relations, which called for the replacement of unions with company associations. The CSU had been born out of the fight against exactly these tactics.

Unlike the government, which centralized all power and effectively eliminated personal freedom to face the war, the CSU took an opposite approach. Rather than limiting democracy, the union sought to extend it in every possible way by building on an important structural change mandated by the 1939 convention to decentralize power to the union's regions. Locals now were called branches, with a new Halifax branch added to the existing organization. The Halifax branch was responsible for the Atlantic seaboard. Montreal covered the St. Lawrence, Thorold took care of the Welland Canal and west to Sault Ste. Marie, Fort William was responsible for the area from the Sault to Lake Winnipeg and Toronto covered the area from Kingston to Georgian Bay. There was no west coast branch because the charter obtained from the ISU — now called the Seafarers' International Union — would not allow it. There were, however, provisions for the organization of fishermen, and the convention directed that fishermen, because of their special needs, should come into the CSU under a special charter.[20]

The areas which each branch had to cover were enormous and at the beginning of the war the CSU moved to increase their effectiveness. The branches set up sub-branches in all smaller towns where there were "enough seamen residents to make union activity possible." During freeze-up, union life would continue through the branches and sub-branches.[21] The campaign to build sub-branches met with immediate success. As soon as union activity was strong enough to warrant it, a full-time meeting hall would be established. In 1939, halls were opened in Kingston, Champlain, Midland, Goderich and Port Colborne, all operated under the direction of a district branch organizer. These were not permanent organizations, but it was hoped they would gain enough strength to develop into permanent branches. In the meantime, they were to "become constructive forces in the life of their respective communities and to stimulate the growth of a progressive labor movement."[22]

In contrast with the growing strength and unity in the ranks of the CSU was the growing split in the Canadian labor movement on the issue of Canadian autonomy. The 1939 convention of the Trades and Labor Congress, held in London in September, faced an ultimatum from the American Federation of Labor: either expel all unions affiliated to the Congress of Industrial Organizations, comprising some 22,000 members, or face a walk-out of the AFL's international unions.

The AFL's 1938 convention in Houston, Texas, had ordered the TLC to oust the CIO unions. The AFL would yield on only one point: the TLC would have the sole right to grant charters to provincial and local labor councils.[23] The 1938 TLC convention had ordered its executive to do everything possible to avoid a split in Canada, but the resolution made it clear that unity would not be at the expense of the AFL. "Action taken," it read, "shall be on terms acceptable to international unions, and thus avoiding any disregard for, or defiance of their laws and policies."[24]

A series of meetings between AFL and TLC representatives proved fruitless. TLC president Pat Draper, unable to attend because of illness, designated TLC secretary-treasurer R.J. Tallon, accompanied by vice-presidents Raoul Trepanier and Percy Bengough, to represent the Canadians. They believed that if the AFL unions made good on their threat to leave the TLC, the congress would disintegrate. They took the position that the only way to save the TLC was to bow to the demands of the AFL.[25] By the time of the TLC's 1939 convention, the CIO unions had been suspended and their delegates barred from the convention floor.[26] All that was left for the delegates to decide was acceptance or rejection of a divisive U.S.-dictated course for Canadian labor.

The seamen had instructed the CSU delegates to fight for a unified congress regardless of the AFL's position. Dewar Ferguson had pointed out that the CIO and AFL unions had picketed in support of the CSU's 1938 Lake strike, and it was this kind of unity that won disputes. The *Searchlight* argued that unity must be maintained and pointed to the unrest that was sure to follow if the congress was permanently divided. The AFL position had to be defeated, the *Searchlight* warned. "The inevitable result of a defeat of the unity forces — raids and jurisdictional squabbles, local councils cracked wide open, a congress diverted from the path of progress — would be enough to warm the cockles of any Tory's heart."[27]

The CSU was not alone in its quest for unity. Forty-four resolutions to the convention were essentially the same, urging the retention of a united congress.[28] Delegate after delegate rose to put the case for the CIO remaining in the TLC. The majority of those who spoke were delegates from Canadian affiliates of international unions.

Tallon looked down on the assembly and addressed those who were demanding a unified House of Labor. "Some will have it," he said, "that we issued the suspension order at the behest of the AFL, but from the circumstances I have related, you will see that it was your own international unions who have made the decision. If these organizations had withdrawn from the congress, some of the delegates who have already voiced their opinion to the action of the executive would not be here at this convention. The question for you as delegates to decide is whether you are going to be inside the congress or on the outside watching other organizations than your own constituting its membership. You might as well know now where you fit in."[29] Tallon was telling the unity forces they could not win. If they achieved a majority, the AFL-linked internationals would leave the TLC. If they voted against unity, the CIO-linked unions would be thrown out. The CSU stood on the side of unity, among the 98 delegates of 231 who opposed the AFL ultimatum.[30]

Had the CIO unions been present, the outcome could have been different. The CIO affiliates accounted for 160 votes and the expulsion had passed by a margin of 133.[31] This was certainly one of the factors which led the AFL to demand that the CIO unions be suspended before the convention convened.

Canada was at war, the War Measures Act was in force and the Canadian labor movement was undergoing one of the worst splits in its history. The AFL had shown once again that no opposition to its policies would be tolerated in the Trades and Labor Congress of Canada. The CSU delegates sadly packed their suitcases and headed for home.

There another tragedy awaited them. Jack Munro had been instrumental in the formation of the union and was the CSU's first president. He had been defeated in his bid for a second term by Pat Sullivan. Then, in June 1939, Munro defeated Tom Houtman by seven votes to become secretary-treasurer of the Montreal branch. An audit of the books the next month found $415 missing from the funds that had been turned over to Munro. He asked for a few days to repay the money. This was granted, but he was immediately suspended from office and Theodore Roy replaced him.

Days passed, but Munro did not repay the money. The national executive met to discuss what action to take. Jack Munro had made important contributions to the CSU, but he had been elected to a position of trust and had mishandled funds that belonged to the membership. He was arrested for embezzlement.[32] The harsh response to Munro's offence reflected the CSU's bitter battles against waterfront racketeering. The seamen would not allow any transgression within the union. Munro's offence was small but it had to be shown that this waterfront union would not be tarnished either by greed or by mismanagement.

Hy Alper was the CSU's accountant in 1939 and runs an active accounting firm today in Montreal. He remembers how carefully the CSU managed its funds. "The CSU was under attack from many points," he recalls, "but I repeat, and this is not on the basis of faded memory, but of fact: at the moment, in Canada, the government has legislation whereby they can verify certain books of a union. At that time, they didn't have the legislation, but the CSU was doubly careful to make sure that every penny was accounted for and everything was certified and tied down properly so that they could never be attacked for having been easy with the money of the membership."[33]

For the CSU, 1939 had been a year of consolidation and growth. While the union's rank and file was building its strength, deepening its education and adjusting to the new challenges of the world war, its organizers were moving to salt water. The drive to organize from coast to coast had begun.

CHAPTER SIX

The Atlantic

LATE IN 1938 the CSU had sent Pat Sullivan and Jack Chapman to Nova Scotia to test the Atlantic waters.[1] A local in Halifax would not only give the union its first contact with the deepsea, but also a base in a year-round port. More importantly, union organization throughout the Canadian merchant fleet was essential if the gains of the Lake contracts were to be protected and expanded. The CSU needed an organizer with sea time and a knowledge of the fishing industry. It was understood that a local organizer could do the job better than a couple of Lake seamen from Montreal. They found Charlie Murray.

Born in Pictou County, Murray came from a religious background. His father and his brother were United Church ministers. A sister worked for the United Church in Japan and he had two brothers and a sister in the medical profession. But by 1939 Charlie Murray was a member of the Communist Party of Canada and deeply committed to the struggles of working people. While other members of his family attended to the spiritual and medical needs of humankind, Murray worked to better the lot of working people through trade union and political action.

In 1980, Murray and his wife Kay lived in the Lower Sackville home they had built in 1940 on the slope of a little valley. Murray was a slim man with glasses that gave him a scholarly look. He had an air of intense discipline. He lit a fire, using wood from two old oak and spruce dories he had sawn up, and remembered the CSU's first official visit to Halifax.

"I was appointed port agent in Halifax. I don't think anyone was happy about it but there was no one else. Pat Sullivan and Jack Chapman came down in very rush order. They got in touch with me and they put it to me: 'Look, it's essential. We must have a port agent in Halifax to start things away, so we are putting you on the payroll.' I don't think I ever got any pay for it. I accepted the position, under protest, on a temporary basis. My background was that I had worked on tugs, but I had a degree in fisheries ... There was a real attempt by the CSU to ensure that the union was a union by and for seamen. I was reluctant because I had no discharges (from deepsea vessels), but there was no one else to do the job."[2]

In February 1939, just months after Murray had taken up his duties, the CSU learned of another organizing effort in Atlantic Canada. McMaster had a man in Halifax and he had successfully signed up a few seamen.[3] The CSU paid little attention until June, when CSU members in Montreal noticed a number of obviously unhappy "down Easterners" hanging around McMaster's Montreal office.[4] What were they doing there? There was terrible unemployment in the Maritimes, but things were not much better on the Lakes. These men could not have come to McMaster seeking employment on the Lakes. His association had agreements covering only about three percent of Great Lakes shipping and he would have to dispatch his own members first. So what were the Maritimers doing at McMaster's office? The answer came from McMaster's Halifax organizer, Kenneth Knickle.

Knickle had shipped out from Newfoundland for more than 20 years. A cook, he had made his first trip up the St. Lawrence in 1938. Anxious to earn more money, he decided to ship out on the Lakes and, being new to the region, asked around the waterfront for leads on a job.

In July he recounted what happened to him in a sworn statement which was reprinted in the *Searchlight*. "One party I contacted," he said, "took me to see Capt. H.N. McMaster, life governor of the Brotherhood of Ship's Employees, the National Seamen's Association and a few other organizations. Capt. McMaster told me that in order to secure employment I would have to pay him the sum of seven dollars for initiation fee and one dollar per month as dues. That only under these conditions could I secure a berth. I therefore paid him the seven dollars necessary to become a member and secure a job. Then I went back aboard the *S.S. Beloeil*. On the following trip I quit the *Beloeil* upon arrival in Montreal and was on the beach for four weeks before Capt. McMaster lived up to his promise to get me a job in return for the seven dollars. He secured a berth for me as a first cook aboard the *S.S. Redfern*, and I held that position until the close of navigation in 1938. The vessel was laid up in the City of Cornwall and upon my return to Montreal, I called at the office of Capt. H.N. McMaster to tell him that my vessel was laid up and that I was returning to see my parents outside Halifax.

"He then approached me with a proposition that, since I was going to Halifax, he would give me credentials as a representative of the National Seamen's Association and he would pay me the sum of $15 a week if I would agree to sign up new members on that coast, telling them that if they would join his organization and pay the initiation fee of seven dollars, he could secure work for them aboard Lake vessels. I was to be given full charge of the East Coast, where I was to tell seamen that the

National Seamen's Association and not the Canadian Seamen's Union had all the Great Lakes steamship companies under agreement with them.

"Not knowing much about Great Lakes conditions and believing Capt. McMaster, I left for Halifax and endeavored to carry out what I thought was correct. I thought that since I had paid for my job and secured it, the others who gave me money would get jobs too. However, during the winter months, I realized that I could make a better living aboard my vessel.

"As I left to resume my duties, I took it upon myself to get a successor to fill my position of being in sole charge of the Port of Halifax and vicinity ... making sure everyone paid their seven dollars...

"Upon my arrival in Montreal, I was astonished to see the change that had taken place. I realized that I had been hoodwinked and that desperate lies had been told to me. I found that I had been placed in the position of taking money from my fellow workers on the East Coast under false pretences, as the McMaster group could never hope to place these men in jobs. I laid out $50 from my own pocket trying to help out some of the East Coast men who I saw starving to death on the beach in Montreal. I had come to realize that the seven dollars which I had taken from them had gone to a bunch of racketeers. It is with this in mind that the foregoing statement and exposure were made."[5]

Knickle did everything in his power to make amends. He exposed McMaster to his replacement in Halifax and to the public through the letters column of the *Halifax Mail*, then agreed to accompany Pat Sullivan on a speaking tour of the region. "McMaster sent this guy down here ... and guaranteed (the Maritimers) jobs in the spring," recalled Murray. "The only way McMaster could guarantee them jobs was if the CSU was broken or went on strike and he supplied the scabs. He was organizing scabs to go to the Lakes in the spring.

"This question came up: would the inshore fishermen go up and would they scab? Well, a lot of them would. This was in the Depression, there were no jobs. The inshore fishermen, according to the *Canada Yearbook*, were getting on the order of $100 a year. So if there was a job on the Lakes, it would look pretty good. The CSU understood this."

It was apparent that the CSU's efforts would have to extend beyond the Atlantic coast seamen. The union's AFL charter gave it jurisdiction to organize fishermen. The CSU's 1939 convention had made arrangements for the fishermen to enter the union with their own structure. The new organization was to be called the Canadian Fishermen's Union. But the CSU had to establish itself among seamen before it could tackle the entrenched vested interests of the Atlantic fishing industry. Two major types of shipping dominated Atlantic trade. Isolated areas and small villages were supplied by the tiny vessels of the "mosquito fleet," ships usually carrying a crew of seven. Working unlimited hours, taking turns at the wheel and handling freight, these seamen had recently seen the number of firemen on their vessels reduced to two men from three.[6]

At the other end of the scale were the Eastern Lady Boats, a fleet of six passenger ships owned by the federal government and operated through the Canadian National (West Indies) Steamships Ltd. They made scheduled voyages from Halifax to the West Indies year-round, carrying general cargo and packaged freight south and sugar, fruit and rum north in addition to their passengers. Most importantly for the CSU, the Lady Boats had the Royal Mail contract for postal service between Canada and the West Indies.

As a result of the mail charter, special conditions applied. An arrangement among the countries concerned required the crews of the Lady Boats to be half Canadian and half West Indian. More often than not, the crew members from the various islands belonged to a union from their home port. There was the British Guiana Labor Union, the Progressive League of Barbados, and the Bustamante Industrial Union that represented many of the Jamaican seamen. Canadian National Steamships would not allow the Black seamen to work on deck. The deck jobs were exclusively for Canadian nationals and the Black seamen were restricted to the "black gang" or the stewards' department.[7]

The "Luxurious Lady Liners," as the CNS called them, catered to every whim of the wealthy passengers. They carried confectioners, bedroom stewards, first class saloon waiters, pastry chefs, butchers and bakers. The seamen were required not only to power the vessel and to serve the passengers, but also to provide an interesting and scenic backdrop to the cruises of Atlantic Canada's upper classes.

Bud Doucette sailed on the Lady Boats for several voyages. "It had been a tradition in the CNS that the crew wear hats," he says, "with RMS Lady Nelson across the band, for instance. The quartermasters were supposed to dress in whites when they were at the wheel. The flags were hoisted at sunrise to a bugle call. Up went the courtesy flag for the country you were in, then up went the Ensign, then up went the company flag, then up went the Pilot Jack on the bow, and then up went a signal flag, say the Blue Peter if it was near sailing time. Then, of course, the flag lowering ceremony in the evening was also done to the sound of a bugle.

"Most of us were experienced seamen, and so far as seamanship was concerned we didn't have a great deal to learn. Seamanship on a passenger vessel is, perhaps, not so exacting and demanding as seamanship aboard a dry cargo ship. The Lady Nelson, for example, carried mixed cargo and first class passengers, second class passengers, third class passengers and, in the West Indies, deck passengers — people who travelled strictly on deck and had no access to the facilities of the ship."[8]

When Connie Munro was a little girl, her father Scotty took her and her mother Alice on a tour of the *Lady Rodney*, where he worked. He showed them around the crew's quarters, the stokehold, the galley and then the first class area. Connie Munro still remembers her father taking her by the hand and leading her out into the dining area. "I'll never forget how impressed I was when we walked out of the area where he worked into this huge, massive room. We were on a sort of balcony. Down below was the dining area and there were big chandeliers. The ship was docked, but everything was laid out with silver and white table cloths.

"It was the most impressive thing. They didn't have television in those days, so everything that wasn't within your scope you had to conceive with your mind. Nothing I had conceived in my mind could compare with walking in and seeing this magnificent dining room. It was beautiful."[9] Neither Connie nor her mother would ever take a trip on the *Lady Rodney*, or dine in that dining room. Those were privileges reserved for another class of people. They would, however, have the job of picketing the *Lady Rodney* in 1949 in what would be the hardest-fought battle in the CSU's history.

From the luxury of the dining room to the harsh conditions of the crew's quarters was like a trip to another world. In 1939, deck crew on the Lady Boats earned $26 a month. The steel bulkheads in the crew's quarters were uncoated and became glazed with frozen condensation during the winter trips in northern waters. Soap was not provided, linen was not changed regularly and meals were served on metal plates. Food was not only below the standards set for the passengers but a cut below that served to officers. On the CNS, the sailors concluded, "anything is good enough for a sailor."[10]

Yet organizing the Lady Boats was no easy task. Murray found a feeling among many of the seamen that they were lucky to have a job at all. Being jobless in Nova Scotia was nothing to look forward to. Some of the seamen felt the company was just too strong to buck. And the crews were divided along racial lines, which led to distrust and suspicion. Some of the Canadians wanted all jobs on the boats for Canadians only, and the Black seamen had cause to believe a Canadian union just might follow this approach. Murray had to take the seamen's existing beliefs and change them. He had to convince them that the company would be forced to give concessions only if the crews were united in a solid organization.

Murray met the seamen from the Lady Boats along the waterfront as they paid off. He called meetings of seamen and fishermen. He listened and discussed and argued. He knew the crews' beefs and he knew the people of Nova Scotia. He argued that changes could be made and that the CSU was the instrument for making those changes. He told the seamen of how conditions had improved aboard CNS vessels on the Great Lakes. He was able to sign up many of the Canadian seamen, but the Blacks remained reluctant.

The Black seamen were shown the CSU's constitution, with its guarantees of no discrimination because of race, creed, color or national origin. Murray showed them the CSU's Hiring Procedures, which prohibited favoritism in hiring or dispatch of members. The policy guaranteed that "members will be shipped out to fill vacancies strictly in rotation."[11] In January 1939, he had a chance to prove his claims. A strike in the British West Indies hit the CNS line and many of the Lady Boats were arriving in Halifax short-handed. The CSU called a seamen's meeting in the Gaiety Theatre in Halifax and Murray made the union's position clear. The ships arriving short-handed as a result of the strike would sail short-handed. The CSU would not use the dispute as an opportunity to turn jobs over to Canadian nationals.[12] It was proof to Black seamen that their jobs would be protected by the CSU, not threatened.

As the organizational drive proceeded, ship's committees were established, delegates were elected and a large section of the *Searchlight* was dedicated to Atlantic coast news. While Murray pounded the docks in Halifax, Sullivan, Chapman and Tom Houtman opened negotiations with the CNS in Ottawa.[13] They immediately made gains. The company promised to caulk the bulkheads to reduce the sweating and freezing; clean linen would be supplied on a weekly basis; ceramic plates and bowls would replace metal ones; all crew's quarters would be heated; soap would be provided and the coffee would be upgraded. For one crew, the changes were not implemented quickly enough. They voted 53 to five for an immediate strike. The union urged the company to speed up the changes and the work stoppage was headed off.[14]

In May, the union was able to negotiate a $5 a month increase for assistant stewards and a five percent raise for all other ratings. The union fell short of its goal of raising all rates by $5, but the gains achieved brought more seamen into the ranks. The CSU's strength was growing daily. With the outbreak of war, the union was able to negotiate a war risk compensation and bonus for CNS crews.[15]

A hall was established near the Halifax waterfront at 6 Birmingham Street and CSU delegates were seated in the Halifax Trades and Labor Council. The Atlantic seamen had been organized in a few months, largely through the efforts of Charlie Murray. As the union grew, more rank and filers stepped in to back him up. The union was ready for its next task. With organization established on the Lady Boats, Sullivan was released from his executive duties to concentrate his efforts on the Maritime fishermen. Murray was transferred out of the CSU to become the first organizer for the Canadian Fishermen's Union.[16] They were taking on the Nova Scotia fish companies — some of Canada's most anti-union employers — in a head-on struggle.

THE CSU HAD STRONG REASONS for seeking to organize the fishermen. A fishermen's union would extend the trade union movement and protect wages and working conditions throughout eastern Canada, as Knickle's experience had shown. But why would fishermen seek to join the CSU?

"There were a series of reasons why our fishermen were anxious, willing and ready to have a trade union," said Murray, "not an association, not a cooperative. They wanted a trade union. From Boston and Gloucester, in Massachusetts, to the south shore of Nova Scotia is not very far. The American fishermen from the ports of Boston and Gloucester fish Georges Bank and the fishermen from Yarmouth, Shelburne and Lockeport fish Georges Bank in the same place. In time of a storm, the Americans run into Nova Scotia ports because they are the closest. In those days, if they happened to be short-handed, they'd pick up a man in Nova Scotia and he fished on the American vessel. He joined the American union because he had to join. In the States, they were considered to be employees and belonged to a union. When they came back to Nova Scotia they had a taste of organization and the benefits of unions.

"There was a guy, for example, who had recently come back from Gloucester. He had been fishing illegally on an American vessel and he was sent back and arrived in Lockeport. He went fishing in Lockeport and was landing haddock from Georges Bank. In Lockeport he got one cent a pound for haddock. When he had been fishing in Gloucester, he had been landing and he was being paid five cents a pound. He was wearing a blue cotton shirt which he had bought in Gloucester for 35 cents, in other words for seven pounds of haddock. In Lockeport, the same shirt would cost him $1.25 or 125 pounds of haddock. Is that sufficient reason for him to join a union?"[17]

Joe West, another CSU veteran, began his life at sea in Liverpool, Nova Scotia, as a fish handler and fisherman. After a lifetime at sea, he moved to Gibsons, British Columbia, about as far as it is possible to get from the fishing banks of the Atlantic coast without leaving the country, but time and distance couldn't dull his memory of conditions on the fishing schooners. His first job was "what they called a 'flunky' on a fishing ship," he recalls. "You didn't get any money. You got the livers from the cod fish and they made cod liver oil from them. They put the livers in a barrel and let it set there and it would render itself out. The oil would come to the surface. It lay there all summer and they would keep adding to it. There would be no cover on it and flies would be in it half an inch thick.

"On a schooner there would be 23, 25 or 27 men, depending on the size of the schooner. Smaller ones would have 10 or 11. From the time you left until the time you got back, you worked. You'd lie down with your clothes on, your boots on, fall asleep and someone would shake you. There would be something to do and you couldn't say no or you'd get a kick in the butt.

"When they delivered the fish the cod livers would go ashore at the same time and the fish buyer would buy them, but it was nothing — 10 cents a bucket maybe. I know the first trip I went on, I made two dollars for two weeks. That was in 1934 and I was 14."[18]

West also fished with his father as a day fisherman. "He'd go out in the morning and come back at night. The two of us left home at two in the morning. We rowed out about nine miles and rowed back in the afternoon. Hand-lining the fish you had two dollars worth of fish." The average inshore fisherman made about $1.80 a day between 1935 and 1939 and for many years the average annual income was as low as $100.[19] Even these wages marked an improvement over earlier years. The fishermen on Capt. Ben MacKenzie's boat, for example, made $70.40 a man for the year 1934.[20] But the fish buyers had effective weapons against organization.

"If you were a little bit bitchy or even talked about organizing, the fish buyer would get back at you," said West. "Just about the time you would get up to the wharf, he'd say 'We're not buying any more.' What are you going to do with your fish? You'd throw them overboard. You only had two dollars worth anyway. I saw that done lots of times. That's how they kept them from getting organized."

Life was just as hard for the fish handlers ashore. West remembers working in the shore plants in his youth: "That's where everyone around the fishing villages worked. We were smoking fish, cleaning fish, packing fish and washing fish. We got 10 cents an hour.

"We'd leave home at six in the morning and walk two miles to the fish plants. We'd get there and there would be nothing to do. We'd sit there until three in the afternoon. A couple of boats might come in and you'd have an hour to unload the fish they had and pack them in ice or something, or bring them in and others that were working there would clean or fillet them. You'd get an hour — 10 cents. If there were some fellows that didn't come in or were late, you'd stay until maybe 9 o'clock and you would work out of the whole day maybe two and a half hours. They paid you for the half hour — five cents."

Scotty and Alice Munro worked the fish plants, too, and well remember the long hours of waiting for a few cents' work. After a lifetime together, they think and talk almost as one person, each giving an individual perspective. "In the fish plants the boats are coming in, eh," says Scotty. "You're called in at say 5 o'clock in the morning. You go down there and maybe the boat doesn't come in until 7."

"And you're there all that time," interjects Alice.

"So you are there until 7 o'clock in the morning waiting for the boat to come in and you don't get paid. When the boat is in, you punch your card and go to work. Maybe there is only three hours' work on the boat. So you have been there from 5 o'clock in the morning until 10 o'clock and you have only three hours pay coming. So the chances are you might get picked up for cutting or filleting or something. If you don't, you get no more work for the rest of the day. But you're an employee of the National Fish Company."

Alice: "It was a heck of an arrangement and you were still an employee."

Scotty: "When a ship came in, if it had a good catch, you might be good until 10 o'clock the next day working on it. If it had a small catch, you might be good for three hours. At that time, from 1934 to 1939, it was 30 cents an hour. You might get paid for four hours, but you ended up putting in anywhere from six to 12 hours to get that four hours' pay. Most of the time you got between $8 and $10 a week because very rarely did you get the full week, except in the fall of the year. Maybe for a couple of months we would get full weeks plus overtime. After that it would go back to what it was."[21]

The fishermen and fish handlers had little trade union experience. Before 1939, they had organized cooperatives rather than trade unions. The Fishermen's Union of Nova Scotia had functioned almost exclusively as a co-op movement, but by 1927 it had virtually disintegrated. It was replaced by the United Maritime Fishermen, which also acted as a co-op but had some of the characteristics of a trade union. It, too, was barely functioning by 1939.[22]

The fishermen wanted a union to give them strength in their dealings with fish buyers. In February 1935 the Fishermen's Federation of Nova Scotia was chartered under the Fishermen's Federation Act of the province. It had limited success, and in places like Lockeport, it could claim the support of 100 percent of the fishermen. Although the fishermen wanted to form a Nova Scotia-wide union, the terms of the act limited them to organization on the basis of "stations" or locals. They were practically powerless in the face of the unity of the Fish Buyers Association.[23]

In 1939, Lockeport had a population of 1,400, including 270 fish handlers and 350 fishermen. The rest of the population was indirectly dependent on the fishing industry for its livelihood. The only two employers, Lockeport Co., headed by B.C. Swanburg and Swim Bros., managed by John and Herbert Swim, were both fish plants.[24] Lockeport had all the elements of a company town. Murray visited scores of such communities in his early days as an organizer. "I had a used car and in the first 10 weeks I put 11,000 miles on it without leaving the province, going from meeting to meeting, backtracking and going to the next meeting."[25]

Later in the summer of 1939, Murray was joined by Sullivan and they completed a joint tour of the fishing villages between Halifax and Yarmouth. Capt. Ben MacKenzie, a leader of the Lockeport fishermen, thought it best to check with the Trades and Labor Congress of Canada to see if these two "had the authority to organize the fishermen and fish handlers. The reply we received from Mr. Draper, president of the TLC, confirmed all Pat Sullivan had told us."[26]

At the end of the tour, the CSU representatives met with Capt. Angus Walters, skipper of the schooner *Bluenose* and president of the Fishermen's Federation. Walters suggested that the stations of the federation should dissolve and become locals of the CSU's Halifax branch, but he wanted the federation's executive to be maintained after the transition. Sullivan and Murray explained that the CSU would have no control over the executive of the fishermen, should they choose to enter the CSU. The fishermen would come in as an autonomous local and hold their own internal elections.

On August 15, Sullivan and Murray addressed a meeting in the Lockeport Community Hall chaired by Capt. MacKenzie. The fishermen present voted to take the entire membership of Station 105 of the Fishermen's Federation into Local 1 of the Canadian Fishermen's Union. The 100 handlers voted unanimously to form Local 2 of the CFU. The handlers elected Robert Williams as their first president and Loren Mackenzie as their secretary-treasurer. Ben MacKenzie was elected president of the fishermen's local.[27]

The joint meeting of the two locals then directed their officers to approach the companies to seek recognition of the union and then to work to raise wages and eliminate discrimination and favoritism ashore and afloat.

"One of the demands in Lockeport was that there should be a policy that they would take the fish in the order they came in," Murray recalled, "or that they would take the same proportion of fish from each person. Maybe they were second or third boat in and they would be told to tie up some place while everyone else sold their fish. He might then be told they were not taking any more fish. That was one of the really big issues and it was quite a common practice."

The companies agreed to meet the union delegation October 13 but then changed their position. They informed the workers that they would close their doors before recognizing a union in their shops.[28] On October 21, fish handlers turned up for work to find signs posted on the Lockeport Co. and Swim Bros. plants informing them the plants were closed "due to union activity."[29] Murray remembered that day vividly.

"You had two locals in Lockeport. The fish handlers had a special notice put up for them: 'Take all your gear, we are going out of business.' The fishermen got another notice: 'We are not buying any more fish, take your gear.' "[30]

Seven hundred people jammed into Lockeport's tiny Hayden Theatre for an emergency meeting October 23. The stage was decorated with banners bearing the crests of the Canadian Seamen's Union and the Canadian Fishermen's Union. The meeting, chaired by Ben MacKenzie, opened with a chorus of children singing union songs. Sullivan, Murray, Lockeport mayor Harold Locke, a majority of the town council and MLA H.R.L. Bill were on the stage. The union understood that the lockout was not only an assault on the workers but on the town itself.

Because the companies had locked out the workers and were referring to them as "ex-employees," the meeting directed the union to try an indirect approach in an effort to re-open the plants and begin negotiations. Sullivan and an elected committee were delegated to approach Nova Scotia Premier Angus Macdonald to seek his assistance in bringing the companies to the table. H.R.L. Bill informed the meeting that he would attempt to get R.H. McKay, Deputy Minister of Labor, to send an arbitrator to Lockeport.[31] In the meantime, Capt. MacKenzie assured the town council there would be no violence because the union would guarantee that order would be maintained.[32]

Just four days later the Lockeport delegation was ushered in to meet Macdonald in the Province Building in Halifax. MacKenzie tried to show the government officials the hardships the people of Lockeport were enduring as a result of the lockout. Macdonald listened coldly, then told the delegates that his government "looked with disfavor on efforts by communists to organize labor unions."[33]

The delegation responded that it was their right, as laid down in the Nova Scotia Trade Union Act, to form a union of their choice. MacKenzie tried to steer the discussion back to the real issue of the locked-out workers, but Macdonald was adamant. Turning away from Sullivan, he asked the workers why they did not form their own local organization without "outside" affiliation. They could call it "Swim Bros. Union" or "Swanburg Union" or any other name they wished and the labor department would gladly cooperate. Sullivan interjected that the Premier clearly was calling for the formation of a company union. Macdonald wheeled on the CSU president, called him a communist and launched into a red-baiting tirade.

MacKenzie tried once more to bring the discussion back on track. He told the Premier he couldn't understand why he wanted the fishermen to withdraw from the CSU affiliation when the CSU was the only organization with jurisdiction in the fishing industry. He didn't know very much about communism, he added, "but he thought there were more fascists in Lockeport than communists."[34] This final barb seemed to strike home. Macdonald agreed to instruct the Deputy Minister of Labor to set up the machinery to arbitrate the case.[35]

It was not their communist beliefs but their effectiveness as organizers and negotiators that turned employers so bitterly against Murray and Sullivan. It was a matter of economics, said the *Searchlight*, rather than politics. "We are not aware of any effort being made by our organization to change the political system in Nova Scotia," the paper editorialized. "The only issue at stake is the living conditions of the fishermen and fish handlers and their right to organize in order to improve these conditions. Any attempt to introduce any other issue can only be construed as an effort to defeat and disorganize the workers and leave them in their present condition of poverty."[36]

The two CFU locals began to picket the plants, organizing the lines to ensure no fish was shipped during the lockout. Although the fishermen and fish handlers were predominantly male, the women of Lockeport joined them on the lines. They saw this as their battle, too, and attended union meetings and sometimes held their own gatherings to plan their actions.[37] Behind the lines were rail cars full of fish ready for market. The companies tried to crack the lines, but they held firm. The fish was returned to cold storage. Despite the provocative company moves, the RCMP reported "everything was very orderly" and there were no reports of rowdyism.[38]

Then the *Halifax Chronicle* reported "a startling development in the conflict." The locked-out fishermen and shore handlers, not content to walk up and down outside the closed plant, had taken out an option on the aged Whiteman Fish Processing plant. Although it had not been operated in years, the CFU planned to renovate the plant and wharf in order to restore the plant to full operation.

Three hundred of the locked-out workers were to be employed on a rotational basis, others would fish for the plant and the entire operation would be run on a co-op basis. The CFU expected to have an annual processing capacity of four million pounds of salt and fresh fish.[39] Markets were secured among the Cape Breton United Mine Workers Local 28 and the Sydney Steelworkers Union. Fish were shipped on trucks decorated with colorful banners bearing CFU slogans.[40] Cape Breton co-op organizers came to Lockeport to teach the workers the fine points of running the organization.[41]

Doug Betts, a CSU organizer in Cape Breton who had some commercial experience, coordinated the sale of fish. Bernie MacDonald, an executive member of the Sydney Steelworkers, and John R. (Blue) MacDonald actively promoted the fish sales among their members. George MacEachern, a steelworker, remembers getting "some orders from steelworkers. The fillets were sold three pounds for a dollar. We would get the orders in advance, the fish would be brought in by truck, and we would deliver it. The steelworkers' and miners' unions played a good part by this means in supporting the Lockeport unionists."[42]

The income generated by the co-op kept the workers alive during the early period of the lockout. "This was during the first days of the war," Murray pointed out, "and people had no backlog of money. The deer hunting helped. They depleted the stock of deer in the woods that fall." Soon new markets opened up further afield.

"Quite a large fish company offered to buy fillets from us in trailer lots," remembers Murray. "The first car of fillets we shipped to Montreal was taken out of the train and put on a siding at a small country station. The first thing we knew was we got a wire that the shipment didn't arrive. So we went looking for it. We had friends in the railroad unions, you see. They found the car for us and put it back on the train and took it into Montreal. Just about the time that the last of the ice was gone, it arrived in Montreal. The buyer refused to accept it without looking at it. We got on the horn and said, 'Look, that fish still has to be good. It's fresher than trawler-caught fish.' They looked at it and it was good. We had a market in Montreal."

The fish handlers believed they could process 20,000 pounds of fresh fish a day. The operation was run on a democratic basis, and the people of Lockeport used the plant to help others. One of their first acts was to vote to send a truckload of fish to the striking miners of Springhill, Nova Scotia.[43]

The fishermen and fish handlers had seized the offensive in short order. Within a month of the lockout, the co-op was up and running and the railcars of company fish remained behind picket lines. The CFU had shown its discipline and its strength. The picket lines had been peaceful, but on November 16, violence came to Lockeport.

More than 300 men and women were picketing the Lockeport Co. that evening when a car "raced up from the Lockeport Co. wharf and roared through the picket line, knocking down four of the pickets and injuring two of them." One man was dragged 200 feet by the speeding car. The pickets immediately approached the Lockeport chief of police, who had witnessed the incident, and demanded that he apprehend the driver of the hit-and-run vehicle. "He ran up the street to the Seaside Inn with the crowd chasing after him demanding that he bring about the arrest of the two in the car," the *Halifax Chronicle* reported, "but he refused to do this and left for home. The mood of the union members, who previously had maintained a demeanor of quiet determination, changed immediately the incident occurred."[44]

There were other signs of a change in the dispute. A few of the fish handlers turned in their union cards shortly after the incident on the wharf and the companies immediately hired them back. But the scabs did not provoke a mass return to work. Pickets treated them to a shower of eggs when they were spotted. Those who respected the picket lines, however, could expect respect in return. When the railroad was unable to move a load of flour because carloads of fish were in the way, 200 pickets pushed the flour-laden cars into position for the conductor.[45]

The workers also sought to build ties with the small businessmen and storekeepers of Lockeport, who were suffering during the lockout because no one had any money to spend. "The prosperity and well-being of any community depends first of all on the wages of that community," said a CFU bulletin. "The amount of money received by the fishermen and fish handlers, hence their purchasing power and the conditions under which they live, will determine the standard of living of the shopkeepers and middle class people of Lockeport, and to a lesser extent, the rest of the county. The fishermen and fish handlers spend their money locally, the profits of the Lockeport Co. are not spent at Lockeport. They are spent elsewhere... It is in this way that a community of interest exists between the workers, fishermen, storekeepers and small business people of the district."[46]

The companies put pressure on the business community to squeeze the new co-op. Shelburne Cold Storage Co. notified the fishermen that they were no longer able to supply the fishermen with bait. This was a setback, but the union fishermen were able to locate a new supply. Then the fishermen moved on another front, demanding a meeting of the ratepayers of the town of Lockeport to investigate the refusal of the police chief to apprehend the driver of the hit-and-run vehicle that crashed the picket line. The CFU also was pressing its demand for an arbitrator to probe the dispute.[47]

The provincial government had approached the union in mid-November with its plan to end the dispute. The province was prepared to appoint a board to settle the matter. As soon as the board was appointed, the plants would re-open, buy and sell fish, and hire as many people as were necessary. The picket line was to come down and there was one more important point: the union would have to cease to exist during the life of the board. Recognition of the union was the workers' one demand and they were not prepared to give it up. The government's proposal was essentially the same as the companies' position and had the same intent: to keep the people of Lockeport unorganized and powerless.[48]

The companies began to lay the legal groundwork for a further offensive. The Lockeport town council, which had been asked repeatedly to support the locked-out workers, wrote to Nova Scotia Attorney General J.H. MacQuarrie asking for an interpretation of the legality of assemblies in the town. MacQuarrie responded the next day, basing his reply entirely on the Lockeport letter. "Such assemblages as outlined in the resolution (of the town council)," he wrote, "whether purporting to be members of a trade union or not, are wrong and unlawful, and it is also wrongful and unlawful for any such assemblages to obstruct, interrupt or interfere with shipments by rail or truck."[49]

The federal government, however, was taking a different tack. Late in November, E. Quirk, a federal mediator with the Department of Labor, was at last appointed to bring the two sides together. The union, seeking to smooth the path to a settlement, dropped charges against Thomas MacLean, driver of the hit-and-run car. The CFU's position seemed strong. The co-op was running at nearly full capacity, fishing was good and scores of unions from all over eastern Canada were responding to the CFU's appeals with letters of support and financial contributions.[50]

But Quirk quickly ran into a brick wall. After his first meeting with the companies, he reported that the employers would make no move as long as the plants were picketed. They argued that the people in front of their plants were not their employees, because they had all been fired when the lockout began. The CFU asked the government to charge the companies with failure to bargain, but the companies argued they had no one to bargain with because they had no employees. Quirk had had enough. He packed his bags and left town.[51] A letter from Murray to Premier Macdonald asking for registration of the CFU under the Trade Union Act was simply ignored. Tension grew. Despite the absolute quiet on the picket lines, monitored by a few RCMP constables from nearby detachments, the town council asked for more police.

"Since the lockout, order has been maintained by the union in spite of provocation, town officials and police," the union replied. "The union is prepared to guarantee discipline and order unless the Attorney General decides to send in the police force as asked for by the town officials. If this force arrives, the union can no longer be responsible for maintaining order in the town."[52]

Mounties began to stream into the area. On December 10, 20 arrived in Lockeport and were billeted in the Seaside Inn, while 40 more were put up in nearby Shelburne. The companies chose this moment to announce the re-opening of their plants. The Lockeport workers had no private army to call to their aid, but they did have the support of CFU locals set up in neighboring communities at the same time they had organized. Four hundred CFU members from Queens and Shelburne counties joined their brothers and sisters on the Lockeport lines in response to the massing of the Mounties.[53]

Confident the RCMP would give them the edge they needed to defeat the workers, the companies repeated their challenge. The plants would re-open, but there would be no negotiations: "We are, now as in the past, willing to bargain with employees, but are not willing to deal in connection with employment matters with outsiders."[54] The workers countered with a petition, signed by the majority of the town's ratepayers, demanding withdrawal of the Mounties. Mayor Locke ignored the petition. The picket line continued to grow. The workers were unwilling to give up their union and they were well aware why the companies so violently opposed the CSU. As the fishermen and fish handlers saw it, the CSU had "shown us for the first time how to establish a sound and permanent trade union."[55]

On the morning of December 11, 1939, there were 700 men, women and children picketing the gates of the plants and the train tracks which led into them. The pickets had turned several trains back during the lockout, and at the same time had been able to maintain good relations with the railroad. They were expecting another train that morning and as it approached, they realized the rules had changed. The train was led toward the line by 50 Mounties marching in two columns. At their head was Inspector MacIntosh, who had so often remarked on the order on the picket lines.

MacIntosh demanded the crowd disperse and allow the train into the yard to remove the carloads of fish. Then the Mounties pressed forward. The pickets fell back a few feet, hesitated, wavered for a moment and then stood firm. The people of Lockeport knew that if the fish was removed from the plants, their struggle was over. They would be forced to give up the union and many of them would never again be able to secure employment in their home town.

"It was then that the 'battle' got under way in earnest," reported the *Halifax Chronicle*. The Mounties swarmed against the pickets to push the men and women from the tracks. Several persons were slightly injured. At one point it was reported stones flew in the direction of the police and after the melee was over, one or two of the police constables emerged from the crowd with blood flowing from facial wounds.

"Also among the casualties were several women and an elderly man. They were Mrs. Clayton Burke, Mrs. MacKenzie, wife of Capt. Ben-

jamin MacKenzie, Fishermen's Union president, and a Mrs. Ward
Tupper Stevens, 74-year-old picket, was said to have been cut considerably in the outbreak. Members of the picket ranks charged last night
that no attempt was made to molest the police until the latter allegedly
attempted to drag the women from the railway tracks, and two or three
women were injured. On the other hand, an official statement released
to the Canadian Press last night by Assistant Commissioner F.J. Mead
of the Royal Canadian Mounted Police indicated that the police used
great forbearance in carrying out their duties, there was incitement to
violence on the part of the pickets and rocks were thrown.

"With the police vastly outnumbered by the pickets, one of whom
climbed a box car and hoisted the Union Jack while others sang God
Save the King, O Canada and other patriotic songs, Conductor 'Happy'
Lennox communicated with railway headquarters at Bridgewater and
the train was ordered to proceed from the town."[56]

The Mounties made a strategic withdrawal and the picket lines held.
Charges were laid against nine women and two men who had been on
the line. Premier Angus Macdonald, meanwhile, dispatched 100 additional RCMP to Shelburne and ordered the companies and the union to
a meeting in Halifax. Still the picket line grew. By December 13, there
were 900 people outside the plants and the next day, as the two sides
met with the government in Halifax, 1,000 marched on the line.[57] Support was coming from all over eastern Canada and protests were
directed at the town council and the provincial government for using the
RCMP as company agents against the people of Lockeport. Then,
recalled Murray, there was still another development which strengthened the union's hand.

"At that time there were approximately 600 American fishermen who
came into Shelburne, which is about 20 miles from Lockeport, to get out
of a storm. I, along with local people, went over and found out who were
the leading union people aboard and asked for support. They were
prepared to come over and join the picket lines or do whatever was
necessary. An international incident was shaping up. Word of this was
sent to Halifax, where the meeting was going on."

In Halifax, the three sides hammered out a tentative agreement to be
ratified by the union membership. It was a significant achievement,
though it fell short of the workers' goals.

The government had followed the companies' lead and ruled that the
fish handlers had all been fired October 21 and were therefore no longer
employees. Since they were not employees, they could not be union
members. But the Lockeport Co. and Swim Bros. agreed to come under
the Trade Union Act of Nova Scotia and to hold a vote of the employees
to determine which organization, if any, would represent the fish

workers. The vote would be taken after picket lines came down and the workers had returned to their jobs.[58]

The fishermen faced an even tougher outcome. Relying on the time-honored legal evasion that fishermen were "co-adventurers" rather than workers because they owned their own boats, the government ruled they could not be employees and therefore could not form a union. The fishermen knew they were workers and no one sitting in an office in Halifax could make a ruling miraculously turning them into something else. The fishermen also were aware that their American counterparts had been unionized for years. The government's goal was to keep the fishermen powerless in their dealings with the Fish Buyers Association.

But, as Murray pointed out, the fishermen could derive strength from their collective action even if they were not registered under the Trade Union Act. "The fishermen on the West Coast were faced with exactly the same problem. They organized a union and they said, 'Look, we want so much per pound for salmon. If we don't get it, we don't fish.' So the companies said, 'All right, you'll get it.' So they fished." The union would not require the government's blessing to benefit fishermen.

The decision to accept or to reject the settlement rested with the fish handlers and it was not an easy one. The entire struggle had been fought on the issue of union recognition. Reluctantly, the fish handlers voted to accept.[59] They could have fought on, but the stakes were very high. On the streets of Lockeport, 1,000 pickets were standing toe to toe with 150 Mounties. The companies and the government had turned to violence before and there was every indication they would again. The CFU agreed to compromise in order to avoid the certain confrontation that lay ahead, a confrontation that could have a disastrous outcome for the workers.[60]

A complete or decisive victory was out of the question, but a base had been established. The fish handlers had their union registered under the act and this would apply to all fish handlers in the province. The fishermen were organized but not registered. Under the circumstances, it was an important victory, achieved with minimum violence. It was by no means the end of the struggle, but the first step forward in a long march.

The plants re-opened December 15 and the companies began to hire back some of the locked-out workers. Charges laid as a result of the picket line skirmish were dropped and the fishermen resumed fishing for the companies. The co-op was a fish buyer, too, and the CFU decided to keep it in permanent operation.[61]

Not only did the people of Lockeport emerge from the struggle with their own plant, but they learned a great deal about politics and power. One of the first acts of the workers after the lockout ended was to take to the polls to elect a new pro-labor mayor and council. M.M. Laing replaced Harold Locke in the mayor's chair and his councillors all had supported the union during the lockout. Clayton Burke was the only fish handler elected because the town bylaws stated that residents must have paid all back taxes to be eligible for election. Burke had been the only fish handler or fisherman able to scrape together the money to pay the town treasurer. No longer would the town council be inclined to turn the RCMP loose on the citizens of Lockeport.[62]

The lockout had been a tremendous challenge to the workers of Lockeport and they had responded with strength and determination. "This lockout, which started out to guarantee that the union would never amount to much, has been characterized as one of the most outstanding labor actions of the decade," said Murray. "On what basis? Not because we won, because there was no way to win, but because it involved everyone in the community and for miles around. We were following, as far as I know, the whole spirit of the Canadian Seamen's Union."

In a year of intensive organizing and struggle, the CSU had extended trade union organization to the seamen, fishermen and fish handlers of the Atlantic seaboard. As 1939 ended, attention shifted once more to the Lake agreement and the growing demands of war. Would the companies and the government accept the union's offer to join forces to defeat fascism, or would seamen once again be asked to sacrifice to protect corporate profit? The answer was not long in coming.

CHAPTER SEVEN

Seamen At War

GLOBE AND MAIL COLUMNIST Judith Robinson was a little taken aback one day early in 1940 when her office door opened and a soldier in full battle dress marched in. He had been on leave, he told her, and it was time to report back for duty, but before he left he had a few things to get off his chest. She told his story to *Globe* readers.

He came to her office, she wrote, because "he wanted to put it straight about the one thing every Canadian deckhand in or out of battle dress is afraid of right now. It's that the owners are going to hide behind the skirts of the government and use the war and the War Measures Act to break the union and call it patriotism." This deckhand had worked on the Lakes before the birth of the CSU and he had seen what the union had done to improve the conditions, wages and self-esteem of the seamen. "That's why," Robinson continued, "he knew the Canadian Seamen's Union was one of the things worth his while going to war for. That's why he didn't like the smell of a lot of this patriotic stuff they were throwing at the Canadian seamen. He wants it straight that the shipowners aren't grabbing a chance to drive unionism off the Lake boats as part of Canada's war effort. He wants it straight that the first gang of Lake seamen who ever had nerve enough to stick together and stand up to the owners aren't going to be smashed in the name of patriotism for doing just that. He wants it straight from someone he can trust. That's all. But it's important."[1]

That nameless seaman was just one of about 1,400 CSU members who left the union to join the Canadian armed forces in 1939 and 1940. The union waived their dues and maintained them in good standing as long as they were in uniform, but both the union and the seamen were concerned about what they might find when they returned to the Lakes at the end of the war.

Although embroiled in their own war for decent wages and working conditions, the seamen had not missed any opportunity to shoulder their share of the struggle against fascism. Many veterans of the Lake organizing drives had had friends in the Mackenzie-Papineau Battalion formed to fight in the International Brigades in Spain. The CSU had been in the forefront of the campaign to end appeasement of Hitler and to cut off shipments of war materials to Japan and Germany.

The August 1939 *Searchlight* reported rumors that CNS ships bound for the West Indies were to be fitted with anti-submarine guns and Dave Sinclair's column noted the admission by the head of a German shipping line that boycott actions were hurting the Nazis. It was proof, Sinclair argued, "that the democratic countries can halt marauding dictators with economic weapons — when they will decide to act instead of 'appease'." The front page of that issue was dominated by a picture of pickets in Victoria halting the shipment of scrap iron to Japan.

The sudden declaration of war, first by Great Britain and then by Canada brought a pledge of cooperation from the CSU. "It is our duty to supply responsible union men in sufficient numbers to man Canada's ships at all times," the *Searchlight* editorialized in October. In a separate article, Sullivan promised the union's cooperation with the government and vowed that "water transportation during the present crisis shall not and will not be interrupted." For the seamen, this commitment assumed similar spirit on the part of the shipowners and the government. It was difficult for the seamen, facing the bitter battles of Lockeport and on the Lakes, to believe that its two opponents had decided at last to tackle the real enemy of the democracies.

The CSU made it clear it would support the war effort but would not allow it to be used as an excuse to crush militant trade unionism. The union's practical proposal — the creation of a tripartite board of union, company and government representatives to coordinate the war effort in the shipping industry — was ignored in Ottawa and in the board-rooms. Instead, CSU members faced continued attacks on their agreements and found that even their access to the docks was curbed under military regulations.

The seamen were not the only Canadians who viewed Canada's involvement in the war with scepticism and even open opposition. Apart from members of avowedly fascist organizations and their sym-pathizers, many groups offered only qualified support, questioning the real purpose and direction of the war effort. The Communist Party, a large section of the Cooperative Commonwealth Federation's member-ship, the vast majority of the people of Quebec and several religious groups, all for their own reasons, either were opposed to Canada's participation in the war or aspects of it.

Many Canadians, drained by the rigors of the Depression, could not see the necessity of moving from the breadlines to the front lines. Others, like members of the CSU, had carried on a constant struggle against fascism at home and abroad. But as a prominent historian concluded many years later, "Canada had gone to war in September

1939 because Britain had gone to war and for no other reason. It was not a war for Poland; it was not a war against anti-Semitism; it was not even a war against Nazism. All that came later, after the defeats in France and Flanders in May and June 1940, after Dunkirk, after the Battle of Britain. However just the war, and it was demonstrably a just war well before its end, Canada did not enter it to fight the good fight."[2]

Many seamen agreed with Jack Chapman, who argued in the October issue of the *Searchlight* that if "this is to be a real war against fascism, our first duty is to ensure that the home front will not be left exposed to the dangers of attack from the forces of reaction under the guise of emergency measures. This means that our trade union movement must be on hand to guarantee the preservation and extension of all our democratic rights."[3]

Unfortunately for the seamen, neither the shipowners nor the government saw things the same way. The survival of the CSU would once again have to rest on the membership's strength and determination. Faced with living costs that soared 15 percent in the life of the old agreement and with the continuing problem of seasonal employment, seamen needed a substantial increase to meet their basic living costs. The seamen asked for a $15 a week across the board increase, a reasonable goal in what was shaping up as the busiest season in the history of the Lakes. The shipowners had already doubled freight rates in response to the war traffic and union research indicated a surge in shipping company profits as 1939 drew to a close.

The seamen also tabled demands for an additional three seamen per vessel, establishment of the "union ship," overtime pay, paid return home at season's end, war zone bonuses and a clearly-outlined grievance procedure.[4]

Sixty days before the contract was to expire on April 15, 1940, the CSU notified the companies of its readiness to bargain. After some stalling, the shipowners came to the table. They were not willing to consider the CSU demands, the operators said, and had counter-proposals of their own — elimination of the ship's delegate and a ban on union officials boarding vessels to inspect conditions or to investigate grievances. The seamen would never "under any circumstances, yield or give up" existing conditions, the union replied.[5] "We will not be deprived of the protection and conditions already obtained."[6] The CSU warned the operators that its 6,500 members were ready and able to take strike action to back their bargaining committee.

It is often the threat of strike action which shakes employers out of their slumber at the bargaining table as they envision the nightmare of profits slipping away. The threat appeared to be having exactly this effect on the shipowners when government action threw negotiations into a tailspin. W.M. Dickson, federal Deputy Minister of Labor, wired the union that a strike would not be permitted. The wire was leaked and quoted in the daily press.[7] The companies promptly walked out of negotiations and cancelled all remaining scheduled meetings. The CSU was furious. Dickson had told them a strike "without application for a conciliation board under the Industrial Disputes Act would be in direct contravention of the Criminal Code of Canada."[8] This delighted the shipowners, who were sure they could break the CSU demands once the union had been disarmed. The union had no court of appeal. Labor Minister Norman McLarty was tanning on a Florida beach.

Unwilling to sacrifice its collective agreement because of Dickson's legal views, the CSU set up strike committees which began mobilizing seamen in all the Lake and St. Lawrence ports. At the same time it sought the opinion of expert labor lawyer Arthur W. Roebuck, Liberal MP-elect for Toronto Trinity. The strike would not be illegal, Roebuck argued, because it did not come under the Industrial Disputes Act. The seamen had been paid off at the end of the last season and had not been re-employed. They were therefore not employees under the act.[9] Sullivan immediately advised Dickson that the CSU had a different view of the law. He outlined Roebuck's argument and appealed to him "to urge employers to cease obstructive tactics and to meet with us at once with a view to concluding proper arrangements."[10] Dickson, who had publicly questioned the legality of a strike, now was overcome with doubts. He asked the Justice Department for a ruling.[11] The seamen were under no illusions about where they stood. Meetings at branches and sub-branches all came to the same conclusion. As the 500-member Sarnia branch put it, the seamen would support the national executive "in whatever action is necessary to secure our demands from steamship concerns."[12]

On April 12, 1940, Sullivan advised a news conference of the union's plans: "I am instructing 6,500 members in all ports that no Great Lakes vessel must be permitted to leave the dock until our negotiating committee informs them that agreements have been signed." The strike was to begin at the opening of navigation at midnight, April 14. It would affect 285 vessels. All was in readiness for the struggle. The publicity-education department began to issue bulletins every 24 hours to keep the seamen informed of developments.[13] The strike fund was well-stocked. In 1938, the CSU had struck with $250 in the treasury, but as a result of the 1939 strike assessment, more than $20,000 was in hand by April 1940.[14]

Once again, the CSU assailed the position of the federal government, contrasting its meek acceptance of corporate war profiteering to its active attacks on labor's rights. "The shipping companies are sitting back relying on the federal government to carry through their designs to eliminate trade unionism from Great Lakes navigation," charged a special issue of the *Searchlight*. "It becomes increasingly clear that the federal government, which has not once, publicly or privately, urged the steamship companies to meet the union, is nevertheless openly fighting the seamen and is now threatening the fundamental rights of labor to strike. This is the most flagrant anti-union stand taken by the federal government in a long while and a serious threat to trade unionism in this country. The government, which backed down before the sit-down strike of the employers, who refused to take war orders on a five percent profit basis, is now threatening labor when we demand but a living wage and traditional trade union procedure in relationships between employer and employees."[15]

The CSU saw other danger signs on the horizon as well. Along with many other trade unionists, the seamen were increasingly concerned about Section 62 of the War Measures Act which empowered the government to declare an organization illegal. Under Section 62, any officer of an organization whose actions were deemed to violate the act was guilty of an offense, "unless he proves that the act constituting the offense took place without his knowledge or consent or that he exercised all due diligence to prevent commission of the act."

The *Searchlight* believed that "these provisions place a trade union at the mercy of a stoolpigeon or an irresponsible member. They will hang like a sword over the heads of all union officers unless we act to force their repeal." While the CSU offered cooperation to fight fascism, the government and the employers were mounting a political and economic offensive against labor at home.[16]

The April 15 strike deadline arrived with no verdict from the Justice Department officials who were pondering the seamen's legal right to strike. The seamen "demonstrated their right to strike by striking."[17] Seamen poured off the ships that were being fitted out or were awaiting the opening of navigation. Picket lines sprang up in every port, and according to the *Toronto Star*, "not a wheel turned on 285 Canadian Lake steamers ... as 4,800 men struck, crippling water transportation from the head of the Lakes to the Gulf of St. Lawrence."

Dickson, still unable to determine whether or not the action was legal, nevertheless "warned that the penalty for illegally striking is a fine of $10 to $50 a day for participants and $50 to $1,000 a day for inciters."[18]

In Ottawa, the government was attempting to maneuver the seamen back to work. Dickson met with Jack Chapman, A.W. Roebuck and conciliation officer M.S. Campbell without the shipowners present. Instruct the seamen to return to work, the government men said, and we will set up a board to hear the dispute. The CSU representatives demanded that the government take the proper course — call the two sides together and insist that negotiations resume. Dickson was inflexible, insisting on a return to work. "This the men rejected," the *Globe and Mail* reported, "claiming that if they went to work they would become employees and would at once come under the Industrial Disputes Act."[19]

Guided by Roebuck and CSU counsel J.L. Cohen, the CSU was navigating through a legal maze designed to frustrate their efforts to win a new agreement. Arrayed against them were the War Measures Act, the Industrial Disputes Act and the Criminal Code. Through careful tactics, the legal guns of the government were silenced.

The nation's attention was rivetted on the picket lines, the battle front in the first strike since the declaration of war which directly affected the war effort. As *Globe and Mail* commentator R.A. Farquharson pointed out, "action taken in settling (the dispute) will be taken as a precedent and government officials are anxious that a course can be established which will avert other war-time disputes."[20] Waterfronts from the Lakehead to the St. Lawrence were picketed by seamen carrying signs bearing slogans like "A Union Ship — A Union Crew," "For a Canadian Standard of Living" and "The Cost of Living is Up — Wages Must Follow." At Goderich, seamen had to jump from the deck of the *William Schupps* to join the picket line as the captain tried to leave port. The vessel was returned and tied up at the dock.[21] As the strike began, two companies had signed agreements, but the remainder stood fast against the union. Attempts to sail ships with strikebreakers foundered when the scabs turned away at the sight of the pickets.

In a score of Lake ports, rank and file committees took charge. By the end of the first week, Sullivan noted with satisfaction that "during the past few days we have seen a preview of our future leadership. From one end of the Lakes to the other, members from the ranks who had never belonged to the trade union movement prior to four years ago stepped into the breach and took charge of ports. These men discharged their duties in a manner which would do credit to a trade union leader of 20 years' standing."[22] The CSU's program of education and consolidation was reaping dividends.

Trade union support was strong as well. The union entered the strike with the backing of longshoremen on both sides of the Lakes. No scab ships were to be loaded in Canada or the U.S. Licensed personnel notified the union through their two associations that they, too, backed the seamen's action. It was an understandable move, because the wages and conditions of the licensed personnel would be tied to those of the crew. They had a direct interest in the outcome of the strike.[23] With the strike solid, the CSU moved to seek a way forward.

On April 17, the union notified the federal government that it was prepared to settle on the basis of the 1938 agreement with some improvements. The demand for a $15 wage increase was reduced to $10 and the call for extra crew was reduced to one additional deckhand from three. The demand for a union ship was non-negotiable. The government, however, refused to transmit the offer. The CSU wired its proposal directly to the 15 hold-out companies.[24] The operators replied with an offer of $5 and a blunt refusal to discuss demands for a union ship, union recognition and other conditions.[25]

The same day the *Globe and Mail* reported that the government had reached a decision on the legality of the strike, but "no word was given out as to the result of the ruling by the Department of Justice."[26] In fact, the government's position that the strike violated the law would not be disclosed until October 16, 1941, a year and a half after the event.[27]

Seamen in various ports kept up their pressure on the government, asking it to intervene and force the companies to bargain in good faith. They knew that a ruling that the strike was illegal would force them to surrender and sail without an agreement, leaving them with nothing.

But the government finally was in motion. An all-day meeting April 17 convened by acting Prime Minister J.L. Ralston brought together Dickson and Campbell for a strategy session. Labor Minister Norman McLarty was unavailable because he was still soaking up the sun in Florida. Ralston directed Campbell to leave immediately for Toronto to break the impasse. He arrived at the Royal York Hotel at 9 p.m. and, within an hour, Sullivan and Roebuck were knocking on his door. It was the government's first move and the union wasted no time in demonstrating its willingness to bargain. Campbell told them to prepare for a morning meeting.[28]

April 18 found the shipowners ready with their solution to the deadlock: a $7.50 raise and submission of all other points to an arbitration board. The amazed *Globe and Mail* declared it to be "the first time in Canadian labor history that advance acceptance has been agreed upon."[29] But the offer held no attraction for the union. It was "confined to a $7.50 increase in wages," Sullivan said. "The terms of last year were to be abandoned *in toto* and the men were to return to work without any semblance of protection or preservation of a single union right. Such an arrangement would be tantamount to abject surrender." The CSU turned the shipowners down. It was the answer the operators had been hoping for. They would break the strike, they declared, putting their fleets to work in "the confident belief that the Canadian public will approve and that the authorities will, in the public interest, ensure the safe operation of the service."[30] The elusive Norman McLarty now hastened back to Canada to intervene directly. The CSU should accept the $7.50, he warned, and the binding arbitration. The message was clear: if the union refused, the government would back the shipowners in breaking the strike.

The CSU tried a last card. It would accept the board, it told McLarty, if it were a conciliation board with non-binding powers. The union had to be recognized as the seamen's legitimate organization. Finally, if the board was used as a shield for the operators' anti-union activities, or if the board's findings were offensive to the interests of the seamen, the strike would resume. All sides agreed to this proposal and the strike was lifted April 20, six days after it began.[31] The CSU had not only won important concessions from the companies and the government, it had established itself as a leading force in Canada's trade union movement in the first major wartime labor dispute.

WHEN THE CONCILIATION BOARD, chaired by Mr. Justice C.A. McTague, convened in Toronto May 13, the CSU was ready with a comprehensive brief that built the union's case with iron logic. Presented and probably written by CSU counsel J.L. Cohen, *Our Case Before the Board* became required reading for the union's membership.[32] Both a history of the industry and an analysis of the CSU's rank and file structure, the conciliation board brief was designed to destroy the shipowners' distortions of the CSU position as well as document the seamen's case.[33]

The main questions before the board concerned the rights of seamen to have an effective union. The shipowners made no bones about their low opinion of the seamen. They told the press that "skill, education and training are not necessary for employees of this type."[34] The seamen were like the boilers of the ship — essential to the operation of the vessel but easy to replace.

If the union was to improve the lot of seamen and to protect their health and welfare, it had to be a force on the ships. The seamen had to have union ships to protect the organization from slow destruction by the hiring of anti-union workers. They had to have ship's delegates to be the voice of the seamen on the job. Yet both of these simple concepts went through great distortions in company propaganda. The employers described the ship's delegates as an "extra union member ... carried on every ship with no other function than to see to the interest of the union."[35] This deliberate lie infuriated the seamen. The shipowners knew full well that the ship's delegate carried out his duties as a seaman. They well understood the ship's delegate system, which was entrenched in the CSU contracts they had previously signed. Far from being a useless extra body on the vessel, the union argued, the delegate could "eliminate petty grievances before they grew into disputes between officers and crew."[36] The organizations representing both the skippers and the mates recognized the validity and value of the ship's delegates and there had never been a complaint lodged against a delegate.[37] But the operators were trying to keep the union off the ships and to do that they had to throw the delegate overboard.

Although the ship's delegate was a familiar feature of existing agreements, the demand for a union ship was new. The expired contracts called for preferential hiring of union members and this had been acceptable until the clause was abused by some shipping companies. The seamen simply were demanding a floating union shop, a permanent solution to the practice of some companies which interpreted preferential hiring as a license "to discriminate against employees because of union membership."[38] Instead, the union proposed a union hiring hall from which the companies would hire CSU members. Companies would be allowed to hire non-union seamen when qualified union members were not available.

The shipowners replied that the union ship existed nowhere in the world "for the simple reason that discipline necessitates absolute control over the crew by the captain while at sea and by the employers." It was typical of the shipowners, the union replied, to substitute their desire for complete control for the legitimate authority of a captain at sea to make decisions on grounds of emergency and hazard. "The employers have consistently sought, by exploitation of the 'safety at sea' consideration, to attach to themselves absolute prerogatives."[39] In any case, the company statement was either based on gross misinformation or a deliberate attempt to mislead. Not only did union ship agreements exist in Great Britain, Norway, Holland and the United States, but the National Maritime Union had a closed shop agreement with the Canada-Atlantic Transit Co., a Canadian National subsidiary. If that example was too remote, the CSU cited the agreement between the CSU and the Quebec and Ontario Transit Co., which was a closed shop agreement on a Lake carrier.[40]

As a result of negotiations centered around the conciliation board hearings, the CSU achieved an agreement June 24 with Canada Steamship Lines, Tree Lines Navigation, Algoma Central Steamships and several other large carriers. The contract recognized the CSU as the sole bargaining agent for unlicensed seamen. It fell short of a union ship clause, but did include a beefed-up preferential hiring clause with union supervision. Union representatives were to be allowed access to ships to investigate grievances and to check conditions. A new grievance procedure provided for three steps in settlement of disputes: first the grievance would be handled at the ship level, then at the union to company level and finally, if still unresolved, it could be referred to the

Maritime Adjustment Board, a tripartite body consisting of appointed company, union and government representatives.

The pact included an additional $2.50 in wages above the $7.50 in the back to work agreement, as well as war zone and dangerous cargo pay. There was to be overtime for non-essential work performed in addition to regular duties and paid transportation back to home port. The agreement was to run until March 15, 1942. Those still refusing to sign included Paterson, Keystone, the Misener group and some other small interests.

By the end of October, the union had a large majority of Lake seamen under contract, but it was not until January 14, 1941, that the board finally handed down its ruling. There were by then only about 50 vessels sailing non-union. The board pointed out that "the adoption of this agreement by such a decisive majority of the industry is itself a recommendation both of its specific terms and the relationship it establishes between the employer and the union. It is the board's opinion, reinforced by three-quarters of the industry, that the specific terms of the agreement are proper, reasonable and constructive."[41]

The board told the federal labor minister that those companies which had not signed "should at once sign and so concur in and complete the industrial agreement which it is our privilege to report to you, sir, is now established policy in the industry of Great Lakes freight navigation."[42] It was a report that vindicated the CSU's strike action and, by implication, condemned the employers. "The abstract rights which it is now conceded belong to labor can only be said to exist in a concrete sense if collective bargaining is practised and collective agreements are concluded. It cannot be said too clearly that labor can no longer be regarded, if it ever was correct to do so, merely as a commodity. Labor is a partner in industry, and as such, it is entitled to have not only the right to organize but the corresponding right and opportunity to utilize its organization for collective negotiations and agreements with employers."[43]

It was a ringing declaration of the rights of labor, but the King government had already demonstrated it viewed matters in a very different light.

THERE WAS AN EERIE CALM over Europe during the winter of 1940. The Allies remained behind France's defense lines and hostilities were so mild that the period was dubbed the Phoney War. In Canada, the King government still harbored hopes of limiting its involvement in the European conflict, but made use of its wartime powers to step up its attacks on its enemies at home. In November 1939 the Communist Party's English and French-language newspapers were banned. By

early 1940, a wave of arrests had hit more than 60 Canadians, communists and non-communists alike, who were charged with violations of
the War Measures Act. On June 6, 1940, the government proscribed the
Communist Party and 15 other progressive and left-wing organizations.

The first indication that the new round of repression would hit the
CSU came in Nova Scotia in mid-June. On June 10, Capt. Ben MacKenzie, president of the Canadian Fishermen and Fish Handlers Union,
wrote to the fish companies requesting a meeting to negotiate herring
prices for east coast fishermen. The reply came not from the employers
but from provincial Minister of Labor L.D. Currie, whose June 15 letter
struck a bizarre and threatening note.

"Dear Sir," Currie began. "It has been brought to my attention that you
are once again endeavoring to mind everybody else's business but your
own. In other words you are trying to stir up industrial trouble among
the workers of the fish plants of Lockeport. If you want to help win the
war and be of some service to the community, jump into your boat and
go out to sea and catch fish, where your talents might display themselves to better advantage than in drawing down a salary from an
outside organization trying to organize a group of workmen that you
don't belong to and I doubt ever will belong to.

"We have stood about all we intend to stand from trouble-makers like
you in this province, and I am warning you now for your own interest,
that we will tolerate it no longer. This country has stood far too much of
crazy agitation from men like you, and it is not in the mood to stand any
more of it. We all welcome proper labor unions and we are prepared to
do anything we can to foster and develop them, but not the type of union
you have in mind."

MacKenzie's reply was blunt and to the point. "Your letter is practically a threat to the organization I represent, as well as myself, and from
the tone of it you are endeavoring to intimidate me, which under existing
law is an offence. The groups I represent are perfectly legal and are the
recognized unions of the country, the Trades and Labor Congress and
the AF of L. From your letter I gather you question my talents. Perhaps I
have not read as much of Shakespeare, Milton, Burns or Kant's *Critique
of Pure Reason* as some other folks, but I still believe I can look after
myself and those who have trusted me in a perfectly legal manner, and
regarding the boat that I could jump into, I will agree to do this, if you
will agree to take a two-wheeled cart and go around the streets of
Halifax and peddle the fish I send you."[44]

Currie had written a similar letter to Charlie Murray, warning him to
"desist from your efforts to create industrial trouble... I warn you too
that your conduct will from now on be very carefully watched and
examined, and if I find that you do not quit this sort of business, then it

will most certainly be the worse for you. I am giving you this final word of warning. My advice to you is to get out of Lockeport and stay out."[45] To save on stamps, Currie enclosed the threat to Murray in the letter to MacKenzie in Lockeport, although Murray was in Halifax at the time.

Were these the ravings of an anti-union cabinet minister gone mad? Events in the following 36 hours were to show they were not. Currie's letters were simply warning shots in a broad assault on the leadership of the trade union movement and Canadian anti-fascists in general.

On the evening of June 18, Pat Sullivan settled into a room at the St. Regis Hotel in Toronto. He had been working hard, constantly moving among the union's various branches and out to the East Coast. His son Bill was shipping out and his wife, Mickey, was still cooking on Lake boats. He may have felt a little more tired and lonely than usual that night. It was his birthday and the increasing grey streaks in his dark hair were the only outward sign that his 46 years were beginning to tell on him. No one was aware, at the time, that he had suffered a series of mild heart attacks.

The loneliness and exhaustion which often stalks over-worked trade union officials were pressing down on Sullivan, but he decided to have a solitary birthday celebration to forget for the moment the daily grind of union work. In lieu of the traditional cake with friends, he was planning to finish off a bottle of brandy.

His plans were rudely interrupted by a sharp rap at the door. It was not a friend dropping by to wish him all the best, but an RCMP officer asking Sullivan to join him for a trip downtown. Sullivan's request to make a phone call was denied, but he was told he would be back in his room within the hour. He had the feeling the brandy might age quite a bit in that time, so without offering the officer a smash, he downed the remaining spirits and left with the Mountie.

Sullivan was kept incommunicado and transferred from jail to jail until finally he ended up in the federal internment camp at Petawawa, Ontario. The hour-long detention was to last from June 18, 1940, to March 20, 1942. No charges were laid, no bail was set and there was no trial. He was dressed in prisoner of war clothing and given a bunk in Hut Number 7.[46] Pat Sullivan was the first trade unionist interned under Section 21 of the Defence of Canada Regulations, but he would not be the last.[47]

It was a full two months before CSU counsel J.L. Cohen could learn why Sullivan was behind barbed wire. The so-called Advisory Committee set up to hear appeals of internment actions would say only that the government had acted on "representations" that Sullivan was a member of the Communist Party of Canada and therefore "it would appear that (he was) disloyal to Canada."[48]

The CSU president would not be lonely in the camp. On July 19 the RCMP grabbed Jack Chapman and sent him to keep Sullivan company.[49] The president and the secretary were joined a few days later by Dave Sinclair, editor of the *Searchlight*.[50] On September 29, Charlie Murray was detained in Nova Scotia. Two days later, Kay Murray gave birth to a baby girl. Murray was allowed a brief visit, then banished to Petawawa. He would not rejoin his family until March 1942.[51] His arrest caused the "widespread feeling that Charlie is being punished for his aggressive leadership in the struggle for justice on behalf of the oppressed fishermen."[52]

The camps quickly filled up. Along with trade unionists and 110 alleged communists[53] were some pro-fascists and even some Jehovah's Witnesses, who were interned, according to some, at the request of ranking officials of the Roman Catholic Church in Quebec.[54]

The nation-wide round-up of anti-fascists, one of the most shameful episodes of the war, had been preceded by two assaults on civil liberties. On January 11, 1940, the King government had amended the Defence of Canada Regulations to give itself the power to arrest and detain citizens without charge or trial.[55] The proscription of the Communist Party and Sullivan's arrest were deliberate steps in a government campaign to cripple the Canadian left in general and the trade union movement in particular.[56]

The CSU had never wavered from its pledge of cooperation in the war effort, provided the government undertook a serious mobilization against fascism and did not use the war as an excuse to assault labor. The Communist Party on the other hand, had altered its stance as the conditions of the war changed and the King government adjusted course. As the Communist Party's historical account of the period acknowledges, the outbreak of the war "led to some confusion in the communist movement."[57] After pursuing a policy of appeasement that produced fascist governments in Spain, Czechoslovakia and Austria, Britain had declared war on Hitler just months after rejecting an anti-Nazi alliance with the Soviet Union. Yet British support continued to flow to the fascist Mannerheim regime in Finland, which was at war with the Soviet Union. When Canada declared war in September 1939, Communist Party leader Tim Buck urged a struggle on two fronts to combine military action to defeat fascism abroad with political action in Canada to control domestic reactionaries. When hostilities finally erupted in western Europe with the Nazi assault on the Low Countries and France, the party called for neutrality based on the assessment that the conflict was an inter-imperialist war that would be fought on the back of the working class.[58] The King government argued that such a position was treason, although it was shared by broad sections of the

Canadian public. The CCF's J.S. Woodsworth had argued for neutrality from the first day of the war.

No evidence of Sullivan's alleged treachery was disclosed until the Advisory Committee responded to repeated demands from Cohen for an explanation. Five charges were brought against Sullivan, charges on which he would never be tried.

The first "crime" concerned an incident in which Sullivan was not even involved. On June 4, 1938, the *Sir Thomas Shaughnessy* had arrived at Port Arthur. When mooring cables were thrown ashore, six men appeared, the committee said, led by Ernest Donne and J.P. Kidder of the CSU. According to the committee statement, "four of the men where chained to the mooring cables which prevented the vessels from departing. The Port Arthur City Police questioned Donne and Kidder, one of whom produced the key and the men were released."

The second incident concerned Sullivan and the *Damia*. According to the committee, a CSU strike was in effect in Cornwall on June 5, 1938. In fact, the 1938 strike ended April 18; the *Damia* affair was an isolated incident. "Members of the Canadian Seamen's Union boarded the vessel, ignoring the orders of the master," the committee charges read. "They were later persuaded to go ashore. A short conference was held on shore, and the men again boarded the ship and endeavored to force crew members to leave the vessel. As a result of rough tactics, a number of the crew, such as deckhands, watchmen, wheelsmen and engine room staff were forced to leave the vessel. This action had the effect of blocking the canal for one day and seriously impeded the progress of general canal traffic. J.A. (Pat) Sullivan was standing on the wharf when the group of men, who he is alleged to have brought with him from Montreal, boarded the S.S. *Damia* with the results above mentioned."

The third charge brought against Sullivan concerned the 1939 "strike of the Canadian Fishermen's Union... in Lockeport." Of course, there was no strike but a lockout precipitated by the firing of all the Lockeport fish company employees. The committee accurately noted that "charges were laid against a number of individuals... but the charges were later withdrawn. The Canadian Fishermen's Union was organized under the direction of J.A. 'Pat' Sullivan and Charles Murray, and these individuals were present during the course of the strike." Clearly, the committee saw something subversive in the organization of a trade union.

Fourthly, the committee charged that the union's revenue was small, that there had been fictitious entries and that the books had never been audited. In fact, the CSU's books were audited regularly,[59] but failure to keep accurate books would not normally count as sedition.

Finally, the committee justified Sullivan's internment on the grounds that the union had conducted an illegal strike in 1940.[60] This charge was based on the government ruling which had been kept secret during the 1940 strike. No one ever was charged for any action during this strike, but the committee's decision was final. For Sullivan, there was no appeal.

If the authorities had hoped to cripple the CSU by jailing its leadership, they were disappointed. The seamen took this latest onslaught in their stride, and were unperturbed by charges that their leaders were communists. Steve Tokaruk, a non-communist CSU ship's delegate, recalls that seamen compared their own union with "what the unions were doing that did not have the CP leadership. At least we knew we didn't belong to a company union."[61]

This assessment was confirmed when Liberal Senator N.M. Paterson refused to sign the Lake agreement on the grounds his employees were not members of the CSU. A Fort William grain merchant and owner of 109 Prairie grain elevators, the Senator was president of Paterson Steamships Ltd., which operated a substantial Lake fleet. He seized on the internments as a way to evade a CSU agreement. At the urging of Tom Moore, president of the TLC, the Department of Labor decided to put the issue to a vote.[62] Paterson's firm agreed to the ballot, but made a final attempt August 24 to influence the outcome. In a letter that day, seamen were advised that "if you vote to have the Canadian Seamen's Union or any other represent you, then you must see that the officers you elect to conduct the union are of the highest type and not of the class that our authorities find necessary to intern."[63]

When the ballots were counted September 10, there were 24 votes against the union and 27 spoiled ballots, but there were 361 votes for the CSU. The ballots of 24 Quebecois seamen had been ruled spoiled because they had written "oui" on their ballot paper instead of marking an x, as the instructions clearly stated — in English. Ferguson and Cyril Lenton delivered the results to Paterson personally in his Fort William office. He signed October 28.[64]

STILL REFUSING TO SIGN the 1940 Lake agreement were Capt. Scott Misener, whose three companies operated 23 vessels, and Capt. Leon Beaupré, who sailed 13 vessels under two company flags. The CSU threatened to renew its strike and appealed to the government to take over the firms which refused to negotiate.[65] Labor Minister Norman McLarty warned Misener that "responsibility for non-acceptance of the board's awards will be entirely and completely yours,"[66] but Misener refused to bargain. Like Paterson, he hoped to use the internment issue to evade union wages and working conditions.

When the CSU held its fourth convention in March 1941, delegates elected Dewar Ferguson as acting president and Ernie Donne as acting secretary-treasurer. They then returned all the interned officials to their posts.[67] When the union asked Misener for a meeting, he responded with ponderous sarcasm: "Might I ask what representatives of the union would attend such a meeting if one were arranged? I note from your letterhead that J.A. (Pat) Sullivan is listed as president and J.A. Chapman as secretary-treasurer. Would these individuals attend such a meeting as representatives of the union? . . . Is Mr. Sullivan as president directing the activities of the union? If so, would he be present at any such meetings as you proposed, and if not, would you be good enough to explain why he would not be present?"[68]

With the government unwilling to intervene and the companies unwilling to bargain, the CSU was forced to take job action. The strike against the Misener and Beaupré interests began with the 1941 navigation season and was limited to their vessels,[69] but it was clear from the beginning it would be a tough struggle. When Lakehead CSU official Aage Antonsen boarded a vessel to inform the crew of the impending shutdown, he was arrested, charged with "inciting seamen to desert," and sentenced to nine months in prison.[70] Misener recruited farm boys to break the strike, despite their ignorance of the sea. "I encourage our captains to hire boys from the farm," he explained, because "they are better sailors than the drifters who sit around wharves."[71] With RCMP assistance to move the scabs across picket lines, by launch if necessary, Misener succeeded in moving several vessels with his inexperienced and short-handed crews.

There remained one stumbling block for the companies: the board order to sign with the CSU. Once again, McMaster came to the rescue. Beaupré signed an agreement with the Captain's National Seamen's Association, despite the board's clear statement that the CSU was the sole legitimate representative of Lake seamen. "I have recognized a bargaining agent of my own choosing," Beaupré said, "and complied with the suggestion of the conciliation board. I have notified my men that if they do not want to work under the agreement which I saw fit to sign with the National Seamen's Association, then they can resign and I will replace them."[72]

With scabs boarding the vessels under police escort, the CSU had only one offensive move left — a general strike of the Lakes with all the risks that entailed. Such a shutdown would undoubtedly be a bloody affair and result in a devastating campaign against the union for undermining the war effort, regardless of the justice of the CSU's cause. It was clear both from union policy and the large numbers of seamen who enlisted that the CSU did not want to strike during the war. In any case, a freeze on shipping would give the opportunity for the government to sink the union once and for all.[73] The only sane course left was to

let the Beaupré and Misener vessels sail non-union.[74] The CSU reluctantly ended its strike and turned its attention to winning freedom for
its interned leaders.

The National Executive had reacted to the internments in a way that
was becoming almost a CSU reflex. Emergency rank and file meetings
were held simultaneously in Montreal, Toronto and Fort William to
inform the membership and to establish rank and file committees that
would "work in close touch with the National Executive in framing the
policies of the union and providing leadership during these tense
times."[75] The union did all it could to publicize the fate of the interned
leaders. Petitions were circulated, defense committees gathered money
for their defense and broadsides were fired at the government for its
anti-union actions. The seamen were well aware their leaders had been
jailed for their union activity and their campaign became part of a
growing public protest against the government's internment policy.

It took the Nazi invasion of the Soviet Union in June 1941 to reshape
the Canadian political landscape sufficiently to open the way for the
release of anti-fascist internees. As the German armies swept toward
Leningrad and Moscow and the Canadian people began to see the Soviet
Union as an ally, the continued imprisonment of Communist Party
members became an embarrassment. The growing public demand for
release of anti-fascist internees was becoming irresistible as the trade
union movement, provincial politicians and the churches took up the
campaign.

The Communist Party too, had drawn new conclusions. Its leadership, dispersed by the War Measures Act ban or incarcerated in
concentration camps, had been unable to shift party policy as the
"phoney war" of 1939 turned into a war of national liberation for the
people of western Europe. The invasion of the Soviet Union left no
doubt as to the anti-fascist nature of the war and Communist Party
policy changed to all-out support for the war effort.[76] From the camps
the communist internees asked for release so they could throw themselves into the war effort.

Late in the summer of 1941, the four interned seamen, along with 43
other interned anti-fascists, wrote to the Dominion government offering
their services to the war effort. "We, the undersigned genuine anti-
fascists, have proven by our words and deed that we are uncompromising
foes of German and Italian fascism," they wrote. "Therefore, we request
our immediate freedom and an opportunity to make our contribution to
the united effort of the Canadian people toward the crushing of the
fascist hordes..."[77]

The CSU internees had worked out plans for the union's role in
supplying, recruiting and training seamen for the demands of wartime

shipping. In October, they were able to get a copy of their program to Dewar Ferguson with the aid of J.L. Cohen.[78] Developed and polished into the union's Victory Program, the proposals included a demand for equal representation with the shipowners in wartime policy-making. A key demand was for the creation of a "distinct and effective merchant marine." The CSU saw the strength of the labor movement as a significant force in the defeat of fascism and warned that "any policy directed at restricting or limiting the labor movement can only have the effect of causing apathy and distraction which would undermine a full participation in war production."[79] The CSU urged more efficient shipping practices on the Great Lakes and a link between inland and deepsea shipping, but it did not forget to point to the necessity of decent wages, conditions and compensation for the seamen.[80] The Victory Program was a logical extension of the proposals made in the war's first weeks, two years before.

The CSU internees were finally released in March 1942 to a warm welcome from the seamen. Indeed, the only rank and file criticism of Sullivan came from some seamen who wondered if their president had not cuddled up to the bosses and the government to gain freedom. Sullivan took on his critics on the front page of the *Searchlight*, arguing that it was pressure from the seamen, organized labor and democratic-minded people across Canada which had secured his release.

Sullivan urged full support for the war effort. "Can anyone say that he is a conscious trade unionist," he asked, "and still fail to be convinced that fascism must be smashed? ... Wherever fascism comes to power it sets about immediately to wipe out the labor movement. Everything that makes life worth living would be drowned in blood, as it has been all over Europe, were the fascist murderers to win out in the present struggle. What should we as labor men, do to ensure the defeat of fascism? Everything we can. I repeat — everything. And by helping to bring about the defeat of fascism in Europe, we are safeguarding our own liberties here in Canada."[81]

A few months after Sullivan's release, the Trades and Labor Congress held its convention in Winnipeg. Sullivan was elected to the post of second vice-president.[82] In 1943, the resignation of the incumbent TLC president moved Percy Bengough into the post of acting president and Sullivan to acting secretary-treasurer. "I could hardly believe what was happening to me," Sullivan wrote later. "It seemed so fantastic — arrested in 1940 as a member of the Communist Party of Canada, released in March 1942, six months later elected vice-president of the Trades and Labor Congress of Canada and finally, less than one year after my release from internment, appointed to take over the job of second-in-command of the largest labor body in Canada."[83]

At the 1943 convention in Quebec, TLC delegates elected both Bengough and Sullivan to their respective positions.[84] It was an indication of how Canadian trade unionists viewed the CSU that the TLC delegates not only unanimously elected the union's president to the secretary-treasurer's position, but also gave him a standing ovation when he accepted it.[85] For the moment the struggle to protect the seamen's gains in Canada was over. At sea, however, the seamen were at war, the vital Fourth Arm of Canada's armed forces.

CHAPTER EIGHT

The Fourth Arm

WHAT PRICE DEATH?

A blacked-out ship zigzags alone
Through the heart of the danger zone.
The threat of submarines is known
To every man on board.
From constant watch, nerves raw and tense,
Sleepless hours filled with suspense,
Striving to pierce the mist so dense,
Before a 'hit' is scored.

The dread alarm is sharply cried,
"Torpedo! on the starboard side!"
A sudden change of course is tried,
In vain to dodge a hit,
Too slow by far to miss its fate,
Unwieldy, turning much too late,
Each one, from cabin boy to mate,
Knows that "This is it."

The strident clang of the warning bell —
For a ghastly moment, a silence fell —
Then a smashing, crashing blast from Hell
As the "tin fish" hit its mark.
An awful feeling of dazed despair.
The fumes of cordite fill the air.
Some of the men who were standing there
Have died in the dark.

Flames shoot up from the after hold,
Fanned by a breeze that's fresh and cold.
Slowly to port the doomed ship rolled,
Her final voyage is done.
"Abandon ship" — the boats are manned.
The men still able lend a hand
To those poor devils who cannot stand —
Cursing the Nazi Hun.

Two boats carry the remaining few,
All that's left of a gallant crew,
And some of the injured won't pull through.

Their lives are the gift they give.
No more watches for them to keep,
No more sailing the salty deep,
From now on, just eternal sleep.
But what of those who live?

Perhaps a few short weeks ashore,
Then carry on, just as before.
There is no rest in this damn war,
For such brave men as he
Who dares to live in this travail.
The Merchant Seaman must not fail,
Though men will die, the ships must sail
Until all men are free.

By Snellie
Searchlight, May 1, 1945

THE NECESSITIES OF WAR forced a transformation of Canadian society. The seamen, probably more than any other civilian group, faced tremendous changes. Canada, which limped through the late 1920s and 1930s with only a shadow of a deepsea fleet, found itself in the same position it had faced at the outbreak of the First World War. There had been no plans for a deepsea fleet and once again it was the spark from the United Kingdom that awakened the Canadian government to the fact that Canada was able to build and man a merchant fleet of its own. In 1940, the United Kingdom placed orders for 26, 10,000-ton merchant ships to be built in Canadian yards.[1] Canada was to follow Britain's lead once more and build a merchant marine.

In 1939 there were only 38 ocean-going vessels of more than 1,000 gross tons under Canadian registry scattered among different companies using them for their individual needs.[2] The Canadian National Steamship Co. had 11 vessels. Imperial Oil owned 10 tankers and Canadian Pacific had a couple of ships under the Red Ensign. Imperial and CPR both were controlled by foreign interests, but because of their Canadian registration they are included in the Canadian total for 1939.[3]

As a result of the desperate need for a bridge of ships to supply Allied troops and to deliver war material, the Canadian government formed the Park Steamship Co. Ltd. in April 1942. It was a fully government-owned company, given the task of constructing and administering a merchant fleet under Canadian registry. The ships were turned over to private companies operated on a management fee basis.[4] The companies were paid for their administrative services, but the government retained ownership and any profits.

The first Park ship was launched in August 1942,[5] and it signalled a new era for Canada and its maritime workers. The *Kootenay Park* was the first of 171 vessels to come out of Canadian shipyards bearing the name of a Canadian park. There were two basic types of Park ship: the 4,700-tonner, of which 18 were built and the 10,000-tonners; a few miscellaneous ships rounded out the fleet.[6]

The war ended the 10-year unemployment crisis. Thousands of the unemployed entered the shipyards. The earliest wartime work was on repair jobs for U.K. vessels damaged in the war. This was followed by construction of British merchant ships, Canadian naval vessels and finally the Park ships. The shipyards had to open up before the shipping industry could ride the wartime boom. It was estimated that 30,000 men and women were drawn into the British Columbia yards[7] and there was similar development in the St. Lawrence and Atlantic yards. Charlie Murray went from the internment camps to the Halifax shipyards along with legions of the single unemployed. Jimmy Bell, one of the leaders of the Toronto Duke Street boys, finally closed the doors to the unemployed organization and was able to go to work.

During the war, Bell was business agent for the Industrial Union of Marine and Shipyard Workers of Canada, Local 3. "The Park ship was an outdated design, even at the time," he remembered years later in the office of the Maritime Workers Federation, "something like the American Liberty ships.

"But the Liberty ship design was more advanced than the design of the Park vessels. They were actually uneconomical. You see on the 4,700-tonner you had a crew of something like 33 and on the 10,000-tonners you had a crew of around 40... They weren't the most efficient type of vessel. They were selected because it was possible to construct them very speedily, a very straight-forward design — expediency more than anything else."[8]

Smiler was working in maintenance in the shipyards around Montreal, testing the new Park vessels as they came off the ways. In 1980, he remembered those years over a couple of beers in Joe Beef's Tavern in Montreal, a drinking establishment he frequented off and on for more than 50 years. The period in the shipyards was Smiler's only steady job ashore and even then he spent 90 percent of his time in the stokehold.

"We were building the Park ships," he said, "and I used to take them on trial. I took 17 on trial. When we went in, it was a shell. Sometimes the boiler was there and sometimes it wasn't. We were assigned to a ship — it had a number, not a name. We went down there and the first thing you knew they might drop the boilers in her and then the engines. The only thing that was in her was the seacocks and the general service pumps. As soon as we had the boilers in we'd light up with wood and keep a little steam on her. After that you might be able to start an auxiliary — the air pumps and all that.

"They ran from here down to Trois Rivières. They'd go down there and turn around in that lake down there (Lac Saint Pierre) and come back. Believe me, I was firing coal in those eight hours. Everything wide open, everything she could. We'd get as high as 14 knots out of a Park ship. Whatever happened to the ships, we'd fix it all up. If it didn't hold up well enough, you might have to bolster it up. Maybe they'd go and examine all the tubes to see if any were leaking or anything. They'd do everything to her. We used to clean all our fires while they tested all the booms, rafts and all that. We'd take her out on trial just before we handed her over to whoever was going to operate her."[9]

Once Smiler and the other shipyard workers had checked out the vessels, they were ready to go into service, but the 6,000 men it would take to form the crews of the merchant marine were not standing on the dock waiting to board. Many of the sailors from the Lakes, probably 2,000 by 1940, had enlisted in the armed forces, and others, like Frank Gallant, were sailing out of British manning pools. Gallant recalls one experience shipping from British pools before the Canadian pools were established. "When I was in England I was in the Dunkirk 'do.' I took a tugboat run in the evacuation of Dunkirk. I was in the British pools and it was a big do at the time. I was a coal fireman and it was a coal boat, so what the hell. It was a bit of excitement anyway. They took them right off the beach, too. It was a total disaster. The guys were dropping in the water coming over. There were all kinds of small boats picking them up. There were planes going over and there were the machine guns. They were the worst — they strafed the beaches.

"We had the small boats and could get them close to the shore. They would have to wade out to get on them. As soon as you got 20 or 30 or whatever the hell you could take, you were gone. You'd go across the Channel and back again. I know I worked 32 hours there at one time. Bloody Jesus, I was never tireder before and I've never been tireder since."[10]

Seamen had to be recruited and trained. For many of the new sailors it was their first job, some because they were only 14 or 15 years old and others because the Depression had denied them employment. People like Joe McNeil, who joined the merchant navy during the war, were among the latter, but they did have the advantage of several years of trade union experience picked up from the Single Men's Unemployed Association. What they lacked in work experience they made up for in political understanding. It could be said they were more red than green. McNeil well remembers the conditions before he went to sea.

"I didn't work much for 10 years. I used to work on an extra gang or something like that to get a pair of boots. But we were organized people, and if the trade unions went on strike we wouldn't think of scabbing on them. In many cases we would shore up their picket lines.

"We were not crowding the labor market. We were organized, we were unemployed but we didn't want to intrude on anyone else's job. Disorganized people are bound to do anything. If you are alone, all you want to do is survive. We weren't like that at all. We were going to do it our way. Until they offered us a job we were going to stay unemployed. ... That was my first introduction to trade unionism."[11]

Canada had very few people with deepsea experience and no institution or organization to handle the influx of workers who had to be trained and shipped. The CSU offered to take on this function. The union suggested that its branch halls could be used as shipping pools and the union would train the new volunteers in seamanship.[12] But Ottawa decided to go it alone and established the Canadian Merchant Marine Manning Pools.[13] The first pool was set up in Halifax in September 1941. The next one opened in Montreal in the Gare Viger on New Year's Day, 1942. In May and July the last two pools were opened in Vancouver and Saint John, New Brunswick.

The seamen who were able to produce discharge papers indicating their competency in the trade or who were trained under the new scheme were dispatched on a rotating basis through the pools. Between trips, they received their base pay and room and board in the pools.[14]

Gerry McCullough was a Lake seaman who went deepsea during the war. He has been a seaman since then and always remained active in his union. Today, as full-time Vancouver organizer for the International Transport Workers Federation, he is responsible for tracking down ships violating basic conditions and bringing them into line. As a result of his work and that of his predecessor, CSU veteran Tom McGrath, Vancouver has an international reputation among deep water seamen as the port in which to stage a fight for union contracts and conditions.

"Once you joined the manning pool you were on wages," McCullough remembers, "but you didn't get your war bonus. They held back so much every week of your wages so that when you shipped out you always had a few dollars when you went aboard a ship. They had, too, what you called a 'two-year agreement' in the manning pools. If you signed the two-year agreement it was like the army, you got all the benefits. I never belonged to the agreement because you had to take the trip they sent you on. You were on continuous wages all the time and when you came off the ship you had to report to the manning pool in a certain amount of time. If you weren't in the two-year agreement, you could take a week off and join the pool whenever you were ready.

"The hiring was pretty fair and there were a lot of jobs. They would put your name on the board and you were supposed to check the board at least once a day. In Montreal the food was very good, I always thought. Every pool was a little different. I was in the pool in Saint John and the food wasn't that good there. You didn't have single rooms. Christ, in Montreal you had a half a dozen guys to a room in bunk beds."[15]

The conditions established by the government in the manning pools were good when compared to the standards the seamen were accustomed to. Seamen were still not eligible for unemployment benefits at the beginning of the war and the payment of base wages with food and lodging between voyages could only be hailed as a great step forward.

These improvements did not fall to the seamen by chance. The CSU continuously pressured the government to improve the shoreside conditions for the merchant seamen and in many cases the government, seeing the wisdom of the arguments, went along with the union's suggestions. It was the same for wages. Even before the union became the bargaining agent for the deepsea fleet it was able to convince the government to bring the deepsea fleet up to the rates paid on the Lakes.

The east coast Park vessels came under contract to the CSU in November 1943.[16] The CSU had always been forced to fight to the last bell to be recognized by any company as the legitimate union of the seamen. Finally, on the government-owned vessels, the union was recognized without even a shrug. There was no work stoppage or unrest because "the CSU was an established organization and the Park Steamship Co. took a very realistic attitude toward the democratic rights of their employees. This company," the union felt, "has not attempted in any way to impede our organizational work, either ashore or aboard ship."[17]

As soon as the CSU was certified on the Park vessels, it set up all the on-board structures it had on the Lakes. Departmental delegates, ship's delegates, ship meetings once a week and in some cases a ship's newspaper were established. On deepsea vessels the on-board organization became even more important as a result of the increased time at sea. Grievances could not be allowed to pile up for months until a patrolman or other shoreside delegate in Canada was contacted. Each ship became a leadership training school. At war's end, when relations between employers and trade unions would return to "normal," the deck-educated delegates would prove invaluable to the CSU.

Canada's merchant seamen had better wages and conditions than their naval counterparts, but they faced all the hardships and dangers that the sea and the enemy had to offer. The merchant vessels were formed into convoys sailing from Halifax's Bedford Basin. The convoys could consist of as few as 40 ships or as many as 150. The Park vessels carried a four-inch gun forward, a 12-pounder aft and Oerlikon guns on the bridge and midships housing. There was a gunnery crew aboard vessels known as DEMS — a naval rating standing for Defensively

Equipped Merchant Ships — but the crews still had to man the weaponry in addition to their normal duties. Of course, any real defense of the
convoy fell to the corvette and destroyer escorts.

The horrors of attack, which could come from under the sea, from
surface raiders or from out of the sky were matched by the violent
forces of nature which pounded and scattered the ships as they steamed
across the Atlantic. Fog, ice, snow, gales and stifling heat all vied to stop
the trains of ships from reaching their destinations on the other side of
the "pit."

Early in the war, the Royal Canadian Navy steered the North Atlantic
convoys as far north as possible, to the very edge of the Arctic ice, in
order to avoid the packs of U-boats prowling the approaches to Europe.
But as the corvettes became more proficient at anti-submarine warfare,
the plan was altered. The emphasis moved away from defending the
convoys to a strategy that used the ships as an element in an offensive
trap. "By the spring of 1943, we were running convoys deliberately right
at the thickest concentration of U-boats, like a fullback running over
tacklers, because this was the best way to kill as many U-boats as
possible. The convoys had become bait..."[18]

Of the thousands of seamen who crewed the merchant armadas, it
can be conservatively estimated that the average age was not over 25.
Hundreds of the young men who put out to sea to fight against fascism
were under 16. Scores shipped out at 14 and 15 — all that was needed
was parental permission. Buddies wrote letters giving the okay for the
kid to ship out, signed the would-be seaman's parents' name and mailed
it to the proper authorities in an envelope bearing the correct home town
postmark. It was that simple and the kid was no longer a kid. He was a
member of Canada's merchant marine.

They lived their adolescence in the world's waterfront haunts and at
sea. They became men. In the fo'c's'le they developed a taste for reading
and education and learned about democracy, trade unionism and politics. Manning the vessels was hard work and months were spent at sea
without a break. Time ashore offered a change from the discipline and
isolation of the ship. It was a time for love and for fun, a time to raise hell
and to see how the peoples of the world lived. Sometimes it was
drinking, fights, prostitutes, nights in the slammer and life lived for the
moment. It was always education.

Wartime shipping was not kind and it did not discriminate between
young and old. Seamen of all ages were blown to bits or interred in
oceanic graveyards with only the memory of the survivor to mark their
resting places. In 1945, the *Searchlight* reported 1,042 Canadian seamen
had perished during the war and 147 were still being held in enemy
prisoner of war camps.[19] More recent figures indicate 1,146 seamen were

killed and 68 merchant vessels sunk.[20] The Company of Master Mariners gives a figure of 1,437 Canadian seamen who died during the war.

But the seamen spent little time worrying about the possibility of death. They had a job to do and a life to live. A fatalistic attitude prevailed. You did your best, but if you were going to get it, you would get it. In the meantime, let's win the war, and if we can, have a good time when there's a break.

Today Clifford Craig and his wife and boys live in Toronto, where he works as a steeplejack. He hasn't shipped out since the 1940s but he still is very interested in the industry and keeps in touch with seamen. A native of Prince Edward Island, Craig is one of many Maritimers who enjoy going down to the Dovercourt Tavern for a beer or two. Every couple of weeks a truck pulls up outside and sells lobster and cod direct from PEI. One evening in the Dovercourt he recalled his first deepsea voyage on the *Point Pleasant Park*, a 10,000-tonner. Craig had shipped coastwise on non-union ships but it was on the *Point Pleasant Park* that he joined his first union, the CSU.

He shipped out from the Saint John pool. The *Point Pleasant* loaded general cargo and explosives in New Jersey and stopped in Trinidad for bunkers, then began her voyage to South Africa — unescorted as was the custom on southerly routes. February 21, 1945, is a day Clifford Craig will never forget. "It was a nice clear day. The water was clear and the temperature was probably in the 80s. I was back aft. It was three in the afternoon and not much to do, so I went forward to midships to get a pack of cigarettes. At one minute after three, the gunner who was on the bridge was changing with the gunner on the stern. They met at midships. That was when the torpedo hit and blew the stern out. It was from a submarine, but we never saw a thing. I got the cigarettes and was coming out of the companionway when the torpedo hit. All I felt was a vibration. The ship shook. I went up on deck and an AB said, 'We've been hit — get your life jacket.' If I hadn't gone for those cigarettes, I would have been gone. They always say smoking is bad for your health, but it saved my life.

"The ship went down so far and then stopped, but we were off her and away from her by then. The submarine came up and shelled the ship to sink it the rest of the way. Down she went, all the way stern first. You could hear explosions, but we figured that was just the boilers... The submarine didn't bother the lifeboats. It was a German U-boat. It stayed on top of the water and never bothered us.

"There was a crew of 54, including the gunners from the Navy and the officers. We had nine killed outright on the ship and one guy died on the lifeboat the first night.

"We had rations on the lifeboats. You got one ounce of water a day roughly, sometimes two but that was all. Just enough to survive. We were in the boats for 10 days and nine nights. In the daytime you'd roast and at night you'd freeze to death. You'd be wet all the time and you'd have to bail steady in rough water. Pretty near every night we got bad weather. There might have been one or two good nights, but some nights were just steady bailing. Two guys would bail for half an hour and then two more. All by cans. They never heard of those little pumps at all. It was bail, bail, bail and bail.

"You had enough food to survive but your stomach was all plugged up. There was fishing gear in the lifeboat and in the daytime we used to fish. We'd catch some fish about like this — six inches long — split them open, lay them out on the side of the boat and let them dry in the sun. You'd peel a little of the meat off and let them dry a little more. If you dug too deep it was still raw. It gave you a little fresh meat and something to do. You couldn't walk or anything.

"Some of the guys in the lifeboat never said anything and nobody ever got hysterical. But what they were thinking in their own minds, nobody knows. We had flares on board and at nighttime we used to set them off. We could hear planes out there but it was too overcast so the planes could not look for us. On the tenth day we saw smoke off on the horizon but we couldn't see a ship. We had a mirror and we kept flashing her with the sun. We saw the ship turn and it picked up two of our boats, but the other boat had gotten two days away from us."

Craig and the others were taken to South Africa where they were hospitalized and treated for exposure and other injuries. They were repatriated in three's and four's when merchant vessels were leaving for Canada short of crew members. In Canada, their reception was brusque.

"Back in Canada you were pretty much on your own," Craig says. "There was never any ceremony or anything like that. We went to the harbor master and got paid off. We put in for the clothes that we lost. No matter if you lost $200 or $500, everybody got exactly $120. I was 14 when I first shipped out and I was 16 when I was torpedoed. It didn't bother me then, but it bothers me today."[21]

Seamen like Craig have a very cool attitude to their wartime service. The struggle against fascism was just one aspect of their war. Another was the fight to keep unionism alive. The CSU, like all unions, took a no-strike pledge in 1942 for the duration of the war. Yet the CSU would emerge from the war stronger than ever thanks to the unceasing efforts of rank and file members to protect union conditions at sea.

One who was in the front line of this quieter battle was Nick Buszowski. Now secretary-treasurer of Local 400, the Seamen's Local of the Canadian Brotherhood of Railway, Transport and General Workers,

Buszowski is tall and thin, bearded and usually wears a snap-brim hat. He walks as if suspended from a sky-hook with a slow, smooth rhythm reminiscent of Django Reinhart. On the wartime Park boats, Buszoswski earned a reputation as something of a "situation specialist" on contract violations.

"If there was any discussion about a beef," he explains, "it wasn't the delegates alone who discussed it. The whole ship's crew would be brought in. There was a meeting of the whole ship's crew every week aboard the ships. The only guys who did not attend were the guys on watch and you'd try to make it so you'd get them the following week. A beef was written up at the weekly meeting and read to the crew. You wouldn't have one beef, you might have 20 or 30. The tactic I used to use, which I think was very good, was to see the chief steward and say, 'Could you type this up in triplicate for us.' Of course, the chief steward would say 'sure.' Then he'd type it out in quadruplicate and give one to the skipper. Then they'd all be primed. But this was a better thing, eh. You wouldn't get them by surprise. You'd go up an hour or two later and start the argument. Sometimes it would last all night. Most would say sure all the way down the line, but some wanted to argue and some just wouldn't listen. Some of the skippers were pretty good, but most of them were shocked. They couldn't believe this, being 'dictated to' by the crew.

"Limeys," Buszowski sighs. "British, baby." Buszowski calls everyone baby. "They tried to institute this British naval formula with the Canadians and it just didn't go across. They had been getting away with it for a number of years. Some of the British were real good, but the majority were shocked. One skipper told me, 'I'm getting the hell off. No way is any goddamn AB going to dictate to me.' "

There were times even during wartime when everything was "normal." There were no big beefs brewing and no anticipated attacks from the enemy. What was the shipboard life like during routine periods? How did the seamen occupy themselves during their time off?

"There was always a ship's library aboard," remembers Buszowski, "which was very educational, Upton Sinclair and things of that nature and the *Communist Manifesto*, of course. There was quite a bit of reading done. You were doing four and eight and only working eight hours a day, so you have eight hours off that you were not sleeping. There might also be weight lifting or boxing. On the odd one we had swimming pools on deck. They were only three or four feet deep, but you could swim in them. We built them ourselves out of canvas and two-by-four's and four-by-four's. You would be amazed at the fun you could have in one of those things. You never played water polo, but it was cool when it was 100 degrees out.

"There were a lot of political discussions. Everybody wasn't a red by any degree. There would be a lot of red-baiting going on. Political discussions were the biggest thing next to playing cards... You'd get into a messroom and there would be six or eight guys arguing. Possibly political discussions were one and card playing was two."

There were times when small beefs could build because of inactivity of the skipper. The company or the government would rarely step in over a beef as small as mattresses, watercoolers or fridges and seamen would have to live with these discomforts for months and even years if they were not resolved.

The union could argue but had no weapon except good will. Resolution of the beef would fall to the seamen. There were instances in which they had to take drastic action in order to have decent living conditions in their floating homes. Buszowski recalls one such incident in 1944 aboard the *Stanley Park* in the port of Montreal.

"We held the ship up for three or four days because of mattresses, cutlery, a frigidaire, water cooler and matches. Matches were a problem. They didn't supply matches. They didn't have a spring-filled mattress, just sort of a donkey's breakfast. But it wasn't straw-laden, it was a piece of felt about two inches thick. The first thing they did was throw me, Charles Fidler and Mel Record into a paddy wagon and drive us around Montreal for a couple of hours. It was a naval police van. Finally they stopped off at the CSU hall. Fergie was the agent, but he was away. They inquired of them whether we were members of the union and whether the union had sanctioned the strike. The angle I was using was that these ships were under a manifest from the shipyards and were supposed to have all these things on it. They had, somehow, been ripped off along the way. They had been grafted.

"They took us back and collected a bunch of naval personnel and a bunch of Park Steamship personnel, you know, the wheels. They started interrogating us and tried to pressure us into sailing. We said, 'No way, baby. We're not going, not until we get these concessions.' Their angle wasn't that we weren't entitled to it. They would certainly give us these things if they were available, but where could they get them. 'We understand what the situation is. We sympathize with you fellows, but we can't get these things. That's why they are not on the vessel.' We said, 'Bullshit. They are in every corner store. Go out and buy them.'

"They told us we were good for two years in jail. They would probably try to get us on mutiny. But you can't mutiny while you are in port, so it would probably be 'disobeying a lawful command.' They kept this up for about three days and then finally caved in. We got spring-filled mattresses and fridges."[22]

The absence of a proper mattress or a watercooler would mean months of discomfort, but in some disputes the stakes were much higher. The deepsea vessels in foreign ports had no recourse to the union ashore and once again, the seamen had to rely on their own abilities. There were many cases in which sick or injured seamen were not properly cared for by skippers who wanted to impress the company by maintaining schedules regardless of the human consequences. There were instances when a seaman went insane, or in another case, was so infected with venereal disease that his life was in danger. They received aid only after the crew took job action.[23]

One of the most important of these incidents took place in Colombo, Ceylon, early in 1944. It had been a terrible ten-month voyage in which the British captain spent a great deal of his time bad-mouthing Canadians and their seamanship. There was rotten food and stretches of up to 70 days without shore leave. According to the *Searchlight*, "on several occasions when the crew members had to go before the chief steward for medical attention he maintained that they were 'bluffing' and 'swinging the lead.' In one instance, a man died because the chief steward ignored the crew's appeal that he receive medical attention, stating that the man had a touch of fever and would recover in a few days."[24] Yet it was another related event on the same voyage that led the seamen to take action.

George Dagesse was a fireman on that trip. Thirty-six years later he recalled that voyage with a couple of friends over a beer in his Montreal home, mimicking perfectly the accent of the stuffy British captain.

"On the way to Colombo, we had a fellow who got smallpox," Dagesse said. "This kid was sick. He was suffering an awful lot. We were supposed to leave as the commodore (lead vessel) of the convoy. Eddie Reid (a distinguished CSU member who was the ship's delegate) went up and tried to get the old man. The old man was in his room but wouldn't open up. I don't know what happened, he just wouldn't open up. Eddie then went to the chief mate and told him all about it. Nothing was done to bring the doctor aboard. We were in the port of Colombo. Eddie tried to get the doctor because the kid had passed out from the pain. He told them that if the kid wasn't seen by a doctor by 7 o'clock in the morning we wouldn't leave. Nothing was done.

"He passed a very bad night. It was after eight in the morning, probably 9 o'clock because I was on the four-to-eight watch and I had the time to go to bed and have some breakfast. After a watch you felt like going to bed, I'm telling you. Everyone else was with the old man on the bridge. I was awakened by the chief mate. He said for me to go on up. I said, 'Good morning, captain, what's going on?' He says, heavy British accent, 'Are you ready to have the boilers ready so the ship can leave this port?' 'Sir,' I said, 'I'm with the fellows and there's nothing doing.' He says, 'You go over there. Chief mate put the flag upside down. This is mutiny! Wilful disobedience of a lawful command.'

"At that everyone was laughing. Then we saw patrols coming to beat hell, guys with bayonets fixed on the ends of their guns. They were Royal Navy patrol from the port of Colombo. We were dismissed when they came aboard. They were at attention with bayonets — no fooling around there. But we were laughing. We were so sure that we were in the right that we thought it was a farce.

"First thing we knew we were taken ashore. He (the sick crew member) was taken ashore and looked after. We were granted leave and given some money. We were supposed to be the head of the convoy the next day. We had the commodore aboard and they had to put him on a different ship. We were waiting about a week for the next convoy.

"The next convoy came and we left and found we had another case of smallpox. We put into Calcutta. A ship right next to us was torpedoed. We were carrying ammunition for the Burma front. It was a good thing we were sitting in position. We never heard about what happened in Ceylon until we came back to Saint John, New Brunswick. The ship was found by the company inspector to be cleaner than when we left Montreal. It just shows you the good standard of the crew.

"When we got to Saint John, we were told to go to the shipping master. So we went in to get paid. There was no pay and all of a sudden the door opened on the side and there was a black maria. There was no escape. 'Please, gentlemen, be seated!' They took us to the district court in Saint John. We were in the cells. Three cells for all 45 of us. We contacted the union right away in Montreal. The union got a lawyer to put up the bail for us, $4,500 dollars for all of us, $100 a piece. We appeared before the judge one afternoon. All the facts were brought out and we had been there a week and a half. In the end our lawyer told us it would be better to plead guilty and after 30 days the pages would be torn off and there would be no record of this — just keep the peace for 30 days and the record would be torn up. The captain was taken off the ship and the chief mate took his place."[25]

It was normal practice to have British officers commanding Canadian crews, a fact which complicated relations between officers and crew. Jack Corrigan was a cook on the Park vessels during the war.

"Not having much of a fleet of any kind previous to the war, we were lacking in trained marine personnel," he explains. "Practically all of the ships' captains and chief engineers were British. Many of them had a very colonial attitude toward the unlicensed personnel. Outside of giving orders, they refused to develop a rapport with the boys. If there was a mistake on the ship there would be snide remarks. If a fuel tank overflowed, the attitude was 'what can you expect from Canadians anyway?' 'Bloody Canadians' or 'bloody colonials' was a remark thrown at us on many occasions. A lot of the seamen became anti-British because of this."

The war was a breathing space for the union in many respects and marked the half-way point in its development. For the seamen, the end of the war would mark the end of hostilities abroad and their beginning at home.

The war was not taken lightly by the seamen or the union. Canadian seamen, more than any other civilian group, were involved in the death and destruction of war. The seamen, who had often been dismissed as drunks, unskilled and the scum of the waterfront in peacetime, became during the war the "fourth arm" of the Canadian forces. The war transformed them from tramps to heroes. And they were heroes, no two ways about it. What many forgot was that they always had been. The war just offered the opportunity for the Canadian people to see them in their true light.

The seamen received high praise for their war service. The Honorable J.E. Michaud, Minister of Transport, credited them with having "maintained the lines of supply across the Atlantic and the seven seas and (having) to a large extent been instrumental in keeping the war from Canadian shores.

"They have endured the hardship of seafaring under wartime conditions and many have suffered from immersion in Arctic waters or in shark-infested seas, and have endured exposure in lifeboats and rafts. They have earned the title of the Fourth Arm of the Fighting Services."[26]

CHAPTER NINE

Deepwater

THE NEW DEEPSEA FLEET and the pressures of war produced a deep change in the membership of the CSU. The CSU had developed ship's committees on the Lakes, but they remained embryonic compared to the stage they reached during the war. The committees on deepsea vessels *were* the union. There were no shoreside officials or patrolmen to come to the aid of the ship's delegates. They were on their own. The delegates handled their beefs guided only by the knowledge and experience of the crew. The committees became self-sufficient and a young, well-informed leadership emerged.

Extended periods at sea increased the educational role of the committees. Inexperienced young men were transformed into well-informed, educated and class-conscious seamen. Many seamen who entered the merchant marine with very little secondary education credit their basic education to their years at sea and a few learned to read and write aboard ship. But education did not stop with literacy. The ship's committees, the *Searchlight*, the on-board libraries and the experience of visiting the other countries of the world all acted upon seamen to develop a critical socialist viewpoint among hundreds, if not thousands, of CSU members.

If society functioned as did the committees, it would be democratically organized, work to solve mutual problems, and move toward common goals. But in their homeland ashore, the seamen found a society which was repugnant to their egalitarian dream. It was divided along class lines. Workers striving to better their conditions were met head on by employers and governments prepared to fight every attempted advance. Many of the deepsea sailors risked their lives in the fight against fascism and had been deeply influenced by many of the countries they had visited during and after the war.

There were common characteristics between the deepsea crews and their brothers and sisters on the Lakes, but there were many obvious differences. The Lake seamen who created the CSU shipped out on voyages of short duration and seldom reached a foreign port outside the United States. There were many women on the Lake vessels employed in the steward's department. There were no women on the deepsea fleet. Deepsea employment was year-round while the Lake fleet worked only seasonally. Lake sailors may have had ties to a family farm or other occupation. This closer tie to the land led to a difference in attitude and lifestyle.

There was, at best, an intermittent deepsea tradition in Canada, although a "laker" might come from a long line of sea-going people. The lack of tradition on the deepsea fleet allowed for the rapid growth of a new sea-going culture. The government and the companies tried to superimpose a highly-disciplined style based on the British model, but the Canadians rejected it as quickly as they rejected the smoked kippers they were fed for breakfast. The Canadian deepsea tradition developed from the firm base of a radical seamen's union. When the vast majority of seamen joined the earliest Park vessels, the union was there waiting. As time passed, the union became even more firmly entrenched in the deepsea fleet. On the Lakes and on the coasts, the seamen fought to create their union, but on salt water the union was creating a new seaman. Almost anyone who works ashore can go to sea, but the wartime deepsea fleet forged a unique type of seaman who can be described with certainty. What percentage of the deepsea men fell into this particular group is impossible to say, but it was more than a minority.

Many of the younger men had hardly worked before shipping out deepsea. Some sailed the Lakes or coastwise for a short time, or worked at other trades, but in general their occupation was seaman. Many of the older seamen had come from other jobs and had union experience, but a large proportion of this age group had worked very little ashore because of the Depression. They brought the ideas and spirit of the Unemployed Single Men's Associations with them. Some of these lads were seasoned veterans of the class struggle like Gerry Tellier, who had been among the leaders of the On-to-Ottawa Trek, the 1935 march of unemployed relief camp workers to Ottawa that ended in a bloody police riot in Regina. But for them too, there was only one occupation: seaman. Of course, there were veterans of the Lake fleets who transferred to the deepsea ships as well. They brought the spirit of the CSU from the Lakes.

It was a fast-moving life. They had the sea, the comradeship of their mates and their union. They had forsaken life ashore and were creating a lifestyle new to Canadians. It was a free-wheeling existence lived over and over in a hundred ports, but at its center was always a social philosophy, a dream and a commitment.

Several diverse elements combined to produce this unique Canadian seaman. This was a man, generally unmarried but maybe considering it if things worked out that way sometime, who wanted to learn and to see for himself. He was a bit cocky and didn't have the greatest respect for society's symbols of prestige or authority. He wanted to teach and to fight for what was right. He was after romance, adventure and love. His attitudes to women were very advanced for his day, but would be somewhat behind today's standard. He did, however, see women as fellow workers and sisters. He liked all kinds of people. He liked to raise hell, drink with the best of them and maybe sometimes smoke a little hashish he picked up in one of a dozen ports.

He liked to read, discuss politics and philosophy and, in some cases, to write. Danny Daniels remembers receiving astronomical amounts of poetry from the ships during his editorship of the *Searchlight*. In most cases, this seaman wasn't a communist. He was one step removed in either direction. To some, he may have suffered from "bohemianism," but he also could be counted on to do double his share when he was needed.

On the other hand there were men like Joe Grabek and Moose Mozdir, who were extremely disciplined and not apt to join in on the wilder side of the seamen's life. They, too, were very proud of themselves as seamen and militants in a left-wing union, but they were not drawn to the hell-raising which most of the group indulged in. Those who did indulge generally kept their antics off the ships. Those who did perform on the vessel were dealt with severely by the union and by the skipper. Yet there was another extreme, represented by Tellier, who remained a living legend for the many capers he pulled off and his fearlessness in standing up for the union.

Canadian seamen learned a lot on their voyage and they saw the world through their own eyes. Joe Hendsbee was one of those seamen and he believes the Canadian seamen differed in many respects from those of other merchant marines. "If you went to a foreign country, Americans were not very well-liked, anywhere in the world. It comes from the fact that Americans come from the richest country in the world and they had a tendency to act like they do when they go to a foreign place. They always have money to blow around, they think they can buy friends.

"Whereas the Canadian seaman, on his ship, was much lower paid during the Second World War," Hendsbee explains. "He made friends with people on the basis that he was in the same exploited position as the people he was visiting. It was true, for instance, in Havana. Many of the Cuban seamen, for instance, were higher paid than Canadians, but they were highly exploited for being Cubans on American ships. Therefore they had something in common with Canadian seamen. They felt the exploitation sitting on their backs.

"So the view that one would have of Havana or Santiago de Cuba was that you would look at it from the point of view of another oppressed person, rather than a playground."[1]

This attitude accompanied the seamen when they were ashore in Canada and they found it hard to keep off the picket lines. Madeleine Parent and Kent Rowley, Montreal organizers for the United Textile Workers of America in the 1940s, were among the many trade unionists who came to know the CSU rank and file from personal contact on the picket line.

"They were one of the most experienced union groups that I ever worked with," Parent remembers. "First of all, they related to each other very, very much and had this way of working in two's. There usually was a ship's delegate. When there were enough of them with us on our picket lines, they wanted to know what we wanted and what we were doing. They would then relate to the captain on the line, the textile worker in charge of the line. They followed the discipline and objective of the group they were helping. There never was any attempt to take over or make a big fuss. They were exceedingly disciplined. Game, but not a wild group in any way. They didn't believe in exerting energies that could be used by the employers in any way."[2]

When a trade union needed some help on a picket line, they needed only to ask at the CSU hall. There was almost always a group which had recently paid off a vessel. The pitch would be made for help, the delegates or other activists would round up a gang and the seamen would head for the line and back up those on strike.

Stan Wingfield was killing time in the Montreal hall one day in 1946 when the call came in for assistance on a United Textile Workers of America picket line. "They were asking for volunteers at Grover Textile Mills," he remembers. "They were on strike there and were having a tough time. They had the cops and private detectives sitting around there in cars and, of course, the scabs would just walk in. The women couldn't do much about that, so they asked for support. Those of us who were waiting for ships immediately volunteered. We said, 'Sure, why not, let's go.' We went over and did picket duty.

"We picketed there for a few hours. Just because we were there fewer scabs were going in. The textile owners sort of frowned on this. I guess they looked out their window and saw a bunch of seamen parading up and down with the women who worked there and thought, 'Who the hell are these characters? Where did they come from?' They found out we were CSUers and blew the whistle.

"My brother and I were walking along a few blocks from there and the detective car pulled alongside us. They said, 'What were you guys doing over at Grover Mills?' We told them we were helping support the textile strike. 'You guys don't work there,' they said. 'No, we don't work there, but they are union and we are union and we are going to help them win their struggle.' With this one of them got out of the car and said, 'Get in the car.' We refused. 'No, we're not getting in that car. What for? What's the charge?' There was no charge. They just insisted we get in. We insisted we wouldn't. At this point, the guy pulled out his '38 revolver. He pointed it at us and said, 'Are you going to get in the car?' With that you don't argue. We went in.

"We were in jail and the law is that within 24 hours you are allowed to use the phone. They kept us right down to the line of 24 hours before they let us use the telephone. We got bailed out almost immediately and then and only then we found out the charge: intimidation. Intimidation for what? All we were doing was picketing. We never did appear in court, by the way. We had shipped out and the lawyer handled it.

"There were so many strikes the seamen volunteered for. We figured it was our struggle, not just their struggle. Nobody had to tell us that or give us a pep talk on it. It was just that the sisters and brothers needed help and would we support them. We did that wholeheartedly. We were proud to do it. I remember when we were down on the Grover's thing, I felt very proud of being there and helping them in their struggles. We knew from our own experiences of sailing who the enemy was and the enemy was the fuckin' bosses."

What was the reaction of the other seamen when they learned where Wingfield had been? "Jealous."[3]

There was a strong bond among the deepsea men that made them a force to reckon with. The bond was built up at sea and strengthened by communal living ashore, especially during strikes. Whenever there was a major strike, the seamen would immediately lose their berths aboard ship and would have to set up their own living arrangements. Tent cities would spring up to accommodate the seamen in various struck ports. But any time ashore usually meant sharing digs with other seamen on the beach. This communalism was reflected in one of the most characteristic aspects of their lives, the "piece off."

A seaman would pay off his ship, usually at the shipping master's office. He would take care of any obligations he had and head for the hang-out where his mates would be waiting, having a few drinks, discussing politics and exchanging stories. In Montreal, it might be Joe Beef's or the Coq d'Or. In Vancouver, there was the Anchor, the Europe, the Pennsylvania or the Patricia. There were similar places in every Canadian port or, for that matter, in any foreign port that had Canadian seamen on the beach.

When the freshly paid-off seaman hit the bar, drinks were on him. He was the "live wire" and he was glad to be ashore and to have the time to have a good time. The other guys in the group were from different vessels and some had not shipped out in a long time. While the live wire had lots of folding money, many of the other guys were just jingling. It was the function of the piece off to eliminate those economic differences. The live wire pieced off those who needed it or, in many cases, everyone who was around.

The piece off was a share of the pay. He knew how much to give and they knew how much to take. The piece off was in no way a loan or even a gift. It was how things were done. It was a link in a chain of events and it carried only one obligation. The seaman who was paid off was expected to piece off whoever was on the beach when he was "live." The money was always in motion and kept the whole scene going. It was an essential part of the camaraderie and made it all possible. The piece off was the economic base of the seaman's life.

IN JUNE 1980, Stan Wingfield fired up his little red car and took the highway north from Montreal to l'Annonciation to talk with Gérard Fortin. Gerry Fortin is an organizer for the Parti Quebecois. It was a beautiful day but unseasonably cold and by the time Wingfield arrived at Fortin's, little cones of snow were blowing around the yard. Fortin had renovated an old 'popote,' a small cook house well back in the woods. The popote is comfortable and warm, a good place to sit and watch the snow fall. Fortin, 56 and greying, opened some beer for his guests and mixed himself a gin and tonic. His physique betrays his days in the black gang when he was a stalwart of the CSU. Later he helped form a union of bush workers, and in 1953, he ran for Parliament on the Labor-Progressive Party ticket against Louis St. Laurent under the slogan of "Le Canada d'abord!" and "A bas les trusts d'américains!" — Put Canada First! and Down with the American Corporations!

Wingfield and Fortin recall their old flame, the CSU. They each know the other's language well and the talk shifts from one to the other, picking the best word or phrase for the occasion. The conversation is animated, boisterous, political and jubilant.

They talk of the process which brought them to a similar way of seeing the world and their stories could be duplicated by dozens of other men who went through the same experiences. They are representative, in a way, of the French and English Canadian seamen who by 1946 were to consider themselves communists even before they joined a political party.

When he was 14, Fortin ran away from home, a small farm not far from Quebec City. He told them he was going to see the world, but his family figured he'd be back soon. After all, he had left school in Grade 4, knew no English and had learned to read by reading the newspaper to his dad, who worked in the asbestos mines and later took up farming. Gérard learned quite a bit about the world from those sessions and was very interested in what he read about the Spanish Civil War. So, *salut* to the farm! In 1938 he made his way to Vancouver and worked in camps at Port Mellon and Woodfibre. He didn't see much of the world from Woodfibre, but he got his first taste of unionism before it was time to move on.

"I tried to join the merchant marine in Vancouver," he recalled, "but my English was no good. I couldn't make myself understood. I went to Halifax by train. A guy told me to go to Imperial Oil. One day they needed a wiper, so I shipped out. But I ended up sailing from the West Coast and was there when the Inland Boatmen's Union decided to merge with the CSU. I had joined the Inland Boatmen's Union, but was at sea when the (CSU) vote was taken.

"At the beginning of the war I was like most French Canadians. We were all anti-British. There was some pro-Nazi feeling. We didn't really know what Nazism or fascism was but we, as French Canadians, wanted to get rid of La Reine — the Queen."

Wingfield found anti-British feeling among the English Canadian seamen as well. "Sometimes aboard the ships you would wonder who the enemy was. Was it the British or the Germans? Because what happened to us, because we had had no merchant marine, was that the majority of the officers on Canadian ships were limeys brought over to Canada. It brought out a lot of Canadianism even in the English Canadians. Although the French Canadians always called themselves *les Canadiens*, the English Canadians would find this sort of strange. 'Well, we are Canadians, too.' That sort of thing. It was the French Canadians who brought up the thing about being Canadian. English Canadians before that would say 'I'm English Canadian,' 'I'm Scottish Canadian,' or 'I'm a Ukrainian Canadian.' But with the Quebecers you'd hear them say, '*Je suis Canadien.*' That was very strong."

In Vancouver, Fortin got his first introduction to Marxism. "I met an old communist by the name of Tremblay. Tremblay is one of the biggest names in Quebec, but I met him in British Columbia. He had the *Manifesto*, the *Communist Manifesto*. He said, 'Read that.' Can you imagine a guy like me? Reading the newspaper, okay, but reading the *Manifesto*? Okay, so I read it and read it, and okay, I became convinced to become a communist, Stalinist, Leninist.

"I used to go to a Vancouver book shop, on Hastings in those days, and buy some books. There were a few in French. Then I said, 'I have to start to learn English.' In Vancouver, you could buy *La Presse* and other French newspapers, but I wound up in Australia, Sydney and Melbourne and it was hard to find anything in French. I had to really make an effort to learn to read in English. I started to buy some English Marxist books about the labor movement and so on. On the ships I had Stalin's and Lenin's picture in my bunk and had many arguments about that."

Fortin remembers the anti-French attitudes he ran into in British Columbia and how rarely he encountered racism or other forms of prejudice on the CSU ships.

"The union fought against those people who were racists. They didn't even know they were racists. The ship's committees dealt with the guy who did discrimination... Don't forget that in Quebec and on the Lakes was where the early union organizing was done. There were a lot of French Canadians sailing on the St. Lawrence River and on the Lakes. I was surprised when I became a patrolman to find out that most of the ships — Paterson, Canada Steamship Line, Upper Lake and St. Lawrence — had sometimes a majority of French Canadians. That must have been the same thing before the CSU and before the war. When the war came, we met a lot of those guys who had sailed on the Lakes and the river and had come to our deepsea ships.

"The union had to fight racism, first because it was part of the union constitution and also because the French Canadians had played a little bit of a role in helping to organize the union. Some of those Lake seamen on the deepsea ships were CSU before we were, young kids like us. Most of the leaders of the CSU were communists and they knew Quebec and they knew from reading the history that we were a big percentage on the Lakes and the river."

By 1945, Fortin had developed his own method to try to get his shipmates to see things in a more political light. To change the brothers from Quebec, Fortin believed, religion had to go. It stood in the way of critical perceptions.

He recounted how he and six shipmates threw their rosaries into the sea as symbols of their rejection of religion. It was only the beginning. He and the other six decided to join the Labor-Progressive Party on their return to Montreal. When the ship docked they had been months at sea and couldn't wait to fulfil their oath. As soon as they were paid off they were ready to head up town and join. It almost ended in disaster.

"We all got dressed, sports shirts and jackets. We weren't going to come in there like a bunch of bums. We ended up at 254 East St. Catherines Street, the party office. We walked into the office and they said, 'You can't join the party like that.' They let us sign applications, but we couldn't join that day.

"That was the biggest payoff I had. We had made a trip around the world. We made the Panama Canal, the Suez and the whole goddamn bit. I had 11 $100 bills in my pocket. We were prepared to pay 50 bucks to join the Communist Party. We were all convinced. Everybody had thrown their rosaries into the sea — one in the Indian Ocean, one in the Red Sea, we had our seven. They refused to take us in and I was so disgusted.

"We ended up in a tavern next to the Viger and started to drink. Some stevedores came in and one beat up one of our guys in the washroom. I took him on and I'm not a fighter, but he hit his head on the floor. I knew they were calling the police because they were worried about the guy. He was unconscious. So I said, 'Boys let's go.' We got outside. 'My fuckin' jacket and my payoff!' I had left it on the chair. So we walked back in. The jacket was still there. Bang! We all took off with my jacket and my payoff."[4]

When Fortin and Wingfield had stopped laughing enough to talk, Wingfield took up the narrative. "In 1946, I ran into a guy called Jake Shaw. Jake and I used to knock around together. He was the ship's delegate and was on deck. I was in the black gang. Jake Shaw wanted me to be the black gang's delegate. Jake Shaw, when it came to getting things done on the ship was the vanguard. Here was a guy who would argue with the old man. He would reason things out, any problems on the ship.

"I remember Jake telling us how we could do away with the bosses. He told us it would be the workers who would run things. It would be working people who would take over and we would have a workers' society. That wouldn't mean you would do away with intellectuals, but seamen, for example, would have their say. We would be the ones to say how to run the ships. We would be the ones to say what kind of conditions there should be on ships. After all, we were the ones who were sailing them. We should know better what was required.

"That impressed me," Wingfield continued, "but what impressed me more, what proved to me that societies don't have to be what they are, is when I went into ports like Takoradi. I saw Black people working at the time for a shilling a day. Takoradi was in the Gold Coast, which is Ghana today. The Black people had sacks for clothes when they came to work on the ships. There were three holes cut in the sack for their head and arms. They were actually gunny sacks. They were fed what you wouldn't feed your dogs. It was a huge basket of rice and a sort of fish mix. They started at seven in the morning and then stopped for a one-hour break around 12 noon. They were allowed two handfuls of this mixture, and it was handfuls, which they would put on bark 'plates' or a large leaf.

"I saw these people and how they were working. It was so obvious to see who the exploiter was. The checker on board the ship was watching the people of the Gold Coast to see they put in a full 12 hours for that big shilling. He was usually a Britisher. This gets back to the English officers, in my eyes anyway, the English officers on the ship. You go into a country like South Africa and the Black people are only a fraction of an inch above the slave level. Here they are, working 12 hours a day, and who was in charge of them, dressed in a white suit? A white guy.

"When we get up town, after we finally got shore leave, what do I see? Tin and grass shacks and up on the hill there are these great big beautiful homes. All painted white, as well. There were white people in them, of course.

"To me that was an education in itself. These people were workers. I was working, they were working. Who was the enemy? The enemy was right there before my eyes. There were the British officers, the lackeys of the bourgeoisie. And here I see it even more pronounced. These bastards are up on the hill looking down on the people who are the majority in the country. And they are treated like dogs or less. As I went around the African coast, I saw how people were treated there. While a few were reaping the benefit of the riches of the countries, the majority of the people were treated like dogs. There would be signs up — this is for whites, this is for non-whites. Nobody had to tell you they were being exploited. We could see that for ourselves and we knew we were being exploited too."[5]

THE EDUCATIONAL AND DEMOCRATIC FUNCTIONS of the committees, coupled with the experience of seeing different societies and different ways of life, were the key factors in developing a truly working class world view among the seamen. Shop committees ashore can do very valuable work and their importance should not be underestimated, but the shop committees do not deal with the problems of life which constantly occupied the committees at sea. Nor do shore-bound workers have the advantage of first-hand experience of how others live. Travel alone can produce the most backward impressions if educated understanding does not put the experience into perspective. Both factors were necessary ingredients in the development of class consciousness among the seamen.

Consciousness means a style of thought which sees causes as well as effects. It is the understanding that there are certain forces at work which shape and change societies. It is the understanding of one's place in the social formation. Consciousness is developed from a critical desire to understand the experience of life. Its development is a process which absorbs trade union and political activity.

Danielle Cuisinier Dionne, editor of the *Searchlight's* French edition was deeply involved in the union's shore-side educationals and schools shortly after the war, saw the seamen's consciousness evolve from the combination of their own experience and the political lessons they learned from each other. "I maybe in a way idealized the CSU," she says today, "but the impression I got was that many of these committees were led at one time or another by people who had ideas about developing people and learning the basics about how society runs. Those committees were very strong in themselves and those guys had self-confidence. It's a natural process if you have one person there with political education who can transmit it.

"I think that's why the CSU was accused of being a 'communist-led' organization. But I don't think there were that many members of the Communist Party. Having been a member, I don't think we were that great in numbers. It wasn't merely the fact that there were communists among the leaders, which was pretty well generally admitted. What was important was that there were young people who had an understanding of class society and an understanding of what racism was all about.

"These guys were going into colonial countries where they would experience it first hand. They would see the contrast. In terms of education, I think the location and the environment were very much conducive to bringing up consciousness. Those guys had a much better chance of becoming conscious because they were together all the time and they were sharing that life experience."[6]

At war's end the seamen, whether salt or fresh water, were members of one Canadian union. While the deepsea fleet was ferrying goods across the oceans, developments ashore had transformed the CSU from an affiliate of the Seafarers International Union, with jurisdiction over eastern Canada alone, into a national union with no 'international' connection. The CSU was no longer limited to the Lakes and the East Coast, but stretched to the Pacific shores of British Columbia — a single union for Canadian seamen from coast to coast.

CHAPTER TEN

The Pacific

THE CSU had always thought of itself as a national, Canadian union. The drive to defend conditions on the Lakes and to organize the unorganized led to the expansion on the East Coast, where the union had organized the Lady Boats and set up the Canadian Fishermen and Fishhandlers Union as an affiliate. The CSU had kept an eye on developments on the West Coast and west coast seamen always were interested in the CSU. Given the similarities between the CSU and its west coast counterparts, merger should have been easy and natural, but employer attacks that decimated the west coast unions, combined with incredible barriers erected by the AFL and its affiliated maritime organizations, delayed the creation of a national union for Canadian seamen by many years. It took the pressures of the war to forge unity.

In 1935, west coast seamen organized a rank and file union called the Seafarers Industrial Union, an affiliate of a council of waterfront workers called the Longshore and Water Transport Workers of Canada.[1] With a constitution that was a model of democracy and rank and file unionism,[2] the seamen built a strong organization based on shipboard committees that fought against all forms of racism and discrimination. They won some remarkable contracts, including one agreement that nailed down the three-watch, eight-hour day.[3] In an era characterized by racist attacks by some unions on Japanese and Chinese workers, the Seafarers Industrial Union established an independent local run by and for its Japanese members.[4]

The Longshore and Water Transport Workers of Canada (LWTW) had the potential to become a significant force in British Columbia. Like the Seafarers Industrial Union, it was extremely democratic and had risen from the ashes of earlier militant waterfront unions that had been smashed during a bitter strike in 1923. The maritime unions had been rebuilt from the ground up in an arduous battle against company associations, strike-breaking and blacklisting of union organizers. By 1935, B.C.'s waterfront workers were again united in a single organization determined to consolidate union wages and working conditions.

Once more the bosses fought back. When longshoremen demanded coastwide union hiring in 1935, the Shipping Federation locked them out and implemented a carefully-planned strategy to run the province's ports with scab labor. When 1,000 waterfront workers marched on Vancouver's Ballantyne Pier on June 18, they were tear-gassed and then assaulted by mounted police massed on the docks. Twenty-eight were injured in the Battle of Ballantyne Pier, which saw club-swinging police pursue the workers down back lanes and up to the front steps of neighborhood houses.[5]

The LWTW, including the Seafarers Union, which had struck in sympathy with the longshoremen, found itself the target of an unceasing campaign of repression by the courts and the police under the direction of Vancouver Mayor Gerry McGeer, who backed the Shipping Federation to the hilt. "I have taken the position that this is not a labor issue but a straight revolutionary attempt to wreck the business of the city," McGeer said when asked why he had unleashed the armed police on the demonstrators. The labor unrest, he declared, was an attempt at "communist revolution."[6] On December 9, 1935, the longshoremen acknowledged they were beaten and declared the strike over.

The strike was a shattering defeat for the marine workers, whose unions were destroyed. With work available only through the company-run associations, more than 500 seamen found themselves blacklisted and forced to leave the province to find work. For many, like Tommy Burnett, the only way back to work was through what the workers called the "fink halls", the hiring halls of the company unions.[7] The Shipping Federation set up an organization almost identical to McMaster's outfit on the Great Lakes. Called the Canadian Amalgamated Association of Seamen, it was run by a west coast version of McMaster named C.D. O'Donovan, who had supplied scabs to the Shipping Federation throughout the strike. To the seamen, it was simply "O'Donovan's union."[8]

It took two years for the seamen to find the strength to begin rebuilding. In a series of secret meetings, they decided to turn south for support. A delegation approached the Washington District Council of the Marine Federation of the Pacific, which decided to send a single industrial union to do the job rather than a number of craft organizations. The federation put the seamen in touch with the Inland Boatmen's Union of the Pacific. An industrial union, the IBU was installed at the old headquarters of the Seafarers Industrial Union between the Europe Hotel and the Anchor on Vancouver's Powell Street.[9] The Canadian seamen had to fund the organization themselves. The initial cash came from Jimmy Thompson who had a fine stamp collection he sold for $400, a great deal of money at a time when union organizers worked for $10 a week. The IBU, a member of the Congress of Industrial Organizations, was one of seven unions, including the Sailors Union of the Pacific (SUP), which formed the Marine Federation. The SUP, however, was affiliated to the American Federation of Labor. American inter-union rivalries soon complicated the situation in B.C.

Within weeks of the IBU's establishment in Vancouver, SUP president Harry Lundeberg sent two organizers of his own to the city even though his organization had been a party to the decision of the Marine Federation. Despite this apparent manifestation of hostility between the CIO's IBU and the AFL's SUP,[10] the Lundeberg organizers found a warm welcome on Powell Street, where the IBU invited them to share the office. Part of the IBU's confidence stemmed from its absorption of the membership of the Seafarers Industrial Union.

Jimmy O'Donnell, a compact Scot whose career on the Vancouver waterfront was to stretch into the 1980s, had a clear memory of the 47 Powell Street offices, which had an SUP crest on one window and an IBU insignia on the other.

Organizers for both outfits worked from the same room, he recalls. "They were all pals with each other. It was just a question of craft union versus industrial union. The men that had to go into the SUP at that time were sailors, but the firemen, cooks and stewards could all go into the IBU. We could have gone with the IBU, too, if Lundeberg hadn't put this charter up for sailors only, which we didn't want, but had to take."[11]

Within four months, the two unions parted company, with the IBU moving east to 164 East Hastings and the SUP a few blocks south to 262 Columbia. The division was symptomatic of the split Lundeberg's action had provoked in seamen's ranks. Two American-based unions now sought their support, one attempting to organize all seamen into one body while the other — Lundeberg's SUP — was interested only in the "sailors" of the deck department.

But the IBU, based in San Francisco, offered the Canadian seamen a decisive advantage while they were rebuilding — the ability to tie up Canadian ships when they entered American waters. From 1936 to 1938, this was virtually the seamen's only weapon to put pressure on the shipowners. The seamen active during that period agree that the IBU's international connection was of great assistance to the Canadians. "It never interfered with anything up here," says Art Ostrum, an IBU veteran who later found his way into the ranks of the CSU. "It may have had the same name, but that was as far as it went, we didn't have any ties with it. It was a good union."[12]

"They helped a lot," adds Norman Coe, who was secretary of the IBU's Victoria local. "They sent lots of funds up here to help organize and any help we wanted, they gave to us."[13]

The Canadians refused to let the organizational division split the rank and file. An example was the crew of the *Border King*. "Everyone was organized on that boat," remembers Jim O'Donnell. "The sailors were all SUP, while the cooks and firemen were IBU. They used to hold joint meetings aboard her. They would send a joint resolution from every meeting to both unions to have a meeting to get together. It was always like that ... but it never came to anything."[14]

The Shipping Federation, aware that seamen were organizing another union to take the place of the old Seafarers Industrial Union, took action. By phoning Trinity 5648, the shipowners could connect with the Industrial Association of B.C., whose offices were in the same Marine Building tower that housed the federation. Billing itself as a "clearing house of industrial information and data," the association produced anti-union propaganda and supplied employers like the federation with spies.

Such a spy infiltrated the IBU, filing voluminous reports that went through the office of the Industrial Association and into the war room of the Shipping Federation. His presence remained undetected for some 40 years until 200 pages of his reports were uncovered in the course of researching this book. His identity remains unknown, despite the efforts of IBU veterans like Tommy Burnett to find the name of the spy they have christened "the fink."

The fink's reports were filed almost every two days between February 1938 and March 1939. After being typed in the association offices, they were turned over to the Shipping Federation, which carefully stamped them with the date received. Close to his fellow workers and a stickler for accuracy, the spy gave the federation a clear picture of the unity of the seamen and their desire for a single Canadian union.

One day in December 1938, the fink joined Jim O'Donnell of the SUP and Jimmy Maskell, secretary of the IBU, in a meeting with employees of the Union Steamship Co.

"They talked to some of the old-time employees of the Union Steamship Co. who were once members of the Seafarers Industrial Union with a view to getting their attitude toward organization," he reported. "These men told them that they did not know which union to join because of the competition between the two, and each representing that the other was useless. Under the circumstances, they had decided to join none for the present and expressed the preference for an all-Canadian union."[15] As Tommy Burnett later put it, the seamen wanted their Canadian union to be rank and file, not rank and filthy.

Once again, however, events south of the border influenced the development of the seamen's organizations. The International Seamen's Union to which the CSU had affiliated three years before was in a state of collapse. Its locals represented seamen shipping primarily from

American Atlantic and Gulf of Mexico ports. Its Pacific affiliate was Lundeberg's Sailors Union of the Pacific. On both coasts, American seamen were deserting the ISU in droves to join the National Maritime Union or, on the Pacific, the Inland Boatmen's Union. Both were affiliates of the surging new movement for industrial unions led by the Congress of Industrial Organizations. Desperate to stop the hemorrhage, the American Federation of Labor intervened directly. AFL president William Green decided in 1938 to move in and take charge. He appointed Joe "King Joe" Ryan, president of the International Longshoremen's Association to do the job.

Ryan moved quickly. Notorious for his own connections with waterfront rackets, Ryan was a natural choice to sniff out corruption. He declared the ISU leadership morally unfit to hold office and called on the union to clean house. When the ISU failed to respond, Ryan lifted the union's AFL charter. The federation created a new union — the Seafarers International Union — and appointed Lundeberg president. It was a fateful decision for the CSU and for Canadian seamen, who are haunted by the SIU to this day.[16]

Lundeberg moved to update the image of his B.C. affiliate. The Canadian section of the SUP was changed to the B.C. Seamen's Union. The CSU and the BCSU now were direct affiliates of the same AFL international union. The IBU had gone on record time and again favoring the creation of a single, dominion-wide union. The CSU, realizing the opportunity was at hand, sent Dewar Ferguson to the West Coast to discuss merger with the two B.C. unions.

Ferguson arrived early in 1939 and convened an informal meeting at the Alcazar Hotel. "Ferguson outlined his ideas on how the two B.C. unions could become united without either losing face," remembers O'Donnell, who attended as a rank and file delegate of the BCSU. Also present were the IBU's Jimmy Thompson and Hugh (Spud) Murphy of the BCSU. "He suggested that the two unions give up their American charters, that the Canadian Seamen's Union extend its charter from the East Coast and the Great Lakes to the West Coast, and that the members of the two B.C. unions join the CSU, thereby making this union a Canada-wide organization.

"He also explained that if this idea was adopted in B.C., the IBU would lose its identity completely; on the other hand, the B.C. Seamen's Union would retain part of their identity because of the fact that the CSU was, at that time, affiliated with the Seafarers International Union of America.

"Thompson said he thought it was a wonderful idea and that he would take it back to his membership with his recommendation. Murphy also said he thought it was a wonderful idea, but he didn't mention membership. He said he would have to confer with his superiors across the line. Accordingly, Murphy wired Harry Lundeberg, president of the SIU, and the answer came back immediately: 'Retain charter at all costs.'

"This answer proved something to me that I had long ago suspected," says O'Donnell. "The Seafarers International Union of America was more interested in dues than they were in the rank and file seamen."[17]

The bid for unity had been foiled by actions outside Canada. The CSU decided to bide its time and to deal with other pressing matters. With contracts signed with the Lake Carrier Association that would not expire until 1940, the CSU had time to consolidate and expand. The charter allowed for a venture into the Atlantic provinces.[18] There, at least, there could be no fear of interference from south of the border. Creation of a single Canadian seamen's union would have to wait.

It took the pressures of war to bring merger. By 1944, the IBU, now renamed the Deepsea and Inland Boatmen's Union, found itself stymied in its efforts to sign agreements for the Park ships sailing from west coast ports. Yet the CSU had won agreements covering all Park Steamship Line vessels in the east. Realizing it was essential to establish uniform conditions, the DIBU wrote to the CSU requesting that a representative be sent to the West Coast to attempt an amalgamation of the two unions.[19]

The CSU sent its president, Pat Sullivan, to investigate conditions in B.C. He concluded that merger could work. Both unions were industrial in structure and both had sought a single union since their independent beginnings. Both were rank and file oriented, with heavy emphasis on educating the membership, although the DIBU was not as advanced in this regard as the CSU. The role of ship's committees and on-board educationals was paramount in both organizations.[20] The DIBU, like the CSU, was an affiliate of an American union, but both organizations believed in the Canadian membership's right to control their own union. The Communist Party was well-represented among the rank and file as well as in the leadership of the two unions and the overall political outlook of the two was similar. It also seemed clear that the DIBU and not the BCSU was the choice of the coastal and deepsea seamen sailing from west coast ports.

The DIBU wished to become a district of the Canadian Seamen's Union with complete autonomy in the Pacific coast region. During Sullivan's visit, it was agreed, pending ratification of the rank and file, that:

— the DIBU would become the west coast district of the CSU with complete autonomy;

— *two west coast representatives would be seated on the National Executive of the CSU;*

— *after ratification of the amalgamation, the west coast branch would apply to be seated in the Trades and Labor Council; and*

— *an east coast organizer would be put on loan to the DIBU to assist in organizing.*

In the meantime, CSU members sailing from west coast ports were to take any and all grievances to the DIBU.[21] The foundation was being laid for a single union of Canadian seamen, but the last link in the chain — the SIU's B.C. Seamen's Union — refused to join. The reasons lay south of the border.

Ferguson and Sullivan had attended the second annual convention of the SIU held earlier that year in New Orleans.[22] Their goal was simple: extension of the CSU's jurisdiction to the Canadian West Coast, effectively uniting Canadian seamen in a single union under the banner of the SIU. The SIU convention, however, was not interested in the unity of Canadian seamen. Content with its efforts to establish the BCSU as a dual union to the DIBU, the international was more concerned with its relationship to the CSU, which was behind in its dues.

The belated discovery that the CSU was in arrears in its per capita payments to the SIU clearly was politically motivated. It had been understood when the CSU affiliated to the International Seamen's Union that its per capita payments would be made directly to the Trades and Labor Congress of Canada. By this device, the CSU secured automatic affiliation to the TLC without the payment of dues to an international, which would have been unacceptable to CSU members. The maneuver suited the leaders of the moribund ISU, who used the existence of the new affiliate to argue they were a vital and growing union. When the AFL finally disbanded the ISU in 1938 to create the new Seafarers International Union, the CSU had quickly been granted jurisdiction for all of Canada east of the Rockies under an SIU charter. Dues were not an issue for six full years, until the CSU sought to unite Canadian seamen in a single organization.

Sullivan and Ferguson stated the CSU's case. It had made all its payments to the Trades and Labor Congress of Canada. Any criticisms of the CSU should be put in writing, the two officers said, so the union's executive committee could respond. Ferguson then persuaded Sullivan that they had fulfilled their responsibilities and they returned to Toronto.[23]

The CSU executive did not have to wait long for the SIU reply. Because of the non-payment of dues, the SIU rejected the CSU request for extended jurisdiction and declared that the Canadian union was no longer a member in good standing. To return to the fold, the SIU convention laid down four conditions.[24] They were:

— that the CSU "establish proper relations" with the affiliated unions in the international and with the international itself;

— that the CSU live up to its financial and moral obligations to the international;

— that the CSU adhere to and follow the policy of the SIU branding the National Maritime Union of the CIO "a dual and hostile organization to the SIU and the American Federation of Labor and the CSU follow a policy of non-cooperation with the NMU/CIO;"

— that the CSU bring itself into line with SIU policy that "the Communist Party on the North American continent is a dual and hostile political set-up, detrimental to the trade union movement as a whole;" and

— that the CSU give its answer and pay back dues by May 1, 1944 if the conditions were acceptable.[25]

The SIU conditions reflected its increasingly bitter conflict with the NMU as well as the rising tide of anti-communism that was to engulf the American labor movement and then Canadian trade unions with the conclusion of the war.

The SIU convention adjourned April 1, giving the Canadians only a month to respond, but the CSU executive was in no hurry. The national executive did not meet until May 12. After conferring for three days, the executive emerged with a unanimous position that condemned the SIU ultimatum as "interference with the autonomous rights of the Canadian seamen to determine their own Canadian policies in accordance with the national needs of our country."[26]

The desire of the Canadian seamen was to have one Canadian union, the executive said. The CSU was to be that union and it was not to be a puppet of the international. But the national executive stated the CSU's willingness to work with the SIU as an affiliate as long as its Canadian autonomy was assured.

The CSU pointed out that it had always maintained an AFL affiliation and had never considered affiliating with the CIO's National Maritime Union, so hated by the SIU for its progressive policies and rank and file orientation. The NMU had never approached the CSU to urge affiliation or to attack the SIU. Nor had the NMU ever entered Canada or wronged the Canadian trade union movement. The problems between the NMU and the SIU, concluded the executive, were the internal problems of the American trade union movement.[27]

As far as communists were concerned, the CSU had many among its leadership and rank and file but could state that it did not have an affiliation with the Communist Party or any other party and that its policies did not necessarily agree with those of the Communist Party. "The CSU determines its policies on the basis of the needs of the Canadian seamen and fishermen and within the framework of the Canadian scene," the executive wrote. "Furthermore, the CSU follows policies *which are completely in harmony with the policies of the Trades and Labor Congress of Canada.*"[28] The fact that the CSU had no problem with the Canadian trade union movement — its president was secretary of the Trades and Labor Congress — indicated that the opposition to the CSU was outside of the Canadian House of Labor. The external opposition was the shipowners, the company unions and the American Federation of Labor's SIU.

The CSU expressed its willingness to adhere to the policies of the SIU provided both sides had the same understanding of the word "policy." "Canada is an independent nation with its own national problems, its own political parties, its own international relationships and its own economic issues," the union statement said. "The workers of Canada, seamen and others, must, therefore, of necessity, have the right to determine their own policies in accordance with the conditions of their respective industries, the existing political relationships and the problems of the country as a whole.

"If by 'following the policies of the SIU' is meant the general policy of organizing and uniting the seamen and fishermen of North America into one union for the improvement of their economic and social conditions and for the ultimate attainment of a united trade union movement on the continent, then, of course, the CSU always was, is at present, and always will be ready to follow such policies." To make their position on Canadian autonomy and relations with the international perfectly clear, the union leaders added that "the inner policies of the Canadian affiliates are a matter for the Canadian membership. Without this understanding, there could be no international trade union movement as now exists between the USA and Canada."[29]

The CSU agreed to bring its financing into line with the international and pleaded its case for jurisdiction over all of Canada as an affiliate of the SIU. But there was one question on which the union was inflexible: "The maintenance of the autonomous right of the Canadian Seamen's Union to determine its policies in accordance with the Canadian conditions and needs, can, of course, not be questioned."[30]

Lundeberg, president of the SIU, quickly notified every labor council in Canada that the CSU charter had been lifted for non-compliance with the demands of the international. The CSU was not interested in sailing the SIU's course, he complained, adding that he had received "numerous pamphlets and publications from Charles Bremner, representative of the SIU of NA, which he picked up during a visit to the CSU's hall, all of which are communist publications and are stamped in red ink, 'Property of the Canadian Seamen's Union.'

"Our representative further reports that the reading room of the CSU was well-stocked with the official organ of the National Maritime Union, CIO, known as the *Pilot*, (and) while the official organ of the east and west coast seamen (SIU) was in the reading room, it was well pigeon-holed."[31] Apparently the CSU slogan that "Freedom of discussion is a CSU tradition," carried in every union membership book, was too much for Lundeberg. The SIU president found strong support from the AFL. AFL president William Green quickly granted the SIU jurisdiction over fishermen and seamen in all waters of North America. Lundeberg demanded that the TLC, whose secretary was the CSU president, refrain from seating the seamen's delegates at TLC conventions.

Although the break between the CSU and SIU was to be an important factor in the years to come, at the time most west coast seamen lost little sleep over the loss of the SIU connection. Art Ostrum recalls his own attitude in a discussion with the SIU's Spud Murphy in Vancouver: "Spud said, 'The SIU was the best union for seamen on the North American continent.' I said, the SIU, as far as I was concerned, was just a bunch of racketeers. It was controlled by the United States. I said, 'I don't see why we as Canadians should belong to your union when we could have our own.' "[32]

What seemed clear to Ostrum was lost on the leaders of the BCSU, who obeyed the directives of Lundeberg and rejected an offer to join the CSU in the creation of a single national Canadian organization. But the amalgamation of the DIBU and the CSU went ahead, creating the first seamen's union in Canada from coast to coast.

On August 28, 1944, Dewar Ferguson, acting president of the CSU, wrote to Digger Smith, secretary of the DIBU in Vancouver. "On the recommendation of President Sullivan in a report to a special meeting of the National Executive committee of the Canadian Seamen's Union, the executive unanimously decided to recognize the Deepsea and Inland Boatmen's Union of the Pacific as the West Coast District of the Canadian Seamen's Union." On September 5, the DIBU held a meeting to endorse the merger officially.[33]

For the west coast seamen, the long-awaited unity was welcome. "At that time the DIBU was a very small, powerless union," remembers seaman Joe McNeil. "At that time, the shipbuilding industry was booming, with all the shipyards here building ships like mad. It was the same on the East Coast. We could see that the Canadian merchant fleet was going to be something big.

"If we wanted to be effective, we had to be organized on both coasts. I think everyone was in agreement with that. We were quite happy when the CSU took us in."[34]

The September 5 merger cleared the deck for negotiation of the first national agreement for Canadian seamen. In October, the CSU was certified as bargaining agent on all Park tankers. It needed only to win certification for the west coast dry cargo vessels to be able to start the process of negotiating the national agreement.[35]

The federal labor department vote to determine which B.C. union would represent unlicensed personnel on west coast Park ships concluded December 31, 1944. The seamen on 52 of a possible 56 Park ships had the opportunity to choose between the CSU — still called the Deepsea and Inland Boatmen's Union on the ballot — and the SIU's BCSU. To be certified, one of the unions had to obtain 51 percent of the ballots of all seamen eligible to vote. When the ballots were counted the CSU had tallied 813 votes to the BCSU's 415, more than 55 percent of the eligible voters and almost double the vote of the SIU affiliate.[36] The SIU was reduced to a handful of ships.

Digger Smith, Dewar Ferguson, H.C. Meade and Conrad Sauras made up the negotiating committee.[37] One stage of the struggle was over. Another was about to begin.

CHAPTER ELEVEN

Eight Hours

CAVALCADE

Back in the days before the war
When Old Man Depression held the floor,
The sailor's life was forlorn.
The steamship trusts had the upper hand,
All talk of unions was quickly banned
'Til the CSU was born.

Slowly but surely it grew in size
And then to the owners' great surprise
There came a reckoning day.
Strong enough to stand up for right,
Defiant of all shipping might,
The Union was under way.

It boosted the scale of all the men
From the black hold gang to the forward end,
Conditions were more humane.
One by one, the Lake ships' crews
Joined the gang and paid their dues.
The union eased the strain.

There was still another wrong to fix,
They were standing watches "six and six,"
Something had to be done.
The new agreements were there to sign
But late in the year of '39,
This bloody war had begun.

Overnight the seamen became
The most needed of all in this wartime game,
Without them, the war was lost.
The CSU had a powerful edge
And yet they voted a "No Strike" pledge
Never counting the cost.

The war is over, the Victory won
The Merchant Seamen's war task is done
What does the future hold?
Must they bow down to those in power

And work for 30 cents an hour
While war-built ships are sold?

Should they "stand watch" twelve hours a day?
And take a drastic cut in pay?
All unions answer "No."
Canada needs a merchant fleet,
To carry our grains and ore and meat
Wherever they should go.

The seamen all should now unite,
No other way will win this fight
For watches four hours long.
Remember, Brothers, the CSU —
Together we are strong.

By Snellie
Searchlight, December 1, 1945

WITH THE END of the war the CSU faced new challenges and new struggles. Within weeks of Japan's surrender, C.D. Howe, federal Minister of Munitions and Supply, told the House of Commons the government was determined to sell the nation's maritime fleet. "As many ships will be sold to private Canadian operators as possible," he said November 19, 1945, "and the probabilities are that if we still have a surplus of ships, it may be necessary to tie them up."[1]

Park ships, built in 1944 at a cost of $1.3 to $1.4 million, would "be offered at about $600,000," Howe said, a windfall for shipowners who already had been paid $5 million in management fees and commissions between April 1, 1942 and August 31, 1945.[2] On November 20, Howe admitted that five tankers had already been sold.

The CSU, by contrast, was campaigning for a significant increase in Canada's merchant marine.[3] The reconstruction of Europe and need for increased employment for returning soldiers amply justified maintaining and expanding the fleet, the union argued. Although the government's first sales had been to Canadian shipping lines, the CSU was determined not to see Canada return to colonial dependency on other nations to ship our exports.

There was another issue facing the union as well. During the war, the Lake seamen had agreed to drop their demand for an eight-hour day until the conflict was over. The seamen had upheld this commitment — and their no-strike pledge — even though their deepsea brothers worked the eight-hour day throughout the hostilities. Now it was the Lakers' turn. The union set its sights on the two main planks of the post-war program hammered out by delegates to the 1944 convention: maintenance of the fleet and implementation of the eight-hour day within "six months after the cessation of hostilities."[4]

THE UNION that took up the struggle for the eight-hour day was a far different organization from the one that had won its first agreements from the shipowners just nine years before. From the Lakes, the CSU had spread to the East Coast, then to British Columbia and ultimately became the only union in Canada's ocean-going merchant fleet. The structure of the union shifted to meet the new demands and the changes were reflected in the national executive that directed the CSU as the storms of the war subsided.

Pat Sullivan, although still elected president of the CSU, was occupied full-time with his post of secretary-treasurer of the Trades and Labor Congress, based in Ottawa. His presence there gave the CSU an important influence in the labor movement and Sullivan could be counted on to assist the seamen when needed. Yet Sullivan, despite his presence at national negotiations and his regular visits to the national office, lost contact with the rank and file and the daily operation of the union.

His place was filled first by Dewar Ferguson and then by Harry Davis, each elected acting president during Sullivan's time in Ottawa. Ferguson had headed the union while Sullivan was interned and carried on after his election to the TLC. In 1944, Ferguson won election as a Toronto alderman, a labor candidate supported by a broad committee. He was known as a member of the Labor-Progressive Party, the party formed by communists in 1943 as they emerged from the illegality imposed on them by the banning of the Communist Party in 1940. In 1946, Ferguson declined nomination to the union's top job and was elected second vice-president, a position that gave him more time for civic work.

Davis had first shipped out in 1939 and he joined the CSU in 1940. He had both deepsea and fresh water experience. Out of work and on the road during the Depression, he had his earliest taste of unionism in the unemployed movement in B.C. in 1936. He had taken an active role in the 1940 Lake strike and Ernie Donne had later approached him to work as an assistant business agent. He worked for the union off and on between 1940 and 1945. He loved the sea, but knew the union needed him ashore and so he divided his time between the two. In 1943, when the manning pools were in full swing, Davis got the job of signing up the deepsea crews. The campaign was very successful, and when Davis and Sullivan went to Ottawa to request a contract with the Park Steamship Company, they obtained it with virtually no difficulty. From there, Davis was sent to Halifax to consolidate the deepsea drive and then to the West Coast to work on the Deepsea and Inland Boatmen's Union merger which was then in progress.

Soft-spoken and unobtrusive, Davis took over as CSU president at the right time. He fully supported Sullivan's role in the TLC, believing "it gave a lot of influence to the seamen . . . and it was great that the TLC had progressive officers during that period," but as the CSU's top officer Davis stayed close to the rank and file, working to harness the wellspring of talent he knew lay there.

Davis replaced Ferguson as acting president in 1946. He was backed by a strong executive. Cyril Lenton, a veteran of the national executive and a Lake seaman with deepsea experience, became national treasurer and Gerry McManus took the post of national secretary.

McManus, only the second non-seaman to hold elected office in the CSU, was an unusual case. (The first elected non-seaman was the union's first president, J.D. Munro.) A communist with a reputation as a Marxist intellectual, McManus had met Sullivan in Petawawa and Hull. He joined the union in 1945, worked as a patrolman, and was used by the publicity and education department as a field representative.[5] Rarely seen on the picket line or leafletting, McManus had technical skills he contributed to the national office. A large man with hornrimmed glasses, he was respected but not well-liked by the seamen.

Jimmy Thompson and Digger Smith had both been active building the Deepsea and Inland Boatmen's Union and had been instrumental in the merger with the CSU. They represented the West Coast on the executive. Captain Ben MacKenzie represented the Atlantic fishermen and Bert Meade the east coast seamen. For the Lakes and the St. Lawrence there were Gregory Saville, Aage Antonsen, Theodore Roy and Eddie Reid. And there was Conrad Sauras.

If ever there was a heroic figure in the Canadian Seamen's Union, it was Conrad Sauras. Medium height, pencil thin and loaded with nervous energy, Sauras was in love with life and absolutely dedicated to the struggles of the seamen. He came to exemplify the spirit of the union. In Conrad Sauras, the seamen had their spark.

Born in Villabragima, Spain, he shipped out at the age of 14 to avoid a life in the military or the priesthood. It is said he joined his first seamen's union in Cuba. While still a teenager he travelled to Mexico, where he became an officer in Pancho Villa's army. When the Mexican revolution was crushed, he worked his way to Canada, eventually opening a restaurant across the street from the Nova Scotian Hotel in Halifax, where he hoped to pick up overflow traffic from the rail station. At first, the restaurant was very successful, even if the waitress did wear Mackenzie-Papineau Battalion badges in honor of the Canadians fighting fascism in Spain. For Sauras, politics always came first. The restaurant's profits were spent feeding the Depression's hungry kids, unemployed workers on the road, seamen on the beach and trade unionists and communists who could use a good meal. Eventually the restaurant went broke and Sauras went back to sea, this time on the Great Lakes.

It was on the Lakes in the 1940s that Sauras joined the CSU. He and his first wife Jessie were cooks and sailed together many times. Sauras quickly became ship's delegate and immediately went to work to better conditions. "They used to keep the English and French separated," Jessie Sauras remembers. "The forward crew were all English and aft, the coal shovellers and the coal passers were French Canadians. Conrad got them all together on the deck. He would get them all out and talk to them. We were only on there two or three months and we were like a family. That's the way he taught them to be. A French Canadian was no better than an Englishman and an Englishman was no better than a French Canadian. We are all one people.

"When we went on the boat the boys had to carry their own mattresses. They ate off rusty tin plates and drank out of tin mugs. Conrad got rid of all that. Conrad used to throw the old mattresses down the St. Lawrence River. If it was now, they'd get him for pollution."[6]

Sauras was known to everyone as an anarchist. He was always ready to act to change the conditions he opposed, but he knew tactics could vary. He was elected to the CSU executive in 1944 and in 1945 was a member of the national negotiating committee which reached a settlement with Park Steamships. He also was assistant business agent for the Port of Montreal.

When things were quiet around the waterfront, Sauras could always be found at the national office at 438 St. Francis Xavier Street. The office usually was humming with activity as seamen dropped in to pay dues, meet up with friends, check on jobs or pick up the latest news. There was a small shipping hall with tables where the seamen could read or play cards and wait for a call. The dispatcher had a little room with a wicket where the jobs were called. If there was a challenge to his interpretation of the shipping rules, a committee would be elected from the men in the hall and a decision would be made immediately.

A small office was available for the patrolmen to write their reports. Then there were the business offices and an outer office where the union's secretarial staff worked. It was there that Conrad Sauras met Dorothy Flaherty, who had a desk by the window overlooking the stock exchange. Her German shepherd named Pancho Villa sat in the window and watched the street below. Dorothy Flaherty became Dorothy Sauras.

Dorothy Sauras saw the fire that burned in Conrad which drove him to work at fever pitch for the seamen's cause. "He was a rebel all his life," she remembers. "This was his problem. When it came to following a decision, it was always very hard for him, it was a real struggle. Discipline was not always commendable to him. His experience in Mexico didn't serve him any because they, too, were relatively anarchistic. It was right up his alley."[7]

Sauras saw life in simple terms. Things were generally black or white. There were the good guys — seamen and workers — and in the other corner were the bosses and the government. On one occasion, he and Daniels, who was 20 years his junior, were arrested and jailed overnight for boarding a vessel without the captain's permission. "There are days in every person's life which are highlighted," Daniels recalls. "That night in jail with Conrad was one of the most beautiful days of my life. He was worried because I was a young kid that I would feel uncomfortable in jail. He figured he had to keep me entertained with stories. He talked about the early conditions of ships when he began to sail, when he was 13 or 14, about the Mexican revolution, about his activity when he was in Cuba and was put down for the murder squad and had to get out and his activities in Halifax when he was a restaurant owner. I would feel very sad if I had gone through life without having spent a night in jail with Conrad Sauras. The police did me such a favor that day."[8]

It was these characteristics of devotion to the union and tireless dedication to the struggle that endeared him to people. Sauras was always ready to go to it and never hid behind rhetorical excuses. He steeled himself against the temptation to take immediate action and used his flamboyant activism as an effective counterpoint to Davis' reasoned arguments. The combination of the two represented the logic and spirit of the CSU.

Rounding out the national leadership as the union entered 1946 was a new head of publicity and education. Percy Newman had been a seaman at one time, but had taken up a career of journalism ashore in 1924. Before he came to edit the *Searchlight*, he had edited national magazines and newsletters and had been the liaison officer for the National Film Board.[9]

IN THE FALL OF 1945, the CSU took its campaign for the preservation of the fleet, the eight-hour day on the Lakes and maintenance of deepsea wages to the Canadian public. The union considered that the main plank in its post-war program was the call for a permanent merchant marine for Canada.[10] At the same time, the CSU wanted to make sure the $44.50 war bonus paid to deepsea merchant seamen was not scrapped with the surrender of Germany and Japan. The war bonus gave the seamen the money they needed to make the base rate acceptable. To combat the rise in the cost of living, the CSU wanted the war bonus rolled into the wage package. Without it, an able-bodied seaman would receive only 27 cents an hour.[11]

The campaign began in earnest September 9, 1945, when a delegation of seamen headed by the CSU sound car invaded Ottawa. "Don't torpedo seamen's wages," the sound truck blared. More than 5,000 leaflets were passed out by picketing seamen led by Conrad Sauras and the seamen's delegation won the right to sit down with the National War Labor Relations Board to plead their case for rolling in the bonus. Meanwhile, seamen stepped up the campaign nation-wide. Fifteen thousand leaflets were distributed in Saint John, New Brunswick. Picketing seamen did the same in Vancouver, and in Halifax a petition was circulated in support of CSU demands for a 300-ship fleet and stable wages. Wives and children set up their own picket lines, telling the public "Merchant seamen are heroes but their wives and kids can't eat medals."[12]

The campaign generated widespread support for the CSU. The negotiating committee of Davis, Sauras and McManus was able to nail down an agreement November 22 covering all the Park ships that rolled the war bonus into the wage package, protecting deepsea crews from wage cuts.

Even more elaborate preparations laid the groundwork for the eight-hour day campaign. An organizational building fund had been set up to collect assessments and contributions for the publicity that would be required. Seamen were ready to strike on the eight-hour issue, but the union knew public support would be essential.

The support of other trade unionists, and in particular the union deepsea crews, could almost be taken for granted. Deepsea crews, with the eight-hour day well behind them, competed to see which could throw the most cash into the building fund. The blue water crews had benefited from the early struggle of the Lakers. Here was a chance to do something in return.

Although most Canadian workers had won the eight-hour day in 1945 and some enjoyed a 40-hour week, Lake seamen endured a 12-hour day based on a two-watch system similar to a two-shift system in a plant running 24 hours a day. At sea the day was divided into "six on and six off," which meant each worker had six hours on the job and six hours off in each 12-hour period. Inevitably, seamen worked much unpaid overtime and a seven day week. There was no paid time off, holidays or vacations. The seamen were working an 84-hour week on the Lakes and the CSU, by fighting for the eight-hour day, was aiming to reduce the working week to 56 hours spread over seven days.

In a system in which profit is derived from the unpaid labor of the workers on the job, a demand for a shorter work period is a direct assault on the bosses' ability to exploit his labor force. On the Lake ships, the eight-hour day not only would reduce the hours of work, it would require the hiring of additional personnel to convert the two-watch system to a three-watch system. Again, the scheduling is identical to that of a factory working three shifts in a 24-hour period. The CSU hoped to increase employment opportunities for Lake seamen returning from the armed forces and for deepsea sailors ready to return to pre-war Lake jobs. The seamen believed as well that the eight-hour day would mean healthier working conditions, better family life and improved safety. But the companies were inflexible. They were determined to maintain the profits they reaped from the two-watch system and refused to bear the extra labor costs of an eight-hour day.

With 12 months to run in the deepsea agreement the eight-hour day issue moved to the top of the agenda. As early as May 1944, the union had put a proposal before the companies to implement the eight-hour day at the end of the war. The companies argued that the post-war period could return Canada to the depths of the Depression. They could not, therefore, commit themselves to the eight-hour day.[13]

In April 1945, the companies again refused to consider shorter working hours. This time the operators told the union that, among other things, the work of the Lake seamen was not comparable to that of factory workers because the seamen's occupation was "healthful." The union stepped up its appeal for public support. The CSU sound car again toured the numerous ports and towns along the canals and Lakes. The Welland Canal area was saturated with 20,000 leaflets and 10,000 more were distributed around Georgian Bay. In addition, 5,000 post cards were distributed for mailing to Prime Minister William Lyon Mackenzie King.[14]

The 1946 convention, held in Montreal February 25 to March 1, warned the operators that the no strike pledge ended the day of Japan's surrender. The executive was instructed to take a strike vote if there wasn't an immediate change in the employers' stand.[15] As the delegates headed back to their home ports, Theodore Roy and Conrad Sauras took the sound car on a two-week tour of Quebec. Harry Davis hit the road as well. "I remember going up and down some of the inland ports driving an old Ford with a loudspeaker mounted on it," he recalls, "having outdoor meetings and speaking about the need to have an eight-hour day." The union appeal was well-received. "The issue was a simple one," Davis remembers, "that most people could understand. People assumed that everyone should have the eight-hour day, while we were still working 12. The fact that we had publicity was important, as was the fact that it was immediately following a war which seamen had played a very important role in helping to win."[16]

With talks stalemated, the union began to take a strike vote April 15 and approached the federal government to request legislation implementing the eight-hour day.[17] The government hesitated, claiming the British North America Act might not empower Ottawa to make such laws. Davis, who knew the matter could be resolved by order-in-council, wondered if "possibly the fact that there were two Liberal senators in the Great Lakes shipping business had something to do with the government's behavior."[18]

Then a breakthrough seemed at hand. Two companies, McColl Frontenac and Imperial Oil, agreed to the eight-hour day and other important concessions. The National War Labor Relations Board still was in session and the employers and the union applied for approval of their new contract. To the fury of the seamen, the board turned them down for fear the eight-hour day was not "reasonable," a decision the *Searchlight* condemned as proof of the King government's eagerness "to help reactionaries."[19] Sheepishly the board reconsidered, announcing on May 6 it approved the contract.[20] Anger turned to jubilation. For the first time in history, the 12-hour day had been smashed on Lake vessels. The three-watch system had been established with no loss in pay.[21]

But far from opening a breach in the employer front, the new contract seemed to stiffen employer resistance. The remaining companies introduced new proposals calling for continuation of the 12-hour day and reductions in pay of $7 to $14 a month. The CSU set a strike deadline of June 7.[22] The vote had been counted and the membership had approved job action 3,019 to 51 with 27 spoiled ballots.[23]

George Donovan, chief negotiator for the operators' Dominion Marine Association, took an increasingly tougher line. The three-watch system would not come to Canada, he said, even though American vessels on the same routes had had the eight-hour day for some time. He insisted that the companies would operate with non-union crews in the event of a strike. But as the deadline moved closer, he appeared to relent. The eight-hour day was no problem, he said, and the association would introduce it in 1947.

What looked like a breakthrough was rejected by the seamen as a smokescreen. They knew that in a year another stall could easily be arranged. Dewar Ferguson told Donovan the proposal was acceptable as a basis for negotiations but would not resolve the dispute.[24] Donovan's proposal had a couple of hidden pitfalls which union officials spotted immediately. The operators planned to add only two seamen to a crew when six were required to put the three-watch system into effect. Their plan was to work the seamen for an hour or two at a time, throughout a 24-hour period, until eight hours had been made up. It was an unworkable approach that marked a step back from the 12-hour day. In addition, a proposed reclassification of existing jobs would have meant a further decrease in wages.[25]

In Ottawa May 21 Sullivan announced that the strike deadline had been advanced to June 3, warning that the seamen had the right to tie up whenever and wherever they pleased.[26] The labor movement pledged its support on both sides of the 49th parallel. American dock workers, members of the International Longshoremen's Association, promised to honor picket lines. From the United States came a telegram from Frank Jones, Lake coordinator for the National Maritime Union. "Your forthcoming struggle to obtain the eight-hour day and a more equitable scale of pay has our firmest support," Jones said. "We recognize that your struggle is an organic part of our own in the spirit of inter-country fraternity with labor in general and maritime workers in particular. We hope you will feel free to call upon us for any and all support within our power to give."[27]

All across Canada, workers were engaged in an offensive to improve their lot. The horrors of war, wage controls and rising living costs had been borne with hardly a shudder. Now trade unionists were out to redress the balance. For 3,700 members of the International Woodworkers of America, May 15 was the deadline for job action to win significant improvements in wages and conditions. Ten thousand rubber workers were set to hit the bricks in Ontario on May 27. Thousands of workers were poised to strike the steel and coal industries.[28] But unlike the Lake seamen, all of these workers had won the eight-hour day. The Lake seamen were no longer prepared to work four hours longer than everyone else. They believed their time had come and they were determined to catch up.

CHAPTER TWELVE

The Battle of the Canals

THE LAKE OPERATORS represented some of the most hard-nosed employers in Canada. Scott Misener, president of Sarnia and Colonial Lines and an officer of the Dominion Marine Association, vowed that strike or no strike his vessels would "continue to operate if we can get fuel and cargo to carry."[1] Captain Norman Reoch's Canada Steamship Lines was equally anti-union, barring union officials from boarding vessels or talking to crews.

Gerry Tellier, a Montreal patrolman in this period, developed his own strategy for getting aboard the CSL ships. "I used to jump aboard them in the locks," he recalled. "If they were going down the St. Lawrence they would have to go through Number 1 Lock and vice versa. I think this ship was going up. I had my literature in my brief case and jumped aboard. I was talking to the guys and giving out literature. Just as the water rose and they opened the front gate to go down to the next lock, I bent down to pick up my brief case. I got a boot in the ass and had to jump or I'd have landed between the ship and the bank of the lock. It was an officer, could have been the Mate or the Chief Engineer."[2]

Not surprisingly, it was Reoch's violations of CSU contract conditions that provided the spark that ignited the Lake strike. On May 24, with negotiations stalemated and the threat of a shutdown hanging over the Montreal waterfront like a fog, CSU patrolman Marcel Gagné was making his usual rounds of the incoming ships. In keeping with the union agreement, he boarded the CSL's *City of Montreal*, a package freighter, just after she had tied up. As Gagné headed up the gangplank, he was blocked by Capt. Legault, who ordered him ashore. To avoid an incident, Gagné stepped back onto the dock and was followed by the crew, who wanted to find out what was up. The meeting took a few moments and the crew returned to the vessel, but Legault again blocked the way. The crew had been locked out.[3]

CSU efforts to win immediate reinstatement of the crew by the federal Department of Labor proved fruitless. Union officers advised all ports that CSL vessels were to be struck. Other lines were to operate without interruption for the time being.[4]

Reoch moved quickly, ushering a scab crew onto the *City of Montreal* and moving her out of port before the seamen could even mount a picket line. "We have won the opening round," Reoch crowed, "and we will win every round after this."⁵ But CSU members were fighting back. By noon the next day, several of the CSL's most important vessels were tied up. In Thorold, the cruise ship *Noronic* was struck in the Welland Canal, stranding 500 American tourists on their return trip from Prescott to Detroit. Almost simultaneously, the crew of the *City of Kingston* walked off their ship in Kingston and the *City of Edmonton* was idled in Toronto.

"We are going to arrest every man who walks off our ships," Reoch warned, and he made good his threat in Montreal, where seven seamen from the CSL's *Battleford* were charged with desertion under the Canada Shipping Act. "The men sign articles when they go aboard and must give the Master seven days notice," Reoch told reporters. "They are liable to arrest without warrant and liable to three months imprisonment." Scabs were on their way to the *Noronic*, he boasted, and the cruise ship would soon sail.⁶

But near Lock 7 in Thorold, where the *Noronic* rocked gently on her lines behind a CSU picket line, all was calm. Thirty crew members who had struck the ship were camped alongside the canal, enjoying food provided by local supporters, singing union songs and taking their turns on picket duty. At 10 o'clock the next morning, however, pandemonium erupted as watchful pickets spotted the *City of Edmonton* steaming toward the *Noronic*, manned by scabs intent on putting a new crew aboard the cruise ship by the back door.

With the *Noronic's* gangways closed, it looked like they would succeed until more than 20 strikers leaped onto the *Noronic's* mooring lines and climbed hand over hand to the deck as startled passengers looked on. Once on board, the seamen turned the *Noronic's* fire hoses onto the deck of the approaching *Edmonton*. The *Edmonton* had no choice but to veer away and continue down the canal. The seamen had defeated Reoch's first attempt to move the *Noronic*.⁷

Within hours, however, the CSL had called the police to its aid. Police swooped on the picket line and arrested the pickets on Canada Shipping Act charges of being absent without leave. After a night in prison, the CSU men were released on $75 bail each, raised by local CIO and AFL unions. The night in jail had not dampened their spirits but it had changed their garb. In protest of the police action, the seamen chalked "jail-bird" stripes on their clothes and proudly wore them on the picket line.⁸ With the seamen's lines reinforced by townspeople and local unionists, the CSL dared not attempt another boarding while the 500 passengers remained on board. The CSL arranged for coaches to pick up the passengers and take them overland to Detroit.

The scene at dockside May 27 as the passengers disembarked was more like a moment from a Broadway musical than a labor dispute. Hundreds of townspeople crowded the dock to witness the event. "The attitude of many of the passengers was a friendly one," reported the *Hamilton Spectator*, "so friendly, in fact, that some were noticed giving them money to 'help their cause.' " The striking seamen responded by singing "Should Auld Acquaintance Be Forgot" and "Pack Up Your Troubles." They were joined in the last number by the departing passengers in a finale that would have impressed Rogers and Hammerstein.[9]

With the strike against CSL heading for the end of its first week, the CSU weighed its options. Only one company — Quebec and Ontario Transportation — had come forward to sign an eight-hour day agreement since the strike began.[10] The others were rallying behind Misener and Reoch, using the time to prepare to break the strike. Once again, the deadline for a general strike was advanced, this time to May 27. Failure to achieve a contract by that date would see 5,000 seamen on strike from the St. Lawrence to Port Arthur on Lake Superior's western tip. The operators gave their answer the same day: an employment office was opened at the CSL's Victoria Square office in Montreal, right across from Joe Beef's Tavern on the Montreal waterfront. The word was out that anyone who would sign with the CSL would have a job waiting for them.[11]

CSU pickets moved in on the CSL office and within moments, 50 police had arrived to break up the line. "The cops were looking for opportunities to take us on," says Danny Daniels, who was picket captain that day. "We had a picket line outside the CSL office and they were bringing scabs. We were, of course, bringing more and more seamen to try to stop this kind of business. We were trying to get the taxicabs to stop. The cops were there with the patrol wagon. An officer came over and said, 'Mr. Daniels, do you mind, I would like to speak to you for a minute.' So, like a naive person, I stepped off the picket line. Three cops picked me up and threw me head first into the patrol wagon. When I arrived at the police station, I asked what I was charged with. They said, 'We'll figure it out.' I was charged with rioting."[12]

By May 30, ships were tied up in many of the smaller ports. In addition to the vessels tied up in Montreal, 16 were struck in Cornwall, 12 in the Welland Canal, 10 in Toronto and 19 at the Lakehead. Reoch, with the help of police and a busload of scabs, had succeeded in moving the *Noronic* out of Thorold that morning, but the seamen served notice they were not finished with the vessel by showering her with rocks from the canal's low bridges.[13] With the strike solid, the CSU once again attempted a negotiated settlement.

In a special meeting in Ottawa, CSU negotiators sat down with federal Labor Minister Humphrey Mitchell, Deputy Minister Arthur MacNamara and Senators G.P. Campbell and George Donovan, representatives of the Dominion Marine Association. On the CSU side of the table were Sullivan, McManus and TLC president Percy Bengough, who had already called on all congress affiliates to give the CSU their undivided support.[14]

The union proposed an immediate end to the strike provided the operators accepted three points — the eight-hour day, 50 cents an hour for overtime and dropping of all charges against the striking seamen. Senator Campbell glanced at the proposal and then gave the Dominion Marine Association (DMA) reply — the companies would not negotiate as long as the strike continued and they would continue to recruit scab crews.[15] Then Mitchell stepped in, urging the operators and the union to meet in an effort to arrange a truce based on a compromise of the union's position. But Misener and the CSL refused, saying they believed "no useful purpose can be served by meeting the present officials of the union."[16]

The CSU had given the nod to the truce, but when the union learned of the operators' statements May 31 they advised the minister that the companies' position amounted to a "declaration of war." The actions of CSL and the Misener companies placed them "in the category of outlaws," the union telegram said. "We are obliged to advise our members to continue their lawful pursuits and halt the lawlessness of these two companies. We shall be ready to meet with you and the other shipowners who are showing a desire to arrive at a settlement which will abolish the 84-hour week and institute a genuine eight-hour day, three-watch system and settlement of other problems. We urge your government to take immediate steps to take over Canada Steamship Lines and Misener's Colonial Steamship Lines to avoid bloodshed."[17]

REOCH'S PLANS to operate the *Noronic* non-union quickly ran aground. In Lock 8, at Humberstone, the cruise ship's progress was blocked by the CSL's *Goderich*, abandoned at anchor in mid-stream by the striking crew. The first and second mates decided to take no part in scabbing the ship, jumped over the side and swam to the picket lines.[18] Despite several hundred Ontario Provincial Police on the banks of the canal, the two ships could do no more than swing to the canal's gentle rhythm. Ontario Conservative Premier George Drew cabled acting Prime Minister J.L. Isley to demand action. Noting the shower of rocks that chased the *Noronic* out of Thorold, he warned he could need additional assistance, including the RCMP to "afford protection which will permit freighters to be moved from the locks and *Noronic* from the canal." If Mounties were unavailable, Drew said, "and it becomes neces-sary to use military force, believe it is of utmost importance that they be well-trained units of the permanent force and that we should not be compelled to rely upon the local militia." In an unconscious tribute to the public support for the seamen, the man the unionists called "Gorgeous George" sought the assistance of professional soliders "in the event of emergency."[19]

When the seamen accused the companies of "declaring war," they meant it figuratively. George Drew went for a literal interpretation and had soldiers standing by in case the shipowners needed them. While the premier readied the Canadian Army to counter the revolutionary threat of rocks being lobbed at a passengerless ship sitting in mid-canal, the Department of Transport dispatched a tug to Lock 8. The tug put a line on the *Goderich* and towed her clear of the lock. The strikers joked with the tug's crew while the maneuver was in progress.[20] The revolutionary threat that inspired Drew to order a full mobilization had been solved by a single tug without even a nosebleed being suffered by either side. With the *Goderich* clear of the lock, the *Noronic* steamed into Lake Erie.

There was a great deal of violence during the 1946 strike, but all of it resulted from direct confrontation between pickets on the one hand, and scabs and police on the other. Many picket lines were entirely peaceful, but those were the spots where no attempt was made to replace the striking seamen. When strikebreakers were used to operate the vessels, it was a different story.

On June 3, a convoy of 38 automobiles brought 200 Mounties, OPP and scabs onto the Lock 8 dock. The scabs were escorted onto the *Goderich* and the *Lethbridge* while the pickets and their supporters looked on from the other side of a police barricade.[21] But for every crew the police helped aboard a struck vessel, another was marching down the gangway to join the picket lines. As the *Goderich* built up steam, the *Mantadoc* was being winched through the locks under the protection of 150 policemen, who were handling her lines and operating the locks. When she pulled into one lock, 13 seamen threw their gear over the side and abandoned the vessel.[22] The police were left holding the lines, wondering who they were protecting as the strikebreakers joined the strike. Time after time, scab crews would move a vessel one day and desert the operators to stand with the CSU the next. In cases in which the crew stayed on board, the vessel would remain in limbo with no place to dock. This was the fate of the *Noronic*, which finally arrived in Detroit only to be advised to leave immediately or face mass picketing by American waterfront unions.[23]

Several times, the companies and the police used Lock 8 to put scabs aboard struck vessels under police protection. On June 4, just after

9 a.m., the CSL's *Glenelg* arrived in the lock with three scab crews, loaded at Port Maitland to replace strikers on Paterson's *Osler* and *Kingdoc* and the CSL's *Teak Bay*. As the *Glenelg* reached the lock, two cooks, Edna Middlebrook and Madeleine Silman, left the vessel and shouted to pickets to head down the canal to the *Osler*, which had been strike-bound for more than a week. When one of the scabs tried to restrain the women, he was hit by one of them with the lid of a metal milk can. One hundred and fifty RCMP and OPP constables formed a line to protect the scabs as they moved to the idled vessels, but pickets broke through and pelted them with rocks and pieces of coal.[24] In the commotion, five strikers were able to board the *Osler*. They hid until the vessel was well under way, then came out and talked the crew into joining the strike. The new crew joined the picket lines at Thorold. The arguments of five seamen had reduced the efforts of 150 policemen to futility.[25]

Why were two women — obviously union supporters — cooking on a vessel carrying 80 scabs to break the strike? The *Searchlight* offers no clues, but an incident that occurred earlier in the strike may shed some light on the affair. The CSU was predominantly a male union. No women sailed deepsea, and on the Lakes they could not find jobs outside the steward's department, where they performed traditional jobs like cooking, serving food or making beds on passenger vessels. Despite their small numbers, the CSU's women members were represented by female delegates to conventions and the 1946 strike committee included women like Dorothy Flaherty, an office worker for the CSU.

Women also played an important role in the CSU's campaigns, picketing and leafletting on issues like retaining the merchant marine and implementing the eight-hour day. During the strike they picketed, carrying signs with slogans like "We Married Men, Not Slaves" and "Our Vets Must Have Jobs." As in many unions in that era, women played an important but stereotyped role during strikes, preparing hot meals and nursing the injured. A sense of propriety and protectiveness on the part of the seamen, however well-intended, in some cases prevented the women from playing a larger role in the CSU.

As one of the first CSL vessels was being tied up, the women from the steward's department walked off with the rest of the crew. A tent city was erected and the strikers began to settle in. But in the small canal town there was no accommodation for the women, and fearing bad publicity if they stayed in camp, the seamen asked them to stay on the vessel. The women were having none of it. They were on strike as well and determined to do their share. After a heated argument, the men prevailed. The disgruntled women returned to the ship but remained true to the strike, passing pies and baked goods to the picketing seamen.[26] The 1946 practice may have become unwritten policy by the time the unfortunate union women found themselves cooking for the scabs on the *Glenelg*.

IN EVERY TOWN and village along the St. Lawrence system, the CSU began to reap the benefits of its careful education campaign about the issues at stake in the strike. Welland was a particular stronghold, where seamen forged lifelong friendships and encountered boundless support and solidarity. The town of Crowland, just east of Welland, was typical of a dozen similar canal towns. Welland clergyman Rev. Fern A. Sayles, a strong supporter of the seamen, wrote later that "Crowland made a name for itself as a place of refuge and support for Canadian sailors, whose service on ships was rewarded by scab replacement and police hunting.

"Homeless pickets around campfires on the windswept canal were cheered by the friendship of Crowland boys, girls, mothers and fathers. Sailors were taken to Crowland homes for hot meals and baths. Their clothes were washed and mended. They were treated as guests at parties and introduced proudly to friends. Day and night, Crowlanders multiplied picket lines and guarded ships in no uncertain manner. In Crowland, sailors from all over Canada were welcomed and supported."[27]

In town after town, community support made it possible for the widely-dispersed seamen to continue the struggle against the operators, their scabs and the police. As the strike began, rank and file leaders took over their areas, coordinated the activities of the strikers and built local support. Town councils, Canadian Legions, ethnic organizations and local unions all contributed to the effort. In many cases, solidarity among all the working people of a community ended trouble before it could begin.

In Collingwood, on Georgian Bay, CSU delegate Fred Bodner was in charge of picket activities. On June 1, the national office warned him that 21 scabs were on their way to take over a vessel in port. "When I heard the news I got in touch with the shipyard workers' union," Bodner told *Searchlight* readers. "We agreed that the yard whistle would be blown as a signal to the townspeople to gather at the station for an interview with the strikebreakers. Seamen and shipyard workers made the rounds of all restaurants, bowling alleys and other open spots telling people about the expected visitors. On my way down to the station, I dropped in at the dance hall and between numbers told the teenagers that scabs were coming to town.

"Almost the whole town crowded the station platform when the train pulled in. Twenty-one flabbergasted scabs stepped onto the station platform at Collingwood. Frightened out of their wits by their welcoming party, they scrambled back aboard. Amidst hysterical laughter of the whole town, they departed for Meaford, dead end of the rail line."[28]

But Cornwall, Ontario, the heart of the St. Lawrence system, was the scene of what became known as the Battle of the Canals, where the strike would be won or lost. CSU strategy called for tying up as few vessels as possible in Duplessis' Quebec. Both political and geographical advantages made Ontario a better province for the main effort, because by tying up as many ships as possible between Montreal and Lake Ontario, traffic on the entire system would be paralyzed. Drawing on union resources in Toronto and Montreal, the CSU could ensure effective strike coordination. The CSU representative in Cornwall would have one of the toughest jobs of the strike.

In many of the inland ports, deepsea delegates or other union representatives went in ahead of the Lake seamen to prepare the ground. Danny Daniels, who was completing a deepsea trip as the strike neared, was one of the members assigned to the Cornwall area. "We had a stroke of luck," he remembers. "I'm paying off a deepsea ship. The delegate on this vessel was excellent. He's got the ship organized perfectly, has been looking after the beefs perfectly, obviously has a very good personality and is very trade union conscious. 'What can I do,' he says, 'to help in this strike that's coming up on the Great Lakes?' I say to him, 'If you really want to help, pay off and hang around until the strike takes place.' "[29]

That man was Mike Jackson. Within days of his decision to leave the *Lasalle Park* to join Daniels on the picket line, the charismatic Jackson was in the thick of the struggle at Cornwall, where he became the most important leader of the strike. With a personality that made people of all kinds gravitate to him, he was able to organize the community to the point that all the trade unions and most of the working people of the region actively supported the strike.

By May 30, 18 vessels were tied up at Cornwall. Any vessel not affected by the strike was allowed to pass, but the decision had been made that none could go by with a scab crew.[30] That day the *W.C. Reynolds* failed in an attempt to run the blockade when the scab crew answered calls from the dock and jumped ship. But they were not prepared to join the picket line. The seamen treated them like prisoners of war. "We marched them through the streets and started them en route to Montreal," Jackson reported. It was commonplace for hundreds and sometimes thousands of townspeople to line the canal with the striking seamen as the ships moved through. Mike Jackson would yell to the crews to leave the ships and repeatedly they would do so. One such vessel was the *John P. Burke*, crewed by scabs who were recruited in Montreal and bussed in to run the vessel. On hearing the plea in

Cornwall, the entire crew left the ship and joined the line.[31] By June 1, 36 vessels were tied up at the Cornwall locks.

Faced with the growing unity between the seamen and the people of Cornwall, the shipowners attempted a desperate tactic to discredit the CSU in the eyes of the public. On May 31 at about 10:30 p.m., Cornwall Police Sergeant James Blackader was about to leave the Royal Café when five men armed with "pulpwood hooks, iron bars and lengths of pipe" pushed through the door.[32] Blackader was just inside. "When they opened the door they were surprised to see a police officer. One of them lashed at me with a gaff hook and several others began hurling iron bars at me. I was lucky to escape death." Blackader had encountered the vanguard of 75 goons hired by the companies from Montreal's "Main," a strip frequented by small-time thieves and thugs.

"I started to fight back and heard glass crashing around me. While I was fighting the hoodlums off, I heard the shouts of the union men coming down the street. Then all hell broke loose. A pitched battle began. Traffic stopped on the street and residents ran from their homes to help the strikers. Storekeepers closed their shops.

"There was blood everywhere, all over the pavement. As more strikers came on the double up the street, the strikebreakers began to retreat. Then the chase began."[33]

As the goons disappeared down side streets, Jackson organized 400 residents and strikers, who tied white handkerchiefs around their necks to distinguish themselves from the Montreal toughs. While seamen armed with clubs patrolled the highway to Montreal, others combed back alleys and streets in search of the intruders. Several were caught, questioned and turned over to Cornwall police.[34]

One of the goons later admitted he was paid $4,450 by E.B. Pride of the operations department of Canada Steamships Lines to organize the attack on Cornwall. Charges laid in connection with the incident were later withdrawn for lack of evidence, but the Searchlight published statements from two of those involved that Pride had paid them to participate in the assault.[35]

Pride's money was wasted. The attempted riot cemented the solidarity of townspeople and seamen still tighter. "It just shows the lengths some groups will go to interfere with the rights of free men," said Cornwall Police Chief Hawkshaw. "The riot started and was over in half an hour. If it hadn't have been for the seamen, cooperating with our men, we probably never would have been able to stop the carnage. The union deserves the credit for stopping the riot."[36] At a mass rally in Cornwall a day later, Pat Sullivan and Atlantic region director Bert Meade announced that Local 100 of the United Autoworkers had thrown $1,000 into the CSU strike fund. The workers of Cornwall, like those in plants across the country, were standing with the seamen.

On June 3, the companies attempted once more to ram their way through the union blockade. The CSL freighters *City of Windsor* and *City of Hamilton* were crewed by professional strikebreakers from the Haney Detective Agency who were determined to break through to the river. It would take more than a shoreside appeal to remove these goons from the vessels.[37]

As the ships approached Lock 17, the seamen hurled a barrage of rocks at the wheelhouse of the *Windsor*, forcing the vessel to reduce speed as glass shattered all over the bridge. As the people on the banks of the canal maintained a covering barrage, five seamen swam out to the *Windsor* "amidst the wildest scenes ever witnessed on the 120-year-old Cornwall Canal," dropped the vessel's anchors and tied her up. The *Hamilton* was trapped behind. Forty scabs were escorted off the ships and deposited on the dock. The RCMP ushered seamen and scabs off the government dock.[38] But the goons' ordeal was not over. They were taken on a humiliating march through Cornwall — under the jeers and taunts of the population — to the city limits, where they were released and beat it back to Montreal.[39]

In Ottawa, CCF members of Parliament demanded an investigation into the riot at the Royal Café. Labor Minister Humphrey Mitchell refused. "Isn't the government aware that strikebreakers from a private detective agency in Montreal were sent to Cornwall to incite strife and promote anti-union activity?" asked Cape Breton South MP Claire Gillis. Mitchell replied with a brusque "No."[40] He would go no further.

There was quiet on the canals. The strength of the union and its supporters had stopped all movement of Dominion Marine Association vessels. Pickets walked the canal banks, the docks of the St. Lawrence and the Lakes.[41] Once again, the union moved to achieve a negotiated settlement to break the deadlock. In a letter delivered to Mitchell an hour before he was to meet the companies, the CSU promised to lift the strike immediately if the operators agreed to recognize the union, drop all charges against seamen and agree to a joint reference of all outstanding matters to a binding decision by the War Labor Relations Board.[42] There was no reply.

McMaster, meanwhile, was doing everything possible to sustain the dispute and break the CSU. Every new crew member hired by the DMA to break the strike was a new dues payer for McMaster's National Maritime Federation.[43] Although charged with inciting to riot in connection with the Royal Café caper, McMaster was able to beat the rap. Another scheme, hatched with Reoch and other shipowners, to break the union with violence foundered when one of the intended participants phoned Sauras and spilled the beans. Statements sworn before the commissioner of the Superior Court of the District of Montreal implicated McMaster in a plot with the owners to discredit the CSU by a campaign of provocations that may have included blowing up part of the canal system.[44]

Yet it was McMaster, with consummate gall, who wired Prime Minister William Lyon Mackenzie King June 16 to warn that "lawlessness along Canada's inland waterfront has reached a state of revolution centered in two constituencies, Welland and Cornwall canals... Local Cornwall authorities are in sympathy with revolt. This is not a trade union matter, but a communist political uprising released through CSU and so far have seized control of authority in these districts so that state of terror now exists on waterfront... If present government does not provide law and order for peaceful Canadian citizens, it should resign and hand over the government to some party who will, as a state of emergency now exists which, if not stopped, will eventually seize the government by force."[45]

Justice Minister Louis St. Laurent refused to be stampeded. Troops in Ontario were placed on alert, but the Liberals were unwilling to send military detachments to the canal.[46] "Gorgeous George" Drew had no such qualms. His attorney-general announced June 5 that 70 OPP would be sent to Cornwall to reinforce the 45 RCMP already on the scene.

Aaron Horovitz had been Cornwall's mayor for 10 years and did not want provincial police in his community. He feared that police in such numbers would "not be conducive to peace but on the other hand might provoke violence."[47] But in spite of the protest of the mayor and the wishes of the people of Cornwall, the heavily-armed police garrisoned the town.[48] It was a case of too much too late. The canals belonged to the CSU and the police presence served to remind people of Mike Jackson's words: "We've just finished a war against Gestapo methods. Will we have to fight another?" No strikebreakers arrived.

The seamen kept peppering away to keep their cause alive in the minds of the public and the politicians. With the shipowners refusing to consider the CSU's settlement proposal, Pat Sullivan called on King to "appoint a controller to take over immediately the Great Lakes shipping industry and apply government formula for settlement."[49] It had become obvious to everyone but the companies that the CSU had won.

As the end of the strike's first month neared, Harry Davis smelled victory: "Even the Minister of Labor said, 'You can no more stop the eight-hour day than you can stop the St. Lawrence.' When I heard that statement I said, 'That's it, we're not going to lose this strike.' "[50] On June 21, with support for the seamen at an all-time high, the federal cabinet approved Order-in-Council PC2556 appointing retired Royal Canadian

Navy Captain E.S. Brand to take over and operate all 29 Lake companies with "uncontrolled discretion and judgment" over the operators' assets and operations. It must have been a tough decision for the government: two of the companies concerned were owned by Liberal senators.[51]

Under PC2556 all employees working for the struck companies prior to May 24, 1946 were rehired and returned to work effective June 24. The companies were ordered to implement the three-watch system at the current rate of pay with any work over eight hours to be paid as overtime.[52] In one of the most dramatic victories in Canadian labor history, the seamen forced an unwilling government to impose their terms on unwilling bosses.

The eight-hour day went into effect as ordered June 24 at 9 a.m. Hiring was through union halls and extended to deepsea vessels with the expiry of the government's manning pools July 31.[53] But there still were no signed agreements on the Lakes.

Brand worked to ease tensions in an effort to achieve a settlement. He persuaded the companies to drop 274 charges of desertion against seamen who had struck their vessels.[54] Union officers Harry Davis, Conrad Sauras, Cyril Lenton, and Aage Antonsen still had charges hanging over their heads, however, and for them the legal harassment continued. As Davis walked into negotiations at Toronto's King Edward Hotel, he was arrested and held in jail for three nights on charges of assault and robbery in connection with the beating of a private detective in Port Colborne June 20. Davis had been miles from Port Colborne, and he, Joe Grabek and Ray Tessier all were acquitted on the trumped-up charges.[55] But Lenton, the union's national treasurer, remained in jail awaiting trial on charges of "holding" a scab, while Conrad Sauras, convicted on a charge of boarding the *City of Montreal* without permission, was sentenced to six months in prison.[56] The seamen responded by setting up a nationwide organization to "Free Conrad."

It was not until August that the companies, first the smaller ones and finally CSL and the Sarnia and Colonial, finally signed an agreement with the CSU granting a small hourly increase, the eight-hour day, union hiring, overtime and union recognition. The agreement ran until December 31, 1947.

Scott Misener, refusing to the last to accept the CSU's existence, had tried a final desperate gambit to tear the union apart. The October 17 issue of the *Searchlight* carried a blaring page one headline reading "$100,000 Offered by Misener to Smash Union."[57] Gerry McManus revealed that he had been offered $100,000 if he would agree to set up a rival organization to combat the CSU. The new organization would sign an agreement with Misener that retained the 12-hour day and conceded cuts in wages. Instead of accepting the deal, McManus exposed the scheme at a conciliation meeting before an Ontario Supreme Court judge. The unflappable Misener acknowledged the offer, but claimed the money was intended as "a gift to assist union officers in their work."[58] What work could a CSU officer do for Misener?

Harry Davis later pointed out that "the price for fighting in the interests of the seamen and refusing to surrender — refusing to be bribed and corrupted — resulted in the imprisonment of our national treasurer, Cyril Lenton, for three months at the Lakehead and of our national director of organization, Conrad Sauras, for six months in Bordeaux Jail. These two brothers were convicted. There were, however, many others who were arrested such as Brother Daniels, our *Searchlight* editor, Brothers Grabek and Tessier, former patrolmen of this union, and myself.

"The strike did not end the attempts on the part of the shipowners to smash us. On the other hand, they laid plans as to how they were going to continue where they had failed before. Some of the more reactionary shipowners plotted and prepared a bombshell with which they hoped not only to wreck our union, but also to do great damage to the labor movement of Canada.

"Prior to the setting off of their explosion," Davis explained, "they carefully prepared the ground by carrying on a red-baiting and smear campaign in the press against our union following the strike. They continued to press charges against officers of the union, thus involving us in legal costs which alone amounted to thousands of dollars. Never did the boss press, whenever they mentioned the CSU in any story, ever fail to refer to us as 'the communist-dominated union.' Red-baiting and slander was the weapon they were using in their attempts to destroy the union. This barrage in the press and radio was the softening-up process which they hoped would result in the collapse of our union once they had set off their bombshell."[59]

"There was no way these backward shipowners, like Misener and the CSL, were going to tolerate the CSU forever," says Danny Daniels. "They were not going to change their fascist mentality to suit the politics of the day. Since McCarthyism was coming to the fore, there was no way they were going to allow a union that had supposed allegiance to the Communist Party to exist — not on the waterfront, it was too important.

"So what we see is an internal attack. In the history of the West Coast, in the 1930s, it worked to smash the waterfront unions. They figured it would work here. They said, 'We'll set up another outfit to replace the CSU, but this time it will be more effective than on the West Coast because we will have a trade unionist with history behind him.' " Misener was looking for a Trojan horse.[60]

CHAPTER THIRTEEN

Man Overboard

ST. PATRICK AND THE SNAKE

Oh, gather 'round you sailors,
    You workers from the deep, deep blue,
And I will tell you of a sailor,
    A worker just like you.

Twelve years ago he came ashore,
    A fugitive from the salty brine,
With big ideas for you and me,
    Ideas brave and fine.

His name was J.A. Sullivan,
    Of whom you probably read,
The man who tried to break your Union,
    But broke himself instead.

The fugitive of the dirty bilge,
    The man who has no shame,
Who sold his fellow workers out,
    And on their Union laid the blame.

Now the ending of this story
    Solves one of the missing links,
You see this guy Sullivan
    Has straightened out the kinks.

For he comes from Erin's shore,
    Whence St. Patrick drove the snakes in days of yore,
But the biggest snake he couldn't find,
    It had escaped to another ground.

And now we have found this long-lost pest,
    I leave it to you brothers, guess the rest.

Anonymous,
Searchlight, April 10, 1947

THE ENEMIES OF THE CSU had tried to use McMaster to skin the seamen but the old Governor was almost out of tricks. In October 1946 they had offered Gerry McManus $100,000 to quit the CSU and set up a rival organization, but he had told them he was a communist, a trade unionist and not for sale.[1] They offered Mike Jackson champagne or rum, but he refused to drink. They offered him blondes or brunettes, but he told them he was happily married. They offered him a job at a salary he could name, a paid vacation, his own office, a private car and "a desk with push buttons." Jackson told them he didn't like push buttons and he preferred his broken-down Ford with the union slogans painted on the side.[2] But Misener and his cronies would not give up. They decided to aim higher.

On March 14, 1947, reporters from every major news outlet in Canada gathered at Ottawa's Alexandra Hotel to receive an extraordinary statement from Pat Sullivan. In a news conference that generated page one headlines right across the country, Sullivan announced his resignation from the Canadian Seamen's Union and the Labor-Progressive Party, the name taken by the Communist Party of Canada when it resumed public, legal activity in 1943. He was leaving the union, he said, because "it has become a front for the Communist Party in Canada."[3] In a rambling 2,000-word release, he traced his trade union career, naming scores of associates he said were members of the Labor-Progressive Party. He declared the CSU to be under the "full control of the Communist Party," and expressed the hope that "honest, decent men who compose the overwhelming majority of the labor movement" would take action "before it is too late."[4]

Warning darkly that he feared an "unavoidable accident to myself" as a result of his revelations, he told reporters that "the Communist Party has many secret agents in different places, including the government service." In answer to shouted questions, he claimed that the LPP secretly financed many strikes, including a recent police strike in Montreal. The reporters stampeded to the phones.

Classing Sullivan's press conference as "a blow-off on Canadian communism second only to the espionage inquiry" into Igor Gouzenko's allegations of a Soviet-controlled spy ring in Canada, Canadian Press reported that Sullivan's allegations included claims that Fred Rose, former LPP Member of Parliament serving a six-year term for violations of the Official Secrets Act in connection with the Gouzenko affair, helped organize the CSU using an alias.[5]

There was more. CSU officers were taking junkets on union money, Sullivan claimed, and funnelling funds from the American National Maritime Union into Canada "in order that they could take the CSU over." During 1946, he said, $10,000 in NMU funds was transferred to the CSU. At least 50 seamen were being paid by the CSU, Sullivan charged, to campaign for the LPP candidate in the Montreal riding of Cartier who was seeking to replace Fred Rose.

Communist control of the CSU was absolute, Sullivan said. At the

1946 convention, for example, "out of less than 100 delegates in attendance, there was a Communist Party fraction ... of over 30 members." A
trade union school taught by American labor educator Leo Huberman
"was confined to Lake seamen in order to extend and develop Communist Party leaders so that in the near future a fight can be developed for
the 40-hour week." Toronto organizer Fred Hackett had been forced to
resign, Sullivan claimed, "although he was popular with all the membership, (and) he was replaced by a Communist Party man." Even
Danny Daniels, who held down a job and a half editing the English
edition of *Searchlight* had a special party assignment: he was considered "a valuable asset as he can speak both languages fluently and
(his) work consists of recruiting members among the young French
Canadians."[6] But perhaps the most serious of Sullivan's remarks was
not contained in his written release. Through the reporters, he appealed
to CSU members to tear up their cards and leave the CSU. Misener, it
appeared, had found his man.

Sullivan wasn't finished. He had intended to hold back the announcement of his resignation from the Trades and Labor Congress to hit the
afternoon editions, but fearing he might run into some seamen who had
read the morning paper, he decided to change his schedule and leave
town.[7] He sent his resignation to Bengough by messenger, jumped in his
Packard and headed north. Bengough had already found Sullivan's
office empty and the keys on the desk while the radio blared Sullivan's
resignation over the speaker.[8] When the letter arrived, Bengough was
puzzled to note the resignation was dated March 1, a full two weeks
earlier. Sullivan had told reporters only the day before that he intended
to run for another term as secretary-treasurer of the TLC.

Sullivan crossed the Ottawa River and drove deep into Northern
Quebec, leaving behind the Lakes and the Montreal waterfront where
he and his wife Mickey, two Lake cooks, had struggled and suffered to
provide the seamen of Canada with a real union and a better way of life.
His career had taken him from the docks of the Welland Canal to the
presidency of a national union, and from the obscurity of dogged
organizational work on the canals to the highest offices of Canada's
labor movement. Now Sullivan was heading into the domain of one of
Canada's most anti-union politicians, "because in my opinion the
Honorable Maurice Duplessis and his government had led and are
leading the fight to stamp out communism."[9]

The CSU National Executive Board promptly wired details of Sullivan's defection to regional offices and ships' crews and then turned to
the task of responding to the avalanche of press attacks the resignation
provoked. Davis, named acting president in the emergency, told reporters in Montreal that Sullivan was out to "sell out the seamen," adding

that the resignation "is only an attempt to smash our union and aid the shipowners."[10] Within two days of Sullivan's news conference, the union executive had confirmed Davis as president and issued a full statement nailing Sullivan's release as a pack of lies.

Davis revealed that Sullivan had been presented with an "ultimatum" by union leaders just days before his resignation to end "collaboration with shipowners. These activities of Sullivan's were not brought to light previously as we had hoped that Sullivan would change his ways and go out and do a job for the labor movement," Davis said. "It is obvious now that our decision not to cover up for him any longer and the laying down of an ultimatum to him about one week before his statement to the press caused Sullivan to decide to choose the way out by betraying his organization as well as the trade union movement in which he had played a leading role for the last few years."

Bengough stood with the union. "Don't desert the ship which has done so much for you," he told the seamen. "Do not listen to the strange advice given by your ex-president. Stand by your union." Labor opinion was not unanimous, however. James Sullivan, president of the London, Ontario, Trades and Labor Council, welcomed the resignation. "Pat has always been loyal to labor," he said. Oliver Hodges, a representative of the CCF's Ontario labor committee, said Sullivan's move was "all to the good of the labor movement." Charles Millard, Canadian director of the United Steelworkers of America and a die-hard anti-communist, said Sullivan's defection was proof that labor could clean its own house.[11]

J.B. Salsberg, LPP member of the Ontario Legislature and the party's labor secretary, saw things differently. Sullivan, he said, "had betrayed the movement in the face of mounting dissatisfaction with his incompetence as a labor leader. I had arranged to see him last Saturday," Salsberg said, "to inform him that because he had not changed we would dissociate ourselves from him. Sensing this showdown on Friday he rushed into the ranks of labor's enemies."

Both Bengough and LPP spokesman A.A. MacLeod hinted that Sullivan's statement appeared to have been written by someone else. Perhaps, speculated MacLeod, it had come from the typewriter of Royal Canadian Mounted Police intelligence man John Leopold, who had infiltrated the party in the 1930s and now headed up the police squad that was handling the Gouzenko investigation.[12]

The seamen's judgment of Sullivan was swift and harsh. On March 16, just 48 hours after Sullivan's defection, his Montreal local gathered to discuss his case. With 99 members present, seaman Johnny Harkin moved to expel Sullivan "as a traitor to the CSU and to the labor movement of Canada.

"I recommend to this meeting that it constitute itself a trial committee and that we, the rank and file seamen, expel Pat Sullivan with detestation and bitterness and a feeling of shame that is in our hearts," Harkin said. "I hope he carries the brand of Cain with him wherever he goes." With a thunderous roar, the meeting carried the motion unanimously, then voted confidence in the national executive and Harry Davis as president. Other locals weren't waiting for a verdict. As the Montreal meeting continued, telegrams arrived from Halifax, St. John, Thorold and Fort William demanding expulsion. The *Searchlight* reported that "Sullivan ceased being a member at 4:30 p.m., March 16, 1947."[13]

Davis and McManus spoke at length to the Montreal meeting and their line-by-line refutation of Sullivan's charges was reprinted in a special 16-page April issue of the *Searchlight* devoted almost exclusively to the defection. All of the charges disintegrated under the slightest scrutiny.

Most transparent were the claims of "communist domination," bizarre from one of the nation's most prominent communists and old news to anyone familiar with the union. None of the communist CSU personalities named by Sullivan — Davis, Sauras, Daniels, Lenton and the rest — had made the slightest secret of their political beliefs. The reaction of the seamen to these revelations was, "So what?" Danielle Cuisinier (Dionne), editor of *Searchlight's* French edition and named by Sullivan as the "editor of the Communist Party paper in Quebec,"[14] had been hired for her literary and political background and was a familiar figure to seamen, who also were well aware that she had been replaced several months before by Raoul Roy.

Sullivan kept stumbling over his facts, offending some CSU activists by suggesting they *weren't* communists! Fred Hackett, who Sullivan alleged had been pushed aside for "a Communist Party man" wrote heatedly from his hospital bed that he "resigned because of ill health and subsequent events have proved it. I have been a communist since 1926," Hackett fumed, "and no one has ever pushed me around or forced me into any action that was not in the best interests of the seamen in particular and the working class in general." All in all, Hackett said, Sullivan's statement was "the most rotten and despicable that any so-called labor man could conceive."

The funds from the NMU were solicited by Sullivan himself, Davis told the Montreal trial meeting, along with solidarity from scores of other unions, to help in the struggle to win the eight-hour day. Every trip taken by union officers was documented and authorized by the elected union leadership. As for the charge of funding the Cartier campaign, Davis stated categorically that "no one is receiving a single penny to work in any by-election."

Then Davis and McManus counterattacked. Twice, Davis charged,

Sullivan had attempted to cut deals with shipowners to end negotiations at the seamen's expense. Only prompt action by the negotiating committee had forestalled a sellout and opened the door to bigger gains.

"Our disagreements with Sullivan started some time ago," McManus told the Montreal local. "During negotiations on the Great Lakes strike settlement, we had to dismiss the negotiating meeting on one or two occasions and take Pat out and try to straighten him out. We told him we would call in the seamen. We said, 'We will expose you to the whole labor movement.' We threatened him with another strike and Pat got sore because he couldn't have his own way and went back to Ottawa and sat on his fanny drinking beer and sulking because we did not agree with him to let the seamen down. We won the eight-hour day and the 20 percent wage increase in spite of Sullivan and the shipowners.

"If we have committed a sin against the membership of our union it is in not coming to the membership and telling them what was going on behind the scenes. Even last week I drove out to see Sullivan and told him to straighten up — come on back to the labor movement — sober up and be a man. And at the very moment I was there, he was plotting and planning how to sell the seamen and their organization down the river.

"The guys with the dough got next to him," McManus concluded. "They now own him, body and soul. They are welcome to him. Traitors come and traitors go, but the movement goes on forever." McManus, who had led off his speech by declaring "I would rather be called a 'red' by the rats than a 'rat' by the reds," would later be haunted by his own words.[15]

It was obvious that many of Sullivan's "revelations" were nothing of the kind. The role of communist activists in the unemployed movement in encouraging the formation of the CSU was well-known to the seamen and to the labor movement. If Fred Rose had been involved in some fashion — using an alias as claimed by Sullivan or under his real name — it would not be surprising, although there is no evidence he was. The party's financial support of strikes was freely admitted by Salsberg.[16]

What of the claims of communist domination? Sullivan backs up his allegation with the statement that 30 of the 100 delegates to the 1946 convention were communists. There is no way to check this statement, but such a figure would not have shocked anyone familiar with the left wing of Canada's trade union movement of the day. The Labor-Progressive Party was a legal political party. Its senior members in the CSU could not have been more above ground. Several, including Sullivan himself, had been interned just six years before because of their beliefs. Since its return to legal political life, the LPP had seen its candidates elected to every level of government, including the House of Commons.

More peculiar were Sullivan's specific statements about party activists in the union, statements which included glaring errors of fact. Daniels, who Sullivan claimed spoke French and English fluently, edited only the English edition of the Searchlight. It was translated and edited in French by someone with real fluency, Danielle Cuisinier (now Dionne). It was Danielle Dionne — not Danny Daniels, as Sullivan claimed — who did "educational work among the young French Canadians." Both were known to the seamen as "Danny." Confusing the two was a mistake Sullivan could not possibly have made. His later assertion that the "statement which I made to the public took many days of anxious preparation" does not hold up.

Sullivan also characterized the CSU trade union school as an affair "confined to Lake seamen in order to extend and develop Communist Party leaders."[17] Not only is this statement utterly false, as Sullivan must have known, it ignores the many seamen who attended the school and were members of the CCF and later the NDP for their entire lives.

Sixty experienced CSU members, elected from the decks of CSU vessels, attended the two-week session during the winter freeze-up of January 1947. On most ships, the crews financed their delegates by passing the hat and deepsea sailors were a small majority. Among the Lake ship representatives were several women.

"Certainly there was class consciousness in the school," Daniels recalls, "a consciousnsess of seamen as workers, shipowners as bosses. But the main emphasis was on how do you handle beefs? How do you conduct meetings?"[18] Chief instructor was American writer and historian Leo Huberman, backed by both Daniels and Dionne. The goal was to give an overall picture of how society worked and how it could be changed. The lessons took effect. Graduates of the Montreal school set up follow-up classes in Toronto, Fort William, Rimouski and Vancouver.[19]

One veteran of that school was Gerry Yetman, who shipped out of his Nova Scotia home port in 1943 at the age of 15. In 1945 he joined the CSU and quickly rose to ship's delegate. Today he is president of the Nova Scotia Federation of Labor. A strong supporter of the NDP, he has never, at any time, been a member of the Communist Party, but he retains an undying loyalty to his first union.

"I left school in Grade 6 with no education," he says today. "I did some reading at sea and found out a few things, like the cause of social justice and belonging to the union of your choice is a long struggle. My early training in the CSU really set me up. I'm not a guy with any big ego and there's no halo over my head, but there's no horns either. I'm just an ordinary guy just trying to do a job, but I wouldn't have been able to do it if it hadn't been for the training in the CSU... It gave me a great start and there were some great people there."[20]

For Yetman and thousands of other seamen, nothing Sullivan said in his lengthy release could shake the fundamental lessons they had learned in the fight for a decent life. As Davis reminded the Montreal meeting, "The monopolies are carrying on a campaign against the labor movement. Standards of living are going down, prices are being boosted on everything. They are trying to prepare the ground, trying to create unemployment as a basis of a drive toward fascism and war. The only way they can succeed is by smashing the labor movement. The CSU is being singled out because we are at the forefront of the fight against these plans." Davis concluded with a ringing challenge: "We will show the ship operators that despite Sullivan's betrayal, their plot to destroy us will backfire and that the CSU will emerge more united and stronger than ever."[21]

The seamen needed no urging. By the time the April *Searchlight* was ready to go to press, thousands of seamen had mailed in their condemnation of Sullivan's betrayal. Sullivan was a man overboard, and no one in the CSU would throw him a life-ring. Crew after crew held meetings to denounce him as an agent of the bosses. Instead of inviting Sullivan to save them from communism, they erected rat guards to keep him off their ships. Years later, CSU veterans remember the strength and unity the defection inspired in an organization that had weathered heavier storms.

"It wasn't the first time he had done things," recalls Moose Mozdir, who saw the resignation as the culmination of a series of events. "He had done a lot of performing before that. We knew he tried to sell out the seamen in the '46 strike. He was going to go along with the companies on the phoney eight-hour day."[22] To seamen who had joined the organization since the war, Sullivan was a distant figure who had never been directly involved in union affairs during their membership.

When Sullivan changed sides, Gerry Tellier, a veteran of the On-to-Ottawa Trek, was a patrolman in Montreal. "I would have liked to kill the son of a bitch," he recalled many years later. "Was I shocked? No, I had been betrayed over the years, since my youth. It was to be expected. At the beginning, like when I was first in the labor movement, there were guys even in the unemployed association. They would be with you and then the next thing you knew they would be special policemen guarding the doors, to try and stop us going in. With Sullivan, I guess he saw his chance — the pot of gold at the end of the rainbow. You name them, they are legion. Sullivan was just another guy. Life does continue."[23]

Bud Doucette was on the *Fort Columbia* in South America as Sullivan dropped his press releases off at the Alexandra Hotel's front desk. When the ship docked in Montevideo "we received communications from the national office of the union advising that Pat Sullivan was no longer president of the union and had, in fact, been replaced by Harry Davis.

"I've heard some analyses from people in the labor movement that this defection had a very serious effect on the morale of the men on the ships, Sullivan having been a rather popular figure. But the facts don't support that theory. Sullivan's defection did not cause a ripple in the Canadian Seamen's Union.

"On that particular ship, the *Fort Columbia*, there was a pretty union-conscious crew. I was the ship's delegate and having read the information we had, a meeting that day or the following day said, 'Sullivan is gone, Davis is president of the union, all power to the union!' The figurehead, the symbol of the union, was not so important as the strength we knew we had in our own unity. Sullivan's departure really was not a traumatic event in the history of the Canadian Seamen's Union."[24]

How could Sullivan have become so divorced from the life of the union he had helped to form? There are many theories and there has been a great deal of speculation, but Tellier's theory fits the facts best. There are legions of people who change their politics every year. Sullivan's change was little different, but attracted a great deal more attention because he held the second-highest position in the Canadian labor movement and his defection was orchestrated to generate as much publicity as possible.

It is also clear both from the statements of McManus and Davis and from Sullivan's own recollections that his change was not an overnight conversion but a years-long development that generated tremendous strains in the leadership of the CSU. Davis' charge that Sullivan clashed with the negotiating committee at crucial moments and urged a conciliatory line is confirmed by Sullivan himself. His autobiography details, from his own perspective, the bitter clashes he had with top union leadership during the 1946 strike and the events leading up to deepsea negotiations in 1947, when he claimed the union set "uncalled-for, exorbitant demands that could not be met."[25]

Much has been made, as well, of Sullivan's heavy drinking. Anyone who knew Sullivan knew of his alcoholism. Seamen were no strangers to the bottle, though drinking was forbidden on ship by union as well as government regulations. The week-long benders at the end of a trip were the exception to the rule of a seaman's life. But charges that the bottle had broken Sullivan carried little weight with the seamen, who had seen many drink just as heavily without betraying their class.

Mike Jackson, the militant young patrolman who had organized Cornwall during the 1946 strike, summed up the seamen's assessment of Sullivan's fall: "I believe that Sullivan made his biggest mistake when he discarded dungarees and donned dress suits."[26] The CSU was at the pinnacle of its success after winning the eight-hour day on the Lakes and the seamen were exhilarated by the joy of victory and the strength that unity had built in their union. This energy communicated itself to the union's officers, moving them forward. But this was an experience that Sullivan did not share. While Sauras and Davis passed their days immersed in the membership, Sullivan sat on boards with government and company officials. While active as president or imprisoned in the internment camp, he had been untouched by Misener's attacks. Life in Ottawa made it possible for Sullivan to transform himself into one of Misener's rats.

Simple resignation after 10 years in one of the labor movement's toughest jobs would have been understood by the seamen, who stood behind him as long as he carried out the policies of the union. Sullivan went much further, urging the destruction of the CSU and then hiding under the skirts of Maurice Duplessis for protection. (His fears were justified. Daniels remembers that "seaman after seaman came to me (saying) 'let's dump him.' We had to be extremely vigilant to make sure no physical violence was used against Pat Sullivan.") Sullivan did not just leave the CSU, he moved to become its most implacable enemy. There is no doubt he was bought off by some person or group of people who had unlimited resources to put toward the destruction of the CSU and everything it stood for.

McManus spelled it out in the *Searchlight*: "I charge Sullivan with being a tool in the hands of the very men who offered me $100,000, and the present publicity campaign indicates that while it is the voice of Sullivan that is being utilized, it is the hand of Misener and Reoch."[27]

Many who were close to Sullivan saw other forces behind his betrayal. Bengough told reporters that there was something strange about Sullivan's parting statement. He had worked side-by-side with Sullivan for five years, a card-carrying Liberal teamed with an acknowledged communist. He knew Sullivan's style and he knew his fellow officer had been absent from his TLC office for almost two months prior to the defection. "I know Sullivan did not write the statements he made to the press," Bengough said. "They are not his style, he couldn't write them."[28]

Eight years later, Sullivan remained secretive about the events that led up to his spectacular press conference. The reporters were called together, he said, by "a friend who even at this date prefers to remain anonymous." This secret ally had powerful connections. "A large group of newspaper reporters had to be called together — some of them from out of town — without their knowing what the assignment was, in order that there be no leak. In this respect, my friend certainly received the cooperation of a large number of the owners and managers of the Canadian press..."[29]

Sullivan's defection was conveniently timed to arouse fears of communist infiltration and treachery and to dovetail with a drive against communists in the Canadian labor movement and a worldwide campaign against communism and the Soviet Union.

A month after the Ottawa news conference, Le Droit photographer Paul Taillefer snapped a shot of Sullivan relaxing with a book in an armchair. He was settling in, it appeared, on his 300-acre property on Lake Baskatong, 25 miles northwest of Maniwaki, Quebec. Le Droit stated in that April 15 edition that Sullivan had purchased the land one month earlier, the date of his defection from the labor movement.[30] It was common knowledge that Sullivan had been broke in the days before his betrayal. He had even attempted to float a loan from the CSU. The source of his new-found wealth never was revealed, but whether or not he was paid, Sullivan went to work for the shipowners to put the CSU to the sword.

The seamen already were engaged in new struggles. While Sullivan made new friends among the shipowners, Conrad Sauras was wasting away in Bordeaux Jail. He had lost several pounds from his already-slender frame. The seamen were writing to Ottawa and picketing under the slogan "Free Conrad." It was left to them to choose their leaders and when the choice was between Sauras and Sullivan, they backed Sauras. "I have no pity for someone like Sullivan," Sauras said. "If I said so, I would be hypocritical. But I am grateful that Mickey (his wife), who passed away not long ago, is not here to witness the betrayal of Sullivan, who tried to destroy what she had helped to build."[31]

Cyril Lenton had done his part for the eight-hour day, and when he was released from prison in Fort William, Mike Jackson picked him up in the union car, which bore "Welcome Home Lenton" signs on each side. The union car was followed by 23 taxis borrowed for the occasion and the caravan honked its way through the streets of Fort William and Port Arthur. Two hundred seamen were waiting for the procession at the CSU hall. Lenton was carried in on the shoulders of Paul Dubec and Sandy Ciffarelli. Lenton did not speak of his time in the pen but of the troubles ahead, and "as he spoke of strength, the audience itself felt the meaning of his words as they passed through the air and became the possession of the men." That night 300 seamen and their friends waltzed at the dance held to celebrate Lenton's release.[32]

CHAPTER FOURTEEN

Skirmishes

12,000 STRONG

There is a story going around, you heard it before I think,
Of Somebody starting a Union, run by a company fink.
Trying like hell to break us, Communists they holler,
Trying to sell us down the line, backed by the company dollar.
We saw them try it times before, we will see it time again,
By Main Street thugs and company bums, sabotaging our gains.
They tried it down in Cornwall, down in 'Frisco too,
But the picket lines were solid, and not a thug got through.
We are in this fight to the finish, they will never put us down,
So pay heed you finks and thugs and Sullivan, the company clown.
We are running on to victory, though the path it may be long,
We are sure to get there, the whole 12,000 strong.

Michael Jackson,
Searchlight, July 17, 1947

WITHIN A MONTH of his defection, Sullivan emerged as president of the Canadian Lake Seamen's Union. Secretary-treasurer of the CLSU was none other than John Harding, a long-time official in McMaster's rackets. Also on staff was Jack Chapman, once a respected CSU leader who had dropped out of sight after Sullivan left for Ottawa. Any affection the seamen had for him was erased when he was re-united with his old comrade.[1]

Misener and Canada Steamship Lines quickly found a role for their new allies. Misener, in particular, violated the agreement at every turn, refusing to allow "communist" patrolmen on his vessels or to meet with union officials he considered communist. A government arbitration board ordered him to grant passes to CSU patrolmen, to pay complete holiday pay and to hire through CSU halls.[2] Misener refused. CLSU members were hired to replace CSU seamen and Sullivan's outfit was freely issued passes. The CSU warned its members not to be provoked but to prepare for a strike. Government investigator L.W. Brockington was assigned to probe the union's grievances.[3]

Sullivan found help from other quarters, as well. The minuscule SIU, with its single remaining west coast local of coastwise **seamen** on Union Steamships, declared itself ready to represent Lake **seamen**. East of British Columbia, the SIU could claim no members.

As Harry Davis told the CSU's 1948 convention, the SIU was answering the shipowners' call to arms. "Following Sullivan's blast," he said, "a new crop of company unions sprang up and the SIU moved into the East Coast hoping to cash in on the shipowners' gravy train. During the threatened strike period, the SIU representative in Montreal publicly stated that his organization would cross our picket lines and that he was behind J.A. Sullivan.

"The SIU and all those company unions waited like vultures to pounce upon what they hoped would be the corpse of the CSU."[4]

On July 17, 1947, Sullivan tried for the first time a tactic that would become familiar during the next two years. The CSL's *Fairmount* needed a fireman. Instead of calling the CSU, as the contract required, the owners asked Sullivan to provide a replacement. The crew refused to sail with the CLSU man aboard. The ship sailed without a fireman, but when the vessel reached the Lachine Canal, the skipper tied her up, paid off the 11 crewmen and allowed a Sullivan crew to board under the protection of police and a gang of Main Street thugs.[5]

By July 25, however, the *Fairmount* was again in difficulty. Sullivan's seamen had been told Canada Steamship Lines had an agreement with the CLSU and that they were replacing scabs, but everywhere they went, crews from other vessels told them they were the scabs. The *Fairmount* crew wired the CSU office and requested the assistance of a patrolman. They were met by CSU officials in Montreal, and in the presence of reporters from the *Daily Herald* and the *Daily Tribune*, they signed CSU cards.[6]

Despite this humiliation, Sullivan moved boldly back into the Montreal waterfront scene he had abandoned during his years in Ottawa and he returned with a bang. Shortly after the *Fairmount* incident, Joe Davis, a 51-year-old CSU member and veteran seaman was settling down at his favorite table at the Coq d'Or, one of the CSUers' favorite Montreal hangouts, when he spotted a familiar face. He looked again to be sure — it was Pat Sullivan, sitting at a nearby table with another man. "I approached Sullivan," Davis said later, "and I said to him, 'Why did you sell out the seamen?' He answered me by reaching for his beer bottle and at the same time yelling to his partner, 'Give me that gun.' Someone took the bottle away from him, but I managed to see Sullivan's partner reaching inside his coat pocket. He pulled out a gun!"

The melee that ensued quickly poured out into the street, where Sullivan himself grabbed the revolver. "Sullivan placed the gun in my stomach and pulled the trigger," Davis recalled. "I figured this was my finish. He pulled the trigger again and again. Somehow, I managed to get the gun off him."[7]

Davis didn't know at the time that Sullivan's companion was Jack Chapman. Both Sullivan and Chapman lost a couple of teeth in the fracas outside the Coq d'Or.[8] Joe Davis was booked, but released on bail. Sullivan's gun was turned over to authorities and CSU Montreal patrolman Joe McNeil had Sullivan charged with intent to maim and attempting to discharge a firearm.[9] The charge was a formality, McNeil said later, because the union knew full well nothing would come of it.[10]

What saved Davis' life? Did the gun fail to fire because it was jammed? Or was it even loaded? The Coq d'Or was a well-known CSU hang-out and a few seamen could always be found around the area of the bar known as Beachie's Corner, perhaps waiting for the next performance of a celebrity dancer like "Princess à la Trixie." Did Chapman pack his gun as insurance against a rough encounter? Not likely.

In July 1947, Sullivan would have been more comfortable with cocktails in Ottawa's Chateau Laurier than with a few beers in the Coq. He had not been on the waterfront in years, and since he and Chapman had recently denounced the CSU and set up a company outfit to do a job on the seamen, Montreal was not a safe place for them. Why, then, did they venture down to the Coq that evening?

Perhaps Chapman and Sullivan were sitting around reminiscing about the old days and decided to hit a few of their old haunts. They considered Joe Beef's, but settled on the Coq because they hoped to see one of the famous dancers. Since it was a CSU hang-out, Chapman decided to pack his roscoe in his belt. Inside the bar, the two ex-unionists were drinking their beer when Davis came over and triggered the dispute. A scuffle and then they end up outside, where Sullivan is handed the gun by his sidekick, sticks it in Davis' belly and pulls the trigger several times. It doesn't fire. Why not? Perhaps it was a 1940s version of the "Saturday night special," a "cheap and nasty" that could not fire until the first shell was put in the chamber. When it fires, it sets the cylinder in motion and the rest of the cartridges will fire in sequence. Perhaps the gun was not loaded, or simply jammed. Whatever the reason, Joe Davis owes his life to the gun not firing.

Another explanation may be closer to the truth. Sullivan may have been slick, but he was no fool. It is unlikely that Sullivan and Chapman would go into the Coq drunk, knowing the likely consequences. Nor is it probable that Sullivan planned to kill someone and risk at least a jail term. But squeezing a trigger while the gun's muzzle was stuck in the seaman's guts could have set off a chain reaction of violence as other seamen stalked the traitor who had tried to kill one of their own. It was a routine with a gun which would not fire. Sullivan could easily beat the rap if there was no corpse in the way and at the same time accomplish his objective. Sullivan's goons would be ready and the waterfront would be turned into a battleground with the police and the government of Maurice Duplessis standing by to intervene against the "communistic" CSU.

To the editors of the *Searchlight*, Sullivan's motivation was crystal clear. It was an intentional provocation to start a waterfront war, the paper told CSU members, a war that would "hide the real fight from the people. The real fight is for higher wages, shorter hours, better conditions and job security."[11]

Meanwhile, the CSU began to prepare the ground for a strike to defend the Lake agreement from Misener's assaults. One hundred and fifty thousand leaflets were issued along the canals, newspaper ads were purchased and radio programs broadcasted the CSU's side of the dispute. The union compared itself to a "guerrilla army fighting for its country's liberation. Unless it has the support of the people, it is doomed to failure."[12]

On August 14, SIU Canadian director Gene Markey announced that his members would cross CSU picket lines and support Sullivan's CLSU. Sullivan told reporters his men would break any attempt to stop ships from moving in the canal.[13] Aware that Cornwall would be the center of any tie-up, Sullivan began to recruit goons along the Main and send them to the town on the St. Lawrence where he had helped the crew of the *Damia*. After a few drinks, they were given union books with the dues stamped paid up, although they had not given Sullivan a dime. The *Globe and Mail* reported that the 200 men who "Sullivan has imported to break any strike called by the rival Canadian Seamen's Union were given money." Among them were a number of legitimate CSU members infiltrated by the union to keep an eye on things. Like the others, they were paid $12 a day and shipped to Cornwall with CLSU books paid up. They were given the day's password and told to "take care of" anyone who didn't know it.[14]

Sullivan quickly ran into problems. "I would probably be seasick if I tried to walk across the lock on the canal," one Main Street scab told the *Globe*. Others admitted they had never been on a ship and had joined the CLSU only moments before boarding the bus for Cornwall. Public support for Sullivan's outfit was at low ebb by August 20, but the situation deteriorated further when Sullivan's bag man was late arriving with the promised cash. Fights broke out in the CLSU ranks, leaving one man with a stab wound and four others in police custody.[15]

As the CLSU mob milled about in a small park near the canal bank, CSU officials and government representatives were meeting nearby with the CSL and Misener in an effort to reach an agreement. Mingling with Sullivan's rag-tag army were local CSU members Johnny Baldwin, Mike McQuarrie, Gerry Tellier and others. Suddenly the beleaguered scabs found all hell breaking loose within their own ranks. Tellier, a big man with day-blue eyes, is remembered by friends as "a gentle person, one of the loveliest human beings, most sensitive and fragile in spirit. He would break down if there was some person who was genuinely hurt or in trouble. But he was ruthless in relation to any person who was against the interest of the seamen or of working people in general."[16] That day, Tellier remembered later, the scabs were dealt with in short order: "We scattered them."[17]

The next evening, August 21, *Searchlight* editor Danny Daniels was cleaning the national office at 438 St. Francis Xavier Street in Montreal with the assistance of two other seamen. Although the office was closed, four men blundered in and asked to see Pat Sullivan. Daniels coolly asked if they were working for Sullivan and they answered that they were. One volunteered that he had been instrumental in rounding up goons for the abortive attack in Cornwall and said he was looking for more action. The CSU men agreed to help. All seven piled into a cab and Daniels told the driver to take them to 606 Inspector. The goons had no idea it was the address of the Montreal CSU local office.

Confronted by the seamen hanging around outside the CSU office, the four hapless Sullivan men agreed to sign statements about their involvement with the CLSU. Union lawyer Albert Marcus took their affidavits in the presence of reporters from the Montreal *Herald*. Alexander Duval, the group's leader, was photographed brandishing a six-inch knife he had hidden under his sweater. Duval said he was not a seaman and listed his occupation as "crook." Only recently released from St. Vincent de Paul penitentiary after serving a two-year term for safe-cracking, he was a craftsman in the trade of blasting caps and come-alongs.

There was one seaman in the group. He proudly produced his SIU card and paid-up dues receipt. Recently paid off from an American ship, he argued that he was not a paid strikebreaker because the SIU's Canadian director had indicated his approval of crossing CSU picket lines. A copy of the receipt, photos of the four men and their affidavits appeared in the *Searchlight*. Sullivan's stumbling attempts to destroy the CSU were turning into a stagger.[18]

The next day, Misener and the CSL agreed to issue passes to CSU patrolmen in accordance with the government's settlement. They further agreed to abide by the contract on all other points, including the use of CSU dispatch halls. But the CSU had to make concessions as well. In order to avert a strike, the union agreed that only non-communist patrolmen would board Misener and CSL boats. The CSU agreed as well to allow a representation vote by the affected seamen. No other unions would be on the ballot in the government-supervised vote — it was either the CSU or no union at all.[19] When the vote was tabulated, the CSU's confidence in its strength proved well-founded. Two hundred and ninety-seven seamen voted for the CSU and only 22 against.[20]

The decision to agree to the companies' demand for non-communist patrolmen was an anguished one. There was no shortage of qualified seamen, men like Mike Jackson and Gerry Yetman, who were never in the Communist Party. But to avoid a tie-up, the executive decided to allow the companies to have an indirect voice in the selection of the union's representatives. With the dropping temperature of the Cold War and the growth of McCarthyism, the CSU wanted to avoid a fight on the issue of "communism".[21] The Lake contract was to run until December. With settlement of a new deepsea agreement on the agenda, the CSU sought to avoid a battle on two fronts. The decision was made to avoid a tie-up of the Great Lakes.

WITH THE LAKE CONTRACTS secured, the union turned its attention to the deepsea fleet, where contracts were due to expire November 15. Meetings in Vancouver with the shipowners' Shipping Federation of Canada produced little progress on the union's demands for a 48-hour week at sea and 40 hours in port. A strike vote gave the bargaining committee a strong mandate and the membership began to lay the groundwork for strike action.[22] Meetings of 300 seamen in Vancouver and 433 in Montreal unanimously endorsed the strike preparations.[23] At the union's request, the federal government appointed a conciliation officer and moved the negotiations to Montreal. Negotiating for the union was a four-person committee including Conrad Sauras, Harry Davis and Nick Buszowski, one of two rank and file members elected to keep the committee directly linked to the membership.

The CSU's hand was strengthened by the creation of a united front with the officers' unions. The CSU, the Canadian Merchant Service Guild, the Canadian Communications Association (a Canadian Congress of Labor affiliate) and the National Association of Marine Engineers, represented by Dick Greaves, all agreed to sign together or not at all.[24] Although negotiations were held separately, Greaves emphasized later that the companies aimed their main fire at the seamen. "The big attack was on them. They were front and center and to some degree we could say that if they got 10 percent, we wanted 10 percent. They had to carry the ball. We were there to give support to the seamen."[25]

The unity among the unions and the government's willingness to pursue a settlement averted a deepsea strike and won an agreement that met the CSU's main demands. The federation agreed to a $20 a month increase, the 40-hour week in port, two weeks paid vacation a year, sick pay and bunk lights. Bunk lights, while a minor financial item to the federation, marked an important concession. Seamen returning from watch had to turn on the overhead light to change, invariably waking their mates. It was impossible to read in the bunk while others slept. Bunk lights made living conditions that much better.[26]

Even more critical was a union security clause that gave the CSU a closed shop. Combined with the union hiring provisions, this clause insured that no one sailed deepsea on a Canadian vessel if he or she was not a CSU member.[27]

It appeared likely the CSU would again reach agreement with the shipowners without a work stoppage, as it had since the inception of the deepsea fleet. But the companies were offering the licensed personnel less than the CSU agreement. The officers rejected an offer that called for a minimal wage increase, fewer holidays and no job security.[28] The three officers' unions and the CSU, meeting together as the Joint Maritime Council decided to wait for the report of Labor Commissioner Mr. Justice D.A. McNiven. If the report did not offer a solution, the council announced, the 1,500 licensed personnel would strike 150 ocean-going vessels.[29]

Although the CSU had succeeded in greatly reducing the number of hours worked on deck, many of the officers still were working up to 84 hours a week while in port. The shipowners, claiming that the three officers' unions did not represent more than 60 percent of the licensed personnel, expected any action taken by the officers would be ineffective.[30] They failed to consider the strength of the Joint Council. CMSG representative S.J. Fisher believed that "with the cooperation of the Canadian Seamen's Union, we can stop any Canadian ship from clearing port."[31] While the commissioner was drawing up his report, the officers flexed their muscles. They did not strike or hamper any vessel already crewed, but they did not sign on any arriving vessels. Those vessels would then be tied up or forced to sail short-handed in violation of Canada Shipping Act regulations. As officers completed voyages, they were not replaced. Those still under articles worked on board but refused to take the ships out. The Joint Council said the action was not a strike, but a case of "no contract, no sail." Christmas Eve in Vancouver saw seven ships idle in Burrard Inlet.[32]

The companies moved quickly. The Canada Shipping Act was dusted off and the ship's masters charged 16 officers in B.C. with "willful disobedience of lawful commands."[33] Then, on the instructions of the shipowners, they told the officers the charges would be dropped if the ships sailed. The officers took the bait and the last of the seven vessels left B.C. waters January 6, 1948.[34]

Mr. Justice McNiven's report was handed down January 27. It called on the companies to recognize the three unions as sole bargaining agents for their classifications and to guarantee preferential hiring, a looser form of union security than the closed shop achieved in the CSU agreement. The report also recommended improved wages and holidays and lump sum overtime payments.[35] The companies turned the report down.

As the dispute headed for a confrontation, the Joint Council held further consultations. The CSU signed its one-year pact with the companies to maintain its gains, but pledged that no CSU member would cross officers' picket lines. Greaves said the assurance was taken for granted; it was well-known, he said, that "the CSU wouldn't scab on anybody."[36]

The three other council unions held membership meetings which overwhelmingly rejected company demands. NAME and the CCA struck immediately. CMSG members followed soon after, hitting the bricks March 3 in Vancouver, Halifax and Saint John. After three days of strike, the companies offered to implement the McNiven report. The strikers turned them down, staying out to win the closed shop and other demands not contained in the latest offer.[37]

On March 15, the unions moderated their stand, offering to end the strike on the spot if the companies implemented the full terms of the McNiven report and accepted conciliation of outstanding items. As a sign of good faith, the officers took down their picket lines and returned to their vessels.[38] But this time it was the employers' turn. They flatly rejected the McNiven report. By March 31, 35 deepsea vessels were tied up.[39]

Finally, 45 days after the deepsea strike began, the dispute was settled. The officers returned to work under the terms of the McNiven report with added protection guaranteeing no discrimination against members for their role in the strike.[40] The officers' strike had been the first to hit any Canadian merchant fleet. To the shipowners, it represented a conspiracy not only against Canada but against the forces of western democracy.

The shipping bosses "linked the present strike of merchant marine officers with a world communist plot to block American shipments of food and supplies to war-ravaged Europe," reported the *Halifax Chronicle*. The Marshall Plan, which funnelled aid for reconstruction to the nations of Western Europe, was directed only at countries willing to meet certain conditions about their political and economic life that were designed to keep them firmly in the United States' orbit. A key objective was the consolidation of non-communist or non-socialist governments.

Although the plan required all American goods to be shipped in American bottoms, the shipowners were developing a theme they were to repeat many times in the coming year. As Harry Davis observed, the maritime struggles were being fought against the "background of the Cold War period."[41] For big business, the enemy was communism abroad and labor at home. The shipowners contrived to combine the two "threats" in a single propaganda offensive.

THE CSU WAS NOT NEUTRAL on the question of what kind of cargo Canadian vessels should carry. The union had consistently opposed shipping arms to fascist forces and as new armed conflicts erupted around the globe the seamen fought hard to deny support to reactionary regimes. Their stand put them on a collision course with the Canadian government.

In 1938, Pat Sullivan had stood before the Trades and Labor Congress convention and demanded that the congress back longshoremen and seamen when they refused to ship scrap iron to Japan. The support was not forthcoming, and at least some of the scrap iron found a final resting place in Pearl Harbor and in the bodies of Allied seamen and soldiers. In 1947, the union took up the cause again, this time over shipment of arms to the forces of Chinese dictator Chiang Kai-Shek.

It took no prompting from the CSU leadership to inspire contempt among the rank and file for the Chiang Kai-Shek regime. When newspaper editorialists concluded the CSU boycott was Moscow-inspired, a rank and filer set them straight with a letter to the St. John *Telegraph-Journal.*

"While it is true that the beliefs and actions of the CSU often differ radically from those of most other Canadians," he wrote, "it is also true that our occupation, which takes us to all parts of the world, makes us that way... During the past year, a number of ships under CSU contract have been trading into Chinese Nationalist ports. This has given us the opportunity to see for ourselves what goes on in the land of Chiang Kai-Shek. Our opinions, formed in China, are therefore nearer the truth than those formed and influenced by biased newspapers.

"It is because we know, beyond a shadow of a doubt, that the government of Chiang Kai-Shek is a rotten, corrupt, harsh and undemocratic dictatorship, which practises some of the worst features of Hitlerism, that we refuse to sail on ships supplying arms to China and thus prolong the agony of China."[42]

The Canadian government's support for the Nationalist cause amounted to more than guns and ammunition. It included Mosquito fighter bombers, airplane ammunition, landing field equipment, small arms and the component parts of a small-arms ammunition factory.[43] What other supplies were involved is unknown. The Canadian government refused to make the lists public for "security reasons."[44]

"We thought we could help the anti-war movement by threatening to refuse to take ships to Chinese ports," recalls Harry Davis. "There were protest actions. There were delays. There were refusals on the part of seamen to go. There was a conference in New York. I went down. There were some leading trade union people there from throughout the world. I spoke and stated we supported the movement to bar shipments to Chiang Kai-Shek.

"I think we were ahead of our time and not too many unions would have taken that kind of a stand, not merely taking a position of condemning a shipment of arms but taking the action of saying we will not let these ships go there with ammunition. Whether we should have gone as far as tying up the ship by protest action, these questions are debatable. It was certainly utilized by the enemies of the CSU."[45]

But the seamen saw the struggles of other workers as their own struggles. They had helped the textile workers in Valleyfield, joined picket lines in India and supported the strike of their own officers, though it meant the loss of thousands of hours of work.[46] It was not remarkable, therefore, that in Vancouver they threw pickets around ships loading arms and munitions for China. The action was led by the Vancouver Labor Council, and included TLC and CCL unions as well as members of the CCF, the Labor-Progressive Party, church groups and students.

In mid-December 1947, the picketing centered on the *Colima*, a vessel worked by a Pakistani crew. Instead of loading cargo, the vessel moved to Burrard Dry Dock for repairs. There, members of the Marine Workers and Boilermakers Industrial Union refused to work the ship.[47] Their action was weakened, however, when CCL president A.R. Mosher ordered Congress affiliates to cease participation in the picket line to allow other trade unionists on to the job. The *Colima* eventually sailed, laden with planes, small arms and munitions.[48]

The focus of the struggle then shifted to Halifax, where the CSU-crewed *Islandside* arrived to load Mosquito fighter-bombers, arms and munitions. An emergency CSU meeting December 22 attended by the *Islandside* crew and 150 other union members voted unanimously "not to sail any ship carrying munitions for fascist China."[49] That same afternoon, the entire crew and all officers, with the exception of the master and first engineer, signed off the *Islandside*. No replacements signed on.[50]

The CSU members understood very clearly the reason for their action. "This is not the first time the government of Canada has helped establish a dictatorship," said Bob Kerr, a CSU member from B.C. "Ten years ago today, the Canadians in the Mackenzie-Papineau Battalion helped to start an offensive to drive back the fascists in Spain. If the Canadian government at that time had sent arms to the democratic forces in that country, the war we have just won would never have occurred. Now democracy is under attack in China, and the Canadian government is willing to send arms to suppress the aspirations of the democratic people of China."[51]

The shipping operators were just as blunt. "To us, it's just another cargo," said one company representative. "It's nothing to get excited about. We take what's booked. If it didn't go on one steamer, it would go on another."[52] Federal Labor Minister Humphrey Mitchell agreed. The union had no choice but to man the vessels, Mitchell argued, because its hiring hall agreement bound it to dispatch men to the ships. The jobs were posted, the CSU replied, but no seamen would take them.[53]

Around the globe, other workers began to respond to the CSU's stand. In Singapore, the waterfront unions were boycotting any Canadian ships that docked. The Hong Kong seamen's union stood with the CSU and the Vancouver Chinese community sent telegrams of encouragement.[54] The Vancouver Trades and Labor Council, the United Fishermen and Allied Workers Union, the steelworkers and miners of Sydney, Nova Scotia and some religious groups and political parties voiced support for the seamen as the New Year was proclaimed.[55]

Early in January, crews from the *Islandside* and other vessels met in the CSU hall in Halifax to consider their position. They had been aware from the start that they would not be able to halt arms shipments entirely. The resolution adopted at the December 22 meeting had concluded that "we fully realize that action on our part alone will not halt the present destructive policy of our government.

"We are, nevertheless, convinced that it is our duty and responsibility to take such action as may be possible, such as refusing employment on ships carrying cargoes of this type. We do this in order that the Canadian people may become aware of this alarming situation and we take our stand confident that when the facts are known, the Canadian people will not stand idly by."[56]

By January, the seamen decided, the time of reckoning had come. They had been ordered back to work and the situation was becoming increasingly tense. The policy of the government and the profiteering of the munitions makers and shipowners had been exposed. The seamen would return to the *Islandside* and would sail it and other vessels to China under protest.[57]

IN DISPATCH HALLS across Canada and in ships' messrooms and galleys around the world, CSU members met early in January to elect delegates to the 1948 convention. On Bud Doucette's ship, the *Lady Nelson*, each crew member chipped in $10 to cover their delegates' expenses to the five-day convention, scheduled to open February 23 in Toronto. When the ballots had been counted, Doucette, the ship's delegate, and engine room delegate Andrew Merriman had been elected to represent their 100 fellow workers.

"The '48 convention was the largest and perhaps the most conscious," Doucette recalled many years later. "The union at that time, in my opinion, had reached its zenith. We were besieged on all sides. We were beginning negotiations to renew the deepsea agreements, the traitor Sullivan had emerged with the Canadian Lake Seamen's Union, the Seafarers International Union had sounded its intention to come in and raid the membership of the CSU and politically the Cold War was acting to our disadvantage.

"There were many problems in 1948, and while it was the very apex of the CSU strength and influence in the labor movement, it was also the year preceding the greatest battle which ever occurred in the North American labor movement, to my understanding. The organization and education of the membership to the size of the problem we faced was the primary concern of the union: to strengthen our forces, as outnumbered as we were, in preparation for the bigger battles that were just around the corner."[58]

The seamen knew they were under attack and they knew they would need the support of the Canadian labor movement if they were going to have any chance of prevailing. Percy Bengough, president of the Trades and Labor Congress, addressed the 95 delegates on the convention's third day.

Bengough had attended the American Federation of Labor's 1947 convention as the fraternal Canadian delegate, his mission to "explain to the delegates attending the convention of the status of the Trades and Labor Congress of Canada as a free trade union center with complete autonomy."[59]

The AFL had put pressure on the Canadian body to recognize the SIU as having national Canadian jurisdiction. The SIU, the argument went, should be seated in the TLC and the Canadian Seamen's Union should be expelled. The TLC, mindful that the SIU had only a handful of members in Vancouver and Victoria, refused. The 12,000 member CSU remained in the congress while the SIU was labelled a dual union. The endorsation of the CSU had come at the TLC's 1947 convention in Hamilton, which heard Bengough describe the $100,000 bribe offered to McManus. The TLC convention voted to condemn the anti-union activities of Pat Sullivan, and when the vote was counted Bengough paused to make certain that "this unanimity of opinion be recorded."[60]

Now Bengough was standing before the CSU's convention. "I have been pretty close to the trials and tribulations of the CSU for a long time," he told the delegates. He was speaking from a podium draped with a banner bearing the slogan that had been with the seamen ever since the union had been launched: "Every Ship A Union Ship! Every Crew A Union Crew!" Overhead was a sign reading "Every Member Is An Organizer!"

"There are many organizations I can think of and that I have seen which would have gone out of business if they had had half the opposition that the CSU has had," Bengough said. "The efforts that were made by the bosses and by treachery to put this organization out of business (have not) succeeded. You emerged stronger than ever.

"I know there has been a lot said by some of the companies that you have tried to do business with who don't like your leadership, and frankly, we are not too fussy about theirs."[61] The seamen leaped to their feet and cheered Bengough. They knew their struggle was just and that the congress was with them.

Elections that week re-elected the leadership with minor changes. Davis remained president. Conrad Sauras became director of organization and Gerry McManus took over the dual position of secretary-treasurer. The new executive included Cyril Lenton, Fort William; Jimmy Thompson and Digger Smith from B.C.; Theodore Roy and Ray Collette from Quebec; Dewar Ferguson, Toronto; Eric Atkins, Montreal; Aage Antonsen, Thorold; Eddie Reid, St. John; and Mike Jackson, director for the Great Lakes.[62]

"There was no question that there were some people in (the executive) that may have been a little more to the left than some others," says Gerry Yetman. "My argument was that we put them in there and if we were not satisfied, it was up to us to put them out.

"Our leadership had told us how the shipowners had tried to buy them off. When you see the shipowners putting out flyers like that by the thousands and thousands of dollars, and people turning them down because they are dedicated to the movement, you don't vote against those guys."[63]

Bud Doucette travelled back to Halifax to report to the crew of the *Lady Nelson*. "It wasn't an optimistic report. We knew that the shipowners were going to do everything in their power not only to stop the advances the Canadian Seamen's Union had achieved in its short history, but were, in fact, going to turn back the clock.

"Acts of provocation were taking place in most ports and on most ships. We knew our jobs were being sold and our ranks thinned by the transfer of Canadian flag vessels to flags of convenience. We called upon the membership to tighten the ranks of the union."[64]

The seamen knew 1948 would be rough. All the signs were there. The struggle began quietly around the negotiating table, spread to the Lake ports, then to the canals and finally reached around the world.

The Canadian Seamen's Union newspaper, the Searchlight. From its first issue on July 1, 1937, the paper carried articles in French. By September 1, 1937, pictured here, it boasted the "Section Française."

Below: Nova Scotia labor leaders discuss aid to the 500 striking fishermen of the Canadian Fishermen's Union, c. 1945. Left to right: Adam Scott, Secretary-Treasurer, District 26, United Mine Workers; H.C. Meade, Secretary of the CFU; J.K. Bell, chief executive officer of the Marine Workers Federation; J.J. MacLean, President of the Allied Trades Council, HMC Dockyard.

The Fourth Arm: Searchlight *special edition,* A Salute to the Merchant Marine, *February 1945.*

Union hall in Toronto, c. 1945.

Vancouver seamen protest Park Steamship's attempt to drop the war risk bonus, 1945. Digger Smith in hat.

Below: Setting sail for the 1946 Lake strike.

A police escort down the Welland Canal for the CSL's Noronic, *crewed by scabs, 1946.*

The City of Windsor, manned by detective agency thugs, attempts unsuccessfully to run the blockade in the Cornwall Canal, June 1946.

RCMP strikebreakers and "Drew's Dragoons" (Ontario Provincial Police) assist the scab supply ship Glenelg, Welland Canal, June 1946.

Welland Canal, 1946 strike: ship traffic at a standstill.

Leo Huberman, former educational director of the National Maritime Union, teaching at the CSU leadership school for ships' delegates, Montreal, January 1947.

Signs of the times — 1947.

CSU cartoonist Jack Derhousoff takes on the shipowners through his main character, Joe Beef.

Among the beefs of the crew of the government icebreaker N.B. McLean — overcrowding. Pictured here, the oilers' room, accommodating six men. The CSU campaigned effectively for improvement of conditions aboard Department of Transport vessels, the "Slums of the Sea."

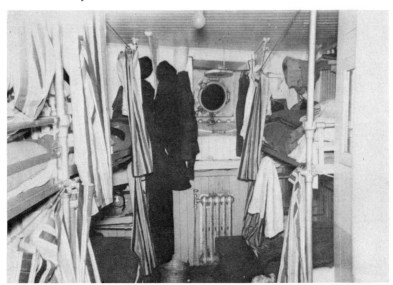

CSU 1948 convention. National executive, below. Left to right, front row: Conrad Sauras, Dewar Ferguson, Harry Davis, Gerry McManus, Theodore Roy, Jimmy Thompson, H.C. Meade; back row: Rocky Rockindale, Mike Jackson, Digger Smith, Eric Atkins, Art Penhale, Eddie Reid, Lucien Labbé, Danny Daniels.

The 1948 strike: CSU flyers appeal for community support against the shipowner-RCMP-scab attack.

Sullivan, Misener, Reoch and Mitchell hang Labour — CSU float, 1948 Lake strike.

Below: Toronto demonstration in solidarity with striking CSU members, 1948.

Halifax picket line in support of the officers' strike, spring 1948.

Before the attack: Lady Rodney *strikers and shoreside supporters, Halifax. Published in the April 8, 1949 edition of the* Searchlight — *the day CN police, SIU goons and scabs attacked the Rodney strikers.*

CSU pickets, Terminal Dock, Vancouver Harbor, 1949.

Seamen on the Mont Alta read injunction commanding them to leave the ship, Montreal, April 1949.

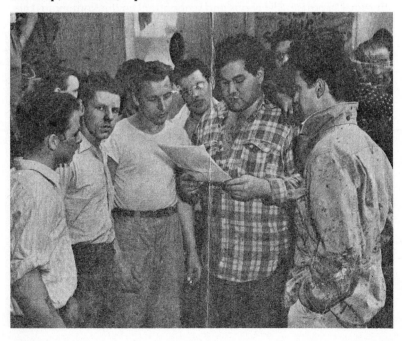

Plant gate collection at Spadina and King, Toronto, 1949. Dewar Ferguson at mike.

Crew of the Canadian Victor, shot at by Cuban gunboats, Havana, 1949.

The Battle in Britain, 1949.

The Beaverbrae.

CSU soundcar, 1949.

Delegates to the last convention of the Canadian Seamen's Union, Toronto, 1950. Left to right, front row: Gérard Fortin, Ireland, Joe Grabek, Dewar Ferguson, Conrad Sauras, Harry Davis, Gerry McManus, David Bentham, unidentified; second row: John Good, Horner, unidentified, Fred Hilson, Gus Genites, Mullins, unidentified; third row: left, Bill Watkins, fourth from left, Lucien Labbé; back row, second from left, William Mozdir.

CHAPTER FIFTEEN

Class Rule, Class Law

ON MAY 12, 1948, Trades and Labor Congress president Percy Bengough went to the microphone at an emergency trade union conference at Toronto's Labor Temple to give Canadian workers a warning. "The fight the CSU is in today is definitely the fight of every trade unionist in this country," Bengough said. "If it is lost, then no union has an agreement worth much if the employer that you are working for has enough money and influence to break it with impunity as these shipping companies have."

Just two years after winning its precedent-setting Lake agreement, the CSU was in a struggle for survival. As Bengough spoke, CSU members were watching scab crews sail former CSU Lake ships under police protection. Pickets on the docks were bathed in live steam hissing from special hoses mounted for the purpose on deck. Three key shipping companies had torn up the Labor Code, refused to negotiate and defied the union to stop them. The federal government was standing idly on the sidelines or so it seemed.

Bargaining for the 1948 season had begun with no hint of the confrontation that was to dominate the Great Lakes. The seamen had entered negotiations seeking a raise of $36 a month on a base rate of $134.50. They also sought a shortened work week of 48 hours at sea and 40 hours in port, a condition already enjoyed by American seamen sailing the same waters. One company found the proposals reasonable: on February 12, Canada Cement signed an agreement granting the closed shop, a 48-hour week and a $55-a-month increase.[1]

But the other shipping companies wouldn't move, offering only seven cents an hour and no reduction in working time. The CSU offered to sign the Canada Cement agreement with the other companies to no avail. A federal conciliation board managed to bring Algoma Central Steamship Lines under agreement but Captain Scott Misener's two companies, Sarnia and Colonial lines, refused even to meet with the conciliation officer.[2]

His companies would "not negotiate with a communistic group," Misener told conciliation officer F.J. Ainscough. "It has been the policy of Sarnia and Colonial companies that we will not deal with or employ men who, to our knowledge, are communists or who belong to any group whose aim is to foment trouble or to disrupt and overthrow the Government of the Dominion of Canada. We have no quarrel with the seamen and unionism, but we have with the executive of the union."[3]

Misener's statement had been released two days before the CSU convention opened in Toronto in February. The seamen had responded by unanimously returning to office the executive Misener so despised. Misener's true interests became plain when it was learned that after refusing to bargain with the legally-certified CSU and turning his back on the conciliation board, he was meeting with Pat Sullivan.[4] At Misener's side was a trusted ally, the Canada Steamship Lines.

Federal labor law and the National War Labor Relations Board recognized the CSU as the sole legitimate representative of the Misener and CSL seamen. Even Labor Minister Humphrey Mitchell declared categorically that the three companies "were bound to bargain with the Canadian Seamen's Union."[5] On March 6, the Labor Board complied with a CSU request seeking appointment of a new conciliation board in an effort to reach a settlement.[6]

The Canada Steamship Lines' reply was swift. Just two days after the announcement of the board's appointment, the CSL announced it had signed an agreement with Sullivan's Canadian Lake Seamen's Union.[7] On March 10, Misener's companies followed suit. It was an "almost unprecedented situation," commented the *Toronto Star*.[8] Not only had the shipowners defied the Labor Board, they had signed collective agreements with an uncertified union in clear violation of federal law.

Misener's concern for democratic freedoms stopped at his own front door. The 3,400 employees covered by the sweetheart contracts had a choice: join Sullivan's outfit or lose their jobs. While the seamen howled in protest, the federal government sat on its hands. Unwilling to condemn the shipowners but unable to condone their actions, federal officials stalled for time. Misener quickly forced them to show their true colors.

Unable to convince CSU members to tear up their cards, Misener announced March 17 his intention of hiring 500 British seamen in time for the opening of the season in mid-April.[9] A telegram to the National Seamen's Union of the U.K. brought the response the CSU had expected: "Under no circumstances will we agree to British seamen being shipped to replace Canadian seamen..."[10]

But Mitchell, questioned in the House of Commons, refused to repudiate Misener's provocative machinations. British seamen had the "perfect right" to enter Canada if they wished, he said.[11]

Bengough saw things differently. Pledging the congress' full support for the CSU, he called on the labor movement "to recognize the facts and not be sidetracked by the propaganda. This particular group of employers, under the guise of combatting communism, are attempting to establish fascism in its worst form."[12]

The new conciliation officer, Leonard Brockington, was no stranger to Misener and his tactics. It was Brockington who in 1947 had attempted to put an end to Misener's claims that the CSU did not represent his employees. At Brockington's suggestion seamen on both lines voted to determine whether or not the CSU should represent them. In a government-supervised ballot, Sarnia Line seamen voted 143 to nine for the CSU. On the Colonial Line, the vote went 154 to 13. Misener simply ignored the vote. His contracts with the CSU were terminated, he declared.

When Brockington again called Misener to the bargaining table, he failed to appear. The union attended the meeting, Brockington reported, but the invitation to the employers "received neither the courtesy of an acknowledgement nor the cooperation of an attendance."[13] Brockington had a new suggestion for the CSU. Since Misener stated publicly he had no quarrel with the union, simply with its leaders, why not remove the union leadership from the bargaining and appoint well-known non-communists to replace them?[14] In one of the most remarkable concessions in the history of Canadian labor, the CSU agreed. It proposed Bengough, TLC secretary John W. Buckley and William Jenoves, vice-president of the TLC and president of the Toronto District Trades and Labor Council, to bargain for them.

Brockington was elated — Bengough was a well-known Liberal and he considered the others excellent choices as well. Then the CSU made another, unprecedented offer. It would agree to have the settlement administered by the TLC.[15]

On March 30, Brockington and the CSU representatives waited expectantly for Misener's bargaining team to arrive. No one appeared. The National War Labor Relations Board decided to press the issue, ordering the CSL to appear before the conciliation board in Montreal April 2. That day, Brockington, assistant board member Douglas McNish and the union's team assembled in Montreal's Confederation Building. At the appointed hour, CSL lawyer Arthur Mathewson entered the room, walked over to Brockington and handed him a notice of petition for a writ of prohibition. The petition was a challenge to the board's right to sit and effectively stopped conciliation proceedings. Mathewson intended to argue that Privy Council Order 1003, which empowered the board to sit and required the parties to bargain in good faith, was no longer applicable. It had been introduced as wartime legislation and Canada was no longer at war.[16]

The courts upheld PC1003, but in the process ruled one conciliation board member ineligible on a technicality. The shipowners had gained precious time. The beginning of the season was drawing relentlessly closer and Brockington's board had to be dissolved. In its place the government appointed an Industrial Disputes Inquiry Commission under Brockington's direction. Again Mathewson challenged its legality, but Brockington pushed on. He found the shipowners guilty of several violations of federal law. Bengough warned that the shipowners' actions left "these unions in a place where there isn't any law. It leaves us in a position where might is right."

Brockington and his fellow commissioners agreed. They told Mitchell in an underlined passage in their report that they were "*unanimous in stating our belief that the defiance of the existing law, the breach of the existing agreement, and the failure to fulfill the promise made by the companies to the government are a serious threat to the recognized practice of labor conciliation, and are moreover, the worst possible weapons any employer could use in a dispute with the legally-constituted bargaining representatives of his employees.*

"*We have reason to believe also that this conduct, which goes to the root of labor relations in this country, raises far wider issues than the isolated dispute with the Canadian Seamen's Union and that there is grave danger that the discord will not be restricted merely to relations between this union and these companies.*"[17]

But Mitchell remained silent. Brockington's report was an appeal for decision. That would be denied. The legal system could no longer claim to be above the interests of contending parties. It would function, without ambiguity, as the arm of the employer class. The legal system, closed to the seamen, would open at the command of the shipowners and the armies of the state would crush any attempts to win justice. Class rule would be supported by class law and the strength of the club.

AS THE LAKE SEASON opened the battle lines were drawn. In March, five more companies signed new agreements with the CSU. The majority of Lake seamen were under contract and all were working a 48-hour week. Still Misener would not bargain.[18]

Joining CSL and Misener were two lines: Transit Tankers and Northwest Transportation. Crews were forced to join the CLSU and those who refused were replaced with scabs. Cornwall CSU business agent Buzz Nuttall warned April 4 that "if any of the vessels of the companies concerned should manage to leave their berths, they will be stopped whenever possible and the non-union crew removed."[19]

On April 15, Branch Lines and Abitibi Navigation signed 48-hour week contracts with the CSU, but more than 700 union seamen remained locked out of their jobs on the ships of Misener and his allies.[20] Slowly the ships began to move.

As in 1946, the CSU intended to protect their agreement by keeping the ships scab-free. In some cases, simple common sense explanations were enough to convince non-union crewmen they belonged on the picket line. On vessel after vessel, scabs joined the picket line or went home. Other crews were "Main Street goons," the dregs of Canada's eastern waterfronts. Their sole interest was doing battle with the pickets.

On April 16, four vessels shipped out of Midland with the help of Sullivan's armed men. Goons beat the local CSU agent and a picketer. Crews of the CSL's *Donnaconna, Gleneagles* and *Stadacona* walked off in protest over the action and to resist a company demand that they tear up their CSU cards to join Sullivan's CLSU.[21]

At first, picket lines were tense, determined, orderly and disciplined. But at Goderich on April 19, 35 crewmen picketing their vessel got a taste of things to come. At 2 a.m. the quiet was broken by the arrival of a squad of Ontario Provincial Police who herded the seamen to one side of the dock. More police approached and at the same instant, 10 taxis rumbled onto the wooden dock, each laden with scabs. The police led the scabs past the pickets, who remained utterly still. CSU picket captain Joe Sullivan stepped forward and called on the scabs to honor the picket line. Of the 50 or 60 heading for the ship, three turned back to join the pickets. The rest headed for the boarding ladders. The pickets moved to head them off, but the police quickly intervened and a brief scuffle resolved itself into a dockside debate as the *Bayton* and the *Laketon*, both owned by Colonial, began to move away.

Moments later, police, reporters and strikers were scrambling for their lives. The *Bayton* had not disconnected its power lines or mooring lines. As the vessel slipped away from the dock, hydro poles snapped and the live lines crackled across the dock. Then the mooring lines broke free and whipped across the dock in a crazy dance with electrical cables. Miraculously, no one was hurt.[22]

The scene at Goderich — the state, dressed in the uniforms of the Ontario Provincial Police intervening on the side of the shipowners — was repeated over and over again throughout the canals and along the Lake ports. Young seamen who had never seen the inside of a jail were sentenced to reformatories and penitentiary for defending the one organization which had stood by them, offered them education and fought for improved working conditions and income.

One of them was Gerry Yetman, who was waiting in Montreal for a trip on a deepsea vessel. With job offers scarce, he decided to head to Cornwall to help on the picket line.

"I left Montreal early in the morning," he recalls, "and by one o'clock in the afternoon I had myself behind bars with 13 charges. When I arrived at the picket camp that morning we decided to go down and picket a ship and talk people into joining the picket lines. There was a plant and a gate there and one of the mates on the boat said, 'You stay there a little while and we'll give you something to warm you up.' He was hooking up a live steam hose to put on us to get us away. We had megaphones and were saying, 'We are in a legal strike. Join us, brothers and sisters.'

"I said to the fellow who was with me, 'By God, he's not going to put any hot steam on me!' He said, 'Me either,' so we went aboard the ship, which was against the law, of course, and we fired the hose in the canal.

"When I was coming off the ship on the port side I saw the RCMP coming on the other side of the canal... The captain came along and said, 'Get off my boat.' I said, 'Okay, captain, I'm just going.' As I was going by him he hit me in the back of the head. I didn't see it coming but he didn't hit me hard enough and I was in pretty good shape. By the time I got up and put a licking on him and ran to catch up with the others, I ran into the arms of the RCMP. Two of them rolled me down the hill. I was in court with 13 charges — assault to cause grievous bodily harm, resisting arrest, you name it — I had it.

"If the occasion came again I would do the same thing. I was defending my right to talk to my brothers to join us. The charge I got convicted of had been in existence from pirate days, that anyone who goes aboard a ship without the permission of the master is liable to a minimum of six months in jail. The judge said he couldn't give us any less than six months even though I had letters from the clergymen in my area that I had a good record. It was a labor dispute. So I was jailed in Guelph for six months as a result of that strike. I served 122 days, four hours and approximately six minutes."[23]

The seamen vowed no vessel would go through the canals with the same scab crew. The Northwest Line found out it was no idle boast. The *Superior* and the *Hudson* both left port with young, inexperienced crews provided by Sullivan. Within 15 days, the *Superior* had gone through seven different crews as CSU delegates made contact and told their story. In each case, the non-union seamen would pack their bags and leave.[24] On April 20, the *Hudson* was sitting idle at the Sydenham River Dock near Wallaceburg, Ontario. Her crew was gone, her anchors had been dropped and the turning keys for the two bridges between the vessel and the Great Lakes could not be found. Steel fitters made new keys overnight, but without a crew, the only move the *Hudson* could make was a gentle rocking. What happened to the crew? "We sent them home to their mothers," picket captain John Torchynuk told the *Windsor Star.* As for the pickets, "they came to get their jobs back," he said, "and as far as they're concerned, the ship stays here until they do."[25]

As in 1946, the CSL's *Glenelg* was a hot spot. Crewed with scabs as the season opened, the vessel was successfully tied up without incident at Thorold. The scabs were taken to the union's picket camp at Humberstone, where CSU Great Lakes director Mike Jackson was giving them an explanation of the strike when the OPP arrived. Jackson continued his pitch. Two of the 18 strikebreakers broke ranks and stayed with the union. The rest returned to the ship with the police. The pickets were warned that if they attempted to tie up the vessel again, they would be bathed with pressurized steam.[26]

On April 22, the *Glenelg* made her way through the Welland Canal. At Lock 7, the scabs began to taunt the picketing seamen. "We're just hoping they will come aboard," one yelled. "There won't be much left to take back to Russia."[27] As the seamen listened to the jeers and ridicule, the scabs showered them with steam and acid from fire extinguishers.[28]

The *Glenelg* reached Lock 5 at 5:45 that afternoon. When the ship was secure in the lock, seamen in the bushes along the canal's east side made their move. Picking up rocks and sticks as they went, they ran across the catwalk spanning the canal, ignoring calls from RCMP officers who ordered them to stop. The seamen pounced on the ship to be met by Sullivan's men armed with iron bars and wrenches. Fights broke out all over the deck.[29]

Jackson and Louis Schmaltz had been at the Thorold CSU office all day. At 5 p.m., they dropped by the picket camp to report on the progress of the lockout and found it deserted. Quickly they headed for the canal and arrived in time to see the fracas under way on the deck of the *Glenelg*. According to Jackson's own account, he went to the canal edge and called on the pickets to leave the ship, an action consistent with the executive's decision to counsel against violence and with Jackson's own strong sense of personal discipline. According to another witness, an employee of CSL, he urged the seamen to "do a good job."[30] Ultimately, it proved irrelevant what Jackson said; it was enough that he opened his mouth.

While the melee continued on deck, the locksman pulled a flood lever, releasing the 30 million gallons of water supporting the ship. It took only eight minutes for the *Glenelg* to drop 65 feet to the bottom of the lock. The CSU seamen were trapped. Their only escape was by way of a maze of tunnels linked by a spiral stairway to the surface. Weights were suspended at the top of the tunnel and the seamen were told that if they attempted to climb out, the weights would be released, crushing anyone below.

The CLSU scabs took to their cabins and locked the doors. Looking aloft, the trapped seamen could see 40 policemen lining the canal's edge.

In their midst stood Corporal J.D. Burger, head of the RCMP detachment, who saw the seamen's predicament and "broke into a hearty laugh." He ordered reinforcements from RCMP detachments in Niagara Falls and St. Catharines and warned the pickets that if "they attempted to get into the maze of tunnels deep under the surface they would flood the area and trap them."[31]

The 34 seamen, along with Larry Boccioletti, a freelance photographer who boarded with them, stood on the deck for three hours before they finally agreed to surrender. It took more than an hour and nearly 20 trips to bring the CSU raiders back to the canal's edge. Twice the police ran out of handcuffs and had to send for more. The seamen emerged from the tunnel joking with the crowd which had gathered.

The seamen were jailed without bail and remanded for a week. CSL attorney Mathewson, who had engineered CSL's assault on the federal Labor Code, announced the company would take every possible measure against the imprisoned seamen. "In addition to charges laid by the police," he said, "civil and criminal actions will be taken by the owners of the Glenelg and the most serious of these charges will be piracy with intent to commit murder." The penalty for piracy was death. CSL managing director Norman Reoch was pleased at the turn of events. "At long last," he told the press, "the proper authorities have stepped in to ensure the proper flow of Canadian produce to centers paid for by the shippers."[32]

The crown prosecutor, however, found insufficient grounds to justify piracy and murder charges.[33] The seamen were charged instead with intimidation and trespass, assault causing bodily harm, mischief, causing damage amounting to $20,000, besetting and conspiracy to beset the officers and crew of the ship.[34] Additional charges under the Canada Shipping Act included unlawful boarding and obstructing the crew and machinery.

"These charges recall the days of Captain Bligh," said CSU president Harry Davis. "They are intended to involve the union's money in all kinds of legal expenses in a further attempt to weaken and destroy the union." The companies were using the charges as a smokescreen, he said "to cloud the real issues — their breaking of the labor laws in this country, their violation of their union contracts, their attempts to force a company union on the seamen and their illegal lockout of CSU members who have been forced on the picket lines because their jobs have been taken away."[35]

On April 24, Jackson was arrested for his role in the Glenelg affair — a shout from the shore. Charged with conspiracy to assault, he was thrown in the Welland jail with the 34 other seamen.

"Gangsters from the worst dens in Montreal have tried to intimidate our men," he wrote in the *Searchlight*. "Our organizer, Jack Howard, was attacked and assaulted by a gang of Sullivan's goons when he was up in Goderich. Our union hall at Thorold was bombed. Live steam and acid from fire extinguishers have been used against our men by the scabs who have stolen their jobs. How come all this is allowed to happen without any arrests being made?

"I am not ashamed of being arrested. On the contrary, I am proud. I am proud because I know I am being arrested for the crime of fighting for the seamen's rights. I have been going to sea since I was 14 and I am well acquainted with hardships, so jail does not faze me. I know the people of this country are with us. I know that working people will help free us. Thus I have no fear of tomorrow because I know that tomorrow belongs to the people."[36]

Sullivan issued a statement as well. CSL was preparing for all-out war. CLSU members would continue to use live steam on the CSU, he told reporters, and "two reinforced hoses would be rigged on all CLSU ships direct to the boilers. Mounted at bow and stern, the hoses would also cover both sides of the vessel."[37]

Transport Minister Lionel Chevrier did not respond to Sullivan's threats, nor to the fact that Sullivan's goons were openly and belligerently armed with heavy clubs. But from his Cornwall home he warned the CSU it was illegal to picket on canal property. All CSU members, he said, would be treated as "unauthorized personnel."[38]

On April 27, the crown set bail for the jailed seamen of $175,000 in property or $87,000 cash.[39] If Davis wanted proof of an attempt to bankrupt the union, he needed to look no further. In the two months since the lockout had begun, 88 seamen had landed behind bars charged with violations of the Canada Shipping Act. The union could not raise the money for bail, but around the canal, farmers and workers put up their homes and farms as security. Still there was not enough money. The seamen came up with a democratic and intelligent solution. One would be released on bail to do what he needed to do on the outside and then return to jail as soon as he could. The bail would be retrieved and another seaman would get a few days relief. It worked well and was not unlike the rotating dispatch of the CSU hiring hall.[40]

There were no speedy trials. The trials of the seamen arrested in the *Glenelg* boarding did not go to court until the end of September. Fifteen were sentenced to seven months, others to nine, and nine were sentenced to serve two years in Kingston Penitentiary.[41]

Mike Jackson, Louis Schmaltz, Basil Dawson and Ray Fougere were tried separately. None of the four had been on board the *Glenelg* on April 22, but all were found guilty of boarding under the Canada Shipping Act because, according to Mr. Justice Henry Hallett, "they were nevertheless aiding and abetting physically and by so doing were principals in the offence under the Canada Shipping Act."[42] The only evidence against Jackson was that of "shouting," but the judge pointed out that "under Section 69, only meager evidence is required to show that they were participants in the act of counselling, aiding or abetting either physically or orally."[43]

The seamen were given a chance to speak before they were sentenced. Louis Schmaltz told the court he would not speak because the court would not believe a union man. Mike Jackson said any hope of union men finding justice in the courts had been destroyed, adding "during the last war we fought in the Battle of the Atlantic to maintain our right to belong to the union of our choice, and now if we fight for the same right, we are sentenced to jail."[44] Mike Jackson and his three companions were sentenced to two years in prison.

Jackson appealed this harsh sentence because he had nothing to lose: he had been given the maximum under the act. There was, however, no way the courts were going to shorten the time given this 25-year-old seaman. When his appeal was heard, the court spliced a three-year "mischief" sentence on his two-year shouting term, to be served concurrently. It added up to three years in Kingston Pen for Mike Jackson.[45]

With the odds as they were, the Lake seamen knew they could not keep the ships tied up permanently. After two months of lockout, new tactics were needed. It was time to change the lockout into a strike. No longer would the seamen's actions be limited to those vessels which had locked them out. Now there would be a much larger target.

CHAPTER SIXTEEN

Red Decks

Your hulls are red, your decks are red
With workers' blood,
You murder agents of the CSL,
You and your RCMPs,
Past masters of the art of scabbery,
And your little boys in blue,
Your swinging clubs won't see you through.
For we are all good union men,
We won't give up come jails or pen.[1]

THE LOCKOUT was two months old when the CSU decided to transform it into a general strike. On June 5 at 11:30 p.m. picket lines went up along the Great Lakes as the seamen went on the offensive for union recognition and the 48-hour week. The strike was aimed primarily at Misener and the CSL, but companies such as Northwest Steamship and Transit Tankers, which supported the outlaw companies, were targeted as well. Within 48 hours, 33 vessels were struck in addition to those already behind picket lines. Many of the vessels were tied up by crews which secretly had maintained their union allegiance.[2]

"We found we could not undo the lockout," recalls Danny Daniels. "There were ships that were not officially part of the lockout but were going along with backing the Canada Steamship Lines (and the) Canadian Lake Seamen's Union. So it was decided to stop the ships altogether instead of having an inept strike against two companies. We would just pull the pin and stop all the ships, as we did in 1946. The shipowners' scheme was to smash the CSU by using a couple of companies as a vanguard. Okay, we'll put a stop to this scheme by tying up the canal."[3]

When Jackson was arrested, the union sent Daniels to Welland to replace him. Jack Derhousoff, the CSU's seaman-cartoonist, divided his time between the picket lines and work on the *Searchlight*. Derhousoff's cartoons, signed with his pen name Der, drew their strength and accuracy from his total immersion in the seamen's life. Der named his central character Joe Beef, recalling both the Montreal waterfront tavern that was a favorite with the seamen and the gripes that the seamen always had to air. Joe Beef, like his real-life shipmates, had gripes, goals, virtues and faults. When they were on strike, so was he, and during the 1948 strike, when so many seamen were landing in jail, Joe Beef went with them.

Daniels was joined in Welland by Eddie Reid, a solid ship's delegate who had become CSU business agent in Saint John, New Brunswick. As the lockout escalated into a strike, Daniels and Reid were bolstered by the arrival of deepsea seamen who began to leave their ships and head to Welland and other ports to do their turn. Among them was Blackie Leonard, a part Cree seaman who grew up in northern Alberta and began his life at sea on the Prairies. Only 19 when he arrived in Welland, Leonard first shipped out from the unlikely port of Fort McMurray, sailing on the river boats to Fort Smith. "I sailed on the *Northland Echo*," he recalled many years later, "a sternwheeler of the Hudson Bay Company, six on, six off, seven days a week for $50 a month plus a $25 a month bonus if you made the season. I did that from when the ice went out in May until the river froze in October or November. You were firing half a cord of wood going down stream and about five-eighths going upstream. You were down in a pit with wood stacked on both sides of you, firing a locomotive boiler carrying 190 pounds of steam. Today what kind of certificate would you have to have to maintain 190 pounds of steam? You'd have to have a first class engineer's ticket, and here they had a kid of 16 doing it."

From Fort McMurray, Leonard moved to the West Coast, shipped out on a fish packer and then went deepsea. VE Day found him off San Francisco and on VJ Day he was in Cardiff, Wales. When he learned of the 1948 strike, he paid off and headed inland. "I went to Welland because I knew if we lost there we would lose the deepsea fleet. Most of the guys on the Welland Canal from the deep water came up on the same theory: if we lose it here, we are going to lose the deep water. I had no other thought of turning to another part of life than what I was doing. I think I got caught up in the trend that was there from the start. The Mounted Police were there to protect the scabs. They were riding the goddamn ships and you just did what was necessary at the time."[4]

Just as Cornwall was the focal point of the 1946 strike, so Welland became the center of the 1948 battle. It was there the seamen made their stand and their survival depended on the degree to which the people of Welland could be mobilized to support them. From the first, there were problems. Thorold longshoremen had refused to handle any ships crewed by scabs and honored CSU picket lines until directed to cross by their national office, under orders from International Longshoremen's Association president Joe Ryan in New York. According to the ILA, there was no strike.[5] Reluctantly, the longshoremen began to unload the vessels. Daniels appealed directly to the longshoremen, to no avail. "They said, 'We all support you, but we can't go against the leadership of our union in the States.' There were four or five ships being unloaded in Thorold at the Q and O dock."

With 200 scabs reported on their way from Montreal to move the ships out, the seamen formulated a plan they hoped would yield a victory. The CSU forces certainly were not strong enough to keep the scabs off the ships. Many of the strikebreakers were thugs recruited from the Main and they would be backed by police. The longshoremen were the key.

Daniels remembers how the plan was formulated: "We were going to crash through the gates leading into the docks. The longshoremen would see this handful of seamen desperately trying to stop 200 scabs and goons. They were going to see us go down fighting and their working class sentiments would affect them. The rank and file long-shoremen would be after their leadership and tell them, 'No way are we going to unload these ships.' Though we were not going to be able to stop the scabs, a change would happen. In our work on the canals, who were we in touch with? Just the leaders of the unions? No, we were in touch with these men. We knew how they felt. We knew they were ashamed of what they were doing. All they needed was just a little push to take that shame and transform it into actions saying, 'Enough is enough.'

"The scabs arrived. The seamen crashed through the gates. They were knocked down, were pummelled. There was no way they could stop the goons and strikebreakers." But the longshoremen could not stand by and watch their brothers go under. The CSU's Thorold office received a call from the longshoremen. They would no longer handle the scab ships. An unexpected benefit was a pledge from the dock company promising that struck ships could no longer use its facilities.[6]

Through hard daily work, the seamen won the community support that could shift the struggle in their favor. Delegates attended community meetings, took collections at plant gates, issued leaflets and prepared radio broadcasts to inform the people of the canals about the issues at stake. The people responded. They knew many of the seamen were from their area and had seen the determined battle they had put up to get a fair shake from the government and the companies. Many of the young seamen who had returned from the war as heroes now were pictured as "aliens," "communist-controlled" and "agents of Moscow." But the reality of the seamen's situation overcame the press propaganda. The people of Welland stood with the strikers. Ethnic organizations fed the seamen, union auxiliaries collected food and clothing, seamen were billeted in workers' homes, dances were organized to show the boys a good time after the hours on the picket lines and workers and farmers turned over the deeds to their homes to raise bail for those in jail.

The seamen put that support to work June 21 in a mass meeting at the Electro-Metallurgical Dock, where the vessels *Sarazen* and *J.P. Burke* were tied up. The *Sarazen* carried a scab crew and was being unloaded. The *Burke* had already discharged its cargo and was awaiting a crew. The CSU called a mass meeting on the dock to protest the *Sarazen's* unloading.

As the 1,000 demonstrators approached the dock they found 75 provincial and Mounted Police guarding the approaches to the unloading area. The demonstrators could go no further, the police advised Daniels and Leonard, because the dock was government property. It was an area used by the townspeople for years for picnics and parking.

The march organizers held a quick meeting, set up a microphone and proposed to the crowd that the people "regain their property." The CSU sound car was rolled up and as union songs played over the speakers, the seamen and their supporters lined up four abreast and followed the car onto the docks.

The noise of the crowd was challenged by the steam-powered cranes as they scooped iron ore from the holds and released it into the waiting gondola railcars on the docks. French and English seamen called to the scabs to come off the ships, but they only watched nervously. The crowd appealed to the crane drivers, all union men, to halt the unloading, but the clamshells continued to bite out tons of ore and drop it into the waiting rail cars. Again, the CSU organizers had a quick consultation and devised a plan. Daniels and two other seamen broke in a fast walk away from the gondolas and the waiting policemen rushed to follow. As they did, Red Rogers and 25 other seamen rushed through the breach left by the police and boarded the gondola. Standing on top of the ore, Rogers called up to the crane operators: "Unload the ship and you'll do so over our bodies."

As the seamen looked up into the steel jaws hanging over them, the crane operator hesitated. One move and the clamshell would open, burying the 26 seamen in tons of iron ore. For three minutes, the operator held the load aloft as the crowd shouted, "Don't kill them, don't kill them." Suddenly, the crane swung away and the load dropped back into the hold of the *Sarazen*. The crane drivers climbed down and went home. Thunderous cheers of relief and victory erupted from the crowd. As the seamen came down from the gondolas, another cheer rose from the demonstrators. The scabs were coming off the ships and joining the strike.[7]

Fern Sayles, Methodist minister in the Welland area, later described the unqualified support the CSU received from the people of Crowland, the community that surrounded the Electro-Metal dock. "Crowland people befriended the seamen and watched the smoke stacks from their homes and factories day and night for any sign of an attempt to get up steam," he wrote. "The *Burke* became a symbol of Welland-Crowland solidarity with the seamen's cause. For 22 days the *Burke* lay helpless. One night a call came from Thorold to help picket two pulp vessels. Only 12 seamen were left beside the *Burke*. At 5 a.m. 50 scabs were brought by truck to 'steal' the ship. Noting the unequal battle from the Electro-Metal factory, furnace men rushed out to help the 12 pickets.

"The battle was furious and the scabs were routed, dispersing in all directions to escape the enraged workers. Some scabs ran down the highway. Others threw their sea bags into the canal and dived in fully clothed, finding safety on the opposite canal bank. Six scabs sought shelter on the *Burke* and the captain, who had his fires ready, started the propeller and immediately pulled the ship from the dock. As the mooring cables stretched, the captain shot the *Burke* out with such power the cable snapped. The cable whipped across the dock like lightning, barely missing the heads of the workers... The *Burke* steamed off manned only by its officers, with six inexperienced and frightened scabs hiding on deck. The sailing of the *Burke* without a crew violated navigation laws. There was, however, neither police nor court action taken against the shipowners or officers. The dock in question is government property. Nevertheless, the Electro-Metallurgical Co. immediately fenced in the whole area, topping it with barbed wire strands."[8]

Despite the growing public support, the seamen were facing escalating violence from the bosses. In Cornwall on June 15, 10 days after the strike began, the CSL's Captain Reoch announced that captains and mates on his vessels would be issued shotguns and revolvers. In addition, he said, "plenty of tear gas equipment is being issued to the boats and steam hoses are being doubled fore and aft. We're making no bones about this: any commie rats who come aboard our boats will get what they're looking for."[9]

The CSU demanded a ruling on the legality of arming Lake vessels during peacetime, pointing out that the issuing of weapons violated the Rush-Bagot agreement between Canada and the United States, which specifically prohibits the arming of ships during peacetime except under mutually-agreed upon circumstances. Ottawa would not intervene.[10] As Blackie Leonard says, "It was war."

The CSU counselled the seamen to avoid violence, but the seamen were not fairytale saints. As TLC president Percy Bengough pointed out, they were from a harsh and violent industry and had been encircled by violence and provocation. "You have read stories of violence on the

Great Lakes," Bengough said. "Even without employer-inspired provocations, the fact that Sullivan could boast quite openly, even on broadcasts, that he had so many men who would go in to see that the seamen did not get a foothold and the companies' assertions that they had live steam hoses — even without all this provocation, it is hardly possible to stage a strike of seamen and make it into a Sunday school picnic."[11]

Education Committees, or flying squads, had first been organized in 1946 to defend the seamen and they were used again in 1947 when Sullivan made his first attempts to break the union. In 1948, they were revived under the direction of men like Eddie Reid, a seaman that fellow-CSU member Gerry Tellier termed a "friendly relations expert." Reid faced a formidable challenge. Scabs were bussed into Welland all the way from Montreal. If not hardened goons themselves, the scabs would be accompanied by armed thugs. The police would be notified of their arrival and would turn out in force to assist them through the picket lines. If the seamen resisted, they would be beaten and clubbed to the ground, then arrested and jailed to await trial on serious charges. Once the scabs were on the ships, they hunkered down behind guns, tear gas, steam and the Canada Shipping Act. A phone call from a high official of the Canadian Lake Seamen's Union gave Reid the tip he needed to set up a lesson for Reoch's scabs.

The CLSU official had decided things were getting too rough. He asked Reid to meet him in a small café halfway between Thorold and Welland. Reid knew the man well and feared a set-up. Two seamen cased the restaurant and gave the all-clear. They sat at the counter and drank coffee while Reid, the CLSU official and his bodyguard met in a booth. There was going to be a big shake-up in the CLSU, the official told Reid, and he wanted out. He wanted to do something to right himself with Eddie. He told him that a large contingent of scabs was coming to Welland and showed him the route of their trip and their schedule.

At 3 o'clock on the morning of June 24 a group of about 12 seamen lay in wait in the tall grass at a crossroads known as Chambers Corners, about nine miles west of Welland. Two vans of scabs slowed to make the turn. The seamen ran out, pulled open the doors and beat everyone within reach. Although outnumbered the seamen had the advantage of surprise. The two van loads of scabs never made it to their destination.

Two men, Charlie Scott and Len Cummings, were brought to trial over the incident at Chambers Corners. Eleven of the scabs were brought in to identify the two seamen, but they failed. On the third try, a twelfth scab identified Scott as an assailant, but the judge remained doubtful because Scott, with pale yellow hair, was the only blonde in the police line-up. The scabs claimed Scott had attacked them with a baseball bat.[12] The judge overcame his hesitancy, found Scott guilty of "wounding with intent to do grievous bodily harm," and sentenced him to three years in penitentiary. Scott was 28 years old and it was his first brush with the law. The judge looked down at him and said, "I can't for the life of me understand why you men with no records break the laws so seriously."[13]

Bats and clubs were standard equipment for Sullivan's goons. For seamen who fought back, there was a jail cell. Seamen were locked up all over Ontario and the Welland jail was packed. In mid-July, the CSU members imprisoned in Welland staged a hunger strike to protest the arrest and detention of Canadian seamen. Daniels and the other Welland-area strike leaders planned a demonstration to back the demands of those in jail. The results proved Daniels' contention that "when trade unionists or others start to blame the people for lack of support, it could well be they did not do the groundwork to get to the people. If you do the groundwork, they are there."[14]

The day of the demonstration was gray and wet. It was pouring rain as 1,500 people crowded into Meritt Park to hear Harry Davis and Danny Daniels update them on the strike. The turnout was good, but the organizers could not hide a little disappointment. They had asked the workers of Welland to down tools in protest and join the demonstration, which was to march to the jail to back the seamen's hunger strike. But as the demonstration began, cheers broke from the crowd. "The factory workers appeared," reported Rev. Sayles, "their faces black with factory dust. It was the first time in the history of the Niagara Peninsula that the workers had left their jobs in support of united action."[15]

The meeting moved to the Hungarian Hall to get out of the downpour. After the speeches, the demonstrators marched down Main Street to the Welland County Jail. A huge picket line formed in front of the jail and the imprisoned seamen sang Solidarity Forever in their cells while the crowd chanted "Free the seamen, free the seamen" in the street outside.

Suddenly a call came from the crowd: "Break down the walls, let's have our Bastille." "As action-oriented as I was, there was no way," remembers Daniels. "I discussed with Blackie Leonard how honest these shouts were. The crowd was picking them up. We took over a bandstand in the area and I made a speech urging the workers against direct action. We had to bring the demonstration to an end. We had succeeded in what we wanted to do. We had carried out every item on the agenda and we didn't want to go far out and lose them."[16]

It was a wise move, but at the time, neither Daniels nor anyone else realized how wise their decision was. They were standing at the mouth of a carefully-set trap. "Behind the jail walls 50 Mounties were stationed," Sayles wrote later, "and inside the courthouse 25 Provincial Police were in hiding. All were well-armed and possessed gas bombs. The authorities could claim no part of the credit that trouble was avoided. The people themselves, expressing militant support for the seamen's cause, though fearless, were disciplined."

But the CSL was determined to make good its threats of violence whether the seamen cooperated or not. Mike Hornak was 23 in 1948. He was from the Welland area but had never sailed on the Lakes, shipping out deepsea in 1943 and working on the North Atlantic run during the war. A third mate and a member of the Canadian Merchant Service Guild, the officers' union, he was working his way to the West Coast. His last ship had been sold in Sorel and he wanted a Lake job to take him to the Lakehead and set him on the road west.

Hornak landed a job on a ship docked in Goderich and he and other members of the crew were driven from Toronto to join her. As they approached Goderich, their vehicle was joined by cars carrying police and other men. When they arrived at the dock they found it picketed by a handful of seamen. More police were scattered around the dock. Hornak and some of the others decided on the spot to honor the picket line. As others crossed the line and joined the ship, Hornak just walked away. A few days later he and a couple of shipmates joined the seamen's picket line.

July 14 found Hornak and four other seamen in Sarnia. After some discussion, they decided to go out to the Point Edwards Dock on the outskirts of town to try to talk the crew of the CSL's *Lethbridge* into joining the strike. It was 3 or 4 in the afternoon when they reached the ship. "I had never boarded a ship before, but it sounded like a good idea at the time," Hornak remembers. "You associated these things with trespassing, and what the hell is trespassing as a charge, anyway? We had intentions of talking to these guys and you couldn't talk to these guys if you didn't go on the ships. None of us were armed in any way, shape, or form. We went up the gangplank together."[17]

Along with Hornak on the gangplank were Curley Jackson, 20, Bob Schumacher, 26, Eddie Rogozinski, 19, George McDonald, 16, and Alex Black, 19. Mike Hornak was the first up the gangplank and onto the deck of the *Lethbridge*. He and Jackson started toward the bow just as the other four were about to step onto the deckplates. Rogozinski, who like Hornak was not in the CSU but had joined the picket lines out of sympathy, later testified that as they reached the deck they "didn't see anyone to ask permission to go on board and didn't hear anyone yell at us."[18] Hornak saw someone and approached him. Although he didn't know it at the time, it was First Mate Alex Houston, who was promoted to captain shortly after the *Lethbridge* incident.

Houston testified he saw the unarmed men coming over the side and was told they wanted to take the crew off. He said they would not and grabbed a club, a tear gas gun and a steam hose to repel them. As he turned on the steam to scald the seamen the hose exploded under the pressure, engulfing the deck in steam.[19] At that moment, Chief Engineer Melville M. Murphy stepped from his cabin between the gangplank and the steam hose. He raised his CSL-issue shotgun, took a bead on the young seamen and pulled the trigger. As the four seamen went down, Murphy turned to his cabin to get another shell for his single-shot gun.[20]

"It happened so fast I didn't see the engineer come out of his room," Hornak remembers. "It was almost like he was waiting for us. He grabbed his gun and came running out. We heard the blast and the kids fell. Rogozinski and Blackie were just coming on board when they got the pellets."[21]

The seamen fled, carrying their wounded and chased on the way by a second helping of lead from Murphy. They staggered to a nearby field, where they were discovered by the Sarnia police and taken to hospital. Black and Jackson had pellets in the chest and abdomen. Rogozinski had more than a dozen wounds in the legs and chest, "some of them penetrating quite deep." Schumacher was carrying a dozen pellets.[22]

Hornak, who was uninjured, "helped get Eddie into the ambulance and to the hospital. I waited for the report on him because I wanted to know if he was all right or going to die or what. I had waited about half an hour to an hour when the Mounties arrested me. I could have taken off, but I never considered it."[23]

Rogozinski was in hospital for three weeks. All five seamen were charged with illegally boarding the vessel without permission. None had any previous convictions. All received six month sentences except Hornak, who had refused to name those who were with him on the ship. The judge accused him of perjury and told the young seaman that in addition to his one-year sentence he would recommend that Hornak be stripped of his citizenship. Hornak was of Czechoslovakian heritage but had been naturalized in 1935 when his father became a Canadian citizen.[24]

"Your honor," Hornak said, "judging from the justice you get in Canadian courts, I feel kind of ashamed to call myself a Canadian," to which the judge responded, "Hornak, you'd better go to Russia to get your justice."[25]

And what of Chief Engineer Murphy, who shot the seamen down without warning? Unlike the seamen, who were charged under the Canada Shipping Act, Melville M. Murphy was tried by a jury. W.A. Donahue, the defense counsel, argued that Murphy fired "in defense of law and order in this country."[26] The *Toronto Telegram* pointed out that

"Murphy admitted shooting the men without warning because he considered it an emergency."[27] It should be remembered that Murphy, like all officers of the CSL, was under orders to shoot "unauthorized personnel" attempting to come aboard.[28] Murphy was found not guilty and returned to his job with the CSL.

In a July 27 comment on the violence of the strike the *Peterborough Examiner* pointed out that "the most blatant evidence of this lawlessness has been the bloody heads of warring seamen, the arming of the ships and the shooting engaged in by one of the ship's officers. Behind this (and this is the primary cause), is the conduct of the Canada Steamship Lines. Its officials have taken the law into their own hands, which is not the ordinary way for law to be administered. The Canada Steamship Lines is chiefly to blame. That is apparent from the Report of the Conciliation Board appointed to deal with the dispute. What is the use of labor laws, labor codes and the like if a company like the Canada Steamship Lines disregards them when it wishes? Is that the way to encourage union members to stick to their contracts and behave like peaceful citizens?"[29]

From the beginning of its attempt to bring Misener and Reoch to the negotiating table, the CSU had tried to induce the government to step into the fray and to bring an end to the dispute. When the Brockington-McNish report was turned in, the CSU began an intensive campaign to persuade the government to implement its recommendations. The federal government did not respond. Instead, it allowed the RCMP to be used as strikebreakers.

The illegal actions of the companies prompted the CSU and the Trades and Labor Congress to call on the government to cancel their shipping licenses.[30] But Labor Minister Humphrey Mitchell declared that it was not within the scope of his department to act against company violence or to cancel the licenses of these companies.[31]

Under the newly-passed Industrial Relations and Disputes Act, the CSU charged four companies with "failing to bargain collectively with the union with the view to completion of collective agreements." After months of waiting, the union received the decision of the board set up under the Act. The CSU complaints were filed under an inappropriate section, the board ruled. Therefore, they were dismissed.[32]

CHAPTER SEVENTEEN

Enter the SIU

AS THE SEAMEN were fighting the battle of the Lakes and the canals, other forces were at work which would affect their struggle to maintain their union, the eight-hour day and the merchant fleet. To hide the reality of class conflict in the strike, the companies, the government and the press portrayed the fight as one between rival unions. Percy Bengough's denunciation of this line was unequivocal. "Let us be fair," he said. "The so-called Canadian Lake Seamen's Union is not wanted by Canadian seamen. Every bit of evidence forces one to the belief that the Canada Steamship Lines and the Sarnia and Colonial Steamship Companies are father and mother to this Canadian Lake Seamen's Union. It has every appearance of being their baby, both in looks and actions."[1]

Bengough's charge was confirmed by Sullivan's closest henchmen, who were deserting the CLSU and then, to atone for their sins, were swearing out affidavits confessing to their own crimes and those of their former employers. One of the most damaging was that of Sullivan's Welland business agent, Robert Lindsay.

Lindsay admitted that on July 3, "at the request of Capt. Misener," he placed "21 seamen aboard the *J.P. Burke* at Welland accompanied by about 20 other persons who were supplied with baseball bats. Each of these persons was told by Jack Chapman and Frank Mimee, respectively vice-president and organizer for the Canadian Lake Seamen's Union, in my presence, to use the bats on any persons who got in his way on the slightest provocation." Lindsay further swore that to his knowledge Sullivan's outfit was "under the control of the companies concerned, namely Canada Steamship Lines, Sarnia and Colonial Steamship Co. Ltd., and North Western Steamship Co." This all was old news to the seamen, but there was a disclosure in Lindsay's testimony which was a bombshell. According to his affidavit, "on July 15, 1948, Capt. Scott Misener made a statement to me as follows: 'We have a move afoot in Ottawa to get rid of Bengough of the Trades and Labor Congress along with certain elements in the CSU.' He also stated to me that he and Capt. Reoch had instructed the Canadian Lake Seamen's Union in Montreal to apply for affiliation with the American Federation of Labor."[2]

Lindsay's charges, which came on July 16, 1948, raised a series of troubling questions. Were the shipowners really powerful and arrogant enough to attempt to get rid of Percy Bengough because of his support for the seamen? Could the Canadian Lake Seamen's Union get an affiliation from the American Federation of Labor? Would the AFL stoop so low as to give an affiliation to an organization which was openly siding with the employers against a locked-out union?

In 1948, as in the past, the support of the Canadian labor movement was the key to the CSU's success and survival. To Bengough, president of the TLC, the shipowners' assault on the CSU was nothing less than an assault on the trade union movement as a whole. He ordered an emergency TLC conference to be held in Ottawa August 5 to determine what assistance could be given to the CSU in its battle with the shipowners. The Canadian Congress of Labor was invited to send delegates as well.

As the labor congresses gathered in one part of the capital, the national Liberal Party convention met in another hotel to bid farewell to William Lyon Mackenzie King and to elect a new leader. Outside, 150 seamen and supporters picketed, handing out a four-page Open Letter to the Delegates of the National Liberal Convention. It outlined the history of the dispute and asked delegates, "Which Side Are You On? Will your party continue to maintain silence in the face of a terrible injustice to Canadian seamen? Does your party approve of giving state police protection to shipping companies who have chosen to defy the nation's laws? Does your party endorse an anti-union policy which may lead to the destruction of all trade unions?"[3]

The seamen pointed to the fact that the authors of the Brockington-McNish report were prominent Liberal supporters and requested that the convention hear a presentation from Harry Davis. Their request was put before the Resolutions Committee by Senator Arthur Roebuck and Mrs. Cecile O'Regan, president of the Ottawa East Liberal Women's Association. There was not enough time, the committee decided, to hear from the union's president. The doors were closed with the seamen outside.[4]

Across town, Bengough was telling 700 delegates representing more than half a million workers that the trade union movement would "never give the employer the right to dictate to us who is going to lead our unions." The emergency conference took the position that the defense of the Canadian trade union movement depended upon labor's ability to defend the CSU.[5]

But the TLC conference was picketed as well, this time by representatives of the AFL unions led by Frank Hall, Canadian vice-president of the Brotherhood of Railway and Steamship Clerks, Freight Handlers,

Express and Station Employees. Hall was a roadman, an officer appointed by the union's American headquarters to represent the international union in Canada. He and eight other roadmen, representing various American-based unions, boycotted the TLC/CCL emergency conference because the meeting was, in Hall's eyes, attended by "about 98 percent communists and two percent fellow travellers."[6] Hall had stretched the already over-extended term "communist" to include anyone backing the seamen's struggle.

Hall was well aware of the companies' actions against the seamen, but that did not concern him or his Roadmen's Association. "Whether the companies are altruistic or not in the positions they have taken is beside the point," he told reporters.[7]

On September 1, Hall made an announcement which staggered the Canadian trade union movement. He had personally conducted a merger between Sullivan's CLSU and the Seafarers International Union. The CLSU was dissolved and its membership transferred into the SIU. Jack Chapman became the first head of the SIU on the Lakes. Sullivan, tainted by the smell of company unionism which clung to the CLSU, was tossed out and returned to his chalet.[8] Hall answered the questions raised by Lindsay's affidavit. The CLSU would get the American stamp through the SIU's international connection. By merging the CLSU with the SIU, Hall could carry the shipowners' campaign against the CSU right onto the floor of Trades and Labor Congress conventions.[9]

Hall's plan was not without drawbacks. The SIU had an ugly history and only one local in Canada — the tiny Vancouver local which had refused to join the CSU four years before. In 1947, the TLC convention had thrown the SIU out and declared it a dual organization in Canada because it had signed back-door agreements with B.C. employers to win certifications from the CSU. The TLC recognized only one seamen's union in Canada, the CSU.[10]

But Hall had a ready reply for this objection. "As an American Federation of Labor union, and thus a sister organization of the great number of AFL unions affiliated with the Congress, the Seafarers' (union) is entitled to equal status with these unions," Hall said. "The Canadian Seamen's Union becomes a dual organization, with no right or recognition from any bona fide group." Why had he intervened to organize a merger of unions in another industry outside his? "It was a choice between the CSU," he explained, "as an organization reputed to be communist, and the CLSU, as one claimed to be a company union. We chose the lesser evil."[11]

Although Hall claimed to have masterminded the merger, he was merely the front man. An affidavit sworn a year later by Frank Mimee, Sullivan's top organizer who subsequently went to work for the SIU, revealed that around "the end of August 1948, in various consultations with Capt. N. Reoch, manager of the Canada Steamship Lines, and with a Mr. Pride, also of that company, I was informed that a conference had taken place in Toronto around the middle of August 1948, attended by Mr. Reoch and Mr. Misener of Colonial and Sarnia Steamships Ltd., and Mr. J.A. Mathewson, K.C., and representatives of the Seafarers International Union, namely A. MacDonald, David Joyce, Harold Banks, and also in attendance was Frank Hall, Canadian vice-president of the Brotherhood of Railway and Steamship Clerks; that at this conference it was decided that the Seafarers International Union would absorb the Canadian Lakes Seamen's Union and take over the contracts which this body had with the Canada Steamship Lines and the Misener companies."[12]

The merger gave the SIU a membership on the Great Lakes for the first time. CLSU members who had been hired off Montreal's Main or had signed with the CLSU at their employers' insistence to keep their jobs were absorbed by the international. But to complete the plan, the Trades and Labor Congress had to be persuaded to throw out the CSU and to welcome the SIU. Those within the congress who supported the CSU had to be discredited or removed from office. With this in mind, Hall and a small group of roadmen formed the Anti-Red Committee. Composed of about 23 paid officials of international unions, the Anti-Red Committee set out to achieve in Canada what the AFL was doing to progressive forces in the American unions: a complete purge of left-wingers, especially communists, from union leadership. The Anti-Red Committee could not count a single representative of a Canadian national union in its ranks.[13] The press praised Hall's initiative. The *Maritime Merchant*, for example, lauded the "loyal Canadians in the TLC who have banded together at long last to fight communism in an organized fashion (who) have the respect and best wishes of all good citizens. They are rendering a service to the nation."[14]

Bengough refused to be deflected from support of the CSU. The TLC executive council reaffirmed its solidarity in an emergency session which upheld the decision of the 1947 convention that had declared the SIU a dual union in Canada. The executive saw Hall's moves as anti-unionism masquerading as anti-communism and considered his actions an overt effort to retain U.S. control over the Canadian labor movement.

The TLC's leadership believed "the question of communism has been brought into the issue by the employers," reported the *TLC News*, "and they took the position they would not do business with an organization having communist officers. Our membership must remember that we asked for a Labor Act giving the right to the workers to have a union of their own choice and bargain through representatives of their own choosing, not the employers' choosing, not Mr. Hall's choosing, but the choice to be made by the membership of the union. If this Congress ever submits that the employers have a right to say who shall represent a union, then all unions will soon become company unions. The present issue is not one of communism. The issue is that the members of an affiliated union are in a legal strike. While on strike with such hostile employers, as government boards have shown them to be, no one with any semblance of trade union principles would condemn the workers and side with the employers."[15]

The executive went a step further. Hall was charged with violation of the spirit and the law of Article 3, Section 8, of the TLC constitution, which prohibited the formation of a dual organization and provided for the suspension of any person or organization which assisted in the formation of a dual organization. For his gross violation, Hall was indefinitely suspended from the TLC.[16]

Hall's union was offered the opportunity to repudiate his actions, but when no reply was forthcoming from the Grand President in the United States, the Brotherhood of Railway and Steamship Clerks joined Hall on the suspension list. Hall, confident of his support from business and the AFL, was defiant. He boasted that the "Congress cannot beat us without wrecking itself."[17] He laid plans to confront the TLC leadership at the scheduled annual convention in Victoria, B.C., in October in an all-out test of the power of the international unions over Canadian trade unionists.

As the congress convention came to order October 11, Hall was sitting outside. One of the first delegates to be recognized by the chair was a representative of an international union. He demanded that Hall and the other Brotherhood of Railway and Steamship Clerks delegates be allowed into the hall. Bengough ruled, in line with the constitution, that the suspended delegates could not be seated. They would, however, be allowed to come into the hall to hear the report of the committee on Officers' Reports. It was that committee which reviewed the suspension decision. It was only proper and democratic to allow the suspended delegates to defend themselves at that time. Until then, they could wait in the lobby.

On the second day of the convention, Hall and his fellow delegates were admitted for the committee's report. Committee chairman J.E. Beaudoin reported that the committee agreed completely with the "executive's statement that the labor movement has been faced during this past year with the most vicious opposition and concentrated smear campaign." He added, "The committee approves the action of the Executive Council in recognizing the decisions of the convention and abiding by them at all times."

The committee then divided its report into two sections. First it addressed itself to the dispute between the CSU and the Lake shipping companies, finding that the CSU had acted properly and legally in all its attempts to reach an agreement. The reason no settlement was achieved, the committee concluded, was because the companies refused to bargain and because the federal government refused to implement the recommendations of its own appointed commissioners. This section of the report received unanimous concurrence from the delegates.

The committee then turned to the second question — the CLSU-SIU merger and the actions taken by the executive in dealing with Hall and his union.[18] It summed up its findings as follows:

"It is most regrettable that while an affiliate of this congress was involved in a desperate struggle for union recognition on the Great Lakes, and the negotiation of new agreements for deepsea shipping, they should also become involved in a struggle for their very existence as a trade union. It is also to be regretted that a senior officer of another affiliate of this congress, without consulting the Executive Council of this congress, was the medium through which an effort was made to substitute a union dual to this congress, for a properly accredited organization of this congress.

"This congress has gone on record as being autonomous in every way, shape or form. The most recent decision in this respect was made at the 1946 convention held in Windsor, Ontario.

"This congress has also gone on record that the Seafarers International Union of America is a dual organization in Canada. This decision was made at the 1947 convention held in Hamilton, Ontario...

"Your committee must concur in the decision of the Executive Council that an officer of an affiliate of this congress rendered assistance to a dual organization to the detriment of a duly and accredited affiliated union. Their only recourse, therefore, was the suspension of the affiliated organization to which the responsible officer belongs.

"It is regrettable that an affiliate such as the Brotherhood of Railway and Steamship Clerks, Freight Handlers, Express and Station Employees should be suspended because of the actions of one person; however, it must be pointed out that there is no definite provision in the constitution of the Trades and Labor Congress of Canada which permits the Executive Council to do otherwise.

"Your committee feels that while many opinions have been expressed publicly and otherwise, the basic question at the present time is whether or not the action of the Executive Council should be endorsed by this convention. Your committee is of the opinion that Article 3, Section 8, of the constitution of the Trades and Labor Congress of

Canada gave the Executive Council the authority to discipline the offending party and they had no other alternative but to suspend the Brotherhood of Railway and Steamship Clerks...

"Your committee, after thorough examination of all evidence submitted, recommends endorsation of the action taken by the Executive Council and that their action in this matter be sustained."[19]

Gerry McManus rose to speak in support of the report, stressing that the question was one of "too much CSU, not too much communism," as far as the shipowners were concerned. He was interrupted by Bengough who asked the secretary to read Lindsay's affidavit into the proceedings. As McManus pointed out, Lindsay's statement had been borne out: an AFL affiliate was challenging the CSU on the Lakes and there was a move afoot within the congress to unseat Bengough and any other CSU supporter.

A.R. Johnson, a representative of an international, challenged the committee recommendation. Quoting from the constitution, he reminded the convention of the requirement that "any international union holding a charter with the American Federation of Labor shall be entitled to affiliate its entire Canadian membership ... to membership in this congress." Bengough refused to accept Johnson's argument, which implied an absolute priority of AFL affiliates over Canadian unions. Johnson's quotation was correct, Bengough said, but the constitution contained important conditions and safeguards. Article 3, Section 5, required that "no international or national union shall be accepted where its jurisdiction conflicts with that of an organization already affiliated." The CSU had been affiliated to the TLC even before the SIU had been created by the AFL executive.

When the SIU had been formed with Harry Lundeberg as president, Bengough continued, "it was given jurisdiction by the American Federation of Labor without any consultation or knowledge of what the situation was in Canada, which was frankly admitted by the Executive Council of the AFL. He (Lundeberg) was given jurisdiction over all fishermen and seamen in the United States and Canada. This congress has never authorized such action. We want the utmost cooperation with the American Federation of Labor, but we certainly must be masters in our own house."[20]

The AFL, with the open backing of the employers, had selected the CSU for a test of its ability to direct the post-war course of the Canadian labor movement. Canadian unions had emerged from the struggle against fascism more strongly organized than ever before. In decisive battles in basic industries, including shipping, unionists had broken through long-standing wage and contract barriers to win large pay increases and reduced working hours. At the same time, Canadian independence had been strengthened by the war effort. Canadian unions were insisting on the right to settle their own affairs, both in domestic and foreign policy.[21]

When Hall was given the opportunity to speak in his own defense, he laid his cards on the table. "I suggest that the question here is not one of recalcitrant and reactionary employers," he said, "the question here is one of revolutionary trade unionism and whether that's the kind of thing we're going to tolerate."[22] He tried to shift the blame away from the shipowners to the seamen and the TLC leadership, despite the unanimous convention support for the actions of both.

Apart from the political question, he argued, "American Federation of Labor unions have the unqualified right of affiliation."[23] The TLC had no power to enforce any sanctions against his behavior, he concluded, for the simple reason that he was "not responsible to this congress, I am responsible only to my own organization."[24]

The next speaker was delegate W.W. Turple. His appearance caused pandemonium in the ranks of Hall's followers. A rank and file member of the Brotherhood, Turple had been elected by his Lodge to speak against Hall's position. Hall hurriedly did an about-face, using his union's suspension to question Turple's credentials. Hall himself had been allowed to speak against his union's suspension, but he relied on the suspension to deny the rank and file delegate the same democratic right. Bengough asked Turple to step down until the Credentials Committee could bring down a report. The committee ruled in Turple's favor the next day, too late for him to speak against his vice-president.[25]

There were many to take Turple's place, but few among the roadmen who were willing to speak against the internationals. One was Kent Rowley, Canadian vice-president of the United Textile Workers of America. Hall and his followers claimed to be innocent, Rowley said, "and yet they attacked the jurisdiction of a bona fide affiliate of this great congress in Canada. Let us make clear that at a time when one of our largest affiliates was out on the front line — on the picket line — fighting for their liberty and that of their members on the Great Lakes, that an international officer in this congress went in with an already-established company organization and endeavored to destroy the established jurisdiction of a body represented by this congress."[26]

The motion was put to a roll call vote so that each delegate would be required to stand and vote publicly. The roadmen voted first. With the exception of Rowley and a few others, they cast their ballots with Hall and against the TLC executive. Then the rank and file delegates took their turn. The result was a smashing victory for the executive, the CSU and the fight for Canadian trade union autonomy: 545 votes in favor of the suspension and 198 against.[27] It was a sweeping denunciation of

Hall's attempt to destroy the CSU and bring the TLC under the complete domination of the AFL.

The Committee on Officers' Reports then proposed a motion to heal the breach. The suspension of Hall and his union would be lifted, but because "of his unwarranted activities detrimental to the Canadian Seamen's Union," Hall would be censured. The question of the SIU's affiliation would be placed before the TLC-AFL Coordinating Committee "with the view of arriving at an understanding whereby the sovereignty of this Trades and Labor Congress of Canada will continue unchanged."[28] The delegates accepted the compromise.[29]

The CSU was safe within the congress for the time being, but remained besieged on every other front. The CSL, Misener and the SIU had not been removed from the Lakes by the TLC vote and the seamen now faced a fight to win contracts on the deepsea vessels. With more and more shipowners registering their vessels under the flags of other nations, the CSU was faced with a battle for the survival of the fleet and every job in it.

CHAPTER EIGHTEEN

Farewell to the Fleet

WINTER FORCED A BREAK in the Lake struggle. As ice finally brought all shipping to a halt from Montreal to the Lakehead, the seamen could assess their victories and their losses. The attack by Hall and the American Federation of Labor roadmen had been beaten back, but the strike itself had cost the union more than $60,000. Many of its best front-line leaders were cooling their heels in jail. The SIU was building its strength on the Lakes and it was certain that Misener and the CSL were not prepared to stop their opposition to the CSU until every vessel on the Lakes was flying the Jolly Roger of company unionism. Now the seamen confronted yet another challenge: negotiations for a new deepsea agreement to replace the contract expiring October 15, 1948. On the East Coast, the union faced the Shipping Federation of Canada. On the West Coast, the employers were organized into the Shipowners Association of B.C. Even before negotiations began, the Shipping Federation of Canada let it be known that the East Coast operators would terminate their agreement with the CSU. Battle would be joined on a new front.[1]

The CSU had always been able to sign deepsea agreements without job actions. In 1948, with the Lake dispute unresolved and the union under siege, the leadership was seeking a one-year agreement which would tide over the blue water fleet until the union was stronger. CSU negotiators were directed to seek a 15 percent wage increase, a ten-cent-an-hour increase in overtime rates and improvements in working conditions. These were modest proposals submitted as "proof of our desire to maintain peace in the industry and for the continued existence of a strong merchant marine," Davis said, warning that CSU demands would rise if the seamen were forced into a strike.[2] No matter how much the union might have liked to avoid a confrontation, there was one issue which could not be brushed aside: the accelerating elimination of Canada's deepsea fleet.

"We saw one of the ways they were fighting the union was (they were) beginning to hire foreign seamen abroad," recalls Harry Davis, "and not only in the West Indies, but wherever they could pick up guys to replace a seaman who got sick or didn't come back aboard ship. They'd keep them on when they got back here. We saw this as part of the whole attempt to weaken the union by replacing Canadian with foreign seamen."[3]

But there was an even more direct attack on the jobs of Canadian seamen. The employers were changing the registry of Canadian ships to the flags of Honduras, Panama or the United Kingdom and paying the entire Canadian crew off in foreign ports without as much as a thank you. The Canadians were replaced by men desperate for work, often displaced persons from Europe with little or no acquaintance with trade unionism. As the flag on the stern was changed, the shipowners slashed wages, rolled back working conditions and eliminated the CSU.

The CSU saw this not only as a move against the Canadian seamen and their union, but as an attack on Canadian taxpayers as well. It was a violation of the entire spirit behind the creation of the Canadian fleet. "These vessels," Davis explained, "built out of taxpayers' money, were sold to Canadian operators at an extremely low cost, under the condition that they would maintain them under the Canadian flag and employ Canadian seamen."[4] The union sought a meeting with the east coast operators to discuss the problem and to negotiate a new agreement. "Canadian firms do not want to sign further agreements with the CSU," the Shipping Federation replied, "until that organization casts out the communists among its leaders and officials."[5]

Eventually, however, after persistent pressure, the east coast operators agreed to meet the union. At the first meeting, the shipowners tabled their demands: a $20 a month cut in wages and a 10 percent reduction in overtime rates.[6] Davis, Conrad Sauras and Gerry McManus were the chief union negotiators, but in line with CSU practice, a number of rank-and-file seamen attended the Montreal bargaining sessions. Bud Doucette was among them. "It was pretty evident to everybody," he recalls, "that the shipowners were not looking for conciliation or settlement. Their intention, of course, was to utilize their power, their strength throughout the Shipping Federation, to harness the opposition to the CSU that existed in the Canadian labor movement, particularly among the AFL roadmen ... and, of course, to use such anti-labor governments as the Duplessis government in the province of Quebec to smash the Canadian Seamen's Union."[7]

While the Shipping Federation was marshalling its allies, it pressed its offensive at the bargaining table. New concessions were demanded, including elimination of the union's hiring hall and the time-tested rotary system of dispatch.[8] "We were in a predicament," remembers Doucette, "and there was no way out of it. The shipowners demanded an end to the hiring hall. He would do the hiring and firing. You can imagine what would happen to me and many, many others who had been active advocates and organizers for the union. They would simply choose not to hire us and they would hire as they had done in the old days: the servile, the voiceless and those who were willing to be pushed around. Besides that, there was an additional provocation. The shipowners refused to back down on their right to sell or transfer flags during the course of a voyage. Every conciliatory effort made by the union was met with a stone-wall opposition. There was absolutely no flexibility in the shipowners' position."[9]

The CSU gave a two-fisted reply. A quick strike vote held in every deepsea port produced a virtually unanimous strike mandate. At the same time, however, the union applied to the federal Department of Labor for the establishment of a conciliation board to assist the parties to reach a settlement. Recommendations of such a board were not binding and carried no legal weight, but under federal law, no collective agreement could be terminated until the conciliation board report was handed down. The seamen would gain an extension of their precious contract protection. The Department of Labor appointed Justice J.O. Wilson chairman of the board. The union named John Kerry as its representative and the shipowners nominated Theodore Meighen.[10]

On the morning of November 23, Davis, Sauras and McManus arrived at Montreal's new court house and proceeded to Room 319, where the conciliation board was waiting to begin its deliberations. One look across the table told the union men all they needed to know about the shipowners' strategy. Seated with the deepsea operators was J.A. Mathewson, the man they were certain had engineered the CSL's anti-union campaign on the Lakes. The CSU's representatives were hardly in their seats when Mathewson began to retrace the course he had steered in the last Lakes negotiations. First he challenged the board's right to sit at all and then he questioned the legal validity of the Labor Code.[11] Both had been upheld in rulings during the Lakes negotiations and Mathewson was simply initiating a strategy designed to set legal windmills in motion while the shipowners developed their offensive. The only way for negotiations to proceed would be for the union to concede the very issues the seamen considered non-negotiable.

Mathewson lit into the seamen with attacks on their wages, their working conditions and their abilities. Conditions established in past contracts would be abolished, he vowed, and seamen would have to do work that historically and contractually belonged to the longshoremen. The seamen would forfeit "dirty money" and clean holds, bulkheads and decks contaminated with bulk arsenic, organic matter such as hides or bones, caustic soda and other dangerous cargoes with no extra compensation.[12] Wages would be reduced $20 to $50 a month and the protection of shoreside delegates would be eliminated. Patrolmen would be denied access to the vessels to handle beefs.[13]

Mathewson still wasn't finished. In front of the board, the CSU leadership, the rank and file members of the negotiating committee and the press, he referred to the seamen as "men of mature years, but probably with a boy's mentality."[14] The seamen grumbled and stirred but did not leave their seats. The shipowners, however, could not contain themselves. They rushed to support Mathewson's slurs with a chorus of derogatory remarks. One of the board members asked J.A. Sauvé, of Canadian National Steamships, how many seamen had died during the war. Three years before, Canada's merchant sailors had been hailed as the "Fourth Arm" of Canada's defense and considered a major factor in keeping the war off Canadian soil. According to Sauvé however, their seamanship was poor and the percentage of Canadian seamen lost was fairly small.[15] The percentage seemed quite high to the seamen, especially when compared to the tally of shipowners who died to protect Canada from Nazism. The ratio worked out to about 1,146 to zero.

That wasn't all. Sauvé complained that before the CSU came on the scene, "we selected the men and got a better class of men. Our difficulty today is that the men that are supplied just cannot be kept to the rail." As he listened to the denunciations and accusations flowing from the shipowners' side of the table, Harry Davis reflected that "the shipowners heard democracy knocking at the gates and they don't like it."[16]

Then it was the turn of the manager of Saguenay Terminals Ltd., the shipping arm of the Aluminum Company of Canada. On the bauxite run his vessels made between British Guiana and Arvida, Quebec, he said, seamen behaved like first class tourists on a West Indies cruise, lying in the sun and tanning.

Conrad Sauras had had enough. He could endure only so much. The tension popped as he leapt to his feet, his body straining and his lean Spaniard's complexion redder than his tie as he barked at the shipowners. "Have you ever sailed? Have you ever been in the engine room when it's 160 degrees? No. I thought not. Then you *cannot* and do not speak for the seamen." He sat down, shaking with anger, but now the seamen were on their feet, applauding him, slapping him on the back and pumping his hand. Conrad Sauras had spoken for every seaman in the room.[17] The rank and file knew the leadership was not prepared to "place the seamen at the tender mercy of the shipowners."[18]

As 1948 turned to 1949, negotiations stalled. The CSU agreement still applied on Canadian deepsea ships as long as the conciliation board deliberations continued, but the shipowners were profiting from the delay as well. They were selling off the Canadian merchant fleet. Knowing that the CSU would demand contract protection against elimination of seamen's jobs, the companies simply refused to bargain.

The process of ridding the Canadian taxpayers of the fleet their dollars had built began a few short years after the first Park ship was launched and reached a fever pitch by late 1948. C.D. Howe had never been happy with the idea of a government-owned fleet. As Minister of Munitions and Supply in 1945, he had warned the House of Commons that he fully intended to sell as many of the Park ships as possible. They would be sold, he said, to "private Canadian operators" for approximately one-half of their cost of construction, even though many of the vessels had been launched only the year before. A vessel built in 1944, he said, cost $1.3 million to construct. It would go on the market for $600,000.[19]

The Liberals were determined to turn the ships over to profit-hungry private operators. Howe appeared committed to ensuring the fleet would remain Canadian by limiting the sale to Canadian companies. In large part this was a concession to the strong CSU campaign against disposal of the fleet, designed to assure opponents of the move that the vessels would remain in Canadian hands.

In keeping with their policy, the Liberals established the Canadian Maritime Commission under the Canadian Maritime Act of 1947. J.V. Clyne, a specialist in admiralty law, was appointed the commission's first chairman.[20] Clyne, like Howe, was opposed to government ownership of the merchant fleet but saw the necessity of maintaining a Canadian fleet under private control. According to Clyne, "Canadian experience during and after the war had clearly shown the strategic and commercial advantages of having a merchant fleet and the dangers of depending on foreign tonnage which would often be unavailable in an emergency. It was for these reasons that the government decided to sell the war-built ships to private Canadian companies for operation under the Canadian flag and to maintain a fleet and shipbuilding facility commensurate with the requirements of national security and external trade."[21]

The future of the fleet and its seamen was placed in the hands of the Canadian Maritime Commission and the Park Steamship Co. The commission was charged with the overall maintenance of the fleet while the Park Steamship Co., by late 1948 devoid of vessels, looked after the payment of mortgages and subsidies owed to the company from the sale of government-owned ships to private corporations. There was no fear of conflict between the two agencies; Clyne not only chaired the commission, he was chairman of the Park Steamship Co. as well. By 1948, the Canadian fleet of approximately 115 10,000-ton dry cargo vessels and 22 4,700-ton tankers was in private hands.[22] It was Clyne's task to ensure that the fleet remained Canadian and that the government collected the money it was owed from the sale of the Park ships. Advising the commission was a non-governmental National Advisory Committee which counselled the commission on policy and practice. It consisted entirely of shipowners, ship builders and their representatives. There was no labor representation.[23]

Harry Davis, along with Dick Greaves and William Doherty of the officers' unions, investigated the sales. Their research laid bare a pattern of profiteering and betrayal of the national interest. The ships had not been sold to private operators at half their cost of production, as Howe had promised, but for 30 percent. "And of this price," the unionists pointed out, "only a scant 25 percent was paid by the purchaser in cash, the rest being financed by seven-year loans extended by the government at three percent interest. Very substantial tax concessions were also given in the form of depreciation allowances: a special 13 percent in the first year, plus 12 percent annually until the end of 1949. Thus, in the first year of private operation the depreciation allowance equalled the entire down payment on the vessel, or to put it otherwise, the down payment was covered out of public funds through tax concessions."[24]

None of this came as a great surprise to the union. The shipowners rarely made a move without raking in a few dollars. But the union investigation did uncover a fact of which most seamen and the general public were unaware: the Canadian Maritime Commission, which was supposed to preserve the Canadian fleet by selling it to Canadian operators, was allowing the ships to fall under foreign control. Davis, Greaves and Doherty found that after the Park Steamship Co. sold the ships, "four-fifths of our dry cargo and tanker fleet (came) under the control of foreign capital. Greek interests alone control two-fifths of our entire fleet. American interests command 17 percent of the ships and British interests 15 percent. And for good measure, there are elements of Danish, Egyptian, French and Italian control aggregating around seven and a half percent. These foreign owners set up Canadian companies to buy our Park ships on the cheap. They have given some Canadian capital just enough of a 'look-in' to provide them with a Canadian 'front.' And now, with the Canadian government looking the other way, and under cover of pious phrases from high quarters, they are moving in a direction diametrically opposed to Canada's national interest." In many cases, there was no actual sale to a foreign flag operator. The "Canadian" seller and the foreign buyer often were subsidiaries of the same foreign holding company. The policy initiated by the Liberal government and administered by Clyne and his commission had ostensibly been established to maintain our fleet. In reality, it was operating at full speed to scuttle it.[25]

The government position against the transfer of Canadian vessels to foreign flags had changed: the commission would allow the shipowners to sell the vessels to foreign owners, but profits from the sales would be held in escrow to be used for the construction of faster, more efficient and more competitive ships. As ex-Park ships approached obsolescence, they could be sold, but the proceeds of their sale would provide the basis for a more modern Canadian merchant navy.[26] The seamen asked: "Why is it we can see the ships being sold and the jobs being lost, but no new keels being laid down in Canadian yards?"

Between 1948 and 1951, the commission collected $36 million for the escrow fund set up to purchase replacement vessels. Sixty-two vessels had been sold by the end of 1951. While the rest of the world experienced a larger ship-building boom than that of 1939, Canada had but one hull under construction and one on the drawing boards.[27] By the end of 1952, 74 Canadian vessels had been sold and the escrow fund had produced exactly two replacement vessels for the deepsea fleet. What had happened to the $41 million collected? The operators had used the money to build Lake boats.[28]

Clyne had been surprised by the 1949 slump in Canada's shipping volumes because he believed that Canadian shipping would cash in on the United States' European Recovery Program, the Marshall Plan which had been set up to assist in the rebuilding of Europe and to establish the dominance of American foreign policy and business interests over its nations. The Canadian fleet sat and waited for a few scraps to fall its way, but Clyne had to admit that instead of tossing crumbs to Canadian ships, "the launching of the European Recovery Program has created many problems for Canadian shipowners. The United States Foreign Assistance Act provides that, subject to the availability of United States tonnage, 50 percent of the European Recovery Program shall be carried in United States flag ships."[29] Canadian shipping was barred from participating in Marshall Plan cargoes because the American fleet was capable of handling the shipments virtually without assistance.

The CSU had campaigned for years for a Canadian policy requiring 50 percent of our exports to be shipped in Canadian bottoms, a move which would protect the fleet and keep the shipyards humming.[30] Clyne considered the union's position "sheer nonsense" and added, "it would be absurd for us to refuse to trade with nations because they don't let us carry the goods in our own fleet."[31] It may have seemed absurd to Clyne, but it was a policy which was filling the holds of American ships.

While some vessels were sold to foreign flag buyers, others were removed from the Canadian fleet by simply switching the registry to other nations. By the beginning of 1949, ships were being transferred as fast as company lawyers could complete the paperwork. In Vancouver, Canadian Transport Co. sold the *Harmac Vancouver* along with two other 10,000-tonners to a buyer it refused to name. The crews were paid off in London, the Canadian flag was hauled down and the Panamanian flag was raised in its place. Kerr-Silver Lines (Canada) Ltd., a subsidiary of the London-based Silver Line Ltd., sold one of its vessels, the *S.S. Manx Marine*, to Greek interests. The Canadian crew was paid off and the Panamanian flag graced her stern where the Red Ensign had flown a few moments before.[32] Seaboard Owners Ltd. sold its six ships to Greek interests along with the entire company.[33] Kerr-Silver followed Seaboard's lead in March 1949 and sold its remaining vessels to South African capital. It was the third B.C. company to do so.[34]

On the East Coast it was the same story. The 10,000-ton *Yarmouth County* was sold to Maritime Compania de Navigation and steamed out of Halifax under Panamanian colors.[35] In Montreal, one deal alone saw four of the ex-Park ships — *Lake Nipigon, Lake Lillooet, Lake Kootenay* and *Lake Cowichan* — sold to Panamanian flag buyers for $3 million.[36] The sale of each ship meant the loss of a minimum of 60 jobs and the fleet was shrinking like a chunk of ice in a stokehold. It was estimated that the transfer to "flag of convenience" nations had meant the loss of $4.5 million in wages and salaries to Canadian seamen and officers, who were joining the unemployment lines while foreign seamen worked their ships.[37] Needless to say, union wages and working conditions were only a dream for the seamen now employed on Canada's former merchant vessels.

By late 1948 the CSU had set up a European field office to assist in handling grievances which arose abroad and to dispatch seamen who were paid off in England or on the continent. Jack Pope had sailed deepsea during the war and paid off in England at the end of the war. Pope was directed to establish the European branch in London and he acquired an office behind a barber shop at 29 Pier Road, North Woolwich, in London's sprawling dock area.[38]

It was to Pope's office that paid-off seamen gravitated during the winter of 1948 when the shipowners began to sell off the fleet in earnest. In Montreal the CSU was trying to get the conciliation board to reconvene and the seamen in the United Kingdom thought they might be able to nudge the operators in the direction of the bargaining table. Accordingly, on January 10, 1949, Pope announced there would be a three-hour work stoppage the next day on all CSU vessels docked in U.K. ports. "This token stoppage," he said, "is a protest against the tactics of some Canadian shipowners in paying off Canadian seamen when their ships reach foreign ports and replacing them with non-Canadian crews who will accept lower wages and bad conditions."[39]

The stop-work action was designed to show support for a stay-aboard strike begun 16 days before by the officers and crew of the *Point Aconi*, who had downed tools when the company attempted to pay them off and replace them with a foreign crew. The men had refused to leave the vessel.[40] The *Point Aconi* was the first vessel tied up by the seamen in the struggle to save the Canadian merchant marine and her story was to be repeated on a score of vessels in as many of the world's ports.[41]

The *Point Aconi* had been built as the *Tuxedo Park*. In the fall of 1948, Italian interests working through the Canadian agency of McLean-Kennedy of Montreal established a Canadian subsidiary named Navico Shipping Co. Navico received a mortgage loan from the Canadian government of $178,000 to purchase the *Tuxedo Park*. Upon purchase, the vessel was renamed the *Angusdale* and she sailed for a few months under Canadian colors before she docked in Barry, a Welsh coal port. There she was sold once more to a non-Canadian operator and renamed the *Point Aconi*. The Canadian seamen were fired and a non-Canadian crew of displaced Poles, Spaniards and a few Britons hired to take their place. The new owners were Navicar Shipping Co., but all evidence indicated that they and Navico were owned by one and the same person in Genoa, Italy.

The seamen refused to leave the ship, arguing it was a violation of the agreement to discharge them in a foreign port against their wishes.[42] If they were forced to leave the vessel, they said, it would be an illegal lockout and a violation of Canada Shipping Act prohibitions against evicting seamen in foreign ports. The company responded by moving stores of food ashore and shutting down steam and sanitary facilities. Once again, however, the seamen forged the essential link with local residents, who came to their aid with food, clothing and an offer of bathing and toilet facilities.[43] The United Kingdom's National Union of Seamen met and resolved not to man any Canadian vessels unless they were paid at the Canadian rate, which was almost twice that paid to U.K. seamen.[44]

On January 11, CSU crews on 10 ships throughout the British Isles struck in support of the *Point Aconi* seamen. Signs were draped over the sides reading "Support Canadian Seamen — Support Trade Union-ism." The demonstration had immediate repercussions in Montreal, where conciliation board hearings resumed. The tie-up was a clear case of "breaking the agreement," Mathewson charged. As for the ship-owners, there was no wrong-doing in the sale of the vessel. "Surely," he said, "the board is not going to suggest that a man cannot sell his property when it is to his advantage to do so."[45] The stay-aboard strike lasted two months before the officers and crew relented, left the vessel and returned to Canada. The *Point Aconi* sailed with a new crew and a new flag.

Like the lightning strikes that precede a forest fire, a series of localized struggles broke out against transfers of flags in January 1949. In some cases, like that of the *Mount Maxwell*, crews took the owners to court in an attempt to recover some of their losses.[46] The crew of the *Pan Trooper* was told the vessel had been sold as they tied up in Philadelphia. They immediately hit the bricks and picketed the vessel, the first time in the history of the port that a foreign crew had taken such action.[47] In some cases, crews which had been hired to replace Canadians struck in support of the Canadian seamen and demanded Canadian conditions and pay rates, as they did in Baltimore on the *Ivor Rita*. Yet the steady hemorrhage did not stop. CSU members had demonstrated they could sustain a long siege, if necessary, but their actions were minor irritants. The transfer of flags continued.

CHAPTER NINETEEN

Battle Joined

WHEN CONCILIATION HEARINGS resumed in late January 1949, the companies tabled new concession demands. The shipowners revived a longstanding campaign to require seamen to produce a continuous discharge book before signing on to a new ship. The discharge book, required by the Canada Shipping Act and by the legislation of most of the world's shipping nations, was known to seamen the world over as the "fink book." It contained a seaman's career record of employment and provided for a captain's comments upon discharge. One bad mark in a book could end a seaman's career and the continuous discharge system was a convenient way for the companies to deal with men who stood up for their rights or were union-minded. The CSU was just as opposed to the book as the employers were in favor. For once the Canada Shipping Act provided some protection for seamen, allowing them to omit the officers' comments in the book. If the seaman so requested, the discharges could be stamped "endorsement not required." The shipowners wanted the union to give up this basic protection, but the union refused.

Equally contentious was a company demand for a clause guaranteeing that the seamen would "cross picket lines in the event of any legal industrial maritime strike."[1] The seamen reacted in typical CSU fashion. Mindful of the government's reaction to seamen's picket lines in general, they picketed the Montreal office of the CSL dressed in prison stripes and wearing handcuffs.[2]

With more than 50 percent of the provisions of the previous agreement in dispute, it became obvious that no agreement was possible. The parties ceased to meet. In private sessions the three board members hammered out a proposed agreement they felt was "a fair compromise and ought to be accepted by the parties."[3] The findings were not legally binding, but the report was unanimous. There would be great pressure on both parties to follow the board's direction. The report was released February 19, copied at CSU headquarters and distributed in every port. The seamen knew at once that the CSU was in for a beating.

First, and most seriously, the report advocated elimination of the hiring hall and its replacement with a new contract provision allowing the employer to hire "either through the office of the union or through the Seamen's Section of the National Employment Service."[4] Given the choice between the government's employment office and the CSU hiring hall, the companies were unlikely to call the union. Men like Nick Buszowski, Stan Wingfield, Eddie Reid, Mike Jackson and Gérard Fortin would never be hired. A second element of the report was impossible for the union even to consider. It called for the parties to "agree that they will cooperate to exclude from the personnel employed by the companies and the union all subversive elements."[5] In the ship-owners' minds, any seaman who stood up for his rights was a subversive. With this clause in the agreement, the union would be required to dismiss its leadership and eat its young. Up-and-coming militants like Yetman, Jackson and Blackie Leonard, who had done time as a result of the Lake strike, would be weeded out. The board also recommended a wage freeze and minor changes in other contract clauses.

On February 28, the Shipping Federation notified Minister of Labor Humphrey Mitchell that it accepted the proposed agreement. The union stalled as long as possible before advising Mitchell on March 28 that it could not accept the board's terms.[6] Gerry McManus had notified . Trades and Labor Congress President Percy Bengough some 30 days earlier that the terms were not acceptable "for the simple reason that the proposals could, in a very short period of time, liquidate the present membership of the union and replace them...

"Our old agreement," he continued, "protected our membership in American ports and provided for Canadians being shipped to American ports where replacements were necessary. The present proposals of the Conciliation Board would allow Canadian members to remain unem-ployed on the beach in Canada while American seamen or non-seamen could be engaged in American ports... This industry is suffering a very grave unemployment situation at the present time due to the policy followed by the Canadian shipowners of selling our ships to dummy companies and engaging foreign seamen in place of Canadians. In spite of this serious situation, the Conciliation Board chose to totally ignore the unemployment situation that was placed squarely before them by the union during the hearings..."

Although the entire hiring proposal was geared toward destruction of the union's established dispatch system, McManus advised Bengough that the CSU was prepared to offer a compromise to avert a strike. "We propose, if the companies so desire, that they may place their orders for unlicensed personnel with the National Selection Service and that the National Selection Service shall relay the order to the nearest union hiring hall which shall then dispatch the men directly to the ships. The union shall undertake, at the end of each day, to supply the names and ratings of all men registered daily. The union further proposes to supply desk space at each union hiring hall for a representative of the National Selection Service." McManus assured Bengough that the union was prepared to sign an agreement if it could get this minimal protection.[7] Harry Davis elaborated on the CSU's proposal in a telegram to Mitchell announcing the union's rejection of the Conciliation Board report. "We now publicly wish through you to advise that a deepsea strike can be averted if the companies are agreeable to the signing of last year's agreement with the one exception of a clause that only Canadian articles will be used, thus maintaining jobs for Canadian seamen."[8] The union was on record revoking its demands for improved wages, conditions and union security. All the CSU asked was for Canadian jobs on a Canadian fleet.

McManus asked Bengough to lend the TLC's assistance in achieving a compromise. The congress agreed and a meeting was set up in Ottawa for March 31 in the offices of Arthur McNamara, Deputy Minister of Labor. If McNamara was satisfied with the union's response to the Conciliation Board report, he would present it to the shipowners. That morning Bengough, Davis and McManus sat down with McNamara, discussed the CSU's proposals and ironed out some minor problems. A formula acceptable to the union and the federal officials was achieved.[9] Confident the issue had been resolved, Bengough returned to his office across town while McNamara left the room to telephone the news to the Shipping Federation. Relaxing for the first time in months, Davis and McManus discussed the ups and downs of negotiations as they waited for McNamara to return. It had been rough going, but they believed the compromise would enable the seamen to keep their jobs and Canada to have her merchant fleet. The deputy minister opened the door and his entrance was like a hammer striking a crystal. The seamen's mirage of hope shattered and crumbled around his feet. "I'm sorry boys, it's too late," he said. "They've just signed a contract with the SIU."[10]

As the deepsea crews had feared, history was repeating itself. In 1948, the CSL and Misener had used this illegal maneuver to begin to purge the CSU from the Lakes. Now the Shipping Federation was attempting the same tack with the salt water seamen. The agreement accepted by the SIU was the same one rejected by the CSU because it lacked protection for Canadian jobs and the merchant fleet. The SIU had no members on the deepsea fleet, but Davis knew that "having once signed with the SIU (the companies) would have prevented us from going on board the ships." The CSU's back was against the wall. "I don't see how we could have survived if we were cut off from the ability to contact the membership. To have tried to fight the signing in court, in my opinion, would have led nowhere."[11] It was the point of no return.

Davis and McManus hurried back to Montreal. In Halifax, the membership already was in action, refusing to sail the CN's Lady Boats because the company would not guarantee them a return trip. The crews believed that if they signed on, it would be a one-way ticket to nowhere.[12] As the two officers returned to headquarters, the rest of the union went into action. "We had already taken a strike vote," Davis recalls, "and when we were told a back-door agreement had been signed, we polled the National Executive Board immediately. It was agreed, we had no choice. Every port set up its own strike committee to work on a local level. The national office had the problem of national policy and relations with the Trades and Labor Congress, which was very vital."[13] The executive exercised its mandate from the rank and file and on the evening of March 31, 1949, a few hours after the companies announced their "contracts" with the non-existent deepsea locals of the SIU, Harry Davis put out the call to strike all deepsea ships owned by east coast operators and flying Canadian colors. By April 1, all Canadian ports and the London office of the CSU, along with most CSU vessels at sea, had received telegrams advising them that all east coast CSU ships were to be tied up as soon as they reached the nearest port. There was one exception. No ships were to be struck in U.S. southeastern ports because of the strength of the SIU and the difficulty of finding supporters in the arch-reactionary political climate of the American South. A strike in that environment would be impossible to win.

The Communist Party of Canada, then the Labor-Progressive Party, opposed a deepsea strike because it believed the issue of "communist domination" would be used to defeat the strike and to destroy the union. Party members in the CSU were told it would be advisable to accept the proposals in the Conciliation Board's recommendations and use the next year to strengthen the union for a postponed confrontation.[14]

The LPP's assessment was logical, but the events of the day would not allow the National Executive Board of the CSU to consider such a course of action. The strike was inevitable and immediate. The seamen had seen the battles of the Lakes and knew the union would not be allowed to survive for a year under the proposed agreement. Besides, the owners said they no longer recognized the CSU and had signed a contract with the SIU. The fleet was disappearing and seamen were being fired. The strike could not be stopped.

As the ships began to tie up, Labor Minister Humphrey Mitchell was asked for his comments on the companies' back-door agreement with the SIU. In a lengthy prepared statement to the House of Commons April 5, Mitchell did not discuss the illegality of the move. Instead, he suggested the shipowners were justified in their actions because CSU members had struck the Lady Boats and had rejected the Conciliation Board report. Then he revealed a new weapon in the shipowners' arsenal. The companies might have signed with the SIU, Mitchell said, because they were being pressured to do so by Joe Ryan, president of the International Longshoremen's Association, which represented longshoremen in every major Canadian and American eastern seaboard port. Most Canadian trade unionists considered Ryan to be little more than a gangster, but Mitchell read the House a letter from Ryan to the shipowners which he suggested had prompted the back-door deal with the SIU.

"You are aware of the controversy involving the Canadian Seamen's Union, the Trades and Labor Congress of Canada, the American Federation of Labor and a number of affiliated A.F. of L. organizations," Ryan's letter said. "The situation has given cause for grave concern to a number of international unions, including those engaged in the shipping and maritime industry. Among these is the Longshoremen's Association, which is anxious to see that this controversy is disposed of in such a way as to eliminate those communist elements which have kept the industry in an unsettled condition for so long. We would be disturbed if your company continues to give aid and comfort to other communist groups, particularly the Canadian Seamen's Union, and we feel that we should advise you of this so that our relations and operations may be continued on an amicable basis."[15]

Ryan had offered the shipowners powerful economic and ideological assistance in their effort to rid the ships of the CSU. The threat was of little consequence; the operators needed no encouragement to pursue their attack. More important was Ryan's implied pledge to work struck ships. Since the east coast longshoremen on both sides of the border were ILA members, the operators believed they could depend on the major ports in both countries. The CSU would thus have little or no base in Canada. With the east coast ports working, with the SIU on the Lakes and Hall and his fellow AFL roadmen working on the congress to expel the CSU, the companies had every reason to believe they could defeat the union in the first round.

Despite Mitchell's suggestion that Ryan prompted the back-door agreement, it was clear that the shipowners had engineered the deal. They had hired the same lawyer used by their Lake counterparts the year before when the Lake operators signed with the SIU. Evidence soon was available which proved that the scheme had been in motion for some time. In fact, it seems likely that the agreement with the SIU had actually been achieved during a break in the Conciliation Board hearings between December 1948 and January 1949.

Frank Mimee, an SIU official who defected from the union during this period, revealed in a sworn statement in May 1949 that "some time at the end of December 1948 or the beginning of January 1949, Dick Deeley and myself went to see Mr. J.A. Mathewson, K.C., at his office because we had heard that he was going down to San Francisco to see Harry Lundeberg and Hal Banks of the Seafarers International Union and the financial situation of the local Seafarers International Union was desperate.

"Mr. Mathewson admitted that he was going to leave in a few days for San Francisco for the purpose of seeing Harry Lundeberg and Hal Banks and we asked him to take up with these officials the question of our financial plight... Mr. Mathewson promised to do this and asked how much money we needed, and on being informed that our payroll was over a thousand dollars per week, he immediately produced and gave us $900 (Nine Hundred Dollars) and asked us for a receipt which we gave him — this receipt was made out with the notation 'to fight communism' and signed by Deeley.

"On the second visit, Mr. Mathewson told us that he was leaving for San Francisco that very day...

"On both of these occasions we discussed with Mr. Mathewson his impending trip to San Francisco and he told us that he was going to take up with Harry Lundeberg and Hal Banks of the Seafarers International Union-Sailors Union of the Pacific the question of a signed collective agreement between deepsea ship operators and the Seafarers International Union.

"On these occasions Mr. Mathewson produced what he said was a draft agreement and read various clauses to us... One of the proposed clauses eliminated the union hiring hall and when Deeley and I objected to this provision, Mr. Mathewson said: 'Don't worry about these clauses — we can polish up any clauses you don't like to suit you.'

"These visits and Mr. Mathewson's trip to San Francisco took place during the adjournment of the Board of Conciliation between the deep- sea operators and the Canadian Seamen's Union, which adjournment lasted for about a month from the middle of December 1948 to the middle of January 1949.

"After Mr. Mathewson had returned and the hearings of the said board had recommenced, I telephoned Mr. Mathewson a number of times and he told me that 'everything was going to be all right and that Hal Banks was going to come up and take charge and stay until everything was ironed out and, if necessary, indefinitely.' "[16]

Mimee's statement proves that the Shipping Federation had no intention of reaching an agreement with the CSU. Hal Banks and the SIU were waiting in the wings for Mathewson to give them their cue and they would come riding in from the American West in white Cadillac convertibles to make the Canadian waterfront safe for gangsterism, extortion and back-door agreements. The only cost would be Canada's merchant marine and trade union rights.

Mimee's charges later were corroborated by Mr. Justice T.G. Norris, who headed an Industrial Inquiry Commission investigation of Banks' role in the violence and corruption that dogged the east coast waterfront for the next decade. "In early 1949," Norris said, "representatives of the shipowners, including Canada Steamship Lines, and prominent trade union officials arranged to have an approach made to Harry Lundeberg, president of the SIU of North America, in San Francisco, to have him send a representative to Canada to provide leadership of another union in opposition to the CSU and it was in answer to this request that Banks came to Canada."[17]

Lundeberg's candidate for the leadership of the new company-backed seamen's union was described by Justice Norris as "very able and ingenious. As in the case of every dictator, he is lawless and is prepared to use any weapon to gain his ends. He has strength and determination and has gathered around him a group of union officials — weak characters — to do his business."[18] His business was the shipowners' business: to get rid of the CSU, to rid the ships of militants, to get rid of waterfront democracy, to get rid of the ships themselves. He was well-suited to the task. A veteran strong-arm man in the SIU, he knew how to break heads and had been in several scrapes with the law since the 1930s. He had beaten charges of burglary, murder and carrying dangerous weapons.[19] A charge of writing bad cheques proved more troublesome. He was convicted, sentenced to 14 years and served three and a half years in San Quentin.[20]

Dominion law prohibited immigration to Canada by any person with a criminal record. How did Hal Banks, a convicted felon, obtain landed immigrant status? The government of Louis St. Laurent admitted that its representatives had met with Banks before his arrival in Canada on January 14, 1949, some two and a half months before the deepsea strike was called.[21] Banks was handed Form 1000, which every candidate for landed immigrant status was required to fill out. Question 17 asked, "Have you ever been convicted of a criminal offense?" This question did not appear on Banks' Form 1000. There must have been a typographical error, the government said, when the document was produced at the King's Printer.[22]

With Banks' arrival in Canada, the government, labor and corporate forces arrayed against the seamen had all their pieces in place. They were not interested in compromise; the destruction of the CSU was their common goal.

The seamen faced a daunting task. The Lake strike had taken a heavy toll and the SIU was digging out all the CSU hold-outs. The federal government clearly backed the shipowners — its Canadian National Steamship Company was one of the first to sign its deepsea fleet over to the SIU. Roadmen from the AFL had not relented in their efforts to break the CSU's links with the Trades and Labor Congress. It would be a fight to the finish, an assault the seamen were determined to meet head-on.

CHAPTER TWENTY

Blood on the Docks

"On March 31, 1949, there began a strike which encircled the world, directly involving eight million workers and indirectly many millions more. The primary causes were simple trade union issues. The consequences of workers demanding their rights were remarkable to say the least."

Don Williams
The Tridale Strike[1]

ON SCORES OF SHIPS in dozens of ports on six continents, Canadian seamen went on strike. For every crew the strike was different, but wherever they stood and fought, the members of the CSU shared common goals, common allies and common enemies. Isolated from each other by thousands of miles of ocean, they drew on their own strength and the support of workers ashore to sustain their cause. Ironically that solidarity was stronger and more dependable in ports far from Canadian shores.

Canada was the weak link in the union's defense. The CSU was aware of large movements of scabs and goons, many imported from the United States. The seamen knew what tactics to expect. They had encountered the SIU on the Lakes, and although Banks was freshly imported, the seamen knew his reputation had been won in battles against rank and file American unions. The SIU had broken a critical NMU strike and had re-established itself in Canada by smashing the 1948 Lake strike. The CSU prepared to do battle with professional union busters.

The seamen's policy was to remain on the vessels until ordered off by court injunction, then leave peacefully and set up picket lines on the dock. It was there the battle would be fought.

The CSU's deepsea strike was absolutely legal, as Humphrey Mitchell made plain: "Under the Industrial Relations and Disputes Investigations Act, the trade union is free to call a strike and the shipowners are free to declare a lockout and attempt to hire new employees... Therefore, the strike declared by the union on March 31, 1949, is a lawful strike."[2]

Then Mitchell added a warning. "This does not permit seamen to violate provisions of the Canada Shipping Act, which prohibits strikes resulting in the disobedience of master's orders on ships at sea or in port abroad nor until the tie-up of the ship and the safe securing of her cargo at her terminal port in Canada upon completion of her voyage."[3] The seamen had the right to strike, but not in foreign ports.

Why then did the CSU call on all ships to strike in the nearest port rather than upon return to Canada? To win a strike the seamen required strong support from shoreside workers, particularly longshoremen. Yet on the eastern seaboard of North America, Ryan's ILA longshoremen had pledged to cross CSU lines and work struck ships. Even before the strike officially began this weakness sapped the CSU's strength.

The deepsea strike began in Halifax when crews on the CN's Lady Boats — the *Lady Rodney*, the *Canadian Constructor*, and the *Canadian Challenger* — staged sit-in strikes to protest CN's refusal to guarantee them returns from foreign ports. The sit-ins were one week old when the strike was officially called, but the Lady Boat strikers had matters well in hand. The deck of the *Lady Rodney* was crowded with 118 striking seamen. They listened to boogie woogie and soap operas competing from two different radios, played cards, smoked and drank pop. Some read and some crowded along the rails to talk to their families and friends alongside on the dock.[4] CN had cut off food supplies to the ships and the shoreside supporters had to make sure the seamen got their meals.

Scotty Munro was the ship's delegate on the *Lady Rodney* and his wife Alice and daughter Connie helped organize the food supply lines. "They (the company) figured they were going to starve them off," recalls Connie Munro. "You can't stay aboard the ship with no food. It started on an individual basis. The wives whose husbands weren't on that particular ship began going down to the union hall with stuff and we would pack it up in shopping bags. They threw a double line down to the dock from the ship and would hoist the groceries up on the line."

At first it was a fairly simple operation. The women and kids would carry the groceries through a cargo shed to the dock where the *Rodney* was tied up. When CN got wise to the scheme, goons showed up on the waterfront. They didn't attempt to take on the striking seamen but tried to stop the flow of food. "They tried to stop us going through," Connie continues. "They would block you off, form a line and not let you through. When we were tromping around with the grocery bags these guys would be walking around with rifles and guns and great long bloody boards. When you walked up to a big guy and he's carrying a board which he is swinging, that's just a little bit intimidating. (There was) name calling — 'Go to hell home.' As a kid, it was all quite intimidating. I was 15." The women changed their tactics.

"What we would do is go to the union hall and pick up a couple of the biggest seamen who were hanging around the hall and take them along with the women... They would go to the outside of the shed and start a bloody ruckus, so that you would get all these characters from the goon squad going up to fight and while they were going up there we would go up the other side of the shed and sneak 'round the back to get the groceries over to the guys."[5] The supply route only was needed for a few days. On April 2 the government shook its own hand and the courts granted CN an injunction against the sit-in. Two hundred seamen aboard the three CN ships obeyed the law and quietly left the vessels, adding their picket lines to those around 11 other vessels already sitting idle as a result of the strike. Only CN police remained on the Lady Boats.[6]

By the next day, the number of struck ships in east coast ports had risen to 19. Fresh from California, Hal Banks boasted of his intentions in Canada. "We have to stop these tie-ups of ships the CSU has been staging." What did he plan to do about the 19 ships already tied up? "Get 'em moving, of course."[7] By April 7, there were 31 ships struck and in the hands of their crews. Vessels were tied up in U.K. ports, Australia, New Zealand, France, Cuba, British Guiana and South Africa as well as Halifax, Louisbourg, Saint John and Vancouver. (Those struck in Vancouver were vessels owned by east coast shipowners docked on the West Coast.)[8]

In their first skirmishes with the SIU, the seamen counted some victories and some losses. In Saint John, Eddie Reid and fellow CSU members learned of a contingent of scabs leaving Montreal for Halifax. The CSU men intercepted the SIU scabs in the small New Brunswick town of McAdam. As soon as the seamen located their quarry, fights broke out. Some of the scabs scattered, but many pushed on to Halifax and Saint John. The attempt to use the harassing tactics of the 1948 Lake strike failed. Reid and some of the other seamen were charged with assault causing bodily harm.[9]

In Victoria, it was a different story. Seamen from the Seaboard Queen were picketing quietly when buses loaded with scabs pulled up on the dock. Police parted the line and escorted the SIU crew on board.[10] The Seaboard Queen quickly got up steam, cast off from Ogden Pier and headed for sea.[11] But the ship was only as far as Royal Roads when her skipper was compelled to heave to. Ten members of the SIU crew apparently had their consciences pricked by the sight of the pickets and decided to return to port. Replacements had to be ferried to the marooned freighter before she could continue on to England.[12] Even fleeting contact with the CSU members could win converts from those recruited by the shipowners. The operators decided to isolate the scabs from working class logic with professional goons.

HALIFAX, APRIL 6, 1949. The strike was six days old. The CSU picket lines were at reduced strength that evening but several seamen were flopping in the nearby CSU hall, able to respond within minutes if they were called. The pickets paced out the long, boring circuits along the docks, chatting about the strike and ports and people they knew. Most tried to pull a little warmth through the end of a tailor-made. It was quiet but cold.

More than 1,000 miles away in Montreal, Robert McEwen and about 100 other would-be seamen climbed into taxis. A member of the SIU for only 24 hours, McEwen was one of the group chosen to go to Halifax to man the struck ships. The taxis took them to a Canadian National Railway siding. As he boarded the special train, McEwen realized his group was one of the last to arrive. In all, "there were about 150 to 200 men," he testified later in a sworn affidavit. "The great majority of the men were in possession of brass chains, about two feet long, which I was informed had been passed out to them on the train."[13]

Few of the men on the train were seamen. Some, like Montreal native Harry Pilgrim, were Canadians. Others were recent immigrants anxious for a job. They arrived in Halifax at 3:30 on the morning of April 8. As they disembarked, "every man was provided with a pick axe handle, many of which were marked 'CNR.' "[14]

There were between 12 and 20 pickets walking the line that night, trying to keep warm and concentrating on making it through the shift. They paid little attention to the shunting of cars as trains were made up on the nearby tracks. The *Lady Rodney* seemed secure, tied up with the gangway down. Between the picket line and the ship ran a railroad track.

Scotty Munro was pacing the bricks that night as he did most nights. He was a veteran of many union struggles from his days as an organizer of the unemployed to the battles at Lockeport, but nothing had prepared him for what happened next: "A train of freight cars pulls in and the first thing anyone knows is that out of those cars come a couple of hundred goons and about as many Canadian National Police. They just made a bee line for the ship. So with this goddamn force coming at you, what do you do? You back up."[15]

"Hundreds of men burst into the freight shed," remembers Arthur Brown, who was picketing that night. "They all wore helmets and had red armbands. I could see later the red bands were worn so that when the fight started they could tell which were their own men. Anyhow, they came along the pier at the double. There seemed to be at least 200 of them flanked by a flying wedge of police. I think they were CNR police rather than RCMP. They shoved us aside while the crew rushed aboard."[16]

The seamen phoned the CSU hall for help, but by the time reinforcements could reach the dock, the goons and scabs were aboard while 200
helmeted CNR police stood guard. As the handful of striking seamen
looked up at the *Lady Rodney*, the goons jeered and brandished their
weapons. Some seemed to be carrying sawed-off shotguns. Dejected, the
striking seamen looked at the scabs who had taken their jobs at gun-
point and then at the CN police, employees of the federal government. At
that moment, a voice on the *Rodney* called out to picket Sammy Walburn: "Hey Sammy! Hey Sammy! You're on the wrong side of the fence
now!" The seamen recognized Harry Pilgrim standing on the bow.
Shotgun blasts illuminated the night air. At precisely the same moment,
the reinforcements from the hall arrived at the dock led by Fred Skelhorn. "When I turned around, I saw the blasting. Pilgrim is on the bow,
but I don't see the gun because I'm trying to get on the way and turn the
hoses on . . . Then boom! Kabloom! Got Sammy in the guts. Another shot
hits Scotty Cranston's son and puts his eye out!"[17]

When the firing ceased, eight seamen were lying in puddles of their
own blood. No one could come to their aid because the other seamen
were "targets for an assortment of rocks, screwdrivers, hammers, nuts
and bolts hurled from the ship."[18] The seamen eventually were able to
turn on shoreside fire hoses to battle those in the hands of the goons, but
it was three hours before the CSU pickets could retrieve their wounded.
They were rushed to hospital for emergency treatment.[19]

As the seamen withdrew, the *Rodney's* lines were slipped and she
moved out into the stream. The scabs were split up and crews transferred to the *Canadian Challenger* and the *Canadian Constructor*. On
the *Challenger* "a number of the members of the crew began making
'molotov cocktails' consisting of a bottle filled with gasoline in which
was inserted a wick, which could be lit."[20] While the scabs prepared
their weaponry, eight CSU members were being treated for gunshot
wounds. Others needed aid for wounds caused by pick axe handles,
bottles and hammers. Donald Cranston lost the sight in his left eye.
Walburn and five others suffered multiple wounds.[21]

Within hours the people of Halifax were aware of what had happened
to the striking seamen. The same morning fish handlers from the plants
and marine workers from the shipyards downed their tools. The waterfront workers began to march to City Hall bearing placards demanding
action against the goons. Tug boat seamen tied up and walked off the job
to protest the shootings, leaving ships in the harbor to fend for themselves. The federal government immediately replaced them with naval
personnel.[22] By the time the marchers reached City Hall their numbers
had swollen to 4,000, most dressed in the clothes of their occupation.[23]
After circling the hall, the marchers halted at the Grande Parade

entrance and demanded that Mayor J.E. Ahern address them.[24]

Ahern side-stepped the issue, insisting the strike was a federal matter and out of his hands. Other speakers went straight to the point. The wife of one wounded seaman reminded the crowd her husband had done nothing wrong. Her husband was shot, she said, "fighting for the rights of the seamen's union." Jimmy Bell, by then head of the Marine Workers Union, closed the rally with a stinging denunciation of the use of goons and guns against workers on a legal strike. He demanded that the government lay charges against those responsible for the shooting.[25]

An emergency meeting of the Halifax District Labor Council issued an appeal for all trade unionists to "rally behind the striking seamen." The "shooting of seamen engaged in a legal strike by imported gangsters is one of the most disgraceful things that has ever happened in the history of Halifax," the council said.[26] The council's appeal was received with silence by one waterfront union. Halifax longshoremen were members of Joe Ryan's ILA and they were under strict orders from their New York headquarters to support the SIU and to work the scab ships. Ryan warned he would take action against any local which did not follow his dictates. The Halifax local executive meekly complied.[27]

For their part, SIU officials crowed over the Halifax massacre and claimed a victory over communism. David Joyce, secretary of the SIU, said nothing would "deter the SIU from their avowed determination to return the Canadian merchant marine to the Canadian seamen and out of the clutching hands of the Kremlin."[28]

Hal Banks later told an SIU convention in his home port of San Francisco how he was able to engineer the battle of Halifax, making it perfectly clear that the take-over of the Canadian National Steamships' vessels had originated in part on foreign soil. His statement so shocked Mr. Justice Norris when he investigated the SIU's activities in Canada that he included Banks' remarks in his report. Banks told the convention-eers that "the Atlantic and Gulf Districts of the Seafarers International Union of North America and the Sailors Union of the Pacific (SIU) gave all-out aid morally, financially and physically, particularly Weisberger came into Halifax with a group of experts and fought a battle they will long remember. They brought in specialists in certain fields. They brought in men who knew their business when it came to drawing up transcripts for radio broadcasts, they brought in experts on public relations and they brought in broad-shouldered boys — in fact, a complete set-up."[29]

On April 9, the day after the shooting, 60 SIU members led by six international officers arrived in Halifax on a chartered plane from the U.S. They cleared customs, got into taxis and disappeared.[30] Were these men brought to Canada to scab on the three CN ships? A.L. Jolliffe, director of immigration, admitted the men were Americans, but wrote to Deputy Minister of Labor McNamara and assured him the men had not been brought to Canada in violation of the Canada Shipping Act. They had been brought into Canada for the "purpose of looking after American shipping interests," but would not be used to man the struck ships.[31] Jolliffe's assertions notwithstanding, the evidence points inescapably to the conclusion that in order to protect American interests the SIU members had come to man the three struck ships owned by the Canadian government. They were needed to replace the goons who had accompanied the scabs aboard. The goons did their job and left the ship. They were gone within hours of the shooting.

In the wake of the public protest, the RCMP instituted a manhunt for the men who had shot the strikers. They were apprehended less than 24 hours after the incident. One was arrested in Newcastle, New Brunswick, and six others were taken from a Montreal-bound train, also in New Brunswick. Among those on the train was Harry Pilgrim, who was charged with attempted murder.[32] The RCMP officers who arrested Pilgrim and the other goons in Moncton seized damning evidence of Pilgrim's part in the incident, evidence that indicated the Canadian government's deep involvement in every aspect of the scabbing and shooting. At Pilgrim's trial, the prosecution introduced in evidence a box stamped "Canadian National Railways" which the arresting officers had removed from the train with Pilgrim. It contained two sawed-off shotguns, one automatic pistol and ammunition.[33]

In Vancouver, where fewer than 100 CSU members were on strike, one newspaper reported Defense Department assurances that "several thousand active force troops can be moved into the seamen's strike centers quickly if violence becomes so extensive that local police cannot cope with it."[34]

Press hysteria did not confuse Nova Scotia workers. In Cape Breton, 13,000 members of the United Mine Workers pledged their full and undivided support to the striking seamen. In Dartmouth, an open air meeting was held at the corner of Portland and King.[35] Young Gerry Yetman, recently released after serving a six-month stretch for his activity in the 1948 Lake strike, addressed the crowd of several hundred shipyard workers. He told them how he was put on bread and water because he complained about the terrible food. The young seaman, who 30 years later would be president of the Nova Scotia Federation of Labor, told how "they treated the union prisoners worse than criminals" on the inside.[36] Jimmy Bell told the marine workers that "when the Government of Canada resorts to strong-arm tactics and brings in armed gunmen and thugs to shoot down innocent picketing men, the time has come for us to take action."[37] The seamen and their supporters would have no time to take action of any sort.

The following day, 18 CSU members were picketing the *Sun Prince*, which was crewed by scabs and docked at the Deepwater Terminals at the north end of Halifax harbor. The pickets were unarmed and peaceful. In the early morning light, 70 Halifax police and 140 RCMP closed in on the seamen. All streets and alleys were guarded and blocked. The police lined up and started for the seamen. "Steel-helmeted and carrying batons (the police) marched in troops to the head of Pier 3, (and) quickly sent men through the sheds from which several citizens, apparently pickets, scurried."[38] As the police closed in on the pickets, the RCMP vessel *McBride*, her gun trained on the dock, moved alongside the *Sun Prince*. The flank was sealed off by Harbor Police Launch *M6*. The seamen were boxed in by gunboats and almost 200 police.

As everyone waited a man dressed in an overcoat and hat walked onto the dock. He was reportedly an official of Saguenay Terminals. The police watched the seamen carefully as the man cast off the vessel's mooring lines. CSU delegate Harry Gulkin asked if he could board the vessel and talk to the scabs, but the RCMP superintendent in charge replied, "No union men are going aboard the vessel this morning." As the vessel began to pull from the dock the tension was shattered by a loud crack. The scabs had neglected to draw up the gangplank, which hung splintered from the ship.[39] One more link in the CSU's chain had been broken.

CHAPTER TWENTY-ONE

The Home Front

WHILE THE COUNTRY'S attention was rivetted on Halifax, seamen in other Canadian ports threw up picket lines and worked to consolidate the strike. Three ships were struck in Saint John, New Brunswick, where the CSU looked to members of Joe Ryan's ILA to honor their strike.[1]

As the picket lines went up, officers on the three vessels demonstrated their support for the seamen in a telegram to Labor Minister Humphrey Mitchell, advising that they would "not be used as strike-breakers. Under no circumstances will we sail with members of the Seafarers International Union."[2] The solidarity of the officers of the *Ottawa Valley, Cottrell,* and *Federal Trader* was appreciated but of little practical consequence. Their position was too vulnerable to bring much pressure to bear on the shipowners. In Saint John, as in every port, the longshoremen held the outcome of the strike in their hands.

Although the Saint John longshoremen were members of Local 273 of Ryan's International Longshoremen's Association, they had a long and close working relationship with the CSU. They refused to handle any vessel behind a CSU picket line. Operators were forced to divert ships to other ports.[3] If the SIU was to be successful, the solidarity between the seamen and the longshoreman had to be broken. From his New York office Ryan ordered his Saint John local members to cross the lines or lose their charter. Ryan threatened the Canadians with trusteeship and boasted that he would order all his locals in the U.S. to boycott any CSU-manned ships if the SIU requested him to.[4] In Saint John the longshoremen paid no attention.

For more than a month the longshoremen honored CSU picket lines. Economic losses mounted, both in lost wages for the longshoremen and for the shipowners, whose vessels were sitting idle with cargoes in their holds. On April 28, the seamen of the CSU Saint John strike committee learned that scabs were on the way. They were being flown into nearby Pennfield Ridge airport.

A group of seamen left immediately to try to intercept the scabs before they met their police escorts. The seamen knew that once the police and the scabs linked forces they would have no trouble breaking up the CSU's picket lines. On the dark country road to the airport the headlights of the strikers' cars picked out something ahead. They pulled slowly up to a police blockade. Cars pulled in behind them and the seamen were surrounded.

They stepped onto the roadway to be greeted by "an estimated 200 steel-helmeted Royal Canadian Mounted Police and city police constables, armed with hardwood axe handles."[5] They had not come to chop wood. The seamen didn't have a chance, holding out only a few moments against the stick-wielding Mounties. Those who could, escaped into the heavy underbrush but others were not able to dodge the carnage of the axe handles. Nine seamen were injured, two seriously.[6]

The blockade opened and four yellow moving vans disappeared into the night. The first held police, the other three were loaded with scabs.[7] They drove through West Saint John and out onto Pier 9. Twenty-five seamen were on the picket line. There usually were many more, but a few hours earlier the police had arrested all the seamen they could round up. The *Cottrell* was tied up behind the thinned lines. The doors to the vans opened and, like cheerleaders at a football game, the police formed two parallel lines for the scabs to run between. Within half an hour the *Cottrell* had moved out into the stream.[8]

No scabs had been hurt. No police were injured. The CSU had nine men injured, but the most damage was done by placing 61 seamen, including Eddie Reid behind bars.[9] Reid, possibly for the first time in his life, was utterly discouraged. He always thought he knew the rules, but he hadn't understood the game. He had led a handful of seamen into a trap where they could be beaten senseless by club-swinging Mounties. He was used to battling the odds, but had never prepared for an action of this magnitude. He threw up his hands in disgust. "It's useless," he swore, "to continue here due to the fact that peaceful picketing is no longer possible."[10] He ordered all picket lines removed from the Port of Saint John. Eddie Reid had tasted despair and it staggered him, but it didn't take him long to shake it off. The next day the pickets returned to the waterfront.[11] The ships had been scabbed, but the seamen still had the support of the longshoremen.

On May 4, ILA vice-president John Galbraith ordered the Saint John longshoremen to work the *Ottawa Valley*. The company dispatched four shifts of gangs to the vessel. The first shift met no picket line and went to work, but when the relief shift arrived to unload the cargo of sugar, they were turned away by the arguments of three women who had joined the restored line. A meeting was called for 1 p.m. that afternoon to settle the question of honoring the CSU strike. At the appointed hour several hundred men and women crowded onto the docks to hear the debate.

Galbraith spoke at length in opposition to Local 273 president William Carlin, who strongly supported the seamen. The argument raged back and forth. The longshoremen were not going to cross legitimate and legal picket lines, Carlin swore. Never. The international representative insisted that the lines would be crossed or the local would lose its charter. The meeting finished with the matter unresolved, but there was an open split among the longshoremen which endangered their ability to maintain their support for the CSU. For a time, at least, the CSU lines would remain sacred.[12]

On May 5, gangs were once again dispatched to the *Ottawa Valley*. They crossed the docks until they reached the CSU picket lines, then came to a dead stop as they had so many times before. This time, two international executive officers, Edward Charlton and Thomas Sullivan, intervened. They told the longshoremen they would lead a back-to-work movement if they could get 16 men to make up a gang. The longshoremen had honored the line for more than 30 days and the international believed they could exploit some of the tension that had built up during the long siege. Frank Crilly, vice-president of Local 273, "flatly declared that Local 273 members should not cross the CSU lines." But the international officers argued that the longshoremen were bound to cross by their contract with the Shipping Federation. Hesitantly the longshoremen began to step forward to join Charlton and Sullivan. First there were only two or three, then nine and finally 12. They needed 16, but they would get a dozen, no more. The attempt to break the line had failed and principles had prevailed. The longshoremen drifted off the dock.[13] The CSU line held until May 9, when a longshoremen's local election was called and the pro-CSU slate was thrown out of office.[14] On May 11, 1949, 64 ILA members crossed the line and worked the *Ottawa Valley*.[15]

The Saint John longshoremen were among numerous groups of rank and file workers and local leaders who resisted the orders of their international unions and supported the seamen. In most cases, however, they could not withstand the unrelenting pressure of their American headquarters. Even though the TLC officially supported the CSU, Canadian locals of international unions faced the threat of loss of their charters or trusteeship, in which international headquarters could set up new locals under the direction of hand-picked trustees. The deepsea strike was confronting the entire Canadian labor movement with a choice between submission to the dictates of the American-based internationals or adherence to a line of independent and militant action.

As the Cold War intensified and the cancer of McCarthyism grew, more and more trade unionists bent under the strain. Some believed that by making political concessions, by purging communists and left-wingers from the labor movement, they could maintain some of the victories they had already won. Canadian trade unionists in international unions faced an incessant drumfire of demands to submit to the anti-communist crusade which by then was reaching into every corner of Canadian society, from the waterfront to the National Film Board.

In the labor movement, the test of loyalty was submission to the domination of the American unions, which had undertaken massive purges of their ranks to meet government and corporate demands for elimination of left influence.

Although inspired and led in the Trades and Labor Congress by the roadmen of the internationals, the anti-communist drive that was paralyzing the Canadian trade union movement had roots in Canada as well. In the Canadian Congress of Labor, where unions like the United Autoworkers, the International Woodworkers of America, the International Union of Mine, Mill and Smelter Workers and the United Electrical Workers had communist or left-center leadership, the right wing of the Cooperative Commonwealth Federation was spearheading the move to purge communists from any union post. By 1949 the purge was almost complete. The result was a labor movement split along lines dictated by the country's political and economic élite and implemented by forces within labor's ranks.

Although the CSU was united — there was no internal division fostered by CCF members — and confident of their leadership, the seamen faced a tough struggle to build the all-important solidarity they needed from Canadian unions. Ryan's International Longshoremen's Association made the CSU its special project, interfering anywhere it could to undermine the seamen's efforts to build support.

Despite pockets of resistance, ILA members on Canada's East Coast obeyed orders to cross CSU picket lines. In Montreal, scabbed ships were worked without question.[16] But on the Pacific coast, longshoremen on both sides of the border backed the seamen wholeheartedly.

Almost all Pacific longshoremen were members of the International Longshoremen's and Warehousemen's Union, an affiliate of the Congress of Industrial Organizations. President of the ILWU was Harry Bridges, a man the U.S. State Department had tried to deport to his native Australia after he led San Francisco longshoremen in a decisive strike for union recognition that culminated in the San Francisco general strike of 1934. Bridges and the ILWU, with its large British Columbia locals, threw their support behind the CSU.

The seamen also could count on the solidarity of west coast ILA locals. President of the small Vancouver ILA local was Jimmy O'Donnell, himself an ex-seaman who had crossed swords with Ryan even before the deepsea strike began. O'Donnell had rejected ILA demands to send per capita to the U.S., arguing his members would be better served if the dues stayed in Canada. As a result of the dispute, Ryan had stopped sending the Vancouver local the dues stamps it required to show that its members were in good standing. All correspondence from the international had come to a standstill. It was as if the Vancouver local had ceased to exist in the mind of the international, a blessing in disguise for the CSU. In addition to honoring CSU picket lines, the tiny Vancouver ILA membership gave a dollar a member to the CSU strike fund. When O'Donnell took the $170 to the president of the CSU's West Coast District, Jimmy Thompson told him, "If we could get this from all the unions, we would win the strike."[17]

The B.C. locals of the ILWU pledged not to cross any CSU picket lines, but to protect their own union and their agreement, they could not afford to boycott ships which were not picketed.[18] Three forces conspired to eliminate the lines: the police, the scabs and the courts.

Although several ships were struck in Vancouver as the strike began, the case of the Riverside illustrated the struggle faced by CSU crews even when shoreside workers provided strong support. The vessel's skipper told his crew on April 3 that "they must join (the) rival union if they wished to retain their jobs."[19] The seamen struck the vessel, which was docked at Vancouver's Lapointe Pier. On Friday, April 8, Andros Shipping obtained an injunction ordering the crew and five officers off the vessel. The seamen obeyed.

The picket line was set up at the entrance to the pier. The seamen set up a small shelter, lit a fire, brewed up a pot of coffee and prepared for the long hours of picket duty. The first cups of coffee were still being sipped when a launch came alongside the Riverside. Police moved onto the dock and scabs were shifted to the struck ship. Dropping their cups, the seamen ran through the police lines and reclaimed the ship. They caught 10 of the scabs and pushed them back down the gangplank. Others already on board were forced to jump the 15 feet to the dock below. The seamen kicked aside the gangplank and held a meeting to consider their next move.

Within minutes the police were joined by reinforcements. The seamen threw a jacob's ladder over the side and helped the police inspector aboard. After a brief conference, the strikers agreed to leave. As they were loaded into the black maria, one of the young lads yelled to a crowd of onlookers, "See you in six years."[20]

The picket lines were beefed up and the next day several attempts to breach the line with truckloads of scabs were turned back.[21] The line held until April 14, when the Riverside was again loaded with scabs from the harbor side.²² Then the B.C. courts stepped in, convicting 34 seamen of illegal assembly for picketing the vessel. In what became a standard method of dismantling picket lines in B.C., the seamen were convicted of illegal assembly for legally picketing during a legal strike.²³

As long as the CSU could muster a line, the ILWU honored its pledge not to work any vessels being picketed. For six weeks, ships lay idle in B.C. ports, marooned behind CSU picket lines. In May, however, the courts handed down blanket injunctions forbidding any picketing of struck vessels and the longshoremen had to give up their 45-day boycott.²⁴

IN MONTREAL, the CSU national office had its hands full. Not only was it coordinating a world-wide strike, it also had the task of negotiating with those Lake companies which had not signed back-door agreements with the SIU. With the exception of Misener's Sarnia and Colonial Lines and the Canada Steamship Lines, things went surprisingly well. Contracts were signed which called for no increase or decrease in wages and hours were reduced. Overtime was to be paid for Sundays worked. The agreements were a compromise designed to give both sides time to cool off after the events of 1948 and they marked a significant achievement for the Lake seamen still under CSU jurisdiction. Those under SIU agreement were working under the concessions exacted by Misener and the CSL. By mid-April, the CSU had contracts with Paterson, Lake Erie Navigation, Alberni Power and Paper, Canada Cement, National Sand and Material and the Quebec and Ontario Transport Co.²⁵ A couple of days later, the union signed the same agreement with the Upper Lakes and St. Lawrence Steamship Co. With the inclusion of the Upper Lakes workers the CSU had more than 2,000 Lake seamen working under the protection of the union's agreement.²⁶

Contracts with generous increases in wages and reduced hours were signed with Shell Oil Tanker and McColl Frontenac Oil Co. The Shell agreement gave the oilers and wheelsmen $185 a month and deckhands $150 a month. These were the highest wages ever paid on the Lakes to that time.²⁷

The union hoped the example of the Lake settlements would spur the east coast operators back to the table, but it did not. Harry Davis advised the federal government that "the CSU is prepared to end its east coast strike tomorrow if the federal government would arrange a meeting with deepsea operators."²⁸ Humphrey Mitchell laughed the offer off. He would not convey the union's desire to resume negotiations with the east coast owners, he said, because "I am not going to be a decoy duck for the Communist Party."²⁹

On the West Coast, where the union was seeking to bring B.C.

deepsea operators to the table, the union dealt directly with the ship-owners. Under the CSU constitution, the west coast district of the CSU was guaranteed autonomy and was free to act independently as long as it followed the general principles and objectives of the national union. The national executive decided that if the west coast district was able to, it should sign an agreement with the B.C. operators.[30] Jimmy Thompson, president of the west coast district and a member of the national executive, followed that directive. The union had signed with the Lake operators, he told the B.C. employers, and was prepared to accept a settlement in B.C. based on renewal of the 1948 agreement. The shipowners stalled. Thompson warned them they would be struck if they didn't sign by April 21 and the operators agreed to the new contract at the last possible moment. It was the compromise the CSU was looking for on the East Coast: a one-year agreement retroactive to October 14, 1948. Davis was pleased with the settlement. The contract contained "identical conditions and hiring hall clause the operators on the East Coast are attempting to abolish," he said. "It is the same contract we offered shipowners on the East Coast."[31]

Dick Greaves, who in 1949 was an official of the National Association of Marine Engineers, believes the west coast operators were prepared to sign the agreement because they had more experience with trade unionism and a healthy respect for the solidarity and militancy of B.C.'s maritime unions. "The viciousness didn't go down here (in B.C.) that went on back east," recalls Greaves, who negotiated with both sets of employers during the same period. "Partially that was because there were some home-grown shipowners here, whereas down east they were not home-grown. There were Greeks and British and you name it... Those negotiations went on and on, but I think truthfully some of the Greek shipowners who were more interested in a fast buck (were willing to sign with the CSU) and had to be whipped into line by the Shipping Federation."[32]

The east coast operators attempted to paint the west coast settlement as a defeat for the CSU, a split in the ranks. In fact, the union was delighted with the contract because it had demonstrated its determination to end the strike based on the old agreement. In addition, 1,000 of its members were sailing deepsea on 19 vessels under union conditions.[33] It was obvious that it was the united front of the bosses which was shattered, not the unity of the seamen. The *Searchlight* pointed out that the agreement "put the lie in the shipowners' teeth about the CSU desiring strikes. It showed that it was the shipowners who were responsible for the shipping strike and that if they wanted peace in the industry all they had to do was renew their agreements as their fellow operators had done on the West Coast."[34] But the strike continued.

THE FOCUS OF THE STRIKE was Montreal, the nerve center for the CSU and for the Shipping Federation. Although ILA longshoremen readily worked struck vessels in Montreal, picketing never let up. The waterfront was the SIU's marshalling yard for scabs and goons and many young CSU members released from prisons and reformatories for their part in the 1948 Lake strike gravitated to Montreal to find their way back into the industry. Some, like Gerry Yetman, stopped briefly on their way to other ports where they could better serve the union. Others, like Joe Grabek, stayed in Montreal once they were released from jail.

Quebec still was ruled by the reactionary government of Maurice Duplessis and Montreal was a tough town. Goons — some imported, some hired off the Main — were all over the waterfront. There were confrontations whenever they met CSU members. The union seamen dodged them and fought only when they had to, but the police were harder to elude and against them there was no defense. They rounded up virtually anyone who even looked like a seaman and the jails were teeming with the union's members. These arrests cost the union both men and money.

When Grabek was released from Guelph Reformatory he hurried to Montreal and joined the strike committee. Before long he was immersed in its work and became its head. The police harassment sticks out in his memory. "All you had to do was walk out the door, step outside and they locked you up for vagrancy," he remembers. "They were trying to drain the union's finances... As a matter of fact, when I got to Montreal, the first morning I was on the strike committee this report came in that there were so many guys in prison in Bordeaux and we either paid the fine or they got one week. Everybody voted to pay it. Okay. The next morning, the same damn thing. So I finally asked, 'What's coming off here?' They answered, 'Well, we do that every morning. We got so many guys in prison, locked up, and we pay $10 or they do a week in prison.

"I put up an argument. I said, 'Let's not pay the fine, let's just send one of the guys to Bordeaux and tell them what the score is, because as long as we keep paying, the cops are going to keep on arresting them — easy money for them.' So that went before the committee and was voted on. I don't think anyone objected to it. We sent people to Bordeaux to inform (the seamen) that this is the policy. The guys said, 'Sure, what the hell is a week?' As a matter of fact, they had better meals than they had on the outside. The funny part is that by the noon hour we got a phone call from the police. 'When the hell are you going to pay the fine?' We told them we are not going to pay. The next morning they only arrested half of the amount. The third morning there were no other arrests."[35]

The police had other ways to harass the seamen. Any trade union demonstration was stopped. When the seamen picketed the St. James

Street office of the Canadian National Steamships, the police screeched up to the picket line and broke it up because the pickets were "impeding traffic on the sidewalk."[36]

In general, the CSU pickets in Montreal played it cool. They stayed as close to the law as possible. When they were pinched for vagrancy, they went to jail quietly, did their time and reported back for picket duty. There were times, though, when things just boiled over. One such incident occurred when Bob Clapper, a former CSU patrolman, switched over to the SIU and went to the press to badmouth the union. He was beaten up by unknown parties and landed in the hospital with concussion.[37] A couple of years later, Clapper got similar treatment in Vancouver on Powell Street, across from the Marr Hotel. He was never forgiven.[38]

SIU members were not the only victims of concussion. The CSU seamen in Montreal got their share. But to the seamen, there were two very different kinds of violence in the dispute. On the one hand was the violence dished up by the goons, a private army hired by the ship-owners to destroy the union. On the other hand was the violence handed out by the seamen in their fight for their ideals and their jobs. Their violence was directed against attacks on the working class. The seamen organized "education committees" to take on the bosses' goons squads.

The education committee's name reflects its primary objective: to convince scabs that the CSU was the way to go. Scabs would be talked to, given CSU literature and urged to mend their ways. Many did. Some joined the union and others simply left the waterfront. There were some, however, who insisted on their "right" to scab and others who simply were goons. These two categories got sterner treatment.

The members of the education committee were not boy scouts. They had been around the block and around the world. They knew how to handle themselves. Size and experience aided in the education they dispensed. Is it not unfair, then, to call one group of heavies a goon squad and the other an education committee? Stan Wingfield sees the distinction as clear and correct because "the goon is hired to take the scab through the lines to take another man's job. The goons did not talk to you. They hit you over the head or shot you in the guts. Usually they are pretty good when there is a gang of them and only one or two of you. That's their approach.

"The name 'education committee' (says) exactly what it was. We would try to reason with them first. The guys we would talk to were seamen and we would try to reason with them. Sometimes it worked and they would come over to join the ranks of the guys who were on strike. Many did not, and these were the ones we had to fight with. Also at that time we had a big education job to do. It was the McCarthy times and everybody was classified as a red with little bombs in our back pockets... Mind you, if it was goons — there's no reasoning with goons — we would try, but some of them were really hoods brought in from the States. They were thugs and some of these guys who were goons had never sailed before."[39]

The goons tangled with the education committees in Montreal on numerous occasions, but the most famous encounter was what came to be known as the "bowling ball caper." It began during a meeting of the education committee. A CSU member burst into the room and reported that goons were being billeted in a Park Avenue bowling alley. The decision was made to stop them before they got to their destination and before they had the assistance of the police.

Gerry Tellier explained what happened. "We stopped the meeting and picked so many to come — bang, bang, you, you and you. Volunteers. We jumped into taxicabs. Al Forde was with us. He used to be a boxer, I knew him from the Thirties. I was a wrestler on the West Coast. We belonged to the same sports club. It was the SUPA — Single Unemployed Protective Association." They swept up Park Avenue and came to a screeching halt outside the bowling alley.

"There were stairs going up to the place and there was all this gear that was there. There were seabags, suitcases, pack-sacks and a whole lot of stuff. They had built a barricade with it. They were living there. We got rid of all these obstructions and went inside. Suddenly, out go the lights. They were at the far end of the alley and we were where you throw the balls. We were charging up toward them. We were going to clean them out. That was the last thing I remember. I got cleaned out. We lost out on that deal."[40]

Tellier had led the charge against the goons, who hurled bowling balls and pins at the onrushing seamen. One of the men charging with Tellier was Spud Haughey. "We went in on the attack and Tellier got hit between the eyes with a pin. It knocked him silly. We got him out of there. Tellier was the leader and when he got conked it threw the whole thing into disarray. We got a cab. He had been knocked pretty well unconscious and we pretty well dragged him into the cab. I had a sister living in Montreal at the time who only lived a short distance from the place. She was a registered nurse. She said to take him to a doctor, it could be concussion. We took him to the hospital and they X-rayed him. It definitely was. They shaved his head and they had to operate to relieve the pressure."[41]

It was some time before Tellier regained consciousness. He realized he was in hospital while there was a strike on. It was no place for him. "I was in there a couple of days," he remembers. "I couldn't pay the bill and didn't know where my gear was or anything. I went over the fence."[42]

Where there were no goons or scabs, there was no violence. In Montreal, as elsewhere, the seamen tied up the ships when they docked and lived a very peaceful existence on the line. This was particularly clear in Montreal in the early days of the strike. When the *Mont Alta* tied up, the crew members lounged around on deck. One seaman entertained the rest of the crew with his lasso tricks. Some worked on their tans. The mood was happy and relaxed. When the captain wanted to go ashore, he went. On his return, the seamen lowered a jacob's ladder and welcomed him aboard. The seamen made it clear, however, that they were on strike for the duration. Police kept people away from the ship and food supplies were cut off.[43] When the shipowners obtained the inevitable injunction, the CSU instructed the crew to abandon ship. According to the *Montreal Gazette*, "the end of the strike on the *Mont Alta* came suddenly and was marked by an impromptu celebration on board the ship during which officers and crew members were seen drinking to each other's health. The drink was bottled beer served by the officers' steward. Apart from the serving of the injunction, there were no formalities, no strife, nor any sign of violence or damage. The men brought their baggage over the gangway and waited for a final goodbye to Captain A.S. Baxter, who shook hands with them as they left the ship..." Members of Montreal's Anti-Subversive Squad watched as the seamen descended the gangplank and set up their picket lines on the dock.[44]

CHAPTER TWENTY-TWO

Cooperation, Yes — Domination, No!

AS THE SEAMEN consolidated their strike in scores of ports in North America and around the world they looked first to trade unionists ashore for support and assistance. In country after country, they were not disappointed. In the United States, however, it was a different story. Whatever their individual feelings might have been, most American maritime workers were unable to extend solidarity because their own organizations were either gangster-ridden or reeling under the pressure of the growing storm of McCarthyism. It was south of the 49th parallel that the CSU's members faced the gravest threat, both to their physical safety and to their union's ability to rally the support of the Canadian labor movement.

The CSU had always considered the National Maritime Union to be its American counterpart, a democratic, militant rank and file organization of seamen. But by 1949, the NMU was undergoing a transformation. Joe Curran, a veteran of the NMU's early days, remained at the head of the organization, but by the mid-1940s he had forgotten his sympathy for the voice of the rank and file and had undertaken a purge of the union that warmed the hearts of the shipowners and the U.S. State Department.

One victim of the purge was Henry Cohen, who shipped out as an NMU member in 1939 and served as a ship's delegate on many vessels before Curran's blacklist drove him from the industry. "All known communists, socialists and Trotskyists were kept from sailing the ships because of their socialist leanings," he recalled during a visit to Vancouver after his retirement. "The government stepped in, not only to break the union but also to establish that leftist officials and leftist members of the union could not ship out at this particular time. They established a special seamen's stamp to clear you, (to show) that you didn't belong to any leftist movement. If they knew about you being involved in the leftist movement, naturally they would not give you that stamp on your seamen's identification."[1]

The destruction of the NMU's democratic traditions stripped the CSU of another important ally in North American ports. The International Longshoremen's Association and the NMU made certain there was little support for the CSU on the U.S. eastern seaboard. On the U.S. Pacific coast, the seamen fared better. Unions like the International Longshoremen's and Warehousemen's Union and the Marine Engineers Association, as well as several smaller seamen's unions, battled in virtual isolation to support the Canadian seamen.

Their assistance, however, was not enough to ensure the strikers' safety. During the strike, three CSU members were found floating in Los Angeles harbor. The body of Leonard Richards was recovered April 9. On May 29, Charles Leslie was pulled from the water with a fractured skull. He could not remember what had happened to him.[2] On June 6, another Canadian seaman was found in Los Angeles bay. He had been in the water for five days when his corpse was recovered. He was Hervé Beauchesne, brother-in-law of Gerry McManus. In ports around the world, seamen picketed United States consulates and embassies. In London, England, they carried signs which read "Murder" and "Gun War On Canadian Seamen." The CSU demanded a full investigation of the Los Angeles deaths and a coroner's jury returned a verdict of "possible homicide."[3] Both deaths later were ruled to be "accidental or suicides."[4] The murder of seamen was not confined to the United States. A few days after Beauchesne's body was recovered, the body of CSU member Theodore Roosevelt Ferguson was found floating in the harbor at the foot of McGill Street in Montreal. The CSU believed two other seamen had been found at the same time, but were denied permission to view the bodies when they went to the morgue to check.[5]

The inability of American trade unionists to render effective support to the CSU in U.S. ports was symptomatic of the cancer that was eating at the guts of the American labor movement. The war on militant, rank and file trade unionism was reaching a peak in the United States and the American Federation of Labor was determined to force Canadian workers to toe the Washington line. The roadmen, the AFL's agents in Canada, were anxious to assist. In a letter to AFL president William Green, the roadmen said their difficulty was not so much "communism" as the "policy of the Trades and Labor Congress, which has become more and more obvious, to depart from the traditionally international aspect and charter and substitute therefore an exclusively national movement." This "trend toward nationalism" had to be halted, they concluded.[6] The roadmen hoped to use the SIU's attack on the CSU as the battering ram to break down the walls of Canadian trade union autonomy.

The officers of the Trades and Labor Congress sounded a warning.

"During the past year our congress has been faced with a serious attempt by the American Federation of Labor to completely ignore our sovereign rights," said TLC president Percy Bengough. "This is not the first occasion by any means... Our present difficulties with the American Federation of Labor only differ in degree with the many liberties taken by the American Federation of Labor at our congress' expense during the past years.

"This is the way it has gone for years: jurisdictional fights, 'breakaways' and 'make-ups.' No consultation or consideration deemed necessary. Just issue orders with a total disregard of how the Canadian membership and the Trades and Labor Congress of Canada was affected."[7]

In a report to TLC affiliates in March 1949, Bengough and congress secretary John W. Buckley recounted their efforts to achieve a reconciliation with the AFL since the stormy convention of 1948, which had recognized the CSU as the seamen's only legitimate union and condemned the actions of the SIU and Frank Hall.[8] Early in 1949, they said, the TLC had welcomed the formation of a Cooperation Committee, composed of three AFL representatives and three TLC delegates, to resolve the conflicts between the AFL and the congress. "In a spirit of cooperation, your congress representatives participated fully in this committee," Bengough and Buckley reported. "While seeking to remove and forestall any possible domination, we strove for a strengthening of real ties of brotherhood between the American Federation of Labor and the Trades and Labor Congress of Canada."[9] Accordingly, the Canadians sought to "take up certain existing differences with the American Federation of Labor at an early meeting of the Cooperation Committee. Among these differences was the question of the Shipping Federation, the Canadian Seamen's Union, the Seafarers International Union and the conduct and action of Frank Hall.

"Following correspondence on this matter a date was set for such a meeting to be held in Miami, Florida. The officers of your congress, acting as members of the Cooperation Committee, arrived in Miami on the set date. They were kept waiting an entire week. The American Federation of Labor had changed its mind. There would not only be no meeting, but it seems that the Cooperation Committee is dissolved."[10]

The AFL's rejection of the reconciliation bid did not deter the Canadians. The AFL's actions were increasingly obnoxious to the congress leaders, but Bengough and Buckley remained committed to the search for a compromise. The AFL executive rewarded their patience by putting them on trial for treason against the American Federation of Labor. As Bengough and Buckley recounted later, "the American Federation of Labor Executive Committee, by a flagrant usurpation of authority, set itself up as a tribunal to try the elected officers of a trade union center representing workers from another country. Still desiring harmony between the American Federation of Labor and the Trades and Labor Congress of Canada, your congress officers appeared before the Executive Committee. Also present for this occasion was Frank Hall and several of his supporters.

"The 'Halls' were invited to present their case, which proved to be made up of some truths, half-truths and many outright erroneous assertions. Their garbled surmises and inferences, both written and oral, were expounded for over an hour and a half. The congress representatives were given less than half an hour to reply, following which the session came to an end. A further session was held where the American Federation of Labor Executive Committee proceeded to render their sentence: 1. Expel all communists; 2. Scrap the present constitution by changing delegate representation at conventions.

"Let us examine this sentence. The issue of communism must be squarely met. The Executive Committee of your congress advises all affiliated organizations to defeat communists aspiring for office on the local union level. The overwhelming majority of Canadian union members are opposed to communism, believing that we can obtain our economic and social aims without resorting to totalitarianism. Although the number of communists in our ranks is relatively small, we call upon our membership for even greater vigilance; local union and general officers must reflect the non-communist membership they represent. In this we are in agreement and advocate the same policy as adopted by the British Trades Union Congress. But communism cannot effectively be dealt with by using the same obnoxious methods we accuse them of. Vigilance in democracy and not mimicking totalitarian methods will meet the threat of communism while preserving and strengthening our Canadian way of life.

"Therefore, on the first point of the sentence rendered we are meeting squarely the threat of communism in our own way. Furthermore, the results of the American Federation of Labor supposed methods of dealing with communism in the United States do not seem to lend themselves too readily as a recommendation for others.

"The second point concerning delegate representation is more easily understood. It perhaps indicates why the issue of communism was raised so alarmingly in the first place in order to cover up the baldness of this demand. The second point is nothing less than an audacious attempt to disenfranchise Canadian members and to make the Trades and Labor Congress of Canada a stifled appendage of the American Federation of Labor."[11]

In Bengough's and Buckley's eyes, the issue of communism was raised to cover the AFL's attempt to destroy the autonomy of the TLC. The two Canadians described the trial in Miami as nothing more than a "kangaroo court." Bengough and Buckley rejected the AFL's attempts to blackmail the TLC by threatening to secede. If the AFL pulled out, the Canadians said, the TLC would simply charter Canadian unions to fill the gap. They concluded their report with an appeal for support: "All affiliated organizations and local unions must act now and notify their respective headquarters that they support the Trades and Labor Congress of Canada in resisting this unwarranted attempt of the American Federation of Labor to dominate the Trades and Labor Congress of Canada. Only by united action on the part of the Canadian membership can your congress remain a free trade union center that can fully represent the aims and aspirations of Canadian workers.

"Cooperation, Yes — Domination, No!"[12]

The TLC statement, issued just days before the CSU strike began, marked a high water mark in the struggle for an autonomous trade union movement. The seamen relied on the solidarity of the Canadian labor movement. It was on this issue that the AFL sought a test of its ability to control Canada's unions. The outcome of the battle for Canadian sovereignty hinged on the effectiveness of the congress' support of the Canadian Seamen's Union in its struggle against the employer-backed SIU.

AROUND THE WORLD, the seamen took on the task of defending their union and the dwindling Canadian fleet. They were rank and file trade unionists, not theoreticians or politicians, but on every ship young men came to the fore who showed they had exceptional talents that had only begun to be tapped. In the national office there was a clear concept of how the strike would unfold. It was a theory based not only on the past actions of CSU members, but as Danny Daniels observes, an "awareness of the role seamen have played historically.

"One aspect that had been rather strongly felt among some of us was the strike of the British fleet at the Nore in 1797 which historically is known as the Nore Mutiny. The entire British fleet went on strike and dismissed their officers. Ship's committees took over the discipline on all ships. I mention this because, to a considerable extent, those of us who were familiar with the Nore strike-mutiny were considerably influenced by it — how they conducted themselves, setting up committees to take over the discipline and control of the ships... We felt that when the strike took place the (Canadian) seamen would be similar. This was not spelled out but it was understood that this type of control was to take place."[13]

The idea and practice of the ship's committee was so ingrained in the

Canadian seamen that it was certain to be the governing body wherever there were groups of seamen together. This model of democratic government was not limited to the ships. When seamen were evicted from their vessels the committees simply transferred to dry land. One of the most sophisticated committee organizations was established in Port Alfred, Quebec.

The seamen were given use of a small plot of land near Port Alfred by a sympathetic farmer. They wasted no time in establishing a camp they called *S.S. Suntan.* Seamen who were hunted for their union activity or who simply had no place to go after their ship sailed with a scab crew made their way to the farm. Tents were pitched and the *Suntan's* committee was established as the governing body. A galley was set up, jobs were assigned and the camp was protected. Everything was administered through the committee, including rules for cribbage tournaments. A softball team called the CSU Stars travelled the vicinity forming lasting contacts with local people. The nearby community and crews from visiting ships from Norway and the United States gave money and food to support the camp. The seamen mixed work with play. Classes were held in trade unionism and courses were offered to train young patrolmen.[14] The union sent seamen who needed a break from the rigors of the strike for a rest at the camp. They returned to the picket lines raring to go.[15]

The *Searchlight* was circulated around the camp as were several other special publications sent out to the various strike centers by the national office. There were strike bulletins and updates as well as an additional weekly christened the *Striker.*[16] But as was the case in other areas, the *Suntan* crew felt it was important to have a local publication. The *S.S. Suntan* was published in both languages as a mimeographed leaflet. Editor Ray Collette urged readers to "give us your light, which we will reflect." The *Suntan* reprinted articles and poetry sent in by the seamen.[17] The camp, like the ships, was run on democratic lines which could be traced back to the early beginnings of the Canadian Seamen's Union.

The organization of the strike around ship's committees, coupled with the past emphasis on training rank and file leaders, gave the CSU a strong base. As Daniels suggested, the similarity with the Nore Mutiny was clear. The British seamen mutinied as a result of unbearable conditions. The crews could find no way short of striking to resolve their grievances. Literally starving, the seamen took the course of last resort and withdrew their labor. They created the ship's committee as a basic unit of self-government in which every seaman had the right to speak and to vote. From their ships, the seamen signalled the shore, proclaiming workers' self-government. In *The Great Mutiny,* James Dugan writes that the seamen's "protest is unparalleled in history... On more than a hundred vessels they raised the red flag of defiance. They swore oaths of extreme fidelity to their cause, deposed His Majesty's officers and elected their own. They established the first government based on universal suffrage that Britain had ever seen, afloat or ashore."[18] By its democratic nature, the strike became a challenge to the monarchy and the entire political system.

In this, too, there was a similarity with the CSU strike of 1949. The seamen were striking for their jobs, their union and a Canadian merchant fleet. In addition to the vested interests they challenged with these goals, the very structure of their organization flew in the face of the established order. The strike gave Canadian workers a taste of a new society based on elected committees nestled in the heart of production. The committees governed every aspect of life — assignment of jobs and tasks, distribution and allocation of food and shelter, strategy and planning, education and entertainment. Everything was decided by workers. It was a society Canada had glimpsed on only a few occasions, such as the Winnipeg General Strike of 1919 and in the unemployed and co-op movements of the Thirties.

The seamen were able to govern themselves in a democratic and disciplined fashion all over the globe and in many instances under the very noses of extremely hostile regimes. The seamen were lifting the curtain of the future and seeing the next act, and they fought to protect it. It was a sight few Canadians had seen. It was democracy without the economic exploitation of one class by another. It was a vision which neither business nor the state wanted transmitted to others, an experiment both were determined to crush.

CHAPTER TWENTY-THREE

Pickets Around the Globe

FOR CSU MEMBERS striking in Canadian ports, the union office was at most a telephone call away. In foreign ports, however, seamen faced obstacles of isolation, language and governments even more hostile than Canada's. But time and again their appeals for support were answered by workers as naturally as if the struggle was their own — as indeed it was. Inevitably the 1949 strike became a global struggle. The story of many of these individual strikes may never be recorded. A few must serve as examples.

THE CSU CREW of the *Tridale* was docked at the New Zealand port of Napier when the strike began. Support from New Zealand's longshoremen, the "waterside workers," was immediate. They promised not to work the ship. But the Canadians, who had intended to strike the *Tridale* then and there, discovered that harbor conditions were unsafe for an unmanned vessel. At the CSU's request, the longshoremen loaded the ship. On April 14, the *Tridale* docked in Wellington and a strike began that was to become a milestone in the history of the New Zealand labor movement.

Once assured that the CSU had the full support of the Trades and Labor Congress, the waterside workers put the machinery of trade union solidarity into action.[1] The seamen put up their strike signs, elected their strike committee and the longshoremen refused to handle the ship.

On board ship, life continued much as before. Under the direction of a strike committee that included able seaman Don Williams, fireman Louis Piveson, steward John Yurechko and carpenter Leigh Hallett, the seamen performed normal duties but refused to sail the vessel. Their strategy was to remain on board without being forced ashore by court injunctions, but they could only delay the inevitable. On April 22, their skipper convened a crew meeting and demanded that the seamen take the vessel to sea. They refused. Charged under the New Zealand Shipping Act with "disobeying the lawful command of the Master," the seamen were taken from the ship and jailed.

Help was not long in coming. Bail was raised by the New Zealand Waterside Workers Union, which arranged for the CSU members to take jobs as casual longshoremen.[2] Despite conviction on the charges April 27 and fines totalling 14 days' pay per man,[3] the crew continued to picket the ship. Then, the *Tridale* skipper made his next move.

"On May 2, we were ordered to return to duty on the ship," remembers Williams. "We realized that if we didn't, we would get another 'lawful command.' Rather than allow the captain the chance to say we had deserted and thus endanger the strike, every man reported for duty."

The lawful command came that afternoon at about 3:30 p.m., but by a remarkable coincidence the crew discovered that the engines had broken down. To a man, they agreed to sail the ship.

"On hearing this, the captain threatened to hire tugs to call our 'bluff,'" recalls Williams, "and he stormed ashore. Little did he know that we had already contacted the crews of the tugs, who had agreed not to touch the *Tridale* until the strike was over."[4]

On May 6, the captain again issued a "lawful command" to sail the ship. The 27 seamen refused. Four days later they were sentenced to a month in prison.[5] The sentences were to be served beginning June 7, but for every weapon the New Zealand courts handed the Canadian ship-owners, New Zealand workers had a ready reply. Donations poured in from worksite collections undertaken by the Waterside Workers Union, the Federated Seamen's Union and other local organizations. The crews of several west coast Canadian vessels, crewed by CSU members, threw what they could into the strikers' kitty. *Tridale* strikers, by now heading a New Zealand-wide committee that coordinated efforts to support the seamen and the strike, were given first priority on dockside jobs by the dockside unions.[6] And when the *Tridale* crew made ready to go to court June 7 to begin a month at hard labor, New Zealand's workers saw them off.

A southern gale lashed Wellington that day, but 200 English seamen and CSU members from west coast vessels marched through the streets with the 27 sentenced seamen to the site of a mass meeting. More than 1,500 marine workers met the Canadians. Williams went to the platform and told them of the struggle in Canada, where seamen were battling armed goons and RCMP officers wielding axe handles. Williams also told them of the magnificent support the dockies in Bristol and Avon-mouth were extending to their Canadian brothers. The New Zealand workers pledged they, too, would stick by the Canadian seamen come hell or high water.

"That afternoon, every man reported to the court on time," Williams wrote later. "We entered with our heads high and our hands clean, proud of what we had done. We knew it was no crime to demand the union of our choice. We knew that as workers we had done the honorable thing in spurning with disgust the company-sponsored outfit responsible for the deaths of our brother seamen when they, too, had refused to bow down to it.

"During our stay in Mount Crawford Prison, the morale of the men was high, as was their determination to continue the strike. A special tribute should be paid the chief cook of the ship, a man 74 years old, who had been employed in Canada's police force for 26 years, during 13 of which he was a police chief in Nova Scotia.

"When asked before he was jailed if he would like to quit on account of his age, his words were: 'I'll never be so old that I'll want to start scabbing.' "⁷

While the seamen served their time, their supporters fought to have them freed. As a result of the New Zealand labor movement's efforts, the Canadians were released a few days early. The sight that met them outside the prison gates was engraved in Williams' memory.

"The crew were met upon release by a fleet of taxis chartered by the Watersiders Union," he wrote, "and upon arrival in town were welcomed by Jock Barnes, the national president, Toby Hill, the national secretary and other members of the union who escorted us to the Royal Oak Hotel to start the celebration.

"That night, all hands slept in great style in one of·the city's leading hotels."⁸

The seamen had little time to relax. Within days the *Ottawa Valley*, manned by an SIU crew which had boarded in Saint John in vans protected by club-swinging Mounties, docked in Wellington. The wharfies refused to touch the vessel and when word of how her crew had found their jobs reached waterfront pubs, the docks became unsafe for the SIU scabs. The Harbor Board Employees Union, the Watersiders Union and the Transport Workers Federation backed the boycott. The CSU crews, secure in the knowledge the two vessels could not be worked, approached the employers' representative and offered a settlement to end the boycott of the *Ottawa Valley* and the strike against the *Tridale*. The terms: the company would sign the 1948 agreement and allow the crew to maintain CSU membership. The company stood firm. The men could sail the *Tridale* back to Canada, but after that there were no guarantees.

The CSU strikers had kept a close watch on events in Canada and the rest of the world. Despite the magnificent support of the New Zealand workers, the seamen realized they could not hold on forever, nor could they stand by and allow the waterside workers to be destroyed by their refusal to work the hot ships. The Canadian executive agreed and the New Zealand strike ended September 7.

"In behind the scenes," Williams remembers, "attempts were being made to use the strike of the Canadian seamen to force a showdown on the Auckland waterfront and smash the Watersiders Union. Rather than allow any reactionary stooges this opportunity, the New Zealand strike committee of the CSU recommended to the Canadian Executive that the ban ... be lifted."

On September 10, the strike committee approached the company and agreed to take the *Tridale* home.

So ended a five-month strike. In Saint John, the CSU sailors were marched ashore and SIU members were escorted aboard. For the new crew there was a little surprise: every wooden object on board — tables, chairs, everything — had been sawed by devilish carpenters. They collapsed at a touch.

The respect and admiration the Canadians developed for their New Zealand fellow workers was reciprocated. The dockies published a booklet called the *Tridale Strike* to commemorate the historic solidarity that developed in Wellington. In his introduction, Waterside Workers Union secretary Toby Hill ranked the *Tridale* strike with the "Home-Boat" strike of 1925 and the New Zealand seamen's general strike of 1934 as historic struggles in the country's labor history.

"More than a history," he wrote, the *Tridale* strike story was "a call to action. Canadian seamen are continuing a struggle which is the first round in defense of workers' conditions everywhere. We owe them a debt which can only be repaid by first strengthening our own unions. The lessons they have left us and the example they have given will not be forgotten."[9]

ON APRIL 7, 1949, two Canadian vessels lay at anchor in the harbor of Georgetown, British Guiana. The *Sunavis* and the *Sunwhit* were the former *Eastwood Park* and the *Wellington Park*, a pair of 10,000-tonners built by the taxpayers of Canada and purchased by the multinational Aluminum Co. of Canada. They were operated by Alcan's wholly-owned subsidiary, Saguenay Terminals Ltd.[10]

The *Sunavis* ship's delegate was Smiler, a veteran seaman who had watched Canada's first merchant marine disappear from under the feet of its unorganized seamen. Smiler and his shipmates on the CGMM fleet had been worked like slaves and when the ships were sold, the seamen had been cast aside like so many worn-out shoes. But in 1949, Smiler and the rest of the crew were union members. Their vessel was organized. This time they would have a say in their future.

The *Sunwhit* was the first to strike in Georgetown and its crew contacted the *Sunavis* urging them to tie up as well. "They sent word over to us they had received orders to go on strike," Smiler remembers.

"Our orders leaving New York were we would take no notice of anybody except straight from headquarters. We were in sort of a jam ourselves. We were ready to sail. We were waiting on the tide.

"We didn't know what we were going to do... They rang down for the engines to stand by. It was time to go but the engines wouldn't turn over. Now that, I know nothing about. There was something wrong in the low pressure cylinders. They took off the LP cover and found a link busted in the ring, so we couldn't go out on that tide.

"By that time we had word from headquarters. It said, 'Hold the ship.' What we did was pull the burners out and hide them, just leaving enough so the auxiliary would go.

"When they rang stand-by from the bridge, we weren't down there. The engineers were there, but they wouldn't answer the telegraphs.

"So the Captain phoned down. 'I'm ringing stand-by, why can't I get an answer?' The engineers told him there was no one down there to run the ship. 'What do you mean?' he said. 'What's wrong with you people?' 'There's nothing to run it with,' they said, 'they've hidden the burners.' "

With that the Captain called Smiler and his mates to the deck. "If you boys don't want to take it out, I'm going ashore and getting warrants for your arrest," the Captain told them. "Are you going to take this ship out?"

"He asked us one by one," recalls Smiler. "We were saying we belonged to a union. 'I didn't ask you that,' he said. 'I asked you if you are going to take this ship out or not.'

"We hemmed and hawed and then said, 'No, we are not.' So he went ashore and got warrants for our arrest."

While the Sunavis crew waited for the warrants to be served, they were able to secure the backing of the British Guiana and West Indies Federated Seamen's Union, which vowed not to touch any CSU ships. The British Guiana Trade Union Council declared that if this action was not sufficient, it would find other means of support.[11] The seamen secured the gangplank and maintained watches. On April 19, two truckloads of steel-helmetted police armed with revolvers, tear gas and rifles assembled on the dock and were loaded into police launches. They cast off and headed for the Sunavis.

But Smiler and the rest of the Canadians were able to defeat this show of force with words. "What we said was, 'This is Canada,' " recalls Smiler. "That place over there is British Guiana. You must deliver those warrants before they are any good."[12]

Amazingly, the police turned and left without boarding or attempting to serve the warrants.[13] The reason, Smiler believes, was that unionized sugar workers ashore had just settled a major strike. The Governor, anxious to avoid any more bloodshed told the police to let the Canadians be. The police contented themselves with a 24-hour watch from a circling boat.[14]

Meanwhile, the owners of the Sunavis and Sunwhit had two scab crews flown in from Canada. It is impossible to say how much the trip cost, but the Vancouver Province estimated the companies spent $125,000 to fly a crew to Brisbane to handle the Triberg. CSU sailors met the SIU crews on their arrival and explained the situation, including the strong support of British Guiana's unions. Possibly because the airlifted crews were used to the higher rates on American vessels, they wired their employers and demanded wages higher than the CSU contract! But the scabs could not be neutralized for long.

On April 11, police served warrants on the crew of the Sunwhit. The seamen were arrested, taken ashore and thrown in prison.[15] The next day they were charged with failing to obey an order and freed on bail of $1,000 each. The SIU crew had already manned their vessel.[16]

Aboard the Sunavis, the crew bided its time and kept a watchful eye on the authorities. By keeping the gangway up and restricting access to ship's officers, they were able to repel several attempts to force them to sail the vessel or to leave so that the scab crew could come aboard.[17]

But ashore, there were splits developing among the local unions. Near the end of April, Waterfront Workers Union members loaded the CNS ship Canadian Challenger, which had arrived with a scab crew. The British Guiana Trade Union Council continued its support, but with longshoremen working scab ships and pressure mounting from the American Federation of Labor to break with the CSU, it was obvious the strike was weakening.[18]

Early in May, the Trade Union Council succumbed and withdrew its support.[19] With the crew now isolated, the Captain moved quickly obtaining an injunction against the vessel on the grounds that it was disturbing harbor traffic. The injunction ordered the crew off the vessel by the following Thursday and directed them to appear in court four days later to explain why they were holding the ship.[20] Then the company sought the services of a watchman who boarded the ship daily. One day late in May, he handed the seamen a copy of the local newspaper. Printed in the paper was the warrant from the Supreme Court of British Guiana, which ordered the crew "upon reading the Writ of Summons ... to forthwith leave the steamship Sunavis."[21] The seamen played a last, desperate card.

Unknown to the authorities, the CSU members had two secret links to the shore. One was Cheddi Jagan, left-wing politician and organizer destined to become Guiana's first premier elected under universal suffrage, who rowed out to the ship in a skiff to bring news and food. Even more secret was the presence on board of seaman Gordie Green.

Although everyone, including those who wrote up the warrants, believed Green was on shore, he actually swam back and forth from the beach to the ship to keep the crew informed on events in the city. Smiler had an inspiration: "I said to this Green, 'Now you're supposed to be ashore. Go and appear in court for us ... go ashore and stand up for us.' "[22]

At 9:30 on the morning of May 30, Green appeared in court. The crew remained on the vessel. The judge was outraged. "I command this colony to have these men, regardless of how, brought ashore and lodged in the prison by Wednesday morning."[23] He then sentenced the 25 seamen to indefinite prison terms, in absentia, for contempt of court.[24]

The *Searchlight* had declared that the stay-aboard strike of the *Sunavis* already was the longest in history, but the Canadians were near the end of the road.[25]

"We had run out of grub by then," says Smiler. "It had been two weeks that we hadn't had anything brought aboard. We put it to the crew. It was up to them. I knew we were going to have a bit of trouble; some of them were young and hungry. I called a meeting and put it to a vote and I told them I would abstain.

"They knew they would be going hungry and I guess they were glad to get out after 53 days. So they said they would acknowledge the fact (of the sentence) and go ashore, give themselves up."[26]

On May 31, the Canadians surrendered and on June 1, they were behind bars.[27] Rousted out of their hotel at 6 a.m. that day, they were driven up the street "like a bunch of cattle to the court.

"We stayed there two or three hours and then they pushed us into a truck, drove us up to the prison."[28] The seamen were held for 16 days, then released. After attending a party thrown in their honor by Cheddi Jagan, they were flown home.[29]

IN JANUARY 1949, the Canadian vessel *Cambrey*, owned by the Elder Dempster Lines, was working the South African coast. Her ship's delegate was 22-year-old Tommy McGrath, who was neither new to the sea, nor to trade unionism. He had shipped out at the age of 14, sailed deepsea throughout the war and joined the CSU in February 1944. On April 11, McGrath was on deck when the wireless operator handed him a message.

"The wording was quite specific," he remembers. " 'Don't put down the gangplank... Be prepared that scabs are ready to board the vessel. They have been hired in various ports.' We carried out the instructions given to us."[30]

The national executive had studied the question of tying up vessels in semi-fascist countries and had decided CSU crews were capable of winning enough support in South Africa to make a strike successful. The telegram had been sent to the *Cambrey* and two other Canadian vessels. Still, the national officers were aware that it took "great courage to strike in South Africa, where the government is semi-fascist and is aping the ways of Hitler."[31] The crew of the *Cambrey* was ready for the test. McGrath told the union the "boys will conduct themselves the way Canadian Seamen's Union members should do."[32]

The *Cambrey* steamed into Table Bay and tied up at the Capetown docks. By the time the hawsers were made fast, picket signs hung from the sides of the ship. "Scabs board this vessel at their own risk," read one.[33] The captain, meanwhile, addressed the crew. "We were asked what we were going to do," McGrath told readers of the *Searchlight*. "He was really going to give us a break, he was offering us the chance to join the SIU. What a joke!"[34]

When the dock police and immigration officials attempted to board, the crew "held the Capetown South Africa police at bay ... with the ship's firehoses and refused to hoist the gangplank for hours."[35] Eventually, port authorities forced the crew to allow a crane to put a gangplank in place, but the seamen maintained wide-awake six-man security watches at all times. Their first setback, however, came not from police but from fellow Canadian workers. The engineers, whose "officers' strike" had been supported by the CSU, turned off the crew's water.[36]

More principled fellow workers were found ashore. The secretary of the Capetown Trades and Labor Council called on all local unions to back the striking seamen and to prohibit scabbing on the Canadians. He assured the seamen they would obtain the support of Capetown unionists.[37]

Within a week, the captain had obtained a court ruling ordering the seamen either to quit the vessel or take it to sea. They stood convicted of "combined wilful disobedience to lawful commands or combined neglect of duty."[38] Sloppy legal work by the shipowners saved the crew. "They were so anxious to get us all in jail they charged us under the British Shipping Act," says McGrath. "When it came to appeal court, it was thrown out. They should have charged us under the Canada Shipping Act."[39]

On April 25 two more Canadian east coasters, the *Cargill* and the *Cumberland County* joined the *Cambrey* in Capetown. To the shock of the South African press, two Black crewmen were on the articles of the *Cumberland County*. "There was an article in the South African papers explaining that the Black crew and the white crew members slept in the same accommodations," recalls McGrath. "The whites in South Africa never thought that was possible."[40] White sightseers began to crowd the docks to gape at the Black and white "reds."

One day, one of the onlookers yelled up to the deck, "what is your position on Blacks?" One of the young white rank and filers put his arm around his Black partner and hollered back, "That's my position. He's my brother."[41] Not suprisingly, the CSU was not popular among supporters of apartheid, but the Canadians' struggle drew broad solidarity from South African trade unionists and progressives. As Danny Daniels noted many years later, the incident was a symbol not only of the CSU's principles "but also of the influence it immediately brought to bear on another country ... that made the CSU not only the scourge of the shipowners, but a scourge to reactionary and right-wing forces in other countries."[42]

For McGrath the support provided by South African trade unionists suggested that their labor movement was more advanced than Canada's despite the backwardness of their political system. "I found it kind of ironic that I ran into three unions where the elected leadership — I mean president and other positions — were all women. I don't find that even in our own country.

"The head of the Fishermen's Union was a woman who gave support financially and otherwise. A union called the Sweet Workers Union, which organized stores in South Africa, was led by a woman, and they were very good, as was the bus drivers' union — also led by a woman."[43]

Solidarity from workers like these kept the strike of the three Canadian crews solid. Watches were maintained and some of the seamen were able to take up lodgings with sympathizers ashore. But in early June, the captain of the Cumberland County obtained an injunction and the police moved against the striking seamen.[44] The crew left without resistance, their spirit intact. Only two seamen agreed to give up the strike and stay on board. The remaining 29 marched off, under police escort, singing, "You can't scare me, I'm sticking to the union."[45] They were incarcerated in the immigration barracks to await deportation.

Two days later, the Canadian vessel Chandler arrived in Capetown with a scab SIU crew. At dockside she was met by the banners of the Trade Union Aid Committee. Nearby, banners signifying the support of Capetown unions for the CSU marked the head of a march to the ship. But as the marchers — local trade unionists and CSU members — made their way down the quay, they were intercepted by the Railway Police. Captain Van Staden ordered his men to "arrest the lot." The entire demonstration was arrested under the Riotous Assembly Act and jailed. The South Africans were released within hours. The Canadians were held overnight, then released without being charged.[46]

On June 21, the authorities arrested the crews of the Cargill and the Cambrey. The Canadians offered no resistance and were held in the Roeland Street Jail. There was no room at the immigration barracks, already filled with the seamen of the *Cumberland County*. The three crews awaited deportation.

Six scabs were found from among the 33 seamen on the *Cambrey* to take the vessel back to Canada. The *Cumberland County* remained tied to the Capetown dock waiting for a crew.

THERE WERE TWO SHIPS at anchor in Cuban waters in April 1949. The *Canadian Victor* and the *Federal Pioneer* both were owned by the Canadian government and operated by its shipping arm, Canadian National Steamships. The *Victor* was anchored at Cayo Frances loading station, 16 miles from Cairbarien, Cuba. Her crew took a strike vote and decided they would join the crew of the *Federal Pioneer* and other Canadian vessels on strike.[47]

For two days the seamen remained on board and refused to move the ship. On April 21, Captain P.L. Scott of the *Victor* informed local authorities that the crew refused to leave the vessel and was "armed and hostile."[48] There was no evidence to support the Captain's allegation of armed mutineers aboard his ship, but the *Victor's* crew was apprehensive. The crew of the *Pioneer* had peacefully walked off their ship only to be thrown into a Cuban prison to await deportation to Canada. They had lost their jobs and there now was one less ship in the Canadian merchant fleet.[49] The "Victors" thought it would be safer to stay aboard than to follow their brothers into the Cuban prison system.

The Cuban government, headed at that time by Carlos Prio Socarras, dispatched a gunboat to remove the striking seamen. The naval vessel was joined by a sister ship and the two gunboats came alongside the idle Canadian freighter. The cautious seamen informed the Cuban marines that they would discuss the issue only with one of their officers. As ship's delegate Paul Campbell later reported, the two gunboats backed off and then, with no warning, both opened fire.

Campbell, the officers and crew of the *Victor* dove for the deck as bullets ricocheted off steel and riddled wood. As the machine gunners continued to strafe bulkheads and funnel, the seamen lowered two jacob's ladders over the side and the marines scrambled aboard.[50] The crew, which was in no position to resist, was rounded up and held at rigid attention by prodding bayonets. Two more men climbed up the ladders and ordered the crew imprisoned. They were Canadian National Steamships officials who had commanded the entire operation from the bridge of a nearby Norwegian freighter.[51] The crew of the *Victor* was transported to the Norwegian ship and locked up. The next day they were removed under an armed guard of 40 marines and locked up in a shoreside prison where they spent the next several days.[52]

The strikers were soon deported. On their return to Canada, the CSU called a news conference to allow the *Canadian Victor's* crew to tell of the Cuban ordeal. Thirteen crew members were telling their story to reporters in the union's St. Francis Xavier Street national office when the Montreal Anti-Subversive Squad crashed into the room, announced that the press conference was over and arrested the seamen for violations of the Canada Shipping Act during their time in Cuba.[53] Danny Daniels argued that the seamen had already done time in Cuba for alleged violations of the act and it would be double jeopardy to arrest them again on the same charges.[54] He was told to "keep quiet."[55] As the seamen were being loaded into the Black Maria, Daniels continued to argue their case. He explained to reporters what had happened in Cuba. For "refusing to re-enter the union hall" he was placed under arrest and thrown into the paddy wagon with the others.[56] The ex-crewmen from the *Victor* were charged with disobeying a lawful command and Daniels with disturbing the peace. They were searched and thrown in jail.[57]

NEITHER LIONEL CHEVRIER, federal Minister of Transport, nor Humphrey Mitchell, the Minister of Labor, had taken any action to arrange a settlement between the CSU and the shipowners. Mitchell simply kept repeating that it was a violation of the Canada Shipping Act to strike in foreign ports. His contribution to ending the strike was to promise that any seaman who contravened the act by striking outside Canada would be punished.[58] The union believed Mitchell was acting in concert with the shipowners by trying to bring the strike back to Canadian soil. Dewar Ferguson said the minister's statements were "all the more despicable when one realizes this is a legal strike. They (the cabinet ministers) are trying to force the crews to sail back to Canada, where with the aid of goons and government police, our picket lines can be smashed and strikebreakers placed aboard the ships."[59] The federal government was prepared to get the CSU any way it could, but the seamen were not about to leave the shelter of the international solidarity in foreign ports to pour their blood on Canada's shores.

While CSU pickets spanned the globe, the forces of the union and the shipowners finally concentrated on a single country's waterfront. It was in the United Kingdom, with its long trade union history and Labor Party government, where the CSU deepsea strike reached a climax.

CHAPTER TWENTY-FOUR

The Battle in Britain

ON MARCH 28, 1949, the Canadian freighter *Gulfside* docked in Avonmouth, England. The stevedores went to work to discharge her cargo and by April 1 the *Gulfside* was standing ready to cast off and make her way out of Bristol Channel.

Forty-nine-year-old Andy "Jock" Brogan called himself the "oldest galley-boy in the CSU." As the rest of the crew readied the *Gulfside* for sea, he was busy cleaning up dishes from the last mug-up and preparing the galley for open water. Brogan was relatively new to the sea. He had grown up in Scotland and spent many years in the Clydeside shipyards, where shop committees, factory councils and trade unions were as old as the working class itself. Brogan was steeped in working class traditions and while in Scotland was a member of the Socialist Labor Party. After his career at sea he was to return to the shipyards, this time as a member of the Marine Workers and Boilermakers Union in Vancouver. That day, however, his main concern was to put the dishes away. On deck was Steve Tokaruk, ship's delegate for the *Gulfside*, who was preparing for the 4 o'clock departure. He was busy at his duties when he was handed a telegram. He unfolded the paper and read, "A GENERAL STRIKE HAS BEEN DECLARED, STRIKE YOUR SHIP, MAINTAIN STEAM AND MAINTAIN SECURITY."[1]

Tokaruk made his way to the galley and handed the message to Brogan, the stewards' delegate. "Within half an hour," Brogan remembers, "we had all the crew congregated and held a meeting. The telegram was self-explanatory and right away we decided the ship was not going to move."[2] Tokaruk went to the bridge and informed the captain of the crew's intentions. The skipper stared at Tokaruk in disbelief and asked if perhaps this was some sort of strange April Fool's prank. Tokaruk assured him it was no joke. The *Gulfside* was marooned in Avonmouth.[3]

The skipper stopped smiling and moved quickly. The officers cut off the water supply so that steam could not be maintained. By April 2 the company had fired the seamen and obtained an injunction ordering them off the ship.[4] They left the *Gulfside* and made contact with the dockers' union. Assured of local support and with lodging nearby, the seamen established picket lines near the dock gates and waited for the next move.[5] An almost identical situation had developed in Liverpool. The *Seaboard Ranger* had docked March 28 and the dockers were working her cargo. On April 1, Jack Pope arrived from London with the news that the world-wide strike was underway. The seamen immediately ceased work and the Liverpool dockers refused to touch the ship.[6]

Canadian vessels continued to arrive in the United Kingdom. On April 4, the *Beaverbrae* maneuvered into the Royal Docks in London. Formerly the *Huascaran*, a German submarine tender, she had come to Canada as war reparations. She had been converted into a passenger/cargo ship which carried Canadian export cargoes eastbound and displaced persons from Europe to Canada on the return trip. The largest Canadian-flag merchant vessel, the *Beaverbrae* was owned by Canadian Pacific Railway and carried a crew of 125. The CPR had many deepsea vessels at the time, but the *Beaverbrae* was the only one registered in Canada. CPR then was 58 percent British owned, 27 percent American owned and five percent in the hands of other non-Canadians. Canadians owned 10 percent of the "Canadian" Pacific Railway.[7]

"We heard on the radio that the strike was on," recalls *Beaverbrae* ship's delegate Bud Doucette, "and we prepared to join the strike in the U.K."

Doucette notified the captain of the crew's intention to strike the ship. The captain "was shocked to the point of being tongue-tied. He'd never had such a statement made to him in all his years at sea. He said we might be on strike, but first we had to move the ship to another dock. We replied that we would take that under advisement, but in the meantime nothing was being moved anywhere. We would do such work as was necessary for the safety of the ship and the members of the crew, sanitation, and the feeding and care of the non-union personnel on board, but there would be no work done in preparation for discharging the cargo, moving the ship, or anything that would be of convenience to the company and against the interest of the union. The cargo in this instance was mainly grain."[8]

The London dockers boarded the *Beaverbrae* and were approached by Doucette. As Jack Dash, a rank-and-file dockers' leader, later recalled, Doucette "explained the situation and made an appeal for international trade union solidarity."[9] The hatch covers were left where they were. The Canadians were told "not to worry" and the dockers walked off the vessel.

As far as Doucette and the rest of the crew knew, there were only two other Canadian vessels in England. The *Gulfside* was tied up in Avonmouth and the *Seaboard Ranger's* crew had struck in Liverpool.

In fact, there were four other Canadian ships in the U.K. The *Lake Atlin* was unloading grain and lumber in Hull. She had arrived from Vancouver and was under west coast articles. Her ship's delegate was a tall, thin CSU militant whose nickname of Stringbean had finally been shortened to Stringer. Stringer MacDonald was grumpy with his friends, clear-cut in his opinions and had a caustic wit. The *Atlin* had been in port for a couple of days when the strike was called. Although bargaining had not broken off with west coast shipowners, the *Atlin* crew tied up. "The next thing we knew," remembers MacDonald, "there was a message from the ship's agent saying there was a long distance call from Vancouver for the ship's delegate. Jimmy Thompson (director of the West Coast District of the CSU) was burning up the wires. He said, 'I'm in negotiations with the west coast shipowners and I've got a chance to sign a contract for west coast ships.' So we had to go back."[10] It was the end of the strike for the *Lake Atlin*, but not for her crew. Like CSU members everywhere, they did what they could to support their brothers who were on the bricks.

There was still another Canadian vessel in the U.K. She was the *Ivor Rita* and she was in London. Doucette and two other *Beaverbrae* delegates were patrolling the London waterfront to see what was up. For the first two days they found nothing. But "on the third day of the strike," Doucette recalls, "we were looking around the Port of London when we spotted a ship flying the Canadian flag at the grain dock not too far from the Royal Docks where the *Beaverbrae* was moored. McNeil, Arland and myself went to visit this ship. Her name was the *Ivor Rita* and we found a peculiar situation. We had never heard of the ship before — *Ivor Rita*: port of registry, Montreal; flag, Canadian — and not a Canadian in the ship's crew. They were mostly East Indian seamen with some North Africans. The officers were British and German.

"We went aboard and talked to the bosun and told him all (East Coast) Canadian ships were on strike. He called his crew together and talked with them. They didn't know their status, so to take the responsibility off their shoulders we went down and talked to the grainhandlers. Their union, following the old terminology, was called the 'corn porters.' The corn porters are a distinct part of the London waterfront unions. We told them the plight we were in and requested them not to handle the cargo in the ship before we were able to determine whether she was black or could be unloaded. So the *Ivor Rita* was declared to be black. That's a common term in British unionism. A job that is in dispute is declared to be black, and of course a ship that is in dispute is black, and that's the end of that. There was no further work done on the *Ivor Rita*."[11] On April 9 the *Argomont* arrived and was struck at the Surrey Docks. Like the crew of the *Beaverbrae*, the seamen remained on board. Again the dockers refused to work a struck ship.

The crew of the *Ivor Rita* was treated in a fashion that allowed the ship to be tied up but made virtually no demands on the crew. The *Ivor Rita's* crew decided they would side with the CSU in the dispute and on April 13 they joined the *Beaverbrae's* crew in a march through London's streets in protest over the shooting of CSU seamen in Halifax the previous Friday. The seamen demonstrated their displeasure by picketing Canada House. They carried signs which read "Stop Gangster Law in Canada, Torpedoed 1939-1945, Shot 1948-49," and "We Fight Clubs and Guns in Canada."[12]

In 1949, Jack Dash was "unofficial" or rank-and-file spokesman for the London dockers. He explained many years later why the longshoremen so readily gave their support to the striking Canadians. It was a tradition based on "an unwritten law in dockland, stemming from the pioneering days of building trade unionism and passing down one generation to another, father to son, that you never do anything to impair another man's strike. Honor the picket line." That principle would be tested to its limit in 1949 and the struggle to defend it would cause great hardship to the dockers and their families. As Dash wrote later, "the spirit of international trade unionism reached a high peak," adding "you can't go into an industrial struggle without getting hurt."[13]

Ships now were tied up in Wales, England, Scotland, Holland, Belgium, Norway, Spain and Italy. It was decided to make London the coordination center for the European strikes. When seamen were evicted from their vessels, they would head to the European Strike Committee in London unless they were deported home. Bud Doucette was elected chairman of the committee and Joe McNeil, Bill Arland, Al MacIsaac, Andy Brogan and Steve Tokaruk were on the executive. Jack Pope carried out liaison duties.[14]

"The strike committee was the most democratic thing I've ever known," Tokaruk recalls. "Nobody was in charge. Nobody was hollering orders at anybody. The area strike committees were formed from the ship's delegates and the crews. They were freely elected... That was one of the things that kept it going. There was no big leadership at the top. There was a collective leadership. All of the rank and file felt they were really involved. It had a sort of syndicalist overtone. I always think that if we had won that strike and become a powerful seamen's union, Canada would have had a merchant marine and the union would have a sort of rotating leadership and would have never become a type of organization that was governed from the top. This was another thing that scared the government. The union was so much ahead of its time and not because someone pushed it. (Its strength) sort of grew out of this moral superiority. We knew we had it over our adversaries. Guys were no longer interested in whether it was a 15 percent increase or a 30 percent increase or anything else. All they were *not* going to accept was a union imposed on them by the federal government (and) run by a convicted gangster, which Hal Banks was."[15]

There were several problems for the committee to contend with. Each crew still aboard ship had to maneuver to stay aboard. Injunctions were avoided in every way possible. Seamen who were ejected from their ships had to have a flop and all seamen, aboard ship or ashore, had to be fed. The seamen's cause had to be publicized and support had to be gathered and maintained. There were virtually no official contacts in the U.K. except for those that Jack Pope had been able to establish since his arrival. Propaganda from the SIU and the American Federation of Labor had to be countered and the morale of seamen on strike thousands of miles from home had to be maintained. It was an enormous task, but the seamen had intelligent leadership seasoned with the experience of the two Great Lakes strikes.

Doucette, always a snappy dresser who now sports a handlebar mustache and a gold earring, well recalls the problems of the European Strike Committee and the methods used to resolve them. It was his job to organize the rank and filers and put them where they could do the most good. "We had to support ourselves," he explains. "We had no funds from the National Office of the union because the National Office didn't have adequate funds to prosecute the strike in Canada. We sent out appeals to the British labor movement and we were invited to many local unions of every description. The requests came in from all over for an explanation of this world-wide strike phenomenon. We went around and explained why we had to be on strike in the United Kingdom, why we couldn't take the ships back home and explained that a Canadian union was being replaced by a union from the United States, over the objections of the people who were sailing Canadian ships and who had sailed them during the war.

"Necessity demanded that we produce people who were capable of going out and explaining the union's position. We had some experienced, politically-astute people on the ships, namely Bill Arland, Joe McNeil, Al Mooney and Nick Carter, who had been in the Lake strikes ...If we had 10 requests for speakers for union meetings in one evening, we had to find 10 speakers to address those meetings. That's when people like Allan MacIsaac and Ken Evans, along with other people in Avonmouth and in Liverpool, and rank and filers like Steve Tokaruk, became good speakers for the union.

"We used to take this position: If someone said, 'I can't get up and speak before people, I get too nervous,' or 'I don't know what the hell to tell them,' well, Jesus, you've been on strike for five weeks and you don't know what you've been on strike for? What are you doing here? He would have to explain what the reasons were behind the strike. It turned out to be a very useful experience and we developed people more rapidly under those conditions than you would normally develop them had there not been a world-wide bloody battle going on."[16]

Seamen like Jimmy Walters, who had no union or speaking experience, learned to speak for the CSU. Walters had done a lot of weight-lifting in Vancouver's Western Gym and could take care of himself in any crowd, but he was shy when it came to addressing groups of people. Out of necessity, he was sent to factory gates to speak to the workers and to try to raise money for the union's cause. It wasn't long before he would jump on the bumper of a car and give the union's spiel without hesitation.

"We call them longshoremen here," Walters says, "but in England they are called dockies. They gave us tremendous support." Now a longshoreman himself in the port of Vancouver, Walters well remembers how British workers responded to his CSU appeal. "They did not work any Canadian ships, realizing what was involved. They would go down to the regular dispatch, just as we do here, and would plug in for different types of work aboard the ships and on the docks. When a Canadian ship came up that the employers wanted worked, all the dockies turned it down."[17]

IN AVONMOUTH, the *Gulfside* sat at her dock, crewless and idle. The longshoremen refused to work the ship. An injunction ordered the seamen off the ship April 21 and the CSU strikers moved into workers' homes near the waterfront, working their picket shifts to maintain the support of the longshoremen.[18] The shipowners loaded an airplane with scabs and flew them to the U.K. to replace the Avonmouth strikers. They arrived May 1, the day celebrated by workers the world over as the symbol of internationalism and solidarity.[19] MacDonald remembers how the *Gulfside* was scabbed: "They shunted a train down onto the dock and part of the train was an open gondola car. The scabs hunched down and the police had the dock cordonned off so that the CSU men couldn't get near her. When the gondola got abeam of the accommodation ladder, they just stopped the train and the scabs piled out and went aboard the *Gulfside*."[20]

Andy Brogan wasted no time. The day after the scabs were put aboard he went to the dockies. "I went over to the open field where the hiring hall was and the men were all there waiting to be dispatched. I got a wooden box out of the hotel and we held an impromptu meeting and the dockers all gathered 'round and I explained the situation — how the scabs had been flown over from Canada. Right off the bat they wouldn't go to work that morning. We held another meeting at the British legion canteen, which was just outside the dock gates. A representative from the dockers' union came down and he tried to get the men to forget all about the CSU. The men booed him out of the place. In fact, he left in a hurry because he was getting such a tough time. I told them to go back to work as usual, as long as we got the guarantee that (they wouldn't) handle the *Gulfside*. That was all right."[21]

The longshoremen warned that they would work no ships in the port if they were pushed on the issue of working the *Gulfside*. The tugboat workers also voted to return to work but to boycott the *Gulfside*. Once the scabs were aboard the freighter, the tugboat crews moved two tugs close alongside to block any attempt to move the ship. Sixteen British crews walked off their ships to show solidarity with the striking Canadians. One vessel's crew vowed not to return to work until the scabs were removed from the *Gulfside*. The memory of the British workers' support would remain with Steve Tokaruk forever: "Never have I seen action of this kind. It was the greatest show of international working class solidarity I have ever seen."[22]

"The scabs were on the *Gulfside* and they couldn't get ashore," recalls Brogan. "It's only a small place, Avonmouth, but the people there would have bloody well crucified them once they found out where they came from. There was a watchman at the gangplank, a local man, a pensioner. He had no time for them and he used to come down and talk to us when he was off duty. They asked him to bring them beer and to bring it on board. There was a girl there who worked in the Army Navy Legion. She was an Irish girl from Cork. Jesus, she was quite a character. She said, 'Sure, come down and get the beer.' He came down with a big can to get it. She filled it up so far with beer and then pissed in the can. The old boy knew but never said a word. He just took it on board and gave it to them ... it was good enough for them, anyway."[23]

Brogan, Tokaruk and the others realized they had little to worry about in Avonmouth and decided to leave the strike in the hands of the longshoremen while they headed for London to get a bunk and link up with the Strike Committee.

In London, the crews of the *Beaverbrae* and the *Argomont* stayed on board but did not work. The *Beaverbrae's* cargo fell under the jurisdiction of the National Amalgamated Stevedores and Dockers. The union's members accepted dispatch to the *Beaverbrae* each morning, but when they arrived at the ship, the crew refused to lower the gangways. The stevedores remained on the dock, outside of the dispute.[24]

Doucette was aboard the *Beaverbrae*, slipping off from time to time to Pier Road to conduct the business of the Strike Committee. Within 10 days of the tie-up, the company had begun court action to evict the crew of the *Beaverbrae*. "We were all served with summonses," Doucette recalls. "We couldn't evade them for evermore." The seamen accepted service of the court orders and were haled into West Ham courthouse to face charges of impeding progress of the voyage, disobeying the command of a ship's master and usurping the captain's authority. CSU lawyer Jack Gaster played a longshot, challenging the court's right to hear the case. He demanded proof that the vessel was registered in Canada. When the captain admitted the Certificate of Registry was in Montreal, the judge dismissed the case because there was no proof of ownership. "That was a temporary victory," says Doucette, "and we celebrated it."[25] By April 24, the crew was back on the *Beaverbrae*, but within two weeks, court proceedings began anew.

"In the interim we went around and secured a church hall in dockland not too far from where the ships were berthed," recalls Doucette. "The hall was big enough to accommodate a couple of hundred for feeding and sleeping purposes. We had about 65 or 70 members off the *Beaverbrae*. Most stayed in the church hall with the crew off the *Argomont*." Crews from Norway, Belgium and France quickly swelled the numbers in the hall. "At one stage we had about 300 seamen to feed and house and in some cases provide clothing. In many cases the fellows were taken off the ships in Europe at night by the police with nothing but the clothes on their backs. Even though many had sailed for six or eight months, they were never paid for the time up to the commencement of the strike. They lost all of their wages."[26]

The *Dingwall* was one of many ships that were scabbed by the SIU in European ports. The crew struck April 14 in Rotterdam and the Dutch authorities had them arrested and held as illegal aliens. An SIU crew was flown to the Netherlands and the *Dingwall* sailed soon after. The authorities then deported the 27 CSU members to England. A similar fate befell the crew of the *Mont Gaspé* when they struck in Lisbon.

It was the *Beaverbrae* and the *Montreal City* which became the focal points of the European struggle. The crew of the *Beaverbrae* resisted eviction for 38 days, leaving the ship on May 12 with a pledge from the dockers not to touch the ship. Doucette considered the strike to be solid because the ships couldn't even be moved to a continental port for unloading "because the tug men have told us they won't allow them to leave."[27] Although the CSU crews in the U.K. were aware that their fellow strikers in other countries had physically resisted eviction, they accepted the advice of lawyer Gaster to avoid such tactics in Britain. "This is a high court injunction," he told the *Gulfside* crew. "You have to get off or they will put you all in prison. You'll lose sympathy if you fight the British police... You'll alienate the labor movement here."[28]

The *Montreal City* provided a different challenge. The vessel was scabbed in Montreal and left that port April 27 bound for the U.K.[29] She discharged cargo in Swansea, Barry and Newport, Wales. The Newport dockers had just begun to work her when delegates from the *Gulfside* arrived and quickly distributed a leaflet asking the longshoremen to hear the CSU side of the story before they returned to work.[30]

"You have allowed yourself to be misled," the leaflet stated, "into believing that the dispute between the Canadian Seamen's Union and the shipping bosses of Canada is a dispute between two unions. You have listened to a tissue of lies and misstatements, written by the representatives of the blackleg Seafarers International Union and spoken by your own trade union leaders... You have accused, sentenced and executed your brother trade unionists, even without the courtesy of a trial. Even a criminal has the democratic right of defense before a reactionary court of law. Surely a trade unionist has the right of a trial before his fellow trade unionists before he is convicted. We appeal to you as one trade unionist to another to give us a hearing."[31]

The Newport dockers downed tools, heard the CSU men out, took a vote and agreed not to work the *Montreal City*.[32] Then the American Federation of Labor intervened. William Green, president of the AFL, demanded that U.K. dockers work the struck ships. Arthur Bird, national secretary of the British Transport and General Workers Union (TGWU), promised to try to persuade the dockers to reverse their stand on the *Montreal City*.[33] After two days on strike, the strength of the rank and file was waning in Newport. Local leaders were able to mount a back to work campaign. The *Montreal City* was unloaded and left for Avonmouth, where she was to take on cargo for the United States. Both the shipowners and the British Ministry of Labor hoped that the defeat of the Newport dockers would serve as an example to the longshoremen at Avonmouth, who stood solidly with the CSU.[34]

The SIU had sent an international representative to London to carry the attack against the CSU into the British labor movement. In a meeting with the TGWU leadership May 7, the SIU's agent claimed that all of the American and Canadian labor movement supported the SIU. As proof he read out a telegram from J.J. Campbell, president of the Halifax local of the International Longshoremen's Association, stating that the CSU had no support·among Canadian longshoremen.[35]

The CSU countered with a telegram from W.L. Carlin, president of the Saint John's chapter of the ILA, who called Campbell a "liar, scab and strikebreaker.

"Rank and file ignore Campbell's orders to work struck ships," he wrote, "and refuse to cross CSU picket lines. My members in Saint John solid behind me in support of CSU. We refuse to cross CSU picket line despite company pressure." It was a convincing account for British longshoremen, who had seen their own leaders turn their back on trade union principles while "unofficial" committees carried on the struggle.

The TGWU attempted to win the London dockers over to the AFL's position, but a waterfront meeting called by Bird to argue his case was abortive. "While Bird was defending (his) attitude," a Canadian reporter wrote, "docker members of his union in Newport and Liverpool were siding with CSU strikers. Officers of the Liverpool Trades Council, a federation of all trade unions in the port, decided the strike should have British backing and offered financial and all other help."[36] British seamen joined the dockers in support of the CSU. On May 11, 150 British seamen left their ships and paraded on the docks with banners supporting the Canadian strike. A wave of police "dispersed the display of international support 'in lightning speed.' "[37]

TGWU leaders descended on Avonmouth, hoping to use the arrival of the *Montreal City* to break the dockers' solidarity with the CSU. To prepare the ground, the national leaders and the Avonmouth Dock District Committee of the TGWU put forward a joint resolution recommending that the *Gulfside* be allowed to sail. A mass meeting of dockers May 12 turned the recommendation down.[38] On May 14, the day the *Montreal City* was to arrive, the dockers gathered at the waterfront once again. This time the speaker was CSU president Harry Davis who had just arrived in the U.K. He explained the situation and the dockers voted "not to permit the *Gulfside* to sail, not to handle the *Montreal City* when it arrived, and not to handle any other Canadian ship arriving in similar circumstances." When the *Montreal City* appeared in the river outside the dock area, the tugboat men and lock gatemen maneuvered her into a safe berth inside the dock and the dockers refused to load her. She was stuck.[39]

On May 16, the Dock Labor Board asked for volunteers to discharge the cargoes from the *Montreal City*'s holds. Fifty-five men answered the call and worked the ship for two or three hours before they were "called off" by other dock workers. When they downed tools, the entire dock was stopped for an afternoon meeting which finally decided to resume work the next morning on all ships except the *Montreal City*.[40] The next morning no workers were called to the Canadian ship and the dockers worked the rest of the port as usual, but on May 18 a gang of grainworkers were dispatched to the *Montreal City* and refused the job. The employers retaliated with a port-wide lockout: no workers would be called for any other ships until the men agreed to work the *Montreal City*.[41]

The Avonmouth docks were controlled by the Port of Bristol Employers' Association. The agents of the *Gulfside* estimated that it cost their company $2,000 a day to have the ship tied up.[42] When that figure was multiplied by every vessel affected by the lockout over the entire Avonmouth port, the cost of the employers' decision must be reckoned in the hundreds of thousands of dollars. Yet G.A. Isaacs, labor minister in the Labor Party government of the day, said there were good reasons for the employers' ultimatum. Had work been allowed on all vessels except the struck ship, "the effect would have been to immobilize that ship indefinitely to the advantage of the CSU strikers," he said. "That was the reason for the repeated suggestion by the CSU that this course should be followed. The employers took the view that it would mean that the dockers would have established a precedent for discrimination against any ship which might be involved in a foreign dispute."[43] It was a battle between the international shipping interests on the one hand and working class solidarity of maritime workers on the other. One thousand British dockers stood firm and refused to perform the one task that would let them return to work.[44]

On May 19, TGWU leaders again advised their members to return to work. Harry Davis addressed the workers outside the hall. They voted 646 to 466 to maintain the strike and elected an unofficial strike committee. Three days later the dockers of Portishead and Bristol stopped work in sympathy with the CSU and the port workers in Avonmouth.[45]

Nothing moved in the three Bristol Channel ports until May 27, when the Labor government decided to intervene on the side of the employers. Two hundred troops marched onto the Avonmouth docks and began to unload 11 million bananas from the British vessel *Bayano*.[46] In addition to the *Gulfside* and the *Montreal City*, there were nine ships in Avonmouth, six at Bristol Docks and one at Portishead. The government decided to work each one and clear them from the ports in an order of priority determined by the ministries of food and transport.

With troops now mobilized to break the dockers' solidarity, Hal Banks stepped up his international offensive. In a telegram to Labor Prime Minister Clément Attlee, the SIU boss threatened that "unless immediate steps are taken to permit free movement of Canadian ships arriving in British ports, we see no alternative but to ask for support of the International Longshoremen's Association." This would result in the complete dislocation of British ships arriving in Canada and the United States. TGWU General Secretary Bird rushed to Attlee's side to promise to do "all we can to end the deadlock and have the Canadian ships unloaded."[47]

On May 31, management personnel of the Port of Bristol Authority opened the dock gates and slipped the *Gulfside* out of Avonmouth. It was a victory for the bosses, but not one tugman, lock gateman or docker had deserted the Canadians or the principles they were defending.[48] In a mass meeting the Avonmouth dockworkers decided other

British port workers should learn of what was happening in the Bristol Channel. Delegates were dispatched to carry the news. In Liverpool, where 1,300 already were on strike over a Canadian vessel, 1,400 more voted to join the job action.[49]

The CSU strike now reached around the world, touching four continents and drawing hundreds of thousands of trade unionists into the struggle. Banks and his allies in the Canadian government, the AFL and among the shipowners had effectively broken the deepsea strike on North America's eastern seaboard, but international support was sustaining the CSU in its battle for justice. The support of the Trades and Labor Congress was proving decisive as trade unionists in a dozen ports around the globe rallied to what they knew was Canada's genuine union of seamen. Ships were tied up in Genoa, Capetown, New York, Vancouver, Georgetown, San Francisco, Avonmouth, Bristol, Southhampton, Liverpool and London. Seamen had been shot, blacklisted, beaten, jailed and killed, but still the struggle continued. The enemies of the CSU launched a final offensive.

IN CANADA, Banks moved against the CSU's last bastion in the East: the Lake companies that had signed CSU agreements. If the "reds" weren't cleared off their ships, he warned, their vessels would be boycotted in American ports. Paterson and Upper Lakes and St. Lawrence agreed to enforce Banks' blacklist, but he ordered their ships boycotted anyway. "We are going to keep communists from Canada from entering American ports," he declared. CSU boycott actions against legally-struck ships had been met with hot steam, police attack and jail terms. When Banks issued his edicts, however, the shipowners rushed to comply.[50]

The AFL, meanwhile, kept relentless pressure on the officers of the Trades and Labor Congress of Canada. Bengough's cry of "Cooperation, yes; domination, no!" was still ringing in the ears of Canadian trade unionists when the CSU announced the beginning of the world-wide strike. Yet within weeks of their defiant challenge to the Americans, Bengough and Buckley, the TLC secretary, appeared to be changing their minds. In mid-May, the TLC executive was summoned to meet the leaders of the AFL in Cleveland, Ohio. They were joined by Frank Hall and the roadmen of his "anti-red committee." The TLC executive returned to Canada from the private meeting and met behind closed doors in Ottawa on May 27. The city was alive with rumors that the CSU was to be thrown to the wolves, but Bengough rejected the idea.[51] "The TLC does not contemplate taking any action against a striking union," he said, assuring the seamen they remained in the good graces of the leaders of the House of Labor. "The CSU strike's legality has been attested to by the federal department of labor," he pointed out, adding that "the TLC cannot condone the actions of the Seafarers International Union in trying to break the strike."[52]

Bengough's statements were welcome news to the seamen, who now were at the apex of their world-wide strike. But they were uneasy at the news that the TLC executive had voted on their return from Cleveland to form a committee of Bengough, William Jenoves and Carl Berg "to make a decision on the issue" of the CSU.[53] If the TLC was firmly behind them, the seamen wondered, why was it necessary to set up a committee to examine the question? The explanation was not long in coming.

On June 3, just four days after he had assured the seamen they could rely on the TLC's continued support, Bengough announced the executive's decision to suspend the CSU from the TLC. CSU strikers were keeping "members of other affiliated unions from the performance of their usual work," the executive council said, and thus were violating "the sanctity of contracts." The strike had been undertaken against the advice of the TLC executive, the statement said. It linked the CSU to a world-wide communist conspiracy and pointed to the British dock strike as proof. The TLC admitted, however, that the threat of 14 international unions withdrawing from the congress had guided the committee's findings.[54]

Banks and his bosses fully appreciated the importance of trade union solidarity to the CSU. While the seamen sought and won the support of workers around the world, the AFL roadmen, armored in McCarthyism and wielding the economic might of the American unions, chopped away at the seamen's Canadian base. Their ultimatum to Bengough was harsh: destroy the CSU or face the destruction of the entire TLC.

In fact, the AFL had demanded the TLC executive both expel the CSU and change TLC voting procedures as the price of continued AFL support of the Canadian organization. Both demands struck at Canadian autonomy and democratic control of the TLC. The AFL's voting procedure would have removed the practice of one vote for each elected delegate and replace it with a bloc voting system that would have allowed one delegate or roadman to vote on behalf of the entire membership he represented. If adopted, the change would have given union leadership the right to eliminate dissent by controlling a union's entire convention strength.[55]

Bengough's reversal was a shattering blow to the CSU. Harry Davis' usually quiet and reasoned demeanor dissolved when he learned of Bengough's betrayal. The committee's decision was not only "a stab in the back against striking seamen," Davis charged, but was "strike-breaking of the most despicable kind in trade union history."[56] The suspension of the CSU amounted to "abject capitulation of Bengough and his executive to the American Federation of Labor and big business."[57]

For his part, Bengough was reduced to plaintive warnings to the shipowners about the SIU, suggesting they might find "they are keeping company with racketeers and gangsters as an alternative to dealing with the CSU and its red-dominated leadership."[58] Although the suspension of the CSU gave the SIU a waterfront monopoly, Bengough grumbled that the TLC didn't like the SIU's style. "Their methods may be good enough for the waterfronts of Chicago or New York, where gangsters operate under the guise of trade unionism, but it is not good enough for a country like Canada. We want no part of the SIU." Big business wasn't listening. The *Financial Post* was exultant about the split in the TLC and gave credit where credit was due. If medals were offered for "meritorious service in the sinking of the Communist Seamen's Union (sic)," the *Post* declared, "the biggest and the shiniest will go to a 56-year-old Montrealer, Frank H. Hall."[59]

In a bitter open letter to Bengough, Davis and McManus wrote the CSU's epitaph to Canadian trade union autonomy. "We have come to the painful conclusion that our suspension was the result of arrogant and humiliating outside interference and foreign dictation in the inner affairs of the Trades and Labor Congress of Canada," they wrote. "What the shipping companies and the Canadian and American government(s) failed to achieve was accomplished by the cynical, reckless and most offensive dictation of a small group of union bureaucrats who lead the AFL in Washington. The suspension of the CSU was, therefore, not merely an attack on our union but a blow at the autonomy, democracy and national dignity of the Trades and Labor Congress and the Canadian trade union movement as a whole.

"Unfortunately the executive failed to resist the combined pressure that came from government and big business at home and the foreign dictation that came from Washington. Thus it came about that despite everything said and done by the congress and its leaders up to that time, despite the Victoria convention decision, and despite the March 1949 document issued by the congress leadership in reply to the AFL, the congress surrendered to this outside pressure."

The CSU did not believe there had been any deliberation after the Cleveland meeting. "They agreed to suspend the CSU," Davis and McManus charged. "The CSU thus became the symbolic sacrifice on the altar of foreign dictation." After the AFL meeting, the TLC had asked the CSU to resign to "cause no embarrassment" to the congress. This the union refused to do because "we felt that the issue involved goes far beyond the limits of our organization and affects the essence of autonomy and inner democracy of the whole trade union movement. We could not lend ourselves to a maneuver which would hide from the eyes of all Canadian workers the crime that was being committed against all of them, their rights and independence."[60]

As the TLC leadership caved in, Davis contrasted their response to the crisis to that of the seamen. "Instead of bemoaning the sad state of affairs in which leaders of the Canadian trade union movement allow themselves to be intimidated into surrendering their rights as Canadians," Davis wrote, "the seamen have plunged into battle, more determined than ever to win the strike which has now become a strike on behalf of our very independent rights as Canadians."

Bengough's blow fell at a decisive moment. The *Searchlight* was forced to resort to point form to compress the global struggle into its columns. "Seven seamen shot in Halifax," the paper read. "Gunboats used against strikers in Cuba. Seamen sit in for 54 days in British Guiana. Armed police seize seamen in Holland. Crew imprisoned for 20 days in Cuban concentration camp. RCMP club pickets with axe handles. Strikebreakers armed with guns. Close to 600 seamen arrested in world's ports. Crews illegally fired in U.S. Shipowners violate the Shipping Act and the Labor Code. Government of Canada actively on side of shipowners. U.S. State Department calling the shots. Gross scab-herding by American Federation of Labor. Surrender of officials of the Trades and Labor Congress of Canada. Red-baiting by CCF leaders. Still the strike continues...

"Almost every possible weapon of strikebreaking has been hurled against the seamen. Murder — goons — police — jails — gunboats — lies — slanders — splits — suspensions — all of this has failed to smash the most amazing strike in world history."[61]

Weakened by the AFL's coup against the TLC and battered by shipowners and government, the seamen made yet another attempt to negotiate an end to the strike. The National Executive announced that the union would return to work if four demands were granted: the rehiring of striking seamen without discrimination; the payment of all wages owed before the strike was called; the holding of a government-supervised vote among rehired seamen to determine which union was to represent them; and the dropping of all charges against seamen.[62] Davis and the rest of the National Executive promised to resign if it would help to end the strike, "so long as those who may replace (us) will be chosen by the members of the union."[63]

The shipowners ignored the June 17 offer. They had signed SIU agreements and considered the matter closed.[64] CSU efforts to get newly-elected Prime Minister Louis St. Laurent to intervene proved futile. He turned the matter over to Deputy Labor Minister Arthur McNamara, who said he would respond to the proposals only when the CSU called off the strike.[65] It was to be a fight to the finish.

CHAPTER TWENTY-FIVE

Internationalism

IN CANADA the labor movement's solidarity lay shattered but in Great Britain thousands more workers were joining what had become an all-out battle with the Labor government. The British workers called the struggle "the CSU strike," but they were also engaged in a desperate defense of their own trade union rights.

In Liverpool, 8,500 dockers remained on strike, while in London, seamen were picketing the U.S. embassy protesting the U.S. intervention in Canadian trade union affairs. In Avonmouth, the *Montreal City* still waited for its load of automobiles for the Canadian market. Avonmouth dockers were asked to put the cargo aboard, but the 2,000 longshoremen held up their union cards in a vote against a return to work. On June 6 military personnel began to work the ship.[1] By June 11, the number of troops on the Bristol docks swelled to 1,200 as the government sought to clear 15 of the 30 vessels tied up in the area.[2] The next day Labor Minister Isaacs issued a radio appeal to dockers in Bristol, Avonmouth and Liverpool to return to work. In Liverpool, where the struggle had not been as sharp as it had been in other ports, the dockers complied, but in Bristol and Avonmouth, the struggle continued.[3] The unofficial committees in the struck ports, however, could not stand by and watch the longshoremen's work be done by soldiers. On June 14 the rank-and-file leadership advised the Bristol and Avonmouth dockers that they must end the dispute, which the government was prepared to settle by use of the military. The next day, the dockers on the Bristol Channel were once again on the job.[4] They had yielded none of their principles in the 10-week battle, but they could do no more. The focus of the strike shifted to London.

In London, the crews of the *Beaverbrae* and the *Argomont* had been cleared from their ships by injunctions on May 12 and May 21 respectively. The strike had moved ashore, where the committee was working from a dockside office. As seamen from various ports migrated to London, the Strike Committee was faced with the task of finding food for hundreds of seamen. On several occasions, the women of London rushed food to the hungry seamen even though the country remained under rationing. "We will never forget," Doucette told them. "We know you working class people are with us and appreciate how much of a sacrifice you are making. It gives us fresh heart."[5]

Tokaruk, who had become a polished public speaker for the union, found support in other quarters. "The students in the universities were interested in what was going on," he recalls, "and Jock Brogan arranged for me to go and speak at a meeting at Bristol University. I really expected to be torn apart there — I was used to the Canadian attitude of the universities, bastions of middle class conservatism. On the contrary, it was just the opposite. A lot of the university students looked at us as rather romantic characters, far away from home, on strike in a near-mutiny... I was interviewed on BBC Radio, and they said, "This is an invasion of private property,' and I said, 'I don't believe in private property.' Of course, the university students ate it up. Believe me, that strike was a university for us, too."[6]

For nearly a month, from May 15 to June 13, the London dockers accepted dispatch to any vessel in port except the two struck Canadian ships. Finally, the government moved. The National Dock Labor Board ruled that "demands from the owners of the *Beaverbrae* and the *Argomont* for dock labor to discharge these vessels must be met."[7] On June 20, 300 stevedores were directed to work the *Argomont*. They steadfastly refused.[8] Isaacs called the executive of the National Association of Stevedores and Dockers (NASD) to his office and demanded an explanation. The union's leadership agreed to instruct their members to work the ships. But when the *Beaverbrae* and the *Argomont* were called at the next dispatch, not one stevedore or docker signed up for the job. The London Port Employers played their last card. All dockers would be locked out, they declared, until the *Beaverbrae* and the *Argomont* were manned and worked.[9]

The CSU moved quickly to break the impasse.[10] As Isaacs recorded later in his report on the strike-lockout, "at 5:30 p.m. Messrs. (Bill) Arland and (Bud) Doucette got into touch directly with the administrative secretary of the Canadian High Commissioner and at their urgent request were received by him. They stated that they had a four-point solution to the difficulties which they would like submitted to the owners of the *Beaverbrae* and the *Argomont*. They said that if the conditions were accepted, they would instruct their members to return to work and would urge the London dockers to unload and handle the *Beaverbrae* and *Argomont*."[11] The secretary agreed to speak to his boss, Canadian High Commissioner, L. Dana Wilgress, and the seamen returned to the Pier Road office to wait. Hours passed as the seamen smoked, talked and waited for the call they hoped would be the first step to achieving a settlement that could influence the outcome of the world-wide strike. The phone rang in the barbershop and the seamen were informed that Wilgress would meet their delegates.

Doucette recalls the meeting. "Bill Arland and I went out together to see the High Commissioner. He saw us smoking English Woodbine cigarettes and offered us Canadian Export cigarettes, Canadian whiskey if we wished, and good will. After all, we were Canadians abroad with some difficulties! He put his good offices at our disposal. We worked out an arrangement that we thought would be adequate. The crew would go back under the original agreement with the companies. We would take the ships back to Canada and there would be no discrimination against anybody for any reason whatsoever. The possibility was that if Canadian Pacific Steamships and the crew of the *Beaverbrae* could work out an agreement that would be acceptable to both parties, this might be a pattern for settlement with the companies that were involved in Southampton, Liverpool and London."[12] The proposals were a variation of the settlement package proposed by the National Executive in Montreal just a few days before.

Doucette and Arland left Canada House with the request that the Canadian High Commission notify the shipping companies of their proposals and inform the strike committee of the companies' decision by 9:30 that same evening. The seamen were to address a mass meeting of London dockers the next morning and wanted to know exactly where they stood so they could convey the decision to the meeting.[13] At the agreed time, Doucette picked up the barbershop phone and placed a call to Canada House. He was informed that the "owners of the *Beaverbrae* and the *Argomont* would accept the four-point proposal." Doucette replied that he would have to check with the seamen to ensure they were satisfied with the deal. At 11 p.m., Jack Pope telephoned the seamen's acceptance and added that the next morning at 7:30 the seamen would address the dockers' mass meeting, inform them that the ships were no longer black and that all work should resume.[14]

The next morning, June 24, Captain R.W. McMurray, the managing director of Canadian Pacific Steamships, told reporters he was "very happy" that the London strike was over. He issued the following message: "Official statement by shipowners of *Beaverbrae* and *Argomont* today says: 1. Crews to go back on the ships. 2. Crews returning at old rate of wages. 3. Owners not to prosecute men on arrival at Canada. 4. Men not required to sign on with any union to go back."[15]

The seamen believed the strike was over. They informed the dockers a settlement had been achieved, that all ships were to be worked and that the seamen would be returning to Canada. The crew of the *Argomont* was in for a surprise. In the words of Isaacs, the agents of the *Argomont* were "willing to subscribe in spirit to the agreement made on their behalf by Captain McMurray on the previous evening (but) they could not carry it out to the letter because the *Argomont* had been sold some months previously, before she arrived in this country, and was not returning to Canada. The new owners were not Canadians and were supplying a crew of their own, who could not be engaged under Canadian articles."[16] The seamen had returned to their vessels on the understanding that they had retained their jobs and their union. They now learned that the crew of the *Argomont* had neither and that Canada's merchant fleet had one less vessel.[17]

The crew of the *Beaverbrae* faced an even grimmer betrayal. The company told the crew it was prepared to ship them back to Canada, but not to the CSU. Once the *Beaverbrae* docked in Canada, the crew would have to join the SIU or leave the vessel.

"We found that the shipowners had in fact decided we were going to come back as one-way passengers to Montreal," Doucette remembers. "We decided no, we were not going to go for that agreement and we would stay and slug it out a little longer. We had been betrayed not only by the shipowners, from whom we expected betrayal, but also by the offices of the Canadian High Commission. We weren't so innocent as to expect support, but we weren't prepared for the bare-faced collusion with the shipowners, to induce us into breaking the strike by bringing her back under the SIU banner. There was a one-day lull and we resumed the strike."[18]

The next day, Saturday, the gangs of dockers and stevedores worked all vessels in the port. Sunday saw only the normal linesmen and overtime employees on the job. On Monday the massive port fell silent until noon, when thousands of workers arrived for a mass meeting to hear the Canadian seamen explain the developments that had forced them to unfurl the CSU's fighting colors once again.

Representatives of the unofficial rank-and-file committees and elected officers of the NASD spoke first. Then Arland stood before the port workers. "Although the Canadian High Commissioner told us the shipowners had accepted greedily our proposals," he reported, "the captain of the *Beaverbrae* told us on Saturday that the non-victimization clause ended as soon as the crew members were back aboard. We immediately got in touch with the High Commissioner and were informed that the shipowners had not understood our proposals."[19] The meeting of 2,000 voted unanimously to work all ships except the two Canadian ones. The TGWU meeting held later the same day ended with a similar resolution. As Isaacs noted later, "it was, of course, known that the employers had decided not to requisition labor for fresh ships until the *Beaverbrae* and the *Argomont* were manned."[20]

It was an extraordinary day. The TGWU leadership had favored a return to work, but the rank-and-file British dockworkers were firmer in their solidarity than their leadership or even Canada's own TLC. By the end of the day, 1,535 men were on strike on the Surrey and Royal Docks and 20 ships sat idle and unworked.[21] The next morning, the workers at the two docks turned-to for the dispatch as usual. They were informed that there was no work until the two Canadian vessels were worked. Four thousand dockers from the Surrey and 3,000 from the Royal and other nearby docks refused the ultimatum and were again locked out.[22] Nineteen Canadians had remained on the Beaverbrae when the CSU members had walked off, a fact much remarked by the press, the government and the shipowners as a rift in labor's ranks. The dockers were unmoved. They refused to touch the vessels.[23]

The dockers formally established a lockout committee on June 30 and laid out their position in a manifesto the same day. The CSU strike, they believed, was an important struggle which had become intertwined with their own. The right to support the CSU was a right they would not surrender. "We claim that this is not a question of the struggle of the CSU. We maintain that in conformity with past customs and practice we should not be called upon to take sides in a dispute between organized labor of the CSU and the Canadian shipowners. We claim the discriminating methods of the London shipowners in conjunction with the London Dock Labor Board in attempting to force us to blackleg is a lockout on their part against the London port workers. We port workers are prepared and demand the right to work on all ships outside of those in dispute in accordance with our known existing practices and traditions as trade unionists."[24]

The London Port Employers were inflexible: there would be no work until the longshoremen worked the Canadian vessels. On July 4, 8,484 London dockers were locked out and 92 ships lay idle in the Port of London. TGWU officials once again attempted to get the dockers and stevedores to return to work, claiming the tie-up was a communist plot. Of the 3,000 present at one meeting only two voted to return to work. The second meeting was an even greater show of workers' solidarity. Three Labor Party members of Parliament told the workers the strike was a skillfully-arranged attempt by communists to cripple the British economy. The dockers shouted them out of the hall.[25] They voted overwhelmingly once again to boycott the Beaverbrae and the Argomont but to work all other ships.[26]

The British workers' solidarity was virtually instinctive. Their own trade union roots ran deep and they recognized in the Central Strike Committee an organization akin to their own rank-and-file committees on the docks. The dockers and the Canadian seamen were trade unionists cut from the same cloth, fighting a common enemy for the same basic economic and political rights. The British solidarity was untouched by a barrage of management and press propaganda playing up developments in Canada, where the TLC had turned on the CSU, east coast ports were working without interruption, and Arthur McNamara, Deputy Minister of Labor, had dismissed the four-point CSU settlement proposals as "communist-inspired."[27]

The Labor cabinet was watching the North American seaboard closely to see if the SIU would be able to make good on the threat to tie up British shipping. An Emergency Cabinet Committee was formed to handle the dock lockout. If the dockers did not return to work, the government warned, troops would be brought in to work the 95 ships.[28] The threat had an unexpected effect. Far from intimidating the port workers, it drew more support to their side. The Watermen, Lightermen, Tugmen and Bargemen's Union, representing workers performing the crucial tasks of berthing ships, moving cargo from midstream vessels and transferring cargo along canals and rivers, voted July 8 to paralyze the port by joining the locked-out dockers.[29] "The government's statement about an emergency was considered," a Lightermen's union officer said, "but we think the emergency of the dockers is greater."[30]

A desperate government moved the same day to smash the dockers once and for all. James Chuter Ede, the Home Secretary, told Parliament that a State of Emergency would be declared unless work was resumed on every vessel in port. "We are faced with a challenge to the whole authority of the state," Ede declared. "We shall carry on," the Lockout Committee replied.[31]

July 9 saw 10,000 London dockers on the bricks. Meat drivers warned that if troops were moved onto the docks, they would not transport any meat contaminated by uniformed scabs.[32] The official leadership of the NASD was branded "communistic" by the press and the Labor government. NASD leaders called another meeting to determine the membership's wishes, but the unofficial lockout committee held a rally just prior to the NASD meeting. The rally was attended by 2,000 dockers who voted to boycott the official vote on the grounds that they had already demonstrated their desires. Five hundred and twenty-one members attended the official meeting and 338 voted to return to work on the employers' terms. It was obvious that the majority of the 7,000 members of the union had voted with their feet. "We have no comment to make," an NASD official told reporters. "We gave them a chance to vote and they have given their answer."[33]

Labor Prime Minister Clement Attlee, who could trace his roots to London's waterfront, had succeeded in splitting the British trade union movement on the question of the dockers' stand. He warned the dockers that if they did not return to work by July 11, the King would be advised

to proclaim a State of Emergency. The government demanded unconditional surrender. Unless there was a 100 percent return to work, the
Emergency Powers Act would be invoked. Although it had been passed
in 1920, the act had been used only twice, once to break the miners'
strike of 1920 and again in 1925 to smash the historic General Strike.
Now labor's own party was dusting it off to use against 10,000 London
dock workers it claimed were communists.[34] The dockers met July 10 to
determine their response.

The Emergency Cabinet Committee waited with Attlee at Number 10
Downing Street while 1,700 troops massed at the gates of the Royal
Docks to receive their orders. Five thousand dockers gathered at the
Victoria Park meeting to debate their reply to the government ultimatum. Special Branch officers mingled with the workers during the
three-hour meeting. NASD officials again appealed to the men to give
up the fight and return to work. Of the 5,000 present only two voted to
follow their advice. The rest voted to work every ship in London with the
exception of the *Argomont* and the *Beaverbrae*. A CSU representative
was introduced to the dockers' meeting, but they voted not to hear him.
"It's nothing to do with him now," they explained. "All we know, and all
that matters, is that there is a dispute, and these two Canadian ships are
disputed ships. We don't work disputed ships."[35] But the dockers knew
that if the troops were put to work on the ships, they would be in a very
weak position. The CSU now was totally at odds with the TLC and
faced three governments — Canadian, American and British — as well
as the SIU doing everything possible to break the strike.

The London longshoremen were in similar straits. The Labor
government had the legal power, the troops and the political will to work
the ships. The dockers were opposed by the Trades Union Congress and
their own official leaders. "We are not communists," the dockers told the
government. "We want to get back to work. There are 105 ships held up
and we are willing to work 103 of them. But we are not going to handle
the two Canadian ships. That's definite. All the government has done by
threatening the State of Emergency is to put our backs up, and it's no
good telling us we are being led by the noses by communists, that's rot.
As soon as the government gets rid of the two Canadian ships, all this
trouble will be over."[36] The dockers had offered the government two
ways out: move the Canadian ships from the port or declare the State of
Emergency, work the two struck ships and the dockers would have no
alternative but to return to work. When the result of the vote reached
Downing Street, Attlee immediately sent a messenger for the King, who
was reposing at Windsor. He was whisked to a meeting with the
Cabinet and the Privy Council in Buckingham Palace.[37]

Still more workers rallied to the dockers. Seven hundred clerical workers from the London waterfront walked off their jobs to join the dockers, the first time the port workers had received such support from white collar workers.[38] A few hours later, 300 more clerical workers followed suit. The meat handlers and drivers confirmed their vow to move nothing that had passed through the hands of troops.[39] Meanwhile, King George VI and the Labor government prepared to bring in emergency powers enabling the government to use troops and volunteers as strikebreakers, granting the government power to stop, search, seize and arrest without warrant, to billet troops in citizens' homes, to stop all mail, gas, electricity and phones and to run the docks with a government-appointed committee of five.[40]

On July 12, while 13,000 dockers waited on their picketlines, Attlee rose in the House of Commons dressed in a blackcoat, knee breeches and powdered wig. In his hand was "a message from the King signed by his own hand." With all the pomp he could muster, he bowed to the Chair, stepped off 10 paces, stiffened, clicked his heels and bowed, stepped and bowed again at the clerk's table and reached the Speaker, where he repeated his click and bow for the third time. There was utter quiet as the Speaker began to read the message which granted the government the emergency powers it demanded. A cry of "Shame! Shame!" came from L.J. Solley, Independent Socialist member for Thurrock who had recently been expelled from the Labor Party for his militant socialist beliefs. He and Phil Piratin (Communist, Mile End) were the only MPs to vote against the Emergency Measures. Willy Gallagher (Communist, West Fife) had been with the miners in his constituency and was hurrying to London to cast his vote, but his train arrived after the Labor Party had sealed the dockers' fate.[41]

London's dockland had a response. One thousand TGWU dockers who had voted to return to work, immediately walked off the job. The Watermen, Lightermen, Tugmen and Bargemen's Union decided its 3,800 members in the port would not handle goods or ships where normal union conditions did not prevail. They decided to touch nothing worked by "imported or service labor."[42] It quickly became obvious that the government was not prepared to use its powers to break the impasse by working the Canadian vessels and moving them out. The Labor government had decided nothing short of unconditional surrender would suffice. "It has been decided by the authorities," explained the *Beaverbrae's* captain, "that the dockers will have to unload these two ships. Only one day's work would be necessary to clear the *Beaverbrae's* cargo. This decision is a tactical move, a test of strength to break the strike."[43]

Not content to clear the Port of London or to assist the shipowners in their fight to smash the CSU, Attlee's government was determined to punish the dockers for their stubborn insistence that they had the right to live and to work as trade unionists. The troops went straight to work. With 13,296 locked out and 126 ships idle, more than 2,500 soldiers attempted to work 15 vessels. Consistent with government policy, the Canadian vessels remained untouched.

Despite the threat of imprisonment and the pleas of their union officials the dockers stood firm. Day by day, more joined the struggle as an increasing number of troops worked the docks. On July 14, 1,400 longshoremen marched five miles through the streets of London to Victoria Park, where they were met by 1,500 more dockworkers. Time and again, the dockers showed their support of the CSU and their determination to see the struggle through to the end. As the lockout headed into its tenth day, there were 15,656 dockers on the bricks and 11,566 troops working the Port of London.[44]

For the seamen, the strike had reached a turning point. If the struggle on the docks continued to escalate there would be serious repercussions for those who continued to support the striking seamen. The dockers had their own grievances to settle with the government and the waterfront employers, but were staking the survival of their organizations on their right to extend solidarity to fellow workers. The CSU had the power to end the entire fight. Behind the scenes the dockers and seamen discussed ways to end the impasse. Bud Doucette remembers those moments of decision:

"At that stage, most of us knew the strike was lost in Canada and the United States. As a matter of fact, the strike was lost in all continental North America, the West Indies, and the north coast of South America. There was still a viable situation in Australia and New Zealand, there were still pockets of resistance in some areas, but we knew there was little hope of coming out with a victory for the Canadian Seamen's Union. It had been decided in the National Office in Montreal that we should try and regroup, reorganize, re-establish the union, demand a vote, oust the SIU and try to save at least the jobs of the Canadian seamen."[45]

The CSU realized that it had to act or there would be very little for the dockers to salvage of their own organizations. Unless the conflict was ended soon the British workers would have sacrificed their own unions in a losing cause. On July 22, the CSU and the Unofficial Lockout Committee called a mass meeting for Victoria Square. Eight thousand dockers attended and were addressed by CSU President Harry Davis. Davis expressed the seamen's thanks and best wishes to the dockers. Canadians would never forget the support they had received from the British working class, he said, and while the solidarity had touched every Canadian worker's heart, it could not continue. "We feel it will be only proper," Davis told them, "in the wider interest of the dock workers and people of London, to make a gesture, even if we suffer ourselves, to enable the wheels of this port to turn again. Our union has therefore decided to terminate the dispute in Great Britain. We accept promises that have been made that there will be no victimization of Canadian seamen and we accept the proposal of Canadian Deputy Minister of Labor McNamara that if the strike is called off in the British ports he will use the machinery of his department to bring both parties together."[46]

The meeting adopted a return to work motion and the dockers celebrated a victorious end to their struggle. They had stood to the end and never compromised their rights and principles. On July 25, they returned to work and 12,796 troops marched off the London docks.[47] The State of Emergency was over, but the dock union's officials exacted a final measure of revenge. Three unofficial leaders were expelled from the union and from the docks, while Jack Dash and two other rank-and-file leaders were barred from holding elected office for two years. The discipline was meted out, Dash said, because "we refused to budge from our principles."[48]

Doucette advised CSU members "to meet at the CPR office in London and those who were acceptable to the company were to make their arrangements for repatriation. The night prior to the return to the ship passions were running high. We were disappointed and felt betrayed, betrayed not only by those from whom treason could be expected, but in some cases by seamen, in some cases by Canadians, who accepted the barrage of propaganda which had been put out by the government, police, the press, and in some cases, by their families. There were certain characters who had played a prominent role in attempting to break the strike. We were having a gathering in the Bridgehouse Tavern in East London and discussing the return to work.

"About nine o'clock some men came along and said the Tidal Basin Tavern was full of scabs. They were former members of the union who had succumbed to the propaganda and who could see the strike was lost. Nonetheless, for several weeks they had been used by the ship-owners, by the press and by certain members of Parliament. They signed documents condemning the union, condemning the strike and so on. In any conflict, in any war, those who join the enemy are treated harshly. Traitors are not respected and are usually shot in wartime. This was a war between classes, a war between some very dedicated spokesmen for the working class and the trade union movement and some very anti-labor elements like Canadian Pacific Steamships.

"Our response upon learning that these characters were celebrating the end of the strike in the Tidal Basin Tavern was to leave them alone and deal with them later on. But by a quarter to 10 there was a demand from our people that we go down and explain to them the error of their ways... We eventually went down to the Tidal Basin Tavern and some punches were thrown. As a matter of fact, three or four of the more repulsive of these creatures were meted out a bit of workers' justice. They were roughed up a bit. When we went to the CPR office the following day, they arrested six of us — Al MacIsaac, Bill Easton, Benny Fisher, Bill McPhedran, Vern Walker and me."[49]

Charges against four of the six were dropped, but Al MacIsaac and Bud Doucette were convicted and sentenced to prison terms of a year and a half each.[50] They served 14 months in Wormwood Scrubbs and upon their release returned to a Canada that had neither a Canadian Seamen's Union nor a job for them. They were like thousands of others — blackballed, seamen without ships.

Why had the seamen fought on for so long against such odds? "We knew, of course, long before, that our chances were very slim," says Doucette. "We could have stuck our tails between our legs and gone whimpering back to the shipowners or we could have very quietly left and slunk away. The SIU had no intention of permitting any militant trade unionist on Canadian ships. As a matter of fact, they had no intention of obstructing the sale of the merchant fleet. That was probably the role that Hal Banks and the Seafarers International Union were brought to Canada to play: to end the opposition to government policy on the waterfront, and the government policy was to liquidate the Canadian merchant fleet."[51]

Tokaruk adds, "It was a cause deeply felt by the leadership and the rank and file. We were not going to be tapered down into a company union, cut down to size and everything else. This may sound conceited, but I also think that we thought that we had to send a signal to the Canadian and U.S. governments and to the right wing of the Canadian labor movement that they could be stood up to. We were destined to set an example for posterity and I somehow feel that the chaps felt that. We *were* striking for posterity. One event of 20th century labor history that will be remembered will be the CSU. In 2049 I think the CSU will be better known than it is today. Most of us knew in 1949 that it was going to be a lost cause in the short term, but in the short term only. Really."[52]

CHAPTER TWENTY-SIX

The Final Round

BATTERED AND DEFEATED but not yet destroyed, the CSU attempted yet again to find a way out. The shipowners had purchased full-page ads in the nation's dailies with headlines that screamed "CSU leaders — not Canadian seamen — are at the bottom of the shipping strike."[1] The seamen decided to call the shipowners' bluff. "The whole leadership agreed that we would resign and let the rank and file decide with the Labor Board to conduct new elections," Davis recalls. The government refused to consider new elections, but the executive resigned anyway. In new elections, the rank and file picked a new executive to negotiate with the shipowners. A government spokesman simply denounced the maneuver as a "new commie plot."[2] Obviously the seamen's enemies would settle for nothing less than elimination of the seamen's union.

As the summer drew to a close, the CSU executive weighed the prospects of continuing the struggle for unity inside the TLC which was meeting in convention in Calgary in September. The question of the CSU's suspension and possible expulsion was certain to divide the convention, but with the internationals firmly in control, the proponents of Canadian autonomy faced certain defeat. The seamen directed Davis and McManus to write an open letter to TLC delegates.

The CSU had the right to demand the continued support of the congress, the letter began, but "we are aware of the painful fact that to bring this issue on the floor of the Calgary convention in the face of iron-clad dictatorial orders from abroad would undoubtedly lead to the most serious division and internal struggle in all congress unions and perhaps even to splitting the trade union movement. Having thus carefully weighed the consequences of our actions, we have decided to act in the interest of unity of the congress and its affiliated unions by eliminating the issue of the executive's suspension of the CSU from the Calgary convention.

"We have, therefore, reluctantly decided to withdraw from the Trades and Labor Congress of Canada, the parent body with which we were affiliated until now... Our decision to withdraw is based on the hope that the removal of this issue, which the AFL bureaucrats are prepared to use as an excuse for either dominating or wrecking the Canadian labor movement, will enable the delegates at Calgary to unite and concentrate on the solution of the many serious problems which now confront Canadian labor.

"We are nevertheless hopeful that the time is not far away when the Canadian trade unions will be unified in an autonomous trade union center, free of all foreign dictation and interference, but in fraternal relations with our brothers in the USA, and that we shall re-occupy our rightful place in such a united, autonomous and democratic congress of Canadian labor.

"Our parting wish," the officers concluded, "is that the congress shall always remain autonomous, united and free and firmly controlled by and for the great membership of the Trades and Labor Congress of Canada so that it will stand as a bulwark against reaction and for a progressive Canada."[3]

The CSU's effort to avoid an open break on the question of the union's suspension was rejected by the TLC leadership. Bengough insisted on a roll call vote to endorse the section of the officers' report on the CSU suspension. Rather than cast their votes in front of the roadmen of the AFL, between 100 and 300 delegates left the hall.[4] Of those who remained, 702 voted with the executive and 77 stood with the seamen.[5] The CSU's exile was complete.

In mid-October, Davis called the CSU's officers to Montreal to review the strike and assess the prospects for continuing. "We had to call off the U.K. strike earlier because we had penalized the dockers way beyond what was fair and reasonable to expect," he recalls. "We said we would attempt to carry on, on our own, in Canada... We had made a concession when they made the issue one of communist leadership. But once the shipowners signed with the SIU they had a 'union' of their own and they were not going to allow a rank and file union to remain... The National Executive was called in from all the ports to discuss the situation. It reached the point that we couldn't carry on any more, financially or otherwise. Meetings were held in the Port of Montreal, and I believe all the other ports, advising them of the National Executive's recommendation."[6]

By that time only a few hundred seamen remained around the CSU hall in Montreal. Fewer still were carrying on the unrewarding task of picketing the Montreal waterfront. The longshoremen of the ILA walked through the line at each dispatch, jeering or taunting the CSU pickets. Neither humiliation nor threats moved men like Tommy Burnett, Jerry Herron, Paddy Slater, Charlie Moore, Big Earl Wasson or Stan Wingfield. They took their turns on the line with pride, sustained by tenacity and belief in their cause. But it was not enough to give them the victory they sought. The National Executive threw in the towel.

Burnett, who to this day has the CSU burning in his heart, well remembers the night of October 15, 1949. The meeting in the St. Xavier Street office was short and solemn. Sitting at her desk in the other room with the office staff, Muriel Davis cried into her hands as she waited to hear what Harry had to tell the seamen.[7] "Harry Davis was there," Burnett recalls. "Danny Daniels was there. Conrad was there. Davis said the best thing to do was to go aboard the ships and try to find jobs wherever we could and get into other unions. After that the meeting broke up."[8]

The CSU made the termination of the strike public on October 20. "The union will continue to struggle to win back the wages and working conditions which were taken from Canadian seamen," the announcement read. The CSU expressed its gratitude for the solidarity it had received from workers around the world, particularly singling out the U.K. dockers, the World Federation of Trade Unions and the World Maritime Federation. On the other hand, the CSU warned, "labor cannot forget the strikebreaking role of the leadership of the American Federation of Labor and the International Transport Federation, who worked hand in glove with the company-dominated and gangster-controlled Seafarers International Union." The seamen laid the blame for their defeat squarely on the shoulders of the TLC leadership, charging that the strike could have been won had the TLC leadership "not capitulated to the AFL bureaucrats."[9]

IN JUNE 1950, Burnett paid off a Norwegian ship and made his way over to the union hall on St. Francis Xavier Street. He paid his dues, rounded up Daniels, Slater and McManus and the group adjourned to a neighboring tavern where Burnett pieced them off. "I gave them all a fin apiece and eventually Slater and I were talking and Danny and McManus were talking and they got in an argument over the Korean War. McManus was all for the South Koreans and the American stand on Korea. It was very, very unusual. He and Danny were having it out and eventually McManus got mad and left. When he left, all of us split up and eventually Paddy and I went to another tavern. When I walked into the hall the next morning, Conrad Sauras had the telegram. It was from Toronto, from McManus, and it said 'I hereby resign my position as secretary-treasurer of the CSU.' "[10]

Despite the defeats and defections, the October 1950 *Searchlight* managed a note of optimism. The few members still working on the Lakes had won pay increases on Shell, Lakeland and Texada tankers and the union had just negotiated the highest wages ever paid to Canadian seamen under an agreement negotiated with Canada

Cement.[11] Yet through the good news could be read the end of the fight. What was to be the paper's last issue was only a single page.

Early in December a friend ran into Nick Buszowski's room waving a copy of *Macleans* magazine. Buszowski looked at the lead article, shrugged and told his friend simply, "McManus sold out."[12] The former CSU secretary-treasurer had stood before seamen just three years before and told them he had turned down a $100,000 bribe because "I'm a communist and you can't buy me." Now the man who had been a Communist Party member long before he joined the CSU repeated the time-worn charge that the union was "communist dominated." Yet his argument foundered on his own evidence. The Communist Party of Canada had ordered the CSU to tie up the *Lady Rodney* and the *Lady Nelson* in Halifax, McManus charged, "as a sign to the government (their owners) that we meant business."[13] Yet Davis, the executive and the seamen had called the world-wide strike, a move the Communist Party had counselled against. Why had McManus performed this eleventh-hour betrayal? Many seamen say he "sold out for a glass of beer," others that he was broken by the struggles of 1949 and 1950: "McManus couldn't take defeat."[14]

Whatever the reason for McManus' treachery, his theme was picked up just six days later in a Canadian Labor Relations Board decision unprecedented in Canadian labor history. Branch Lines Ltd. had a contract with the CSU that expired in November 1950. Rather than renegotiate, the company sought to have the CSU's bargaining rights removed. There were only two grounds for decertification of a union under the law: evidence that the union no longer represented the employees or proof that the union was employer-dominated.

Branch Lines did not even attempt to claim that its employees did not want the CSU to represent them. To decertify the union, the board would have to find that it was company-dominated.[15] The CSU had been called many things, but "company-dominated" was not one. A bit of creativity was required to make the case fit the law. The CSU did not meet the definition of a union, the board found, because it had called a world-wide strike and received international solidarity. This confirmed what the board termed "common knowledge in Canada that the respondent (CSU) is a communist-directed organization." An organization's political affiliation "does not affect its status as a trade union," the board said, "but the frequent transformation made by communist elements of organizations formed for other purposes, over which they obtain control, into organizations whose real and ulterior purpose becomes the promotion of communist objectives, is well-known in this country."

Because of these ulterior motives, the board concluded, the primary purpose of a communist-directed organization "is not such as to bring the organization within the definition of 'trade union' or 'union' under the act." The CSU's right to represent the seamen employed by Branch Lines Ltd. was revoked.[16] The decision was not subject to appeal.

The Branch Lines decision went further than any previous ruling in the United States or Canada. Under the notorious American Taft-Hartley Act, all officers of American unions were required to swear an oath that they were not members of the Communist Party. Yet in the United States no union had lost a certification for reasons of political affiliation.[17] The board's decision effectively sentenced the CSU to death. Within six months, the union's remaining certifications were revoked. The union that had done the most to end racketeering on the waterfront and bring democracy to the maritime industry was wiped out. In its place was an employer-dominated organization led by an American racketeer.

THE CANADIAN SEAMEN'S UNION ceased to exist as a legal entity in 1951. The seamen had carried out an historic struggle which was lost to insurmountable foes, and with the death of the CSU, the hopes of saving Canada's merchant fleet came to an end.

During the war, Canada built 363 deepsea dry cargo vessels with taxpayers' dollars. Ninety were sold to the United States for lend-lease to the United Kingdom. Two were sold directly to the United Kingdom and thirteen were lost. Of the 258 vessels still in operation at war's end, Park Steamships operated 150. Sixteen were on loan to the United Kingdom and one was loaned to Australia. Ninety-one were chartered by the British Ministry of Transport.[18]

J.V. Clyne, in his dual role as president of Park Steamships and Chairman of the Canadian Maritime Commission, had carried out the government's policy of selling off Canada's deepsea fleet. The third largest fleet in the world was consistently eroded. By 1957, Canada was left with only 15 obsolete vessels engaged almost entirely in Canadian trade.[19] The last vestiges of the merchant fleet withered away. Clyne had stated that vessels lost to foreign flags would be replaced by modern ships constructed in Canadian yards, but not one ever appeared. To this day the federal government still adheres to a no-Canadian fleet policy.[20]

The Canadian Seamen's Union had argued that the transfer of flags would bring disaster to the Canadian maritime industry. But the sell-out policy carried the day. A longshoremen working on the west coast docks some 30 years later could clearly see the results. If he were standing at Vancouver Wharves he might glance over to Burrard Dry Dock, which had employed thousands of workers during the 1940s. Instead of bustling shipyards he might see a skeleton crew of marine workers doing a minor repair job. One or two yards in Burrard Inlet might have enough work for 20 or 30 workers, the rest would be idle.

If he were at Vancouver Wharves on the right day, he would see a huge 40,000 ton plus bulk carrier, resplendent in Maple Leaf red and white. The vessel, owned by Canadian Pacific Railway, would be loading either nickel ore or another of Canada's raw materials for export. True, it wouldn't be a government-owned ship, but at least, as Clyne had predicted, it would be a ship owned by a Canadian company and bearing Canada's colors. Walking up the gangway to start his shift our longshoreman might have a word with a couple of crew members and maybe one of the officers. If he did, he would learn that the crew was from Spain and every one of the officers was British. On his lunch break he could walk away from his hatch and perhaps take a peek at the vessel's registry. There he would see the crest of Bermuda. And when he left the ship at the end of his shift, he could glance over the bow for a glimpse of her name. There, in foot-high letters, he would read *J.V. Clyne*. Clyne's policy has conjured up an image which is the true symbol of present-day Canadian shipping — it bears his signature.

The shipowners and the federal government worked together to get rid of the Canadian Seamen's Union and the Canadian fleet. In its place a maritime nation was left with only domestic shipping under her flag, and a waterfront under the domination of racketeers.

With Hal Banks and the SIU in control and working as the hand-maiden of the shipping companies and the federal government, virtually every active member of the Canadian Seamen's Union was blacklisted in the shipping industry. Canadian shipping was taken back to a barbaric pre-union stage. Threats, intimidation, beatings and killings once again became the norm. In 1962, the Honorable T.G. Norris was given the task of investigating Banks' operation in Canada. As he looked over the human carnage of Banks' rule he observed: "In these modern times the days of the old rough and tough life at sea and in the ports of Canada are over. The Banks' code of violence — revived as it was in 1949-1950 and again during the last two or three years — is an uncivilized relic of deepsea sailing conditions of over 75 years ago."[21]

It is not within the scope of this book to relate the story of Hal Banks and the SIU after 1949. It is, however, necessary to glimpse some of their activities in order to see what replaced the Canadian Seamen's Union.

Justice Norris' investigation of the SIU's activities resulted in 108 volumes of testimony which are, in themselves, a devastating account of the differences between the CSU and SIU. The strong-arm tactics and ideological warfare used to eliminate the CSU continued long after the CSU was put to the sword. Banks improved on the techniques and used them against any person or organization that did not kow-tow to his supremacy. "The cry of communism," Justice Norris observed, "which

was successfully levelled by Banks against the CSU in those days —
doubtless with some truth at that time (there were differences of
opinion as to whether in fact such a cry was really a proper one to raise
in Canada in such a dispute) — has been raised by Banks throughout
the years since, against those who opposed him, even in the hearings,
against persons the tenets of whose philosophy are far removed from
Marxian philosophy."[22]

The same tactics the SIU had used to destroy the CSU were used
again in the late 1950s as the SIU continued to raid Canadian maritime
unions. In 1959, for example, Canada Steamship Lines, whose licensed
division was legally represented by the National Association of Marine
Engineers (NAME), announced that it had cancelled its collective
agreement with NAME and had signed with the SIU.[23] Within a few
months, all the companies belonging to the Association of Lake Carriers
had turned their NAME employees over to the SIU in spite of prohibit-
ing legislation.[24]

Among the Norris Commission's major findings were: The SIU (Canadian District) never held a convention of members.[25] Of those seamen
who were able to gain entry into the SIU, some 4,000 were on Banks'"Do
Not Ship" (DNS) List. Anyone who crossed the SIU in even the most
trivial matter could end up on the DNS List. Justice Norris referred to
this scheme as "one of the most cruel and oppressive instruments of
control used by Banks."[26] Salaries of Banks and top SIU officials in
Canada were approved "by a conference of paid officials of the
union — the very persons whose salaries were under consideration."
No rank and file members were present.[27]

In addition, Banks and his top flunkies used union funds for their
own personal enjoyment — Cadillacs, first class air fares, vacations,
and the like. Justice Norris cited Banks' expenses between 1959 and 1962
as an example. Banks turned in vouchers totalling $8,220.45. He
received from the union an amount ten times greater, a staggering
$80,205.45.[28]

Justice Norris itemized the various means by which the SIU under
Banks' direction, was able to control the rank and file: "...lavish use of
union funds to gain influence and support ... a system of brainwashing
members of the union by untruthful propaganda," the employment of
persons out of union funds who were "entirely subservient to him, and
carried out his orders without question," the DNS List which gave
Banks the "power to decree 'industrial death' to seamen against whom,
for one reason or another, he wished to discriminate," fraud, and unfair
trials.[29]

However, the SIU's most important tactics were beatings and intimidation. Justice Norris, in speaking of the period after the death of the

CSU, observed: "Men and women were attacked and beaten, and in most cases the beatings were extremely brutal. They were cowardly, inasmuch as the attackers were either more numerous or stronger than those attacked, or were armed with weapons of one sort or another... In this generally law-abiding country where we boast of our culture and our freedom, decent citizens were afraid to walk the streets and were afraid to take a stand in support of their rights. Witnesses came to give evidence still bearing the marks of beatings — some were crippled or marked for life."[30]

Justice Norris concluded that the violence on the Canadian waterfront dated back to the entry of the SIU into the Canadian maritime theater. He added, "Banks has been lawless from the beginning, and it was a mistake to bring him to Canada. His early lawlessness led him to further lawlessness."[31]

It may have been a mistake, but Harold Banks did the job he was brought in to do. The Canadian fleet was scuttled. The shipowners pocketed millions of dollars that would have gone to pay Canadian taxes. More millions were raked in by the shipowners as they hired seamen from Third World countries at below-poverty wages to replace Canadian seamen. The movement for an independent Canadian trade union movement was set back.

By 1964, events in Canada began to catch up with Hal Banks. He had been convicted of a "manifest act of gangsterism" in conspiring to assault a trade union organizer, but was released on a $25,000 bond. He was also wanted for a 30 day jail term in a contempt of court conviction on an unrelated incident. When attempts were made to serve a warrant for the latest infraction, Banks fled. For over a year law enforcement officials tried to track him down. They were unsuccessful, but a Toronto newspaper reporter found him being harbored in Brooklyn, New York by the SIU President Paul Hall. In 1967 Banks was ordered by a U.S. court to be extradited to Canada to face a charge of perjuring himself before the Norris Commission. However, Dean Rusk, then U.S. Secretary of State, had the order quashed. Banks never returned to Canada to face any charges.[32] He died in San Francisco in 1985.

A CRUSHING HOLLOWNESS weighed upon the members of the CSU as they saw their union, their jobs, their lifestyle and their vision taken from them. But even before the CSU was legally dead they began to regroup and carry on their mission.

As early as 1949 ex-seamen began to set up unemployed committees in four major centers under the banner of the Union of Unemployed Workers.[33] They carried with them the CSU tradition of rank and file militancy that the CSU had inherited, in part, from the unemployed groups of the 1930s. But the "first organization of unemployed since the depression of the Thirties"[34] was not to be long in existence. Demonstrations held at National Employment offices demanding "work projects to create jobs, maintain rent controls, jobs, and security" were broken up by police. In Toronto, 24 carloads of police swept down on a demonstration of about 100 and arrested six seamen who were held on $1,000 bail. Among those arrested were former Quebec City business agent Ray Collette and Stan Wingfield.[35] The fledgling unemployed movement, headed up by rank and filers fresh from the waterfront picket lines, had been followed closely by the authorities and they had laid plans for the seamen. The Union of Unemployed Workers was not able to organize effectively because "police agents planted in the organization fed information on the plans of the group to the police."[36]

In Quebec, under the leadership of Danny Daniels, Harry Gulkin, Andy Mickey, Roger Messier and Gérard Fortin, the Union of Unemployed Workers attempted to organize the unemployed, but under the hostile conditions of the period it could not survive. Also in the east, seamen like Eddie Reid, Buzz Nuttall, Pete Jones and Red Burnham set up the Canadian Brotherhood of Seamen — it fared somewhat better than the Union of Unemployed Workers, but it too was doomed to extinction.[37]

In Vancouver, the last vestiges of the CSU remained. The West Coast District of the CSU, with the support of the National Executive, had won an agreement with the employers in 1949. As a result, it survived the devastation which had been inflicted on the rest of the union. The west coast fleet was dissolved at the same time as the rest of the Canadian fleet, and the Vancouver local was soon limited to coastal shipping. The union went through a name change to become the West Coast Seamen's Union (WCSU) but maintained its CSU leadership under the direction of Jimmy Thompson and Digger Smith. The rank and file remained strongly CSU and eastern CSUers were readily admitted into the WCSU.

The WCSU was not without problems. It was relatively isolated from the mainstream trade union movement and was in constant struggle with the SIU local. This friction was to last until 1956 when the "year of mergers" saw the Trades and Labor Congress join with the Canadian Congress of Labor to form the Canadian Labor Congress of today.

That same year, discussions were undertaken to merge the WCSU with the SIU. The Seafarers promised it would allow all WCSU members to enter the SIU without discrimination, despite past hostilities. After much stormy debate, the WCSU membership voted to dissolve the West Coast Seamen's Union and enter the SIU en masse. The decision was a bitter pill to swallow. The SIU honored its pledge and accepted the WCSUers as members, but the volatile unity lasted only four years.

In March 1959, the SIU attempted to take over the Northland Navigation operation which was under contract to the International Longshoremen's and Warehousemen's Union (ILWU). SIU members were ordered to cross ILWU picket lines or be stripped of membership in the SIU. The CSUers refused to scab and the dispute became the catalyst that led to a breakaway from the Seafarers International Union and the founding of Local 400 of the Canadian Brotherhood of Railway, Transport and General Workers as a Seamen's Section. CSUers such as Tommy Burnett, Dave West, Jimmy Cocks, Red Hill, Jimmy Thompson, Matty Allen, Moose Mozdir, Bill Sikie, Tommy Dunn, Dave Crain, Bill Brannigan and many others were instrumental in this development.

Local 400 (or Vocal 400 as it was known for years in the B.C. labor movement) elected a CSU executive and once again the seamen were in a Canadian union and part of the Canadian trade union movement. Local 400 has made Vancouver internationally known as the port where Third World crews can get support to win collective agreements with flag of convenience employers.

Through their work with the International Transport Workers Federation, CSUers like Dave West, Tommy McGrath, Gerry McCullough and others have kept alive the spirit of international solidarity they learned as teenagers in the Canadian Seamen's Union. Today, Local 400 continues to struggle in a shrinking coastal industry for fair play for seamen, and CSUers Bill Sikie, Tommy Dunn, Nick Buszowski, Dave Crain and Cyril McCormick sit on its executive board.

After the defeat of 1949, with Hal Banks riding roughshod over the Canadian maritime industry, most CSUers never went to sea again. A few became successful entrepreneurs. The majority went to work in other industries. CSUers still may be found as active rank and filers in the Marine Workers, Longshoremen, Laborers, Ironworkers and other unions. Others have been elected to leadership positions: Tommy McGrath is a national vice-president of the Canadian Brotherhood of Railway, Transport and General Workers and Gerry Yetman is president of the Nova Scotia Federation of Labor and a vice-president of the Canadian Labor Congress. Still others work as sociology professors, secondary school principals, aldermen, art dealers, film producers, newspaper editors and reporters, poets and playwrights.

CSUers can always be found actively working in the peace movement, in co-op housing, in civic reform organizations and community groups.

The spirit of the Canadian Seamen's Union continues to percolate through the fabric of Canadian society. We have been left a legacy and a vision. It is our inheritance and it's up to us to use it as best we may.

Notes

Notes

Preface

1. Fred Skelhorn, interview with the author and Stan Wingfield, June 17, 1980.

Chapter 1
Shipping Out

1. Paul Barford, *Fighting Ships and Prisons: Mediterranean Galleys of France in the Age of Louis XIV*, Minneapolis, University of Minnesota Press, 1973.

2. Canadian Maritime Commission, *Second Report*, Ottawa, 1949; Canadian Maritime Commission Act, 1947, p.12.

3. *Second Report*, p.13.

4. Hedlin, Menzies and Associates, *Canadian Merchant Marine: Analysis of Economic Potential*, Ottawa, Canadian Transport Commission, 1970, p.24.

5. Joe West, interview with the author, Smiler and Two Points Murray, May 14, 1980.

6. Canada Shipping Act, Ottawa, 1934, p.98. All quotes are from the 1934 act. The 1970 revised act is essentially the same, although the section numbers differ.

7. Ibid., p.99.

8. Ibid., p.100.

9. Ibid., p.99.

10. Danny Daniels, interview with the author, June 18, 1980.

11. Canada Shipping Act, p.91.

12. Stan Wingfield, interview with the author, June 16, 1980.

13. Nick Buszowski, interview with the author, Mean Maxie Smith and Gerry Tellier, July 23, 1980.

14. Dave Crain, interview with the author, Sheila and Mike Linke, July 27, 1980.

15. Stan Wingfield interview.

16. A.W. Currie, *Canadian Transportation Economics*, Toronto, University of Toronto Press, 1967, p.618.

17. *Report of the Royal Commission on Coastal Trade*, Ottawa, Queen's Printer, 1958, p.53.

18. Currie, p.620.

19. *Royal Commission on Coastal Trade*, p.53.

20. Currie, p.20.

21. *Royal Commission on Coastal Trade*, p.53.

22. Smiler, interview with the author, May 14, 1980.

23. Ibid.

24. *Worker*, August 13, 1935.

25. *Searchlight*, July 1, 1937.

Chapter 2
Beginnings

1. *The Canadian Pocket Encyclopedia*, 33rd ed., 1978-79, Toronto, p.161.

2. *Searchlight*, July 1, 1937.

3. J.A. Sullivan, *Red Sails on the Great Lakes*, Toronto, Macmillan, 1955, p.11.

4. Gus Genites, interview with the author, June 29, 1980.

5. George Dagesse, interview with the author and Stan Wingfield, June 15, 1980.

6. Stan Wingfield, conversation with the author and Bill Charney, June 20, 1980.

7. George Dagesse interview.

8. Smiler, interview with the author, June 17, 1980.

9. J.K. Bell, interview with the author, June 5, 1980.

10. H.A. Logan, *Trade Unions in Canada: Their Development and Function*, Toronto, Macmillan, 1948, p.288.

11. *Globe*, August 10, 1935.

12. Ibid.

13. *Worker*, August 15, 1935.

14. *Globe*, August 12, 1935.

15. Charles Lipton, *The Trade Union Movement of Canada 1827-1959*, Toronto, NC Press, 1973, p.255.

16. Dewar Ferguson, transcript of tape. Unless otherwise noted, quotes from

Dewar Ferguson in this section are from this source.

17. Rita Tanche, interview with the author and Nick Buszowski, January 21, 1980.

18. Danny Daniels, interview with the author, June 18, 1980.

19. *Daily Clarion*, May 2, 1936.

20. Sullivan, p.12.

21. "In the Matter of the Defence of Canada Regulations, and in the Matter of John Allen Sullivan," p.3., in J.L. Cohen papers, Public Archives of Canada, Ottawa.

22. *Daily Clarion*, May 2, 1936 and October 5, 1936.

Chapter 3
Victory on the Lakes

1. H.A. Logan, *Trade Unions in Canada: Their Development and Function*, Toronto, Macmillan, 1948, p.370.

2. Ibid. p.342.

3. William Dodge, interview with the author, June 9, 1973.

4. J.A. Sullivan, *Red Sails on the Great Lakes*, Toronto, Macmillan, 1955, p.21.

5. Sullivan to Tallon, September 12, 1936, Canadian Labor Congress Collection, Public Archives of Canada (PAC), Ottawa.

6. Sullivan, *Red Sails*, p.24.

7. Tommy Burnett, interview with the author, January 29, 1980. All quotes from Tommy Burnett in this chapter are from this source, unless otherwise noted. Burnett's account may be verified by: "The Short, Short Journey from the ISU to the SIU," in the NMU *Pilot*, April 25, 1937; pamphlets: *Labor Spies in the NMU*, Pilot Education and Publicity Department, NMU, n.d.; *The NMU Fights Jim Crow*, NMU, August 1944; *Equality for All: The Stand of the NMU on Discrimination*, New York, Pilot Education and Publicity Department, NMU, n.d.; books: Joseph Goldberg, *The Maritime Story: A Study in Labor Relations*, Cambridge, Harvard University Press, 1959; Charles Rubin, *The Log of Rubin the Sailor*, New York, International Publishers, 1973.

8. Sullivan, *Red Sails*, p.22. Substantiated by Hy Alper, interview with the author, June 11, 1980.

9. Morrison to Moore, March 27, 1921, CLC Collection, PAC, Ottawa.

10. Ibid., April 11, 1921.

11. Madeleine Parent, interview with the author, June 27, 1980.

12. Sullivan, p.56, and "In the Matter of the Defence of Canada Regulations and in the Matter of John Allen Sullivan," p.30, J.L. Cohen papers, PAC.

13. *Searchlight*, December 1, 1937.

14. Ibid., July 1, 1937.

15. Ibid., August 16, 1937.

16. CSU leaflet, "To all Canadian seamen," April 2, 1937.

17. Danny Daniels, letter to the author, January 27, 1980.

18. *Searchlight*, October 15, 1937.

19. *Toronto Star*, June 28, 1937.

20. *Searchlight*, July 1, 1937.

21. Ibid., July 15, 1937.

22. Madeleine Parent interview, and Rick Salutin, *Kent Rowley, The Organizer: A Canadian Union Life*, Toronto, James Lorimer, 1980, pp. 16,17.

23. *Searchlight*, November 15, 1937.

24. J.K. Bell, interview with the author, June 5, 1980.

25. *Searchlight*, July 15, 1936.

26. "In the Matter," p.50.

27. Wesley Jack et al. to the CSU, J.L. Cohen papers, PAC.

28. *Searchlight*, August 16, 1937.

29. Kenneth McNaught, *The Pelican History of Canada*, Markham, Ont., Penguin Books of Canada, 1978, p.250.

30. Danny Daniels letter.

Chapter 4
The Right to Choose

1. *New York Journal of Commerce*, April 15, 1938.

2. *Globe and Mail*, April 15, 1938.

3. *One Big Union Monthly*, February 1938.

4. CSU Constitution.

5. Ibid.

6. McMaster to K. Knickle, February 4, 1938, J.L. Cohen papers, PAC.

7. CSU Constitution.

8. Ibid.

9. *Daily Clarion*, February 21, 1938.

10. Ibid.

11. Ibid., February 18, 1938.

12. "In the Matter of the Defence of Canada Regulations and in the Matter of John Allen Sullivan," p.58, J.L. Cohen papers, PAC.

13. *Windsor Star*, April 20, 1938.

14. *Toronto Star*, April 11, 1938.

15. *Port Arthur News Chronicle*, April 13, 1938.

16. McMaster to Scott Misener, June 14, 1938.

17. *Port Arthur News Chronicle*, April 13, 1938.

18. *Windsor Star*, April 15, 1938.

19. *Montreal Star*, April 16, 1938.

20. *Toronto Telegram*, April 21, 1938.

21. *Toronto Star*, April 12, 1938.

22. *Port Arthur News Chronicle*, April 13, 1938.

23. *Daily Clarion*, April 15, 1938.

24. *Windsor Star*, April 15, 1938.

25. *Toronto Star*, April 14, 1938 and *Daily Clarion*, April 15, 1938.

26. *Daily Clarion*, April 16, 1938.

27. *Toronto Star*, April 16, 1938.

28. Ibid.

29. Ibid.

30. Ibid.

31. *Ottawa Morning Citizen*, April 16, 1938.

32. *Daily Clarion*, April 16, 1938.

33. "In the Matter," p.58.

34. *Daily Clarion*, April 19, 1938.

35. Ibid., April 16, 1938.

36. *Evening Telegram*, June 6, 1938.

37. "In the Matter," p.58.

38. *Daily Clarion*, June 6, 1938.

39. "In the Matter," p.60.

40. Sullivan, *Red Sails*, p.49.

41. *Evening Telegram*, June 6, 1938.

42. Sullivan, p.51.

43. Mathewson to Rogers, June 7, 1938, J.L. Cohen papers, PAC.

44. Statement of J.M. Osborne, July 2, 1938, J.L. Cohen papers, PAC.

45. *Searchlight*, July 1, 1938.

46. *Daily Clarion*, September 16, 1938.

47. *Proceedings of the American Federation of Labor 1938 Convention*, p.431.

48. Ibid., p.432.

Chapter 5
Knowledge is Power

1. J.A. Sullivan, "Special Bulletin to all crews of the Sarnia, McKellar and Colonial Steamship Lines (Scott Misener interests) from the National Executive," and *Searchlight*, June 1939.

2. *Searchlight*, August 1939.

3. Ibid., April 1939.

4. "Ship's Delegate Bulletin," CSU Publicity and Education Department, July 21, 1939.

5. *Searchlight*, July 1939.

6. Ibid.

7. Billy Boyd, interview with the author, May 6, 1980.

8. *Searchlight*, October 1939.

9. Ibid., August 1939.

10. Ibid., November 1939.

11. Ibid., July 1939.

12. Ibid., October 1939.

13. H. Blair Neatby, *William Lyon Mackenzie King: The Prism of Unity*, Toronto, University of Toronto Press, 1976, p.315.

14. *Searchlight*, October 1939.

15. Ibid.

16. Ibid.

17. Ibid.

18. Neatby, p.317, and "War Measures Act," *Revised Statutes of Canada*, Ottawa, King's Printer, 1927, p.4085.

19. Stephen J. Scheinberg, "Rockefeller and King: The Capitalist and the Reformer," in *Mackenzie King: Widening the Debate*, eds., John English and J.O.

Stubbs, Toronto, MacMillan of Canada, 1977, p.94.

20. *Searchlight*, March 1939.

21. Ibid., December 1939.

22. Ibid., February 1940.

23. *Proceedings of the American Federation of Labor 1939 Convention*, p.451.

24. *Proceedings of the Trades and Labor Congress 1939 Convention*, p.47.

25. Ibid., p.48.

26. Charles Lipton, *The Trade Union Movement in Canada 1827-1959*, Toronto, NC Press, 1973, p.262.

27. *Searchlight*, September 1939.

28. *TLC 1939 Proceedings*, p. 148.

29. Ibid., p.151.

30. Ibid., p.157.

31. I.M. Abella, *Nationalism, Communism and Canadian Labor: The CIO, the Communist Party, and the Canadian Congress of Labor 1935-1956*, Toronto, University of Toronto Press, 1975, p.40.

32. *Searchlight*, July 1939 and December 1939.

33. Hy Alper, interview with the author, June 11, 1980.

Chapter 6
The Atlantic

1. *Searchlight*, January 1939.

2. Charles Murray, interview with the author and Kay Murray, June 3, 1980. All quotes are from this source unless otherwise noted.

3. *Searchlight*, February 1939.

4. Ibid., June 1939.

5. Ibid., special supplement, July 1939.

6. Ibid., August 1938 and June 1939.

7. Bud Doucette, interview with the author, Grace Doucette and Brenda Ferguson, July 1, 1980; Charles Murray interview; and Scotty (Alex) Munro, interview with the author, Alice Munro, Connie, Merv, Kay and Karen Fydenchuk, June 28, 1980.

8. Bud Doucette interview.

9. Connie Fydenchuk interview, June 28, 1980.

10. *Searchlight*, July 1939.

11. Ibid., June 1939.

12. Ibid., January 1939.

13. Ibid., February 1939.

14. Ibid., March 1939.

15. Ibid., May 1939 and October 1939.

16. Ibid., November 1939.

17. Charles Murray interview.

18. Joe West, interview with the author, Smiler and Two Points Murray, May 14, 1980. All quotes by Joe West in this chapter are from this source.

19. Tom Burger and Bill McKiggan, "The Finest Kind," a 28 minute videotape, 2048 Cline St., Halifax, N.S.

20. Gene Barnett, "History of the Nova Scotia Fishing Industry," MA thesis, Dalhousie University, Halifax, n.d., p.114.

21. Scotty and Alice Munro interview.

22. Barnett.

23. Capt. Ben MacKenzie, "History of the Fishermen's Unions at Lockeport," 1941, J.L. Cohen papers, PAC.

24. Lockeport Fishermen's and Fish Handlers' Strike Committee, Canadian Fishermen's Union, Lockeport, N.S., "To all trade unions and trade unionists," November 10, 1939, J.L. Cohen papers, PAC; and *Halifax Chronicle*, October 24, 1939.

25. Charles Murray, conversation with the author, June 4, 1980.

26. MacKenzie.

27. *Searchlight*, September 1939 and MacKenzie.

28. CSU press release signed J.A. Sullivan, October 28, 1939.

29. *Halifax Chronicle*, October 2, 1939.

30. Charles Murray interview. The wording of the lockout notice is in the *Halifax Chronicle*, October 24, 1939.

31. *Halifax Chronicle*, October 24, 1939.

32. Ibid., October 25, 1939.

33. *Halifax Clarion*, October 28, 1939.

34. CSU press release, October 28, 1939.

35. *Halifax Clarion*, October 28, 1939.

36. *Searchlight*, November 1939.

37. Ibid., December 1939.

38. *Halifax Chronicle*, November 6, 1939.

39. Ibid., November 10, 1939.

40. Sullivan, *Red Sails*.

41. *Halifax Chronicle*, November 10, 1939.

42. George MacEachern, letter to the author, June 22, 1980.

43. *Halifax Chronicle*, November 14, 1939.

44. Ibid., November 17, 1939.
45. Ibid., November 19, 1939.
46. *Searchlight*, December 1939.
47. *Halifax Chronicle*, November 17, 1939.
48. Ibid., November 21, 1939.
49. Ibid., November 25, 1939.
50. *Searchlight*, December 1939.
51. *Halifax Chronicle*, December 1, 1939.
52. *Searchlight*, December 1939.
53. *Halifax Chronicle*, December 11, 1939.
54. Ibid.

55. Statement of the Lockeport Fishermen's and Fish Handlers' Strike Committee, Canadian Fishermen's Union, Lockeport, N.S., November 10, 1939, p.2.
56. *Halifax Chronicle*, December 12, 1939.
57. Ibid., December 14, 1939.
58. Ibid., December 15, 1939.
59. *Searchlight*, January 1940.
60. *Halifax Chronicle*, December 16, 1939.
61. Ibid.
62. *Searchlight*, February 1940.

Chapter 7
Seamen at War

1. *Searchlight*, May 21, 1940.
2. J.L. Granatstein, *Canada's War: The Politics of the Mackenzie King Government 1939-1945*, Toronto, Oxford University Press, 1975, p.420.
3. *Searchlight*, October 1939.
4. "Brief: Board of Conciliation and Investigation," May 20, 1940, p.29. Published as *Our Case Before the Board*, Toronto, 1940, special supplement to the *Searchlight*. References are to the original Brief.
5. Ibid., p.27.
6. Ibid.
7. *Toronto Star*, April 13, 1940.
8. *Globe and Mail*, April 15, 1940.
9. Ibid.
10. Ibid.
11. *Toronto Star*, April 15, 1940.
12. *Windsor Star*, April 11, 1940.
13. *Searchlight*, March-April, 1940.
14. *Toronto Star*, April 13, 1940.
15. *Searchlight*, April 19, 1940.
16. Ibid., February 1940.
17. Ibid., April 23, 1940.
18. *Toronto Star*, April 15, 1940.
19. *Globe and Mail*, April 15, 1940.
20. Ibid.
21. *Evening Telegram*, April 15, 1940.
22. *Searchlight*, April 23, 1940.
23. *Toronto Star*, April 16, 1940.
24. Ibid., April 17, 1940.
25. *Evening Telegram*, April 17, 1940.
26. *Globe and Mail*, April 17, 1940.
27. "In the Matter of the Defence of Canada Regulations and in the Matter of John Allen Sullivan," J.L. Cohen papers, PAC.
28. *Globe and Mail*, April 18, 1940.
29. Ibid., April 19, 1940.

30. Ibid.
31. *Searchlight*, April 23, 1940 and *Globe and Mail*, April 18, 1940.
32. *Searchlight*, May 1940.
33. Brief.
34. *Globe and Mail*, April 15, 1940.
35. Brief, p.30.
36. *Searchlight*, May 21, 1940.
37. Brief, p.31.
38. Ibid., p.44.
39. Ibid., p. 49.
40. Ibid., pp.50-51.
41. *Searchlight*, February 1941.
42. Ibid.
43. Ibid.
44. Benjamin MacKenzie to L.D. Currie, June 28, 1940.
45. L.D. Currie to Charles Murray, June 10, 1940.
46. Sullivan, *Red Sails*, pp.71-73; and J.L. Cohen, report to the union beginning "Following Mr. Sullivan's arrest..." n.d.
47. Sullivan, pp.71-73.
48. J.L. Cohen report.
49. *Searchlight*, July 22, 1940.
50. Ibid., September 1940.
51. Kay and Charles Murray, interview with the author, June 3, 1980.
52. *Searchlight*, October-November 1940.
53. Ivan Avakumovic, *The Communist Party in Canada: A History*, Toronto, McClelland and Stewart, 1975, p.142.
54. Granatstein, *Canada's War*, p.102.
55. William Repka and Kathleen Repka, *Dangerous Patriots*, Vancouver, New Star Books, 1982, p.13.
56. *Canada's Party of Socialism*, Toronto, Progress Books, 1982, p.137.
57. Ibid., p.134.

58. Ibid., p.135.

59. Hy Alper, interview with the author, June 11, 1980.

60. *Searchlight*, November 1941.

61. Steve Tokaruk, interview with the author, November 1980.

62. *Searchlight*, August 24, 1940.

63. Paterson Steamship Ltd., "To all employees" August 24, 1940, J.L. Cohen papers, PAC.

64. *Searchlight*, October-November 1940 and *Port Arthur News Chronicle*, October 29, 1940.

65. *Telegram*, April 12, 1941.

66. *Globe and Mail*, April 11, 1941.

67. *Searchlight*, March and April 1941.

68. Scott Misener to Canadian Seamen's Union, March 14, 1941.

69. *Telegram*, April 14, 1941.

70. *Globe and Mail*, April 11, 1941 and *Proceedings of the Trades and Labor Congress 1941 Convention*, p.101.

71. *Star*, April 21, 1941.

72. *Toronto Telegram*, April 16, 1941.

73. Ibid., April 22, 1941.

74. "The Story of the CSU," in *A Salute to the Merchant Marine, Searchlight* special edition, February 1945, p.12.

75. *Searchlight*, July 22, 1940.

76. *Canada's Party of Socialism*, p.141.

77. *Searchlight*, August 15, 1941.

78. Sullivan, Chapman, Murray and Sinclair to Dewar Ferguson and Ernest Dunn, October 11, 1941.

79. Dewar Ferguson, "Report to the CSU Executive Meeting," November 27-28, 1941.

80. CSU, *A Victory Program for Canada's Inland and Deepsea Shipping*, CSU Publicity and Education Department, May 1942.

81. *Searchlight*, June 1942.

82. *TLC 1942 Proceedings*, p.230.

83. Sullivan, *Red Sails*, p.108.

84. *TLC 1943 Proceedings*, p.300.

85. *TLC 1944 Proceedings*, pp.257-8.

Chapter 8
The Fourth Arm

1. Canadian Maritime Commission, *Second Report*, Ottawa, King's Printer, 1949, p.17.

2. *Report of the Royal Commission on Coastal Trade*, Ottawa, Queen's Printer, 1958, p.53.

3. Hedlin, Menzies and Associates, *Canadian Merchant Marine: Analysis of Economic Potential*, Ottawa, Canadian Transport Commission, 1970, p.25.

4. Canadian Maritime Commission, *First Report*, Ottawa, King's Printer, 1948, p.17.

5. *Canadian Seamen*, August 18, 1944 (official organ of the Deepsea and Inland Boatmen's Union, Vancouver).

6. *Victory Program*, p.10, and *Second Report*, p.20.

7. Pacific Maritime Council, "The Canadian Merchant Marine and a Shipbuilding Program for Canada," March 8, 1949.

8. J.K. Bell, interview with the author, June 5, 1980.

9. Smiler, interview with the author, June 17, 1980.

10. Frank Gallant, interview with the author, June 30, 1980.

11. Joe McNeil, interview with the author, Nick Buszowski and Kirsten McNeil, April 3, 1980.

12. Sullivan, Chapman, Murray and Sinclair to Dewar Ferguson, October 11, 1941.

13. *Labor Gazette*, May 1941, p.957.

14. Hon. Lionel Chevrier, Minister of Transport, *Canada's Merchant Seamen*, Ottawa, King's Printer, 1945, p.6.

15. Gerry McCullough, interview with the author, April 21, 1980.

16. *Searchlight*, February 1945.

17. *The CSU and You*, p.3. The first of three pamphlets with the same title. The second deals with how to conduct union meetings at sea. The third, published in 1949, is a statement on the CSU's relation to the TLC.

18. James B. Lamp, *The Corvette Navy: True Stories from Canada's Atlantic War*, Toronto, MacMillan of Canada, 1977, p.58.

19. *Searchlight*, February 1945.

20. John Stanton, *Life and Death of the Canadian Seamen's Union*, Toronto, Steel Rail, 1978, p.24; and "The Company of Master Mariners" in *Seaports and Shipping World*, Montreal, Galley Publications, 1980, p.48.

21. Clifford Craig, interview with the

author, June 26, 1980, and *Searchlight*, June 18, 1945.

22. Nick Buszowski, interview with the author, Stan Wingfield and Blackie Wolkowski, September 11, 1980, and *Searchlight*, May 1944.

23. Joe Grabek, interview with the author, July 2, 1980; Jack Corrigan, interview with the author, December 10,

1980; and *Searchlight*, July 5, 1945.

24. *Searchlight*, July 1, 1944.

25. George Dagesse, interview with the author and Stan Wingfield, June 15, 1980, and *Searchlight*, July 1944.

26. Hon. J.E. Michaud, Minister of Transport, in *A Salute to the Merchant Marine, Searchlight* special edition, February 1945.

Chapter 9
Deepwater

1. Joe Hendsbee, interview with the author and Donato Coletta, July 6, 1973.

2. Madeleine Parent, interview with the author, June 27, 1980.

3. Stan Wingfield, interview with the author, June 16, 1980.

4. Gérard Fortin, interview with the author, Marie-Paul Fortin and Stan Wingfield, June 10, 1980.

5. Stan Wingfield interview, June 16, 1980.

6. Danielle Dionne, interview with the author, June 16, 1980.

Chapter 10
The Pacific

1. *Ship and Dock*, November 19, 1935 (official organ of the Longshore and Water Transport Workers of Canada).

2. Seafarers Industrial Union, *Constitution*, November 4, 1934.

3. *Ship and Dock*, May 4, 1935.

4. Ibid., April 20, 1935.

5. James O'Donnell, interview with Peter Chapman, March 9, 1976, Provincial Archives of British Columbia, Victoria; *Vancouver Sun*, June 19, 1935; Ben Swankey, *Man Along the Shore*, Vancouver, 1975, pp.83-85.

6. *Vancouver Sun*, June 20, 1935.

7. James O'Donnell, interview with the author, February 20, 1980, and *B.C. Workers' News*, September 6, 1936.

8. Gerry Tellier, interview with the author, Nick Buszowski and Lis Partington, January 30, 1980, and *Ship and Dock* (any issue).

9. James O'Donnell, "The SIU," in *Seamen's Voice* (official organ of the Canadian Brotherhood of Railway, Transport and General Workers, Local 400, Vancouver).

10. *Inland Boatmen's Union of the Pacific: Its Birth and Growth*, San Francisco, n.d. (1938).

11. James O'Donnell interview, February 20, 1980.

12. Art Ostrum, interview with the author, March 31, 1980.

13. Norman Coe, interview with the author, February 14, 1980.

14. James O'Donnell, interview with the author and Tommy Burnett, April 24, 1980.

15. Charles P. Larrowe, *Harry Bridges: The Rise and Fall of Radical Labor in the U.S.*, New York, Lawrence Hill, 1972, pp.47-50,128.

16. Unless otherwise noted, information in this section is from the "Fink Report," covering the period February 1938 to March 1939. There is a copy of this report in the Vancouver Archives, B.C. Maritime Employers Association, under the heading "IBU."

17. O'Donnell, "The SIU."

18. *Searchlight*, January 1939.

19. *Canadian Seamen*, September 1, 1944.

20. Sheila Thompson, interview with the author, April 4, 1980.

21. *Canadian Seamen*, September 1, 1944.

22. Harry Lundeberg and T. Skinner to "All labor councils in the Dominion of Canada affiliated with the AFL," August 11, 1944.

23. Cyril Lenton, interview with Bill (Moose) Mozdir, n.d.

24. "Report of the Seamen's Organization Committee SIU/AFL re Canadian Seamen's Union," n.d., p.1.

25. Ibid., p.2.

26. Sullivan, Ferguson and Lenton to Executive Committee, SIU, May 16, 1944.

27. Ibid., p.2.

28. Ibid., p.3. (emphasis added).

29. Ibid.

30. Ibid., p.4.

31. Lundeberg and Skinner.

32. Art Ostrum interview.

33. *Canadian Seamen*, September 15, 1944.

34. Joe McNeil, interview with the author, April 3, 1980.

35. *Canadian Seamen*, October 27, 1944.

36. Ibid., January 19, 1945.

37. *Searchlight*, March 1, 1945.

Chapter 11
Eight Hours

1. *Hansard*, November 19, 1945, p.2261.

2. Ibid., November 19 and 20, 1945, pp.2264, 2285.

3. *Searchlight*, May 1, 1945.

4. Ibid., April 1944.

5. Ibid., January 1, 1946.

6. Jessie Sauras, interview with the author, June 7, 1980.

7. Dorothy Sauras, interview with the author, June 1980.

8. Danny Daniels, interview with the author, June 20, 1980.

9. *Searchlight*, February 14, 1947 and June 18, 1945.

10. Ibid., May 1, 1945.

11. Ibid.

12. Ibid., October 15, 1945.

13. Ibid., May 1944.

14. Ibid., November 1, 1945 and April 4, 1946.

15. Ibid., March 21, 1946.

16. Harry Davis, interview with the author, Muriel Davis and Stan Wingfield, May 30, 1980.

17. *Kingston Whig Standard*, April 11, 1946.

18. *Searchlight*, May 2, 1946.

19. Ibid., April 18, 1946.

20. Ibid., May 16, 1946.

21. *Sarnia Canadian Observer*, May 8, 1946.

22. Ibid., May 7, 1946.

23. *Searchlight*, June 7, 1946.

24. *Canadian Transport*, May 1946.

25. *St. Thomas* (Ont.) *Times Journal*, May 8, 1946.

26. *Ottawa Morning Journal*, May 22, 1946.

27. *Kitchener Daily Record*, May 23, 1946.

28. *Halifax Mail*, May 10, 1946 and Charles Lipton, *The Trade Union Movement of Canada 1827-1959*, Toronto, NC Press, 1973, pp.269-276.

Chapter 12
The Battle of the Canals

1. *Welland-Port Colborne Evening Tribune*, May 23, 1946.

2. Gerry Tellier, interview with the author and Nick Buszowski, June 23, 1980.

3. Danny Daniels, interview with the author, June 20, 1980, and *Searchlight*, July 11, 1946.

4. *Woodstock* (Ont.) *Daily Sentinel Review*, May 25, 1946.

5. *Chatham Daily News*, May 25, 1946 and *Evening Telegram*, May 25, 1946.

6. *Toronto Daily Star*, May 25, 1946.

7. *Woodstock Daily Sentinel Review*, May 27, 1946.

8. *Toronto Daily Star*, May 29, 1946, and *Hamilton Spectator*, May 29, 1946.

9. *Hamilton Spectator*, May 27, 1946 and *St. Catharines Standard*, May 27, 1946.

10. *Quebec Chronicle*, May 25, 1946.

11. *Chatham Daily News*, May 27, 1946, and *Montreal Daily Star*, May 27, 1946.

12. Danny Daniels interview, and *Montreal Daily Star*, May 27, 1946.

13. *Stratford Beacon-Herald*, May 30, 1946.

14. Percy Bengough, "To all officers and delegates and to all Trades and Labor Councils affiliated to the TLC," CN telegram, May 30, 1946, CLC papers, PAC, Ottawa.

15. *Ontario Intelligencer*, May 30, 1946.

16. *Moncton Daily Times*, May 31, 1946.

17. Sullivan to Bengough, copy of telegram sent to Humphrey Mitchell, Minister of Labor, May 31, 1946.

18. *Searchlight*, July 11, 1946.

19. George Drew to J.L. Ilsley, acting Prime Minister, telegram, May 30, 1946, Mackenzie King papers, PAC.

20. *Woodstock Daily Sentinel Review*, May 31, 1946, and *Owen Sound Daily Sun Times*, May 31, 1946.

21. *Cornwall Daily Standard Freeholder*, June 3, 1946, and *Toronto Daily Star*, June 3, 1946.

22. *Kitchener Daily Record*, June 3, 1946.

23. *Owen Sound Daily Sun Times*, June 4, 1946.

24. *Peterborough Evening Examiner*, June 4, 1946 and *Globe and Mail*, June 5, 1946.

25. *St. Catharines Standard*, June 5, 1946.

26. *Brantford Expositor*, May 30, 1946; *Port Arthur News Chronicle*, May 30, 1946, and *Hamilton Spectator*, May 27, 1946.

27. Rev. Fern A. Sayles, *Welland Workers Make History*, Welland, Ont., 1963, p.161.

28. *Searchlight*, July 11, 1946.

29. Danny Daniels interview.

30. *Stratford Beacon Herald*, May 30, 1946.

31. *Cornwall Daily Standard Freeholder*, May 30, 1946.

32. *Woodstock Daily Sentinel Review*, June 1, 1946.

33. *Searchlight*, July 11, 1946.

34. *Port Colborne Evening Tribune*, June 1, 1946.

35. *Searchlight*, July 11, 1946 and June 12, 1946.

36. Ibid., July 11, 1946.

37. Ibid.

38. *Ottawa Evening Journal*, June 3, 1946.

39. *Searchlight*, July 11, 1946.

40. *CCF News*, June 6, 1946.

41. *Sarnia Canadian Observer*, June 6, 1946.

42. *Cornwall Daily Standard Freeholder*, June 5, 1946.

43. *St. John* (N.B.) *Telegraph Journal*, June 3, 1946.

44. John M. Osborne, Affidavit, Superior Court of Montreal, June 14, 1946; Arthur Walter Smith, Affidavit, Superior Court of Montreal, June 7, 1946; and Muriel Fishman, Affidavit, Superior Court, District of Montreal, June 17, 1946, Mackenzie King papers, PAC, Ottawa.

45. H.N. McMaster to Acting Prime Minister, CP telegram, June 6, 1946, Mackenzie King papers, PAC.

46. *Galt Daily Reporter*, July 8, 1946, and *Montreal Star*, June 6, 1946.

47. *Globe and Mail*, June 5, 1946.

48. *Kitchener Daily Record*, June 6, 1946.

49. Sullivan to Mackenzie King, CN telegram, June 16, 1946, PAC.

50. Harry Davis, interview with the author, Muriel Davis and Stan Wingfield, May 30, 1980.

51. Order-in-Council P.C. 2556, June 20, 1946, Government House, Ottawa.

52. National War Labor Board, Case File 3N-219, June 21, 1946; and E.S. Brand to J.A. Sullivan, June 21, 1946, Mackenzie King papers, PAC, Ottawa.

53. *Halifax Daily Star*, July 26, 1946.

54. *Montreal Daily Star*, August 1, 1946.

55. *Searchlight*, August 1, 1946 and December 1, 1946.

56. Ibid., October 10, 1946.

57. Ibid., October 17, 1946.

58. John Stanton, *Life and Death of the Canadian Seamen's Union*, Toronto, Steel Rail, 1978, p.92, and *Globe and Mail*, July 22, 1947.

59. Harry Davis, "Report to the Seventh Biennial Convention CSU," n.d. (1948).

60. Danny Daniels interview.

Chapter 13
Man Overboard

1. *Searchlight*, April 10, 1947.

2. Ibid.

3. J.A. Sullivan, *Red Sails on the Great Lakes*, Toronto, Macmillan, 1955, p.172.

4. Ibid., p.189.

5. *Vancouver Sun*, May 14, 1947.

6. Sullivan, p.186.

7. Ibid., p.174.

8. Madeleine Parent, interview with the author, June 27, 1980.

9. Sullivan, p.174.

10. *Vancouver Sun*, March 15, 1947.

11. Ibid., March 17, 1947.

12. Ibid.

13. *Searchlight*, April 10, 1947.

14. Sullivan, p.188.

15. *Searchlight*, April 10, 1947.

16. *Vancouver Sun*, March 17, 1947.

17. Sullivan, p.188.

18. Danny Daniels, interview with the author, June 18, 1980.

19. Leo Huberman, mimeographed examination paper, January 1947.

20. Gerry Yetman, interview with the author and Dan Morrison, June 6, 1980.

21. *Searchlight*, April 10, 1947.

22. Bill (Moose) Mozdir, interview with the author, March 17, 1980, and

Searchlight, April 10, 1947.

23. Gerry Tellier, interview with the author, Stan and Jeannette Wingfield, February 28, 1981.

24. Bud Doucette, interview with the author, Brenda Ferguson and Grace Doucette, July 1, 1980.

25. Sullivan, p.188.

26. *Searchlight*, April 10, 1947.

27. T.G. McManus, "Charting the Course," *Searchlight*, July 17, 1947.

28. *Globe and Mail*, March 15, 1947.

29. Sullivan, p.172.

30. *Le Droit*, April 15, 1947.

31. *Searchlight*, April 10, 1947.

32. Ibid., April 24, 1947.

Chapter 14
Skirmishes

1. *Searchlight*, April 24, 1947.

2. Ibid., July 17, 1947.

3. Harry Davis, "Report to the Seventh Biennial Convention CSU," n.d. (1948), and *Searchlight*, July 31, 1947.

4. Davis.

5. *Searchlight*, July 17, 1947.

6. Ibid., July 31, 1947.

7. Ibid.

8. *Globe and Mail*, July 22, 1947.

9. Ibid., July 23, 1947.

10. Joe McNeil, interview with the author, February 26, 1981.

11. *Searchlight*, July 31, 1947.

12. Ibid.

13. Ibid., September 11, 1947.

14. John Atkinson, Affidavit, reproduced in *Searchlight*, September 11, 1947 and *Port Arthur News Chronicle*, August 11, 1947.

15. *Globe and Mail*, August 20, 1947.

16. *Searchlight*, September 11, 1947.

17. Gerry Tellier, interview with the author, Jeannette and Stan Wingfield, February 28, 1981.

18. *Searchlight*, September 11, 1947.

19. Ibid.

20. Ibid., October 16, 1947.

21. Danny Daniels, interview with the author, June 18, 1980.

22. *Toronto Evening Telegram*, October 25, 1947.

23. *Halifax Chronicle*, October 21, 1947.

24. *Searchlight*, October 16, 1947.

25. Dick Greaves, interview with the

author and Lis Partington, February 24, 1981.

26. *Searchlight*, November 20, 1947 and December 4, 1947.

27. Ibid., December 4, 1947.

28. *Vancouver Sun*, December 15, 1947.

29. *Halifax Herald*, December 16, 1947.

30. *Halifax Star*, December 16, 1947.

31. *Montreal Herald*, December 20, 1947.

32. *Vancouver Sun*, December 22, 1947, December 23, 1947 and December 24, 1947.

33. *Vancouver Province*, December 30, 1947.

34. Ibid., December 31, 1947 and *Vancouver Sun*, January 6, 1948.

35. *Halifax Herald*, January 27, 1948.

36. Dick Greaves interview.

37. *Montreal Daily Star*, March 2, 1948, and *Halifax Mail*, March 3, 1948.

38. *Globe and Mail*, March 17, 1948.

39. *Montreal Daily Star*, April 1, 1948.

40. *Vancouver Province*, April 16, 1948.

41. Harry Davis, interview with the author, Stan Wingfield and Muriel Davis, May 30, 1980.

42. *St. John* (N.B.) *Telegraph Journal*, January 1948.

43. *Stratford Beacon Herald*, December 30, 1947.

44. *Nanaimo Free Press*, December 31, 1947.

45. Harry Davis, interview with the author, June 16, 1981.

46. *Searchlight*, January 26, 1948.

47. *Toronto Star*, December 20, 1947.

48. *Searchlight*, January 8, 1948.

49. *Halifax Chronicle*, December 23, 1947, and *Searchlight*, January 8, 1948.

50. *Halifax Star*, December 23, 1947.

51. *Toronto Daily Star*, February 28, 1948.

52. *Vancouver Province*, December 31, 1947.

53. *Halifax Herald*, December 27, 1947.

54. *Montreal Herald*, December 27, 1947.

55. *Searchlight*, January 8, 1948.

56. Ibid.

57. Ibid.

58. Bud Doucette, interview with the author, Grace Doucette and Brenda Ferguson, July 1, 1980.

59. *Proceedings of the 1947 Convention of the Trades and Labor Congress*, p.141.

60. Ibid.

61. *Searchlight*, March 18, 1948.

62. Ibid.

63. Gerry Yetman, interview with the author and Dan Morrison, June 6, 1980.

64. Bud Doucette interview.

Chapter 15
Class Rule, Class Law

1. *Windsor Daily Star*, January 15, 1948 and *Montreal Gazette*, February 7, 1948.

2. *Searchlight*, February 12, 1948 and *Galt Daily Reporter*, February 19, 1948.

3. *Welland Evening Tribune*, February 21, 1948.

4. *Globe and Mail*, February 20, 1948.

5. Humphrey Mitchell to T.G. McManus, July 22, 1948, PAC, Ottawa.

6. *Montreal Gazette*, March 6, 1948.

7. *Montreal Herald*, March 8, 1948.

8. *Toronto Daily Star*, March 8, 1948.

9. *Stratford Beacon Herald*, March 17, 1948 and *Toronto Daily Star*, March 24, 1948.

10. *Windsor Star*, March 24, 1948.

11. *Fort William Daily Times Journal*, March 24, 1948.

12. Percy Bengough, "Speech delivered by the President of the Trades and Labor Congress of Canada at the Labor Conference held Wednesday, May 12, 1948, at Labor Temple, Toronto."

13. Leonard Brockington, "Report in the matter of an Industrial Disputes Inquiry Commission to inquire into a dispute between Colonial Steamships Ltd. and the Canadian Seamen's Union," p.6., n.d.

14. Ibid., p.2.

15. Ibid.

16. *Globe and Mail*, April 3, 1948 and Brockington.

17. Brockington.

18. *Toronto Star*, March 20, 1948 and *Owen Sound Daily Sun Times*, March 10, 1948.

19. *Cornwall Standard Freeholder*, April 5, 1948.

20. *Globe and Mail*, April 16, 1948.

21. *Toronto Star*, April 16, 1948.

22. *Globe and Mail*, April 19, 1948.

23. Gerry Yetman, interview with the author and Dan Morrison, June 6, 1980.

24. *Searchlight*, May 6, 1948.

25. *Windsor Star*, April 28, 1948.

26. *Globe and Mail*, April 21, 1948.

27. Ibid., April 23, 1948.

28. *Toronto Star*, April 23, 1948.

29. *Globe and Mail*, April 23, 1948; *Toronto Star*, April 23, 1948, and *Searchlight*, May 6, 1948.

30. *Welland-Port Colborne Evening Tribune*, December 15, 1948.

31. *Toronto Star*, April 23, 1948.

32. *Montreal Gazette*, April 23, 1948.

33. *Hamilton Spectator*, April 23, 1948.

34. *Toronto Star*, April 24, 1948.

35. *Globe and Mail*, April 24, 1948.

36. *Searchlight*, May 6, 1948.

37. *Ottawa Morning Journal*, April 26, 1948.

38. Ibid.

39. *Toronto Star*, April 27, 1948.

40. *Searchlight*, May 20, 1948; and Blackie Leonard, interview with the author, Nick and Pat Buszowski, April 6, 1981.

41. *Kitchener Waterloo Record*, September 28, 1948.

42. *Toronto Telegram*, October 1, 1948.

43. *Toronto Daily Star*, October 2, 1948.

44. Ibid.

45. *Welland-Port Colborne Evening Tribune*, December 15, 1948 and *Ottawa Morning Citizen*, December 15, 1948.

Chapter 16
Red Decks

1. Gerry Tellier, interview with the author and Stan Lowe, April 1, 1981. This poem was conceived by Gerry Tellier during the 1948 strike, but never published. It was recited on the occasion of Stan Lowe's 71st birthday. Stan Lowe and Gerry Tellier were both members of the five-man committee which made the decision, based on a motion put forward by Stan Lowe, to launch the On-to-Ottawa Trek in 1935. Stan Lowe was a member of the CSU and stopped sailing only in the late 1970s.

2. *Searchlight*, June 10, 1948.

3. Danny Daniels, interview with the author, June 20, 1980.

4. Blackie Leonard, interview with the author, Nick and Pat Buszowski, April 6, 1981.

5. *Toronto Star*, April 19, 1948.

6. Danny Daniels interview.

7. *Searchlight*, October 22, 1948; Danny Daniels interview, and Rev. Fern A. Sayles, *Welland Workers Make History*, Welland, 1963, p.173.

8. Sayles, p.174.

9. *Vancouver Sun*, June 16, 1948.

10. *Ottawa Morning Journal*, April 28, 1948 and *Searchlight*, May 20, 1948.

11. "Canadian Seamen's Union vs. Frank Hall," *TLC News*, n.d., p.1.

12. *Globe and Mail*, December 13, 1948 and *Welland Evening Tribune*, December 11, 1948.

13. *Welland-Port Colborne Evening Tribune*, December 18, 1948.

14. Danny Daniels, interview with the author, June 21, 1980.

15. Sayles, p.175.

16. Danny Daniels interview.

17. Mike Hornak, conversation with the author, April 29, 1981, and *Moncton Daily Times*, July 15, 1948.

18. *Toronto Daily Star*, December 7, 1948.

19. *Sarnia Canadian Observer*, December 7, 1948.

20. *Globe and Mail*, December 8, 1948.

21. Mike Hornak conversation, and *Toronto Daily Star*, December 7, 1948.

22. *Toronto Daily Star*, December 7, 1948.

23. Mike Hornak conversation.

24. *Owen Sound Sun Times*, October 7, 1948.

25. *Hamilton Spectator*, October 7, 1948.

26. *Montreal Daily Star*, December 9, 1948.

27. *Toronto Telegram*, December 9, 1948.

28. *Chatham Daily News*, June 30, 1948.

29. *Peterborough Examiner*, July 27, 1948.

30. *Toronto Telegram*, May 13, 1948 and *Toronto Star*, May 13, 1948.

31. Humphrey Mitchell to T.G. McManus, July 22, 1948, PAC, Ottawa.

32. *Globe and Mail*, November 27, 1948.

Chapter 17
Enter the SIU

1. "Statement made by Percy Bengough, President of the Trades and Labor Congress of Canada. The Case of the Canadian Seamen's Union," n.d.

2. Robert Lindsay, Affidavit, "In the matter of the Wartime Labor Relations Regulations P.C. 1003, and in the matter of the Canadian Lake Seamen's Union," July 16, 1948, sworn before Commissioner George D. McPhedran, Toronto.

3. National Executive of the CSU, "An Open Letter to the Delegates to the National Liberal Convention," n.d.

4. *Montreal Gazette*, August 7, 1948.

5. *Searchlight*, August 12, 1948.

6. *St. John's Evening Telegram*, August 6, 1948.

7. *Montreal Gazette*, August 7, 1948.

8. *Amherst Daily News*, September 1, 1948.

9. CSU, "An Exposé of Company Unionism: A Story of the SIU in the USA and Canada," n.d.

10. *Proceedings of the 1947 Convention of the Trades and Labor Congress*, p.284.

11. *Moose Jaw Times Herald*, September 3, 1948.

12. Frank Mimee, Affidavit sworn

before I.R. Prazoff, Commissioner of the Supreme Court of Canada, District of Montreal, May 17, 1949.

13. *Chatham Daily News*, September 3, 1948 and *Moose Jaw Times Herald*, September 3, 1948.

14. *Maritime Merchant*, September 9, 1948.

15. "Canadian Seamen's Union vs. Frank Hall," *TLC News*, n.d.

16. "Executive Council of Congress Meets," *TLC News*, n.d.

17. Frank H. Hall, "'To All Canadian Lodges of the Brotherhood of Railway and Steamship Clerks ...'" September 22, 1948.

18. *Proceedings of the 1948 Convention of the Trades and Labor Congress*, p.147.

19. Ibid., pp.148-9.

20. Ibid., p.157.

21. Charles Lipton, *The Trade Union Movement of Canada 1827-1959*, Toronto, NC Press, 1973, pp.274-279.

22. *TLC 1948 Proceedings*, p.168.

23. Ibid.

24. Ibid., p.170.

25. Ibid., p.228.

26. Ibid., p.206.

27. Madeleine Parent, interview with the author, June 27, 1980, and Rick Salutin, *Kent Rowley, The Organizer: A Canadian Union Life*, Toronto, James Lorimer, 1980, p.74.

28. *TLC 1948 Proceedings*, p.214.

29. Ibid., p.217.

Chapter 18
Farewell to the Fleet

1. *Telegram*, August 6, 1948.

2. *Searchlight*, September 4, 1948.

3. Harry Davis, interview with the author, Muriel Davis and Stan Wingfield, May 30, 1980.

4. *Hamilton Spectator*, September 10, 1948.

5. *Montreal Gazette*, August 7, 1948.

6. Ibid., September 1, 1948.

7. Bud Doucette, interview with the author, Grace Doucette and Brenda Ferguson, July 1, 1980.

8. *Ottawa Evening Journal*, October 26, 1948.

9. Bud Doucette interview.

10. Department of Labor (Dominion), "News Release No. 3451," February 19, 1949, PAC.

11. T.G. McManus to Percy Bengough, November 23, 1948, CN telegram, PAC.

12. *Montreal Daily Star*, January 24, 1949.

13. Ibid.

14. *Searchlight*, February 10, 1949.

15. Ibid.

16. Ibid.

17. Dick Greaves, interview with the author and Lis Partington, February 24, 1981, and Stan Wingfield, conversation with the author, September 12, 1980.

18. CSU, "To the trade union movement of Canada," April 15, 1949, PAC.

19. *Hansard*, November 20, 1945, p.2285.

20. Canadian Maritime Commission, *First Report*, Ottawa, 1948, p.5., and *Hansard*, November 19, 1945, p.2264.

21. *First Report*, p.5.

22. Canadian Maritime Commission, *Second Report*, Ottawa, 1949, p.5.

23. *First Report*, p.7.

24. Dick Greaves, William Doherty and Harry Davis, "An Appeal for Action on Canada's Disintegrating Merchant Marine," n.d. (March 1949).

25. Pacific Maritime Council, "The Canadian Merchant Marine and a Shipbuilding Program for Canada," March 8, 1949.

26. *First Report*, p.9.

27. Canadian Maritime Commission, *Fifth Report*, Ottawa, 1952, p.6.

28. Ibid., *Sixth Report*, Ottawa, 1953, p.9.

29. *Province*, December 19, 1949.

30. *Vancouver Sun*, December 16, 1948.

31. *Toronto Daily Star*, January 22, 1949.

32. Eric G. Adams, "Canadian Deepsea Fleet Shipowners and Their Corporate Connections as of January 1949," February 10, 1949 (an 86 page study, excellently researched, apparently commissioned by the CSU).

33. *Vancouver Sun*, December 16, 1948.

34. Ibid., March 12, 1949.

35. *Ottawa Evening Journal*, January 5, 1949.

36. *Globe and Mail*, January 13, 1949.

37. Greaves, Doherty and Davis.

38. *Searchlight*, December 24, 1948.

39. *Toronto Evening Telegram*, January 10, 1949.

40. Ibid.

41. *South Wales Echo*, January 6, 1949.

42. *Searchlight*, January 20, 1949.

43. Adams, pp.5,74.

44. *Barry and District News*, January 7, 1949.

45. *Vancouver News-Herald*, January 20, 1949.

46. *Montreal Daily Star*, January 28, 1949.

47. *Philadelphia Inquirer*, January 8, 1949.

Chapter 19
Battle Joined

1. *Port Arthur News Chronicle*, February 5, 1949.

2. *Welland Evening Tribune*, February 4, 1949.

3. J.O. Wilson, T. Meighen and John Kerry, "In the Matter of the Industrial Relations and Disputes Investigation Act and of the Dispute Between Various Deep Sea Cargo Shipping Companies ... and the Canadian Seamen's Union (TLC) (bargaining agent)," p.2.

4. "Memorandum of Agreement for Dry Cargo Freight Vessels ... between Acadia Overseas Freighters Limited (and 23 other companies) ... and the Canadian Seamen's Union ..." signed J.O. Wilson, T. Meighen and John Kerry, Section 2(b), n.d.

5. Ibid., Section 3.

6. Humphrey Mitchell, "To all trade unionists and interested citizens," May 16, 1949, PAC.

7. T.G. McManus to Percy Bengough, February 24, 1949.

8. *The CSU and You*, Montreal, CSU National Office, n.d. (1949), pp.12-13.

9. Ibid., p.16.

10. Harry Davis, interview with the author, May 30, 1980; see also *The CSU and You*, p.16; *Hansard*, April 5, 1949, p.2335; and Humphrey Mitchell, "Memorandum in answer to wires and communications addressed to Minister of the Dominion Government," April 19, 1949.

11. Harry Davis interview.

12. *The CSU and You*, p.13.

13. Harry Davis interview.

14. Dick Greaves, interview with the author and Lis Partington, February 24, 1981; Danny Daniels, interview with the author, Lis Partington and Sue Moorhead, June 24, 1980; and Ellen Davis, "The Canadian Seamen's Union and the Deep Sea Shipping Strike of 1949," March 29, 1976, essay, University of British Columbia.

15. *Hansard*, April 5, 1948, p.2335.

16. Frank Mimee, Affidavit sworn before I.R. Prazoff, Commissioner of the Supreme Court of Canada, District of Montreal, May 10, 1949.

17. T.G. Norris, *Report of Industrial Inquiry Commission Concerning Matters Relating to the Disruption of Shipping on the Great Lakes, the St. Lawrence River System and Connecting Waters*, Ottawa, Queen's Printer, 1963, p.49.

18. Ibid., p.105.

19. *Toronto Star*, December 4, 1974.

20. Norris, p.184.

21. *Toronto Star*, December 4, 1974.

22. *Macleans*, February 15, 1955.

Chapter 20
Blood on the Docks

1. Don Williams, Louis Piveson, John Yurechko and Leigh Hallett, *The Tridale Strike*, Wellington, N.Z., New Zealand Strike Committee, CSU, n.d.

2. Humphrey Mitchell, "To all trade unionists and interested citizens," May 16, 1949, p.3.

3. Ibid., p.2.

4. *Truro* (N.S.) *Weekly News*, March 31, 1949.

5. Connie Fydenchuk, interview with the author, Scotty and Alice Munro, June 28, 1980.

6. *Vancouver Sun*, April 2, 1949.

7. *Montreal Standard*, April 2, 1949.

8. *Prince Rupert News*, April 2, 1949.

9. *Edmonton Journal*, April 7, 1949.

10. *Vancouver Sun*, April 6, 1949.

11. *Vancouver Province*, April 7, 1949, and *Vancouver News Herald*, April 8, 1949.

12. *Vancouver Sun*, April 7, 1949.

13. Robert McEwan Jr., Affidavit declared before A. Feiner, Commissioner of the Supreme Court of Canada, District of Montreal, May 14, 1949.

14. Ibid.

15. Scotty Munro interview.

16. *Moncton Transcript*, April 8, 1949.

17. Fred Skelhorn, interview with the author and Stan Wingfield, June 17, 1980; also, Scotty Munro interview and *Searchlight*, May 26, 1949.

18. *Quebec Chronicle Telegram*, April 8, 1949.

19. *Ottawa Evening Citizen*, April 8, 1949.

20. Robert McEwan Jr., Affidavit.

21. *Searchlight*, May 26, 1949.

22. *Edmonton Bulletin*, April 8, 1949.

23. *Searchlight*, May 26, 1949.

24. *Halifax Chronicle Herald*, April 9, 1949.

25. *Halifax Mail Star*, April 9, 1949.

26. Ibid.

27. Ibid., and April 11, 1949.

28. Ibid., April 11, 1949.

29. T.G. Norris, *Report of Industrial Inquiry Commission Concerning Matters Relating to the Disruption of Shipping on the Great Lakes, the St. Lawrence River System and Connecting Waters*, Ottawa, Queen's Printer, 1963, p.50.

30. *Halifax Mail Star*, April 11, 1949.

31. A.L. Joliffe, Director, Department of Mines and Resources, to A. MacNamara, April 12, 1949, PAC.

32. *Montreal Herald*, April 11, 1949, *Halifax Mail Star*, April 9, 1949 and *Winnipeg Citizen*, April 9, 1949.

33. *Searchlight*, May 26, 1949.

34. *Vancouver News Herald*, April 13, 1949.

35. *Sydney* (N.S.) *Post Record*, April 9, 1949.

36. *Halifax Mail Star*, April 12, 1949 and Gerry Yetman, interview with the author, June 6, 1980.

37. Ibid.

38. *Halifax Mail Star*, April 13, 1949.

39. Ibid.

Chapter 21
The Home Front

1. *Halifax Chronicle Herald*, April 5, 1949.

2. *St. John Telegram Journal*, April 11, 1949.

3. *Moncton Daily Times*, April 16, 1949.

4. *St. Thomas* (Ont.) *Times Journal*, April 27, 1949.

5. *Toronto Daily Star*, April 29, 1949.

6. Ibid.

7. *St. John Telegram Journal*, April 29, 1949.

8. Ibid., and *Toronto Daily Star*, April 29, 1949.

9. *Welland Evening Tribune*, April 29, 1949.

10. *British Columbian*, April 29, 1949.

11. *London Evening Free Press*, April 30, 1949.

12. *St. John Evening Times Globe*, May 5, 1949.

13. Ibid., May 6, 1949.

14. Ibid., May 10, 1949.

15. *Ontario Intelligencer*, May 12, 1949.

16. *Montreal Gazette*, April 14, 1949.

17. James O'Donnell, interview with the author, July 31, 1981.

18. *Vancouver Sun*, April 11, 1949.

19. *Vancouver Sunday Sun*, May 28, 1949.

20. *Vancouver News Herald*, April 9, 1949.

21. *Vancouver Province*, April 9, 1949.

22. *Vancouver Sun*, April 14, 1949.

23. *Vancouver Sunday Sun*, May 28, 1949.

24. *Prince Rupert News*, May 18, 1949.

25. *Woodstock Sentinel*, April 12, 1949.

26. *Sault Daily Star*, April 14, 1949.

27. *Stratford Beacon Herald*, April 19, 1949 and *Sault Daily Star*, April 27, 1949.

28. *St. Thomas Times Journal*, April 27, 1949.

29. *Montreal Daily Star*, April 28, 1949.

30. Harry Davis, interview with the author, Muriel Davis and Stan Wingfield, May 30, 1980.

31. *Vancouver News Herald*, April 22, 1949.

32. Dick Greaves, interview with the author and Lis Partington, February 28, 1981.

33. *The Fisherman*, April 22, 1949 and *Vancouver News Herald*, April 22, 1949.

34. *Searchlight*, May 26, 1949.

35. Joe Grabek interview with the author, July 2, 1980 and Stan Wingfield, interview with the author, June 16, 1980.

36. *Montreal Daily Star*, April 18, 1949.

37. Ibid.

38. Common Vancouver waterfront knowledge.

39. Stan Wingfield interview.

40. Gerry Tellier, interview with the author, Stan and Jeannette Wingfield, February 28, 1980.

41. Spud Haughey, interview with the author, June 27, 1980.

42. Gerry Tellier interview.

43. *Montreal Daily Star*, April 11, 1949.

44. *Montreal Gazette*, April 13, 1949.

Chapter 22
Cooperation, Yes — Domination, No!

1. Henry Cohen, interview with the author, July 23, 1981.

2. *Toronto Telegram*, June 9, 1949 and *London Evening Free Press*, June 9, 1949.

3. *London Evening Free Press*, June 9, 1949; see also *Toronto Daily Star*, June 11, 1949 and *Toronto Telegram*, June 9, 1949.

4. *Niagara Falls Evening Review*, June 15, 1949.

5. *Montreal Gazette*, June 18, 1949.

6. Frank Hall et al. to William Green, February 1949, PAC.

7. Percy Bengough and John W. Buckley, "An Informed Membership Will Strengthen Democracy and Defeat Domination," *Trades and Labor Congress Journal*, March 1949, pp.2,3 (reprinted in pamphlet form in March 1949).

8. *The CSU and You*, CSU National Office, n.d. (1949), p.8.

9. Bengough and Buckley, p.3.

10. Ibid., p.4.

11. Ibid., pp.4,5.

12. Ibid., p.7.

13. Danny Daniels, interview with the author, Lis Partington and Sue Moorhead, June 24, 1980.

14. Ray Collette, "Les Membres des Union Nous Supportent," *S.S. Suntan*, n.d. (1949), trans. Jaquelin Rutherford.

15. Gerry McCullough, interview with the author, April 21, 1980.

16. *The Striker* (published by the CSU), September 2, 1949.

17. Ray Collette, "Pourquoi un Journal Du Camp?" *S.S. Suntan*, n.d. (1949), trans. Jaquelin Rutherford.

18. James Dugan, *The Great Mutiny*, New York, G.P. Putnam Sons, 1965, p.36.

Chapter 23
Pickets Around the Globe

1. *Moncton Transcript*, April 11, 1949 and Percy Bengough to K. Baxter, Secretary, New Zealand Federation of Labor, telegram, April 22, 1949, PAC.

2. Don Williams, Louis Piveson, John Yurechko and Leigh Hallett, *The Tridale Strike*, Wellington, N.Z., New Zealand Strike Committee, CSU, n.d., p.3.

3. *Toronto Telegram*, May 10, 1949.

4. *The Tridale Strike*, p.10.

5. *Toronto Telegram*, May 10, 1949.

6. Two Points Murray, interview with the author, Stan and Jeannette Wingfield, September 8, 1980.

7. *The Tridale Strike*, pp.12,13.

8. Ibid., p.14.

9. Toby Hill, foreword to *The Tridale Strike*, p.1.

10. Eric G. Adams, "Canadian Deepsea Fleet Shipowners and Their Corporate Connections as of January 1949," February 10, 1949, p.57.

11. *Halifax Mail Star*, April 8, 1949.

12. Smiler, interview with the author, Two Points Murray and Joe West, May 14, 1980.

13. *Searchlight*, May 26, 1949.

14. Smiler interview.

15. *Province*, April 25, 1949.
16. *St. John Telegraph Journal*, April 11, 1949.
17. *Montreal Herald*, April 12, 1949.
18. *Halifax Chronicle Herald*, April 25, 1949.
19. *Kingston Whig Standard*, May 2, 1949.
20. Smiler interview.
21. Supreme Court of British Guiana, 1949, No. 252 Demerara, Civil Jurisdiction, between James Wilson Sutherland, Master of the Steamship *Sunavis* (Plaintiff) and Jack Hurrell, Zenna le Lievre, Richard Moore, Robert Rudolph, Etienne Robichaud, George Orr, James Kerry, Fleming White, Ross Melbourne, Joseph Hitchen, Mickey Knihnicki, Raymond Labatt, Harry Underhill, Edmond Hebert, James Quinn, Lloyd Green, Gabriel Dufour, Fred Hobbs, Roland Reny, Jacques Tessier, Arthur Dubreuil, Victor Martin, Lawrence Gagnon, Hugh Maguire, Lawrence Know, Gordon Green, Cyrille Thibodeau, Edward Carey, Jean M. Miller and William King (Defendants).
22. Smiler interview.
23. Ibid.
24. Supreme Court of British Guiana.
25. *Owen Sound Daily Sun Times*, May 31, 1949.
26. Smiler interview.
27. *Windsor Daily Star*, June 1, 1949.
28. Smiler interview.
29. *Montreal Herald*, June 17, 1949.
30. Tommy McGrath, interview with the author, January 18, 1981.

31. *Searchlight*, May 26, 1949.
32. Tommy McGrath, "Strike Report *SS Cambrey*," n.d. (April 1949).
33. *Guardian* (South Africa), April 21, 1949. The *Guardian* is no longer published; its editor, Brian Bunting, lives in exile in London, England.
34. McGrath, "Strike Report."
35. *Montreal Herald*, April 12, 1949.
36. McGrath, "Strike Report."
37. *Guardian*, April 14, 1949.
38. Ibid., April 21, 1949.
39. Tommy McGrath interview.
40. Ibid.
41. Ibid.
42. Danny Daniels, interview with the author, June 24, 1980.
43. Tommy McGrath interview.
44. *Guardian*, June 2, 1949.
45. Ibid., June 9, 1949.
46. Ibid.
47. *Vancouver Sun*, April 21, 1949 and *Kingston Whig Standard*, April 19, 1949.
48. *Chronicle Herald*, April 21, 1949.
49. Ibid.
50. *Canada's Weekly*, May 6, 1949 and *Chronicle Herald*, April 21, 1949.
51. *Searchlight*, May 26, 1949.
52. Ibid.
53. *Montreal Daily Star*, April 29, 1949.
54. Danny Daniels interview, June 25, 1980.
55. *Montreal Herald*, April 29, 1949.
56. *Montreal Gazette*, April 29, 1949.
57. *Montreal Daily Star*, April 29, 1949 and *Montreal Herald*, April 29, 1949.
58. *Globe and Mail*, May 4, 1949.
59. Ibid., May 5, 1949.

Chapter 24
The Battle in Britain

1. Steve Tokaruk, interview with the author, November 4, 1980.
2. Andy Brogan, interview with the author, May 11, 1973.
3. Steve Tokaruk interview.
4. G.A. Isaacs, Minister of Labor and National Service, Command Paper 7851 of the 1948-49 Parliamentary Session, "Review of the British Dock Strike of 1949," December 14, 1949, p.32.
5. Andy Brogan interview.
6. Isaacs, p.8.
7. Eric G. Adams, "Canadian Deepsea Fleet Shipowners and Their Corporate Connections as of January 1949," February 10, 1949, p.28.
8. Bud Doucette, interview with the author, Grace Doucette and Brenda Ferguson, July 1, 1980.
9. Jack Dash, *Good Morning Brothers!*, London, Lawrence and Wishart, 1969, p.68, and *Peterborough Examiner*, April 4, 1949.
10. Stringer MacDonald, interview with the author and Tommy Burnett, August 18, 1981.
11. Bud Doucette interview.
12. *St. Thomas Times*, April 13, 1949.

13. Dash, pp.63,71.

14. Steve Tokaruk, written on the back of Andrew (Jock) Brogan's 1949 Deepsea Strike CSU Picket Card, #2631, Leith, Scotland, June 15, 1949.

15. Steve Tokaruk interview.

16. Bud Doucette interview.

17. Jimmy Walters, interview with the author, May 21, 1980.

18. *Searchlight*, May 26, 1949.

19. Isaacs, p.33.

20. Stringer MacDonald interview.

21. Andy Brogan interview.

22. *Searchlight*, May 26, 1949.

23. Andy Brogan interview.

24. Isaacs, p.9.

25. Bud Doucette interview; Steve Tokaruk interview, and *Sherbrooke Daily Record*, April 23, 1949.

26. Bud Doucette interview.

27. *Galt Evening Reporter*, May 12, 1949.

28. Steve Tokaruk interview.

29. *Vancouver Sun*, April 20, 1949.

30. Isaacs, p.10.

31. "Dockworkers of Newport, What Have You Done?" Central Strike Committee, CSU, London, n.d. (May 1949).

32. *Welland Evening Tribune*, May 6, 1949 and Andy Brogan interview.

33. *Ottawa Evening Journal*, May 7, 1949.

34. Isaacs, p.10.

35. *St. John Evening Times Globe*, May 7, 1949.

36. Ibid.

37. *Toronto Star*, May 11, 1949.

38. Isaacs, p.10.

39. Ibid., pp.10,35.

40. Ibid., p.11.

41. *Evening Telegram*, May 19, 1949.

42. *Searchlight*, May 26, 1949.

43. Isaacs, p.11.

44. *Searchlight*, May 26, 1949.

45. Dash, p.69 and Isaacs, p.11.

46. *Victoria Daily Times*, May 27, 1949.

47. *London* (England) *Daily Herald*, May 28, 1949.

48. *Guelph Daily Mercury*, May 31, 1949.

49. *St. John Evening Times Globe*, May 31, 1949.

50. *Windsor Daily Star*, June 1, 1949.

51. *Vancouver Sun*, May 27, 1949.

52. *Ottawa Evening Citizen*, May 30, 1949.

53. *Calgary Albertan*, May 30, 1949.

54. *Moncton Transcript*, June 4, 1949.

55. *Halifax Chronicle Herald*, June 4, 1949.

56. *Stratford Beacon Herald*, June 4, 1949.

57. *St. Thomas Times Journal*, June 4, 1949.

58. Ibid.

59. *Financial Post*, June 4, 1949.

60. Harry Davis and T.G. McManus, "Letter Sent to President Percy Bengough and the Executive of the Trades and Labor Congress of Canada, for Immediate Press Release," September 1, 1949.

61. *Searchlight*, May 26, 1949.

62. *Halifax Chronicle Herald*, June 18, 1949.

63. *Edmonton Bulletin*, June 18, 1949.

64. *Montreal Herald*, June 18, 1949.

65. *Globe and Mail*, July 5, 1949.

Chapter 25
Internationalism

1. *Galt Evening Reporter*, June 8, 1949 and G.A. Isaacs, Command Paper 7851 of the 1948-49 Parliamentary Session, "Review of the British Dock Strike of 1949," December 14, 1949, p.37.

2. *Daily Times Gazette*, June 14, 1949.

3. *Halifax Chronicle Herald*, June 13, 1949.

4. *Moncton Transcript*, June 15, 1949.

5. *Searchlight*, May 26, 1949.

6. Steve Tokaruk, interview with the author, November 4, 1980.

7. Isaacs, p.16.

8. *Stratford Beacon Herald*, June 21, 1949.

9. Isaacs, p.16.

10. *London* (Ont.) *Evening Free Press*, June 24, 1949.

11. Isaacs, p.17.

12. Bud Doucette, interview with the author, July 1, 1980.

13. *London Evening Free Press*, June 24, 1949.

14. Isaacs, p.17.

15. Ibid., Appendix XVII, "Press Statement Issued by Minister of Labor and National Service."

16. Ibid., p.18.

17. Eric G. Adams, "Canadian Deepsea Fleet Shipowners and Their Corporate Connections as of January 1949," February 10, 1949, p.42.

18. Bud Doucette interview.

19. London Evening Free Press, June 27, 1949.

20. St. Thomas Journal, June 28, 1949 and Isaacs, p.20.

21. London (England) Evening Times, June 27, 1949 and Isaacs, p.19.

22. Toronto Telegram, June 29, 1949.

23. Isaacs, p.21.

24. Ibid.

25. Globe and Mail, July 5, 1949.

26. Toronto Telegram, July 5, 1949.

27. Globe and Mail, July 5, 1949 and Star London, July 7, 1949.

28. Globe and Mail, July 7, 1949.

29. London Daily Express, July 9, 1949.

30. London Daily Mirror, July 9, 1949.

31. London Daily Graphic, July 9, 1949.

32. London Daily Mirror, July 9, 1949.

33. Ibid.

34. Ibid.

35. Ibid., July 12, 1949.

36. London Daily Mail, July 11, 1949.

37. London Evening Standard, July 11, 1949 and London Evening News, July 11, 1949.

38. London Evening Standard, July 11, 1949.

39. London News Chronicle, July 12, 1949.

40. Ibid., and London Daily Mirror, July 12, 1949.

41. London News Chronicle, July 12, 1949 and London Daily Express, July 12, 1949.

42. London Daily Graphic and Daily Sketch, July 13, 1949.

43. Ibid.

44. Searchlight, August 4, 1949 and Isaacs, p.44.

45. Bud Doucette interview.

46. Searchlight, August 4, 1949.

47. Isaacs, pp.25,44.

48. Jack Dash, Good Morning Brothers! London, Lawrence and Wishart, 1969, pp.68,71.

49. Bud Doucette interview.

50. Isaacs, p.26.

51. Bud Doucette interview.

52. Steve Tokaruk interview.

Chapter 26
The Final Round

1. Vancouver Sun, April 18, 1949.

2. Searchlight, August 4, 1949.

3. Harry Davis and T.G. McManus, "Letter sent to President Percy Bengough and the Executive of the Trades and Labor Congress of Canada, for Immediate Press Release," September 1, 1949.

4. Labor Gazette, November 1949, pp.1355-1366; Canadian Tribune, October 3, 1949.

5. Report of the 64th Annual Convention of the Trades and Labor Congress, p.252.

6. Harry Davis, interview with the author and Stan Wingfield, May 30, 1980.

7. Muriel Davis, interview with the author and Stan Wingfield, May 30, 1980.

8. Tommy Burnett, interview with the author and Stringer MacDonald, August 18, 1981.

9. "Statement re Termination of the Strike," October 20, 1949.

10. Tommy Burnett interview.

11. Searchlight, October 1950.

12. Nick Buszowski, interview with the author and Blackie Wolkowski, Stan Wingfield and Yippie Joe, September 11, 1980.

13. T.G. McManus, "Death of a Union," Macleans, December 1, 1950.

14. CSU Bulletin 438, Montreal, n.d. (December 1950).

15. Canada Labor Relations Board, "Between Branch Lines Ltd., Applicant, and Canadian Seamen's Union, Respondent," December 7, 1950.

16. Ibid.

17. Globe and Mail, December 12, 1950.

18. Canadian Maritime Commission, Report, 1947, p.20.

19. Ibid., 1957, p.8.

20. Vancouver Sun, September 30, 1982.

21. T.G. Norris, Report of Industrial Inquiry Commission Concerning Matters Relating to the Disruption of Shipping on

the Great Lakes, the St. Lawrence River System and ·Connecting Waters, Ottawa, Queen's Printer, 1963, p.93.

22. Ibid., p.50.

23. Dick Greaves, interview with the author and Lis Partington, February 24, 1981.

24. Norris, p.54.

25. Ibid., p.106.

26. Ibid., p.184.

27. Ibid., p.107.

28. Ibid., p.108.

29. Ibid., p.127.

30. Ibid., pp.203-204.

31. Ibid., p.302.

32. Toronto Star, December 4, 1974.

33. Ibid., December 29, 1949.

34. Globe and Mail, December 29, 1949.

35. Stan Wingfield, interview with the author, September 9, 1982.

36. Globe and Mail, December 29, 1949.

37. Red Burnham, interview with the author, Stan Wingfield and Smiler, June 17, 1980.

Index